THE BIBLE FOR TODAY'S CHURCH

THE CHURCH'S TEACHING SERIES

Prepared at the request of the Executive Council of the General Convention of the Episcopal Church

THE BIBLE
FOR TODAY'S
CHURCH

Written by
Robert A. Bennett and O. C. Edwards
with the assistance of a group of
editorial advisors under the direction of the
Church's Teaching Series Committee

THE SEABURY PRESS / NEW YORK

Second Printing

1979
The Seabury Press
815 Second Avenue
New York, N.Y. 10017

Printed in the United States of America

Library of Congress Cataloging in Publication Data

Bennett, Robert A 1933-
The Bible for today's church.

(The Church's teaching series; v. 2)
Includes index.
1. Bible—Criticism, interpretation, etc.
2. Bible—Study. I. Edwards, Otis Carl, 1928-
joint author. II. Protestant Episcopal Church in the U.S.A.
Editorial Committee. III. Title. IV. Series.
BS510.B4   220.6   78-31570
ISBN 0-8164-0419-4
ISBN 0-8164-2215-X pbk.

Grateful acknowledgment is made to the following
publishers for permission to use the material listed:

American Bible Society—maps: "Ancient World," "United
Israelite Kingdom," and "Palestine in the Time of Jesus."
From *Good News Bible*. Maps © United Bible Societies,
1976.

Cambridge University Press—map: "The Fertile Crescent";
diagram: "Cross-section of Palestine." From *Old Testament
Illustrations* by Clifford M. Jones, © Cambridge University
Press 1971.

Harcourt Brace Jovanovich, Inc.—map: "The World of the
apostle Paul." From *The New Testament: An Introduction* by
Norman Perrin, © 1974 by Harcourt Brace Jovanovich, Inc.

Foreword

The series of books published for the most part in the 1950s and known as the Church's Teaching Series has had a profound effect on the life and work of the Episcopal Church during the past twenty years. It is a monumental credit to that original series and to the authors and editors of those volumes that the Church has seen fit to produce a new set of books to be known by the same name. Though the volumes will be different in style and content, the concern for quality education that prompts the issuing of the new series is the same, for the need of Church members for knowledge in areas of scripture, theology, liturgy, history, and ethics is a need that continues from age to age.

I commend this new Church's Teaching Series to all who seek to know the Lord Jesus and to know the great tradition that he has commended to us.

John M. Allin
PRESIDING BISHOP

Introduction

This is one of a series of volumes in the new Church's Teaching Series. The project has been both challenging and exciting. Not only is there a wide variety of opinions regarding the substance of the teaching of the Church, there are also varying and conflicting views with regard to the methods of communicating this teaching to others. That is why we have tried to pay close attention to the various movements within the Church, and to address them. The development of this new series, therefore, has involved hundreds of men and women throughout the Episcopal Church and is offered as one resource among many for the purposes of Christian education.

While it is neither possible, nor perhaps even desirable today to produce a definitive series of books setting forth the specific teachings of a particular denomination, we have tried to emphasize the element of continuity between this new series and the old. Continuity, however, implies movement, and we believe that the new series breaks fresh ground in a creative and positive way.

The new series makes modest claims. It speaks not so much *for* the Episcopal Church as *to* it, and not to this Church only but to Christians of other traditions, and to those who wait expectantly at the edge of the Church.

Two words have been in constant use to describe this project from its inception: affirmation and exploration. The writers have affirmed the great insights of the Christian tradition and have also explored new possibilities for the future in the confidence that the future is God's.

Alan Jones
CHAIRMAN OF THE
CHURCH'S TEACHING SERIES
COMMITTEE

THE BIBLE FOR TODAY'S CHURCH

Contents

NOTE TO THE READER

· 1 ·

Why Read the Bible?

Why read the Bible? At one level the answer is obvious. We have abundant statements on the subject, statements that vary from the private testimonials of satisfied users to the most authoritative of official pronouncements to the infinitely careful efforts of theologians to get the matter exactly right. All join in a mighty chorus to extol the values of reading the Bible.

A sample of these could begin with the Catechism in the Prayer Book:

> Q. Why do we call the Holy Scriptures the Word of God?
> A. We call them the Word of God because God inspired their human authors and because God still speaks to us through the Bible.

We could also look at an official statement that goes back to the time of the English Reformation. It comes from the Thirty-nine Articles of Religion that were framed to express, as tactfully as possible, our differences from the Calvinists on the one hand and the Roman Catholics on the other. In the sixth of these articles we read:

> Holy Scripture containeth all things necessary to salvation: so that whatsoever is not read therein, nor may be proved thereby, is not to be required of any man, that it should be believed as an article of Faith, or be thought requisite or necessary to salvation.

Next we could examine the rites by which bishops, priests, and deacons are ordained and see that everyone who is ordained signs a statement that attests:

> I solemnly declare that I do believe the Holy Scriptures of the Old and New Testaments to be the Word of God, and to contain all things necessary to salvation.

Indeed, we could look throughout the new Prayer Book and see that whenever the Bible is read the reader may conclude the lesson by saying, "The Word of the Lord," to which the response is, "Thanks be to God."

Such exalted claims about the Bible are not limited to official statements. Church history furnishes us with an abundance of individual Christians—great saints and ordinary churchmen, high officials in the church and laypeople, brilliant theologians and uneducated believers—who have combined in making superlative assertions about the value of Bible reading and study for their lives. Saint Augustine, for instance, referred to the Scriptures as "letters from home." And, something which gets closer to our own day, most of us have known some fellow Christians who have told us and others about how much time they spend with the Bible and of the guidance it gives to their lives and the joy it brings to their souls.

Why do we read the Bible? There is obviously no end of testimonials to the value of doing so, but these testimonials may be like letters of reference we have read about certain people: the extravagant words of praise are not consistent with our experience. Certainly they are not consistent with the experience of the majority of contemporary Christians. There is what has aptly been described as a "strange silence" of the Bible in the church. We continue to hear it read at most of our services, but we usually do not listen carefully and expectantly to what is being read. As for reading it ourselves on a regular basis for our own spiritual nourishment, either that is an idea that has never occurred to us, or we have tried it and, far from finding it helpful for understanding other things, we have not been able to make heads or tails of it. Or, if we did understand it, it seemed to tell us of a God who may have been all right in the bow-and-arrow league, but who sounded merely quaint in the role of creator and controller of a universe in which we can land a space ship on Mars and send television pictures back to earth from there.

A case in point for all of these difficulties may be found in the passage from Galatians 4:21–31 that was appointed to be read as the epistle for the Fourth Sunday in Lent in the 1928 Book of Common Prayer:

> Tell me, ye that desire to be under the law, do ye not hear the law? For it is written, that Abraham had two sons, the one by a bondmaid, the other by a freewoman. But he who was of the bondwoman was born after the flesh; but he of the freewoman was by promise. Which things are an allegory: for these are the two covenants; the one from the mount Sinai, which gendereth to bondage, which is Agar. For this Agar is mount Sinai in Arabia, and answereth to Jerusalem which now is, and is in bondage with her children. But Jerusalem which is above is free, which is the mother of us all. For it is written, Rejoice, thou barren that bearest not: break forth and cry, thou that travailest not: for the desolate hath many more children than she which hath an husband. Now we, brethren, as Isaac was, are the children of promise. But as then he that was born after the flesh persecuted him that was born after the Spirit, even so it is now. Nevertheless, what saith the scripture? Cast out the bondwoman and her son: for the son of the bondwoman shall not be heir with the son of the freewoman. So then, brethren, we are not children of the bondwoman, but of the free.

It is unlikely in the extreme that anyone who has ever heard that passage read in church has understood it without a great deal of study, much less felt that it immediately cleared up all of the unsolved mysteries of life. Merely to understand this passage from Galatians requires a good bit of background information. You have to know that it alludes to a story in Genesis 16 and 21 about Abraham, the ancestor of the people of Israel.

God had promised that he would be the ancestor of a great nation, but when Sarah his wife was well past her menopause and the possibility of any children at all began to look very remote, they decided to help God keep his promise. Sarah had a slave by the name of Hagar (the *h* was dropped off when the name was translated into the Greek of the New Testament). Sarah suggested that Abraham have his son by Hagar, a suggestion that was in accord with the customs of the time. After Hagar gave birth to a son named Ishmael, Sarah herself had a son who was called Isaac. Sarah then became very jealous for her son's inheritance and forced Abraham to drive Hagar and Ishmael out into the wilderness so that Hagar's son would not share Sarah's son's inheritance.

With that background information you can go on to see that in the passage from Galatians Paul sets up a series of equivalencies.

$$\frac{\text{Hagar}}{\text{Sarah}} = \frac{\text{mother after the flesh}}{\text{mother by promise}} = \frac{\text{old covenant}}{\text{new covenant}} = \frac{\text{earthly Jerusalem}}{\text{heavenly Jerusalem}}$$

The point of these equivalencies is to suggest that Christians are related to Jews as Isaac is related to Ishmael. This is to say that the church rather than Judaism is the true people of God and thus the church is the legitimate heir to all of God's promises to Israel.

It has taken this much effort merely to discover what point Paul was making. That says nothing about (a) whether the point is valid, and (b) what difference it makes to us. To establish its validity we would have to show that the true meaning of the story in Genesis did not have so much to do with Isaac and Ishmael as it did with Christians and Jews. We would have to go even further than that: the quotation that Paul makes toward the end of his argument, which begins, "Rejoice thou barren," is from Isaiah 54:1. A full validation would have to show that Isaiah also was talking about Christians and Jews in addition to Isaac and Ishmael.

Even assuming the soundness of Paul's argument, though, we are still left with the question of what difference it makes to us. It had never occurred to most of us to worry about whether Christians are the true people of God or not, so Paul's elaborate proof that we are answers a question that we did not ask.

Which brings us back to our original question: Why read the Bible? This whole book was written to answer that question and a closely related one: How do you read the Bible? While it takes the entire book to state that answer in full, a brief summary of it can be stated here.

Most of the Bible is narrative. Even the parts that are not, such as the writings of the prophets or the letters of St. Paul, are addressed to particular historical situations and have the function of dialogue in that history. Both individual Christians and the church as a body have discovered over the past 2,000 years what the people of Israel had discovered before them: when the people of God read these stories and try to discover the meaning of their own lives in the light of them, understanding comes. Through these stories they have felt that they heard God talking to them and telling them his will for them. Out of this experience they have come to regard the Bible as "the Word of God" and have been able to say, in the words of the Catechism, that "God still speaks to us through the Bible." Part of the purpose of this book is to see how this can be.

Obviously, not all Christians have had this experience of using the Bible to see their lives through God's eyes. That is why part of this book is on learning how to read the Bible; learning that can help remove impediments to the experience of hearing God speak through the Scriptures.

The section of the book that deals with how God can speak to us through the stories of the Bible is the second division of Chapter 4. Chapter 2 will be devoted to removing some impediments to reading the Bible by going over the process by which, from a human point of view, the Bible came into existence. The writing of the individual books, their recognition as Scripture, and their translation and transmission to us will be described as a way of discovering what kind of books they are.

Other impediments will be removed by a discussion of how the Bible has been interpreted in the past and how it is interpreted by scholars today. It will be seen that the purpose of most modern study techniques is to eliminate the sort of misunderstanding that arises from the differences between the historical and cultural circumstances of the world of the biblical stories and those of our own world.

Since it can no longer be expected that biblical stories will be familiar to Christian people, Chapters 5–7 will give a brief summary of them, together with a sketch of a modern understanding of the historical framework into which these stories are to be set. The beliefs about God and his people that are set forth in these stories will occupy Chapters 8–10. Finally, Chapter 11 will be devoted to situations in the church and home today in which the Bible is read and studied, and will make suggestions about how that can be done more effectively.

To summarize, then, the purpose of this book is not just to convey information about the Bible. Rather, it is written to help Christian people to read the Bible so that they can hear God speaking to them through its stories. We should admit in advance, however, that his voice is more easily discernible in some parts than in others. As it turns out, the passage we quoted from Galatians, in which Paul explains the relation of Christianity to Judaism in terms of the relation of Isaac to Ishmael, is not one of the stories that has the worst acoustics for hearing the Word of God. In fact, we will return to it again and again throughout the book to illustrate the principles that are being discussed. When you have gone through the whole book, it is our hope that you can hear God speaking to you through the Bible.

· 2 ·

How the Bible Came to Be

Visitors to the Holy Land are often amazed to discover that the Samaritans mentioned in the Bible still survive. A group of less than a hundred still live in the territory of their ancestors and even sacrifice their Passover lambs every spring, something that the Jews have not done for 1900 years. The tourist-pilgrim often gets taken to their area, being shown Jacob's well where Jesus met the Samaritan woman; the ruins of Sebaste, the Roman city that Herod built where the ancient city of Samaria had been; and modern Nablus (ancient Neapolis) where the remaining Samaritans live.

One may be taken to a shop where a Samaritan priest sells antiquities: a pottery flask that goes back to the time of Moses, a graceful terra-cotta figurine of a Greek lady, and clay lamps by the score, all dug up nearby and none rare enough to have its sale forbidden by the government. Then, after suitable arrangements, one may be taken up to the Samaritan temple where the current high priest is willing to show the Torah scroll, the copy of the first five books of the Old Testament, from which the Samaritans read during their worship. His son, the priest who sold you the pottery and the member of the family who speaks English, will all assure you that this is the original copy that Moses himself wrote.

Of course, any student can tell you that it is not. Our knowledge of ancient writing is detailed enough to date this scroll to the thirteenth century A.D. rather than to the same century B.C., the century in which some scholars place Moses and the exodus from Egypt. Polite tourists do not say so, however, although they may ask to see the scrolls the Samaritans use for the other books in the Bible. If they do, they are in for a surprise: there are no others. The Samaritan Bible consists exclusively of Genesis, Exodus, Leviticus, Numbers, and Deuteronomy. The Samaritans broke away from the Jews during the time between Alexander the Great and the Maccabees (323–167 B.C.) and they accepted as their inspired books only those that were so regarded by the Jews at that time.

The realization that there are still people of our religious tradition who have a Bible of only five books, and that they have had it since the time when no one recognized more than five biblical books, can be startling. It can shake all of our preconceptions about what the Bible is. We are accustomed to thinking of the Bible as a single volume. Perhaps we visualize it as having a black leather binding and pages edged in gold or red. Yet now we are told that it has not always been that way. That raises questions for us, questions of how certain books came to be regarded as books of the Bible, of how these books came to be written in the first place, and of how books written so long ago came to be a part of the familiar landscape of our religion today.

In order to answer the questions raised by the Samaritan Pentateuch* we will begin with the Bible familiar to us today, trace it back through the steps by which it came to be translated into English, through the process before that by which the various books came to be recognized as part of the Bible, to the way those books came to be written in the first place.

God's Word into English

MODERN TRANSLATIONS

In recent years there have been so many efforts to get the Bible into more up-to-date and accurate English that one al-

---

* *Pentateuch*, derived from the Greek for "five books," means the first five books of the Old Testament, which the Jews refer to as the Torah or Law.

most needs a score card to keep track of them. The New English Bible (New Testament 1961, Old Testament 1970) was produced by British biblical scholars to make the Bible speak in the English that is currently idiomatic on their side of the Atlantic. Its American counterpart is the Good News Bible (NT 1966, OT 1976), subtitled The Bible in Today's English Version.

Roman Catholic scholars have been as active as Anglicans and Protestants. Their pioneers were the French Dominican scholars who, by 1956, had completed and published in one volume the translation they called La Bible de Jérusalem after the city in which it was produced. An English translation made directly from the Hebrew, Aramaic, and Greek original (but compared with the French) appeared in 1966, carrying also an English translation of the footnotes to the French edition. We know it as The Jerusalem Bible. American Roman Catholics have also produced The New American Bible (1970).

To demonstrate the value of these new translations, let us look at the first paragraph of our passage in Galatians in which Paul compares the relation of Christianity and Judaism to that of Isaac and Ishmael. The virtually incomprehensible translation of it that we read in Chapter 1 is from the King James Version. See how much more sense it seems to make in the Good News Bible:

> Let me ask those of you who want to be subject to the Law: do you not hear what the Law says? It says that Abraham had two sons, one by a slave woman, the other by a free woman. His son by the slave woman was born in the usual way, but his son by the free woman was born as a result of God's promise. This can be taken as a figure: the two women are two covenants, one of which (Hagar, that is) comes from Mount Sinai, whose children are born in slavery. Hagar stands for Mount Sinai in Arabia, and she is a figure of the present city of Jerusalem, a slave with all its people. But the heavenly Jerusalem is free, and she is our mother. (Gal. 4:21–26)

The Living Bible, it should be noticed, is not a translation but a paraphrase. This is to say that it represents an effort to render the sense of the original rather than exactly what the original says word by word. The quality that makes it so easy to understand is thus the very one that makes it least reliable for accurate interpretation. It should therefore be used with caution, especially since there are also traces left of the special theological interests of the author.

Most prominent among these modern English translations (and the one from which biblical quotations in this book are taken) is the Revised Standard Version (NT 1946, OT 1952). It represents an effort to alter the classic and beloved King James Version in only those places where it is necessary to do so either because English usage has changed or modern scholarship can make the translation more accurate. An intermediate step lies between the King James Version and the Revised Standard Version (RSV), a revision made by British scholars at the turn of the century, which was quickly revised by Americans. The need for the RSV was evident very soon, though, because, as someone pointed out at the time, the Victorian revisers knew Greek very well but, unfortunately, they did not know English.

OLDER ENGLISH TRANSLATIONS

If we are to begin our journey back to the original writing of the biblical books with the Bible familiar to us today as our starting point, the chances are good that, in spite of all these recent translations, the familiar Bible will still be the leather bound one with gold- or red-edged paper. In the last quarter of the twentieth century, the most familiar single translation of the Bible into English is still one that was made in 1611.

The King James Version is so called because when that king came to the English throne he had a controversy with the Puritans. When they objected to the Prayer Book on the grounds that it contained inaccurate translations of the Bible, he called for a new translation that everyone would recognize as accurate. (Incidentally, it is the *King* James Version, not the *Saint* James Version. James I has never been recognized as a saint by any Christian body and he is not likely to be.) This translation is also known as the Authorized Version, which means that since its first appearance it has been authorized to be read at services in the Church of England.

The King James Version was by no means the first English translation, nor was it an entirely new one. Nor, for that matter, was its future popularity in any way foreshadowed by its first reception. Just as contemporary translations have a hard time winning out over the King James Version, it had great difficulty in supplanting the Geneva Bible (1560) in popular favor. This translation receives its name from having been made in the city of John Calvin by English Protestants who fled there when Mary Tudor ("Bloody Mary") came to the throne. This edition was small and handy for private study. It was the first English Bible to adopt the verse divisions that had been so recently introduced in a Greek New Testament. It also had marginal notes of a militantly Protestant flavor.

The immediate ancestor of the King James Version was the Bishops' Bible of 1568, which in turn was a slight revision of the Great Bible of 1539 which was published to comply with an order of the Archbishop of Canterbury for "one boke of the whole Bible, of the largest volume, in Englyshe, and the same sett up in summe convenient place within the said churche that ye have cure of, whereat your parishners may most commodiouslye resort to the same and rede yt." It is this Bible that is behind our Prayer Book (which accounts for the difference between the Prayer Book translation of the Psalms and that of the King James Version).

Without too much violence to the evidence, one could take the Great Bible as a symbol of Anglicanism and the Geneva Bible as a symbol of the Puritan tradition that has had so much influence on the piety of American Protestantism. In some ways Anglicanism can claim to be the most biblical denomination on earth because the Bible so dominates our public worship. No one else reads so much of it in their services. But our Bible is the lectern Bible, the one that is read in church. We have never been able to cultivate within our people the habit of private Bible reading for devotion and study that has characterized the Protestant practice of religion at its best.

The Great Bible was edited by Miles Coverdale, who had previously published the first complete Bible in English

(1535). His earlier work was not his own rendering of the original languages, because he did not know them. The Great Bible (1539), however, is based on the work of William Tyndale, who did know Hebrew and Greek, and who only three years before had been martyred by the Holy Roman Emperor, Charles V. He had fled to the continent for fear of persecution in England for his efforts to get the Bible into English. It must have given him pleasure in heaven to see his recent persecutors placing his work in large lectern editions in every church in England.

Even Tyndale's translation was not the first in English. John Wycliffe, an Oxford professor in the fourteenth century, came to doubt the authority of the church, which was the basis for all religious teaching at the time, and said that the only authority for religious belief is the Bible. He thus launched a movement that produced a translation of the Bible from Latin into English in 1382 and that sent a group of wandering preachers called Lollards all over England to teach his doctrines.

THE REFORMATION AND TRANSLATIONS OF THE BIBLE

What we have just seen about Wycliffe could leave the impression that before the Reformation the Bible was not recognized as the source of authority for Christian belief and that translations of it were discouraged by the church. Both inferences are false. The question was not whether the Bible was authoritative but who was to interpret it. All agreed that its teaching was normative, but they did not agree as to what that teaching was, because its meaning is not always obvious. The question was: Who is to say what the teaching of the Bible is when that teaching is not clear? The papal position was that the hierarchy of the church was divinely empowered and enabled to make such decisions. The position of Luther and Calvin was that each person should interpret for himself or herself. Even they, however, did not think that the meaning of the Bible was always clear to the unaided human intellect. Rather they thought that it was clear to those guided by the Holy Spirit or those who were predestined to salvation. At first the reformers naïvely expected that those so guided would all agree with one another (and with their leaders), but they were disillusioned in time.

Before the Reformation the openness of the church to translations of the Bible into the language of the people varied with the experience the particular country had with such translations. In England where the Lollards had used the Wycliffe translation to undermine the church's authority, such translations were looked on with great suspicion. In Italy, though, ten different translations appeared in the last quarter of the last century before the Reformation. Fourteen translations of the Bible into High German and four into Low German appeared in print in the less than a century that elapsed between Gutenberg's invention of printing and the publication of Luther's Bible. France, however, has never produced a single translation that has preempted all others. Calvin did not make a translation of his own, but his cousin, Pierre Robert Olivetan, did, and Calvin and his successors in Geneva subjected it to a number of revisions through the years.

EARLY VERSIONS

Efforts to get the Bible or parts of it into the language of the people were made in every period of church history, sometimes on the highest authority. In the ninth century, for instance, King Alfred either translated the Ten Commandments himself into Anglo-Saxon or had it done so that it could be placed at the beginning of his country's code of law. He was also responsible for a translation of the psalms. At about the same time a priest wrote an Anglo-Saxon paraphrase between the lines of the Lindisfarne Gospels, one of the most beautiful manuscripts in the British Museum. Other early Anglo-Saxon translators include the Venerable Bede, who wrote the history of the English church up to his time, and the seventh-century poet, Caedmon.

THE VULGATE

Translations go back to the earliest days of Christianity. There is reason to believe, for instance, that during the second century much of the New Testament was translated into Syriac, a Semitic language close to the Aramaic that Jesus spoke. The New Testament began to appear in the Coptic language of Egypt in the third century and in the language of the Goths in the fourth. Surprisingly enough, the New Testament did not begin to appear in Latin until the late second century and then in North Africa rather than Rome. The Christian community in Rome spoke Greek and thus had no need for a translation. There was no one standard translation into Latin at first and by the end of the fourth century there was such a chaos of renditions that in 382 Pope Damasus asked St. Jerome, the great Bible scholar, to restore order by making a revision of the existing texts that would be the standard Latin text. His edition is called the Vulgate because it was the established form of the Bible in Latin, the vulgar tongue or language of the common people. This was the official Bible down through the Middle Ages. It was the Vulgate that the translations into European languages were to replace. Until very recently, Roman Catholic translations were required to be from it rather than from the Hebrew and Greek.

THE GREEK OLD TESTAMENT

Since the New Testament was originally written in Greek, the Old Testament is the only part of the Greek Bible that is a translation. This translation was made before the time of Christ and was necessitated by the fact that Hebrew ceased to be familiar to Jews. Even in Israel at synagogue services the lessons were read in Aramaic paraphrases called *targums*. By this time, though, there were more Jews outside Israel than in it. A large colony of these were in Egypt, especially in the great city of Alexandria, which was fast becoming the literary and cultural center of the world. Since the foundation of the city by Alexander the Great, its language was Greek, the language that had also become the *lingua franca*, the international language of government and trade. Jews there ceased to be familiar with Hebrew and needed a Bible in their everyday language. The Pentateuch at least was translated into Greek by the early third century B.C. A charming but unhistorical tale that the translation was made at the request of the Egyptian king by seventy or seventy-two scholars sent from Israel has led to the designation of the translation as the Septuagint (from the Latin word for seventy). This designation is often abbreviated in print by the Roman numerals LXX.

The Writing of Holy Writ

THE BIBLE AS LIBRARY

Our discussion of the Samaritan Pentateuch showed us that there was a time when the Bible consisted of just five books. A lot of questions are raised by that realization, as we have already seen. One is how books came to be recognized as being inspired and authoritative for the religious community. Before that process can be studied, however, it is necessary to see how the books came into existence in the first place (and thus perhaps to get straight in our minds exactly which books those are and what each is about). Even before we get to that, however, we need to recognize that for many people the shock will be, not that there was a time when the Bible consisted of only five books but rather that the Bible is more than one book.

The problem is that it all comes bound in one cover. The impression is thus left that the contents are of a unity. In a very important way, they are, but they do not have a common origin, humanly speaking. This lack of original unity is implied in the word *Bible* itself, which in Greek means "books."[1] The appropriateness of this plural form would be very obvious if we could be transported through time and space to a synagogue in the first centry A.D. If we asked in such a place to see their Bible (our Old Testament), and the congregation was rich enough to possess an entire one, we would be shown a chest in which were stored twenty-two to twenty-four parchment scrolls. This would be their library of books that "defiled the hands"—that is, books whose very touch was sacred. It was only during the Christian era that writing materials, whether parchment or papyrus, were cut into pages and sewn together as books, thus making it possible to bring together a number of biblical books in one volume.

When the books of the Bible are listed in the order in which they appear in Anglican and Protestant editions,* it can be seen that the library is divided into a number of major collections of documents, each of which has its own characteristic content or literary form.

OLD TESTAMENT
    Law
        1. Genesis (Gen.)
        2. Exodus (Ex.)
        3. Leviticus (Lev.)
        4. Numbers (Num.)
        5. Deuteronomy (Dt.)
    History
        6. Joshua (Jos.)
        7. Judges (Jg.)
        8. Ruth (Ru.)
        9. 1 Samuel (1 Sam.)
      10. 2 Samuel (2 Sam.)
      11. 1 Kings (1 Kg.)
      12. 2 Kings (2 Kg.)
      13. 1 Chronicles (1 Chr.)
      14. 2 Chronicles (2 Chr.)
      15. Ezra (Ezra)
      16. Nehemiah (Neh.)
      17. Esther (Est.)
    Poetry
      18. Job (Job)
      19. Psalms (Ps.)
      20. Proverbs (Pr.)
      21. Ecclesiastes (Ec.)
      22. The Song of Solomon (S. of S.)

---

* Since the order of books is different in Jewish and Roman Catholic editions of the Bible, those are listed in Appendices I and II (pp. 37–40).

Prophets
 Major
    23. Isaiah (Is.)
    24. Jeremiah (Jer.)
    25. Lamentations (Lam.)
    26. Ezekiel (Ezek.)
    27. Daniel (Dan.)
 Minor
    28. Hosea (Hos.)
    29. Joel (Jl.)
    30. Amos (Am.)
    31. Obadiah (Ob.)
    32. Jonah (Jon.)
    33. Micah (Mic.)
    34. Nahum (Nah.)
    35. Habakkuk (Hab.)
    36. Zephaniah (Zeph.)
    37. Haggai (Hag.)
    38. Zechariah (Zech.)
    39. Malachi (Mal.)

APOCRYPHA (omitted in many Protestant editions)
    1. 1 Esdras (1 Esd.)
    2. 2 Esdras (2 Esd.)
    3. Tobit (Tob.)
    4. Judith (Jdt.)
    5. The Additions to Esther (Ad. Est.)
    6. The Wisdom of Solomon (Wis.)
    7. Ecclesiasticus (The Wisdom of Jesus the Son of
       Sirach) (Sir.)
    8. Baruch (Bar.)
    9. The Letter of Jeremiah (Let. Jer.)
    10. The Prayer of Azariah and the Song of the Three
        Young Men (S. of 3 Y.)
    11. Susanna (Sus.)
    12. Bel and the Dragon (Bel)
    13. The Prayer of Manasseh (Man.)
    14. 1 Maccabees (1 Macc.)
    15. 2 Maccabees (2 Macc.)

NEW TESTAMENT
 Gospels
  1. Matthew (Mt.)
  2. Mark (Mk.)
  3. Luke (Lk.) ʼ
  4. John (Jn.)
 History
  5. The Acts of the Apostles (Acts)
 Letters
  Attributed to St. Paul
   6. Romans (Rom.)
   7. 1 Corinthians (1 Cor.)
   8. 2 Corinthians (2 Cor.)
   9. Galatians (Gal.)
   10. Ephesians (Eph.)
   11. Philippians (Phil.)
   12. Colossians (Col.)
   13. 1 Thessalonians (1 Th.)
   14. 2 Thessalonians (2 Th.)
   15. 1 Timothy (1 Tim.)
   16. 2 Timothy (2 Tim.)
   17. Titus (Tit.)
   18. Philemon (Philem.)
  Attributed to Others
   19. Hebrews (Heb.)*
   20. James (Jas.)
   21. 1 Peter (1 Pet.)
   22. 2 Peter (2 Pet.)
   23. 1 John (1 Jn.)
   24. 2 John (2 Jn.)
   25. 3 John (3 Jn.)
   26. Jude (Jude)
 Apocalypse
  27. Revelation (Rev.)

---

* While tradition associates Hebrews with St. Paul, it is generally recognized as non-Pauline.

THE PENTATEUCH

As the Samaritan Pentateuch showed us, the first five books in the Old Testament in order of appearance were for some time the only books to be regarded as inspired and authoritative. Not surprisingly, they also were the first to be written. Later tradition named Moses as the author of these books. For a number of reasons, including the fact that they report his death (Deuteronomy 34:5–8), scholars have come to assign a much later date to the completed form of the Pentateuch. The attribution of these books to him, however, is very understandable, since he is their chief character.

There are four main events that are recorded in these books: (1) the exodus of Israel from slavery in Egypt, (2) the gift of the Torah or Law to Moses on Mt. Sinai,* (3) the wandering of the twelve tribes of Israel in the wilderness for forty years, and (4) the entry of the tribes into the promised land of Canaan. The account of these events is prefaced by the stories of the patriarchs or ancestors of the Israelites who were slaves in Egypt, Abraham, Isaac, Jacob, and Joseph. This record of the patriarchs in turn is prefaced by a "pre-history" that goes back through the time of Noah to creation itself. These two prefatory bodies of material make up Genesis while the account of the mighty events beginning with the exodus are recorded in Exodus and the books that follow.

There was a long time between the occurrence of these events and the setting down of any of them in written form. Before that the stories were passed down individually by word of mouth. Many of the older stories, such as those of the patriarchs, came into existence to account for the origin of something, such as the association of a particular act of worship with the place where it was performed. Others were preserved to tell why a certain place bears the name that it does or how one tribe is related to another.

---

* This Law is not understood just to have been a legal code, but all of the Pentateuch. For this reason the entire five books are designated as Law or Torah even though they seem to us to be much more history than legislation.

When these stories were first written down in the time of David or Solomon, they were not written down in the form in which we now have them. Rather, our present edition of them is the result of the blending of four different strands of tradition over a period of several centuries. The most ancient oral traditions of Israel from the time of Moses and the somewhat later traditions of Israel about the patriarchs before Moses were brought together in two different places by two different groups during the early tenth and late ninth centuries B.C. Later these two versions of the traditions about the patriarchs and the exodus under Moses were brought together into one conflated account. Some of the same material was covered in a different work that came to light in the late seventh century B.C. Finally, a century or more after that, the conflated version was edited by a different hand. Thus there are four different layers of the tradition. Scholars designate them by letters of the alphabet; they are:

J. The J document is so-called because it seems to be connected with the land of Judah and it refers to God as Yahweh (English transliterations of biblical names beginning with either J or Y refer to the same initial letter in Hebrew; that is part of the reason why Yahweh has been mistransliterated as Jehovah). The J document represents the first effort to collect all of the stories in the tradition about Moses. Its writer was also the first person to think of joining to this record of the exodus event the stories about Abraham, Isaac, Jacob, and Joseph, the patriarchs. He united this material on the basis of an exalted theological vision of the interrelation between the patriarchal material and the material about the exodus.

E. The designation of this document comes from its reference to God as Elohim and its connection with Ephraim. After the death of Solomon, his kingdom was divided and the northern part was called Israel or Ephraim and the southern part was called Judah. The E document thus comes from the break-away northern kingdom, while the J document was written before the separation. E is pietistic in its attitude and more self-consciously theological in its statements than J.

D. The D document is not intertwined with the others

but consists of the core chapters of Deuteronomy 12–26. *Deuteronomy* comes from the Greek for "copy of this law." This book is written as the speech that Moses gave to the Hebrew people on the eve of their entry into the promised land. This document is identified with a book discovered in 621 B.C. during the reign of King Josiah and this date is the basis of the relative chronology of the other dates.

The group that composed the D document were under the influence of such great prophets as Amos and Hosea. The work of the group seems to have been done in two stages: the first of these produced the Book of Deuteronomy and thus belongs to our study of the Pentateuch, while the second stage was a gathering of traditions of Israelite history and the incorporation of them into the historical books of the Old Testament from Joshua through 2 Kings. This latter stage will be considered when we deal with the Prophets section of the Old Testament.

P. The P document is so designated because its interests are such Priestly matters as the temple ritual, the priesthood itself, and liturgical practices from circumcision to religious festivals. It is assigned to the sixth century B.C., a time when Israel no longer had political independence and the priesthood was becoming the focus of national identity. Even though it incorporates traditions that go back to patriarchal days, the P work was the final stage of the editing of the Pentateuch and it was the P writers who put the Pentateuch into the form in which we now have it. These writers are not thought of as having written a long and consecutive account as the J and E writers did, but as having made additions to an edition of the tradition in which J and E were already merged.

Material that is peculiar to P includes the creation story of Genesis 1 and additions to the story of Noah and the flood in Genesis 6–9. Representing as they did the Temple clergy, it is only natural that the P writers should have linked the Sabbath rest to creation (Gen. 2:1–4) and have given in such detail the religious laws of the people that make up the Book of Leviticus.

This analysis of how the Pentateuch came to be written

down can sound pretty abstract stated in this bare bones way, but the logic behind it becomes very clear when we apply it to a particular story. The account of Abraham's two sons, Isaac and Ishmael, to which Paul referred in the Galatians passage previously alluded to, makes a good case in point. The story is told in chapters 16 and 21 of Genesis. In chapter 16, Hagar is driven out immediately after she becomes pregnant because she becomes contemptuous of her barren mistress. In chapter 21, she is driven out when Sarah saw Ishmael and Isaac playing and did not wish her slave's son to be an heir with her own.

Even though Hagar is told by the angel of the Lord to return from her first exile (16:9), there is something that sounds very suspicious about the idea of two separate expulsions, especially since on each of them Hagar has a religious experience in which it is explained to her that her son will also become the ancestor of a great tribe. Our suspicions are confirmed when we notice that in chapter 16 the revelation to Hagar is made by the angel of the Lord, but in chapter 21 it is made by God himself. Since Lord is the usual English translation for *Yahweh*, and God is the rendering of *Elohim*, we know that we have what were originally two different accounts—the J and E versions—of the same story of the expulsion of Hagar. The editor who blended J and E together treated them as distinct occurrences in order to preserve both forms of the story intact.

The Priestly (P) additions to this story make an account that could almost stand by itself:

> Now Sarai, Abram's wife, bore him no children. So, after Abram had dwelt ten years in the land of Canaan, Sarai, Abram's wife, took Hagar the Egyptian her maid, and gave her to Abram her husband as a wife. And Hagar bore Abram a son; and Abram called the name of his son, whom Hagar bore, Ishmael. Abram was eighty-six years old when Hagar bore Ishmael to Abram. Abraham called the name of his son who was born to him, whom Sarah bore him, Isaac. And Abraham circumcized his son Isaac when he was eight days old, as God had commanded him. Abraham was a hundred years old when his son Isaac was born to him.

The difference in the spelling of names (Abram/Abraham, Sarai/Sarah) is a result of P editorial activity. The shift is made in 17:5,15 amid the P version of God's covenant with Abraham, in which circumcision is commanded. It is the P writer who has recorded Isaac's experience of this bit of ceremonial surgery. Indeed, the strict observance of circumcision appears to have begun near the time of the Priestly writer, since Deuteronomy, which was written earlier, is much more interested in what it calls "circumcision of the heart." It will be noticed that the P account has very little story but supplies most of our chronology. It is little more than a chronicle. Yet this chronology shows us what a blending of sources we have here, since the dates given would make Ishmael seventeen years old at the time of the expulsion, while the E account has him a child that Hagar can hide under a bush (21:15).

Behind all of the editing that has obviously gone on, we can still see vestiges of the earliest forms of the story. We said that these stories often came into existence to account for the association of a particular act of worship with the place where it was performed, to tell why a certain place bears the name it does, or to tell how one tribe is related to another.

We see all these principles at work in our story. The appearance of God to Hagar became attached to the shrine at Beer-la-hai-roi. The name of the place, which means "the well of one who sees and lives," is explained by Hagar's question in 16:13: "Have I really seen God and remained alive?" Ishmael is predicted to be a wild ass of a man who will be against all other men and have them against him, and who will live in enmity with all his kinsmen (J, 16:12) and as one who would live in the desert of Paran, intermarry with the Egyptians, and be a great archer (E, 21:20, 21). In other words, this story accounts for the tribe of Ishmaelites who were known to live that kind of life in that vicinity. Thus we see that each of the stages of pentateuchal composition may be observed in the story of Isaac and Ishmael.

THE PROPHETS

After the settlement of the tribes in the promised land of Canaan and the eventual establishment of a monarchy under David, the prophetic movement had the next great impact on the growth of the Hebrew Bible. We see that impact not only in the books that are named after the prophets and contain their oracles but also in the books that record the history of Israel from the entry into the promised land until the end of the monarchy at the time of the exile in Babylon. For this reason, the second section of the Hebrew Bible is known simply as "The Prophets" even though it includes works that we think of as historical in addition to the prophetic books themselves.

The historical record of the nation begins with the conquest of Canaan itself and continues through the time before the monarchy (Joshua, Judges, and Samuel), but calls special attention to the story of David's descendants upon the throne in Jerusalem up to the time of the end of that kingdom in 587 B.C. Thus the Book of Kings gives a prophetic interpretation of the political movements affecting this kingdom throughout its history. The writers of these historical books used a number of sources that went back to the time of the events they recorded. It is clear, for instance, that from the time of David on, official court records were used. Some of these sources from the tenth century B.C. achieve a standard in historical writing that was not to be rivaled until Thucydides and Herodotus began to write Greek history five centuries later. As we noticed above, however, the compilation of these ancient sources into a continuous narrative, and the interpretation of the events recorded from a prophetic point of view, were the accomplishment of the Deuteronomist school.

The books by and about the prophets themselves grew out of a movement of inspired men who wished to help their people to understand what was going on in the life of their nation from the perspective of God. In a way, they broke the tradition of the Pentateuch which had emphasized God's guidance of Israel and began to say that being called by God carried special responsibilities and that God would judge even his chosen people if they failed to do what he had called them to do. These prophets did not believe that their insights into the political situation of the country were the achievement of their own analytical skills, but instead they felt that the oracles they pronounced were words that had been given to them by God to pronounce to his people.

The books that bear the names of the prophets (the "Major Prophets," Isaiah, Jeremiah, and Ezekiel, and the so-called Book of the Twelve "Minor Prophets," Hosea to Malachi), then, grew out of smaller collections of oracles and sermons that had been preserved and they were given their present form during and soon after the exile. We have hints within these books themselves that the prophets had disciples who had collected and passed down the oracles and life stories of their masters. For instance, Isaiah tells his followers: "Bind up the testimony, seal the teaching among my disciples" (8:16). And in Jeremiah 36:4 we read: "Then Jeremiah called Baruch the son of Neriah, and Baruch wrote upon a scroll at the dictation of Jeremiah all the words of the Lord which he had spoken to him." Apparently the reason these oracles were written down so soon was that when the predicted event came to pass, the prophet could say, "I told you so." All of the oracles in a prophetic book do not go back to the original prophet. His disciples in later generations felt that they could add insights into the events of their own times and thus speak in the spirit of their master and say what he would have said if he could have been there.

We can see the process of the composition of a prophetic book at work in Isaiah. Scattered throughout the book there are some titles that are obviously designed to mark off different sections (e.g., 1:1; 2:1; and 13:1). Pronouncements about Israel occupy chapters 1–12 and those against foreign nations are found in chapters 13–23. There are beautiful lyrical poems in chapters 42–44 and there is a stern pronouncement in chapter 65. As a matter of fact, scholars have decided that chapters 1–39 are basically the oracles of one prophet who pronounced them during the time of the Assyrian aggression in the eighth century B.C., and that chapters 40–66 reflect the time of the release from exile in the sixth century. These two prophets are referred to rather unimaginatively as First and Second Isaiah. Other scholars suggest that there was a Third Isaiah who was responsible for chapters 56–66. The work of these two (or three) prophets is linked by their call to the nation to trust in what God was about to do for his people. Thus preexilic words were joined to postexilic ones. The people continued to see the relevance of these words to their own situation even in much later times. For example, the doctrines of the Messiah and the Suffering Servant—which were crucial to New Testament efforts to find an adequate way to speak of the impact of Jesus—are both drawn from the Book of Isaiah.

There were also interchanges within the prophetic literature. The oracle on beating swords into plowshares and spears into pruning hooks appears in both Isaiah 2:4 and Micah 4:5. A reversal of it occurs in Joel 3:10, when the people are told that plowshares will become swords and pruning hooks spears. Jeremiah 26:18 recalls an earlier prophecy on the destruction of Jerusalem in Micah 3:12. Thus the prophets were aware of and referred to their own literary tradition much as New Testament writers were later to appropriate parts of the prophetic tradition in their writings.

THE WRITINGS

We have been following the divisions of the Hebrew canon because they reflect the order in which Old Testament books were written better than Christian sequences do. The third section of the Hebrew Bible comes from the last period of Israel's witness to the hand of God in her life. That period was initiated by the tragedy of the exile of the people from the promised land into captivity in Babylon. The sorrow associated with this period in the nation's history may be heard in the plaintive lament of the psalmist: "By the waters of Babylon, there we sat down and wept, . . . How shall we sing the Lord's song in a foreign land?" (Ps. 137:1, 4). Yet this experience of the sixth century B.C. produced a whole new literature of affirmation and trust in God. The Writings, as this section is called in the Hebrew Bible, contains the remaining books of our Old Testament: Psalms, Job, Proverbs, Ruth, Song of Solomon, Ecclesiastes, Lamentations, Esther, Daniel, Ezra, Nehemiah, and Chronicles.

These miscellaneous works were also for the most part older traditions that were given their final literary form in the centuries following the return from exile. The hymns or sung prayers of the Psalms, though used in the Second Temple (the one that was built after the return from exile), had in large proportion been used before the exile in the Temple built by

Solomon. The tale of the innocent sufferer in Job was an ancient one that was put to new use in a protest against the narrow view of divine retribution that says that suffering is always a sign that one has sinned. Ezra-Nehemiah and Chronicles are closely related to one another and together bring the history of Israel up to the time of the restoration of the Temple at Jerusalem and the rebuilding of the city walls after the exile. Ezra's reading of the Torah to the people in Nehemiah 8 signals that the final editing of the Pentateuch by the P writers was completed by the end of the fifth century B.C. Chronicles is based on the Deuteronomic history of Israel, but it is written from a point of view nearer to that of the P document than that of the Deuteronomist. This late period of the Old Testament also saw the completion of poetic works such as Proverbs and the Song of Solomon and of tales like Ruth and Esther.

The last Old Testament book to be written was Daniel. It reflects the oppressed situation of Israel when the Seleucid successors of Alexander the Great in Syria dominated Israel. Although the scene of the story is set in the exile in Babylon, internal indications show that it was written in the reign of the Seleucid king, Antiochus IV Epiphanes, between 167 and 164 B.C. The prophetic tradition that had preceded and followed the exile of the sixth century had more or less ceased to function by the time of Daniel. In his book, however, a new spirit may be seen, in which the writer looks for God's dramatic intervention in history to bring to an end the oppression of his people. This expectation is expressed in the latter part of the book in the form of a vision that reveals the future course of history. Daniel was thus the beginning of a new kind of literature that was to be important during the period between the Testaments and was to have a considerable influence on the New Testament. That kind of literature is called apocalyptic, after the Greek word for revelation.

THE LETTERS OF ST. PAUL

Unlike the very long period during which the Old Testament was formed, the New Testament took shape in a relatively short time. Barely a hundred years separate the ministry of Jesus from the last New Testament book to be written, yet some eight centuries transpired between the time of Moses and Ezra's establishment of the Torah of Moses as the authoritative norm for the life of the people after the exile.

The first New Testament books to be written were not the Gospel accounts of the life and teaching of Jesus. Rather, Paul, the great missionary to the Gentiles ("people of the nations" or non-Jews), was the earliest author of New Testament books. His epistles or letters were written at least a decade before the earliest Gospel. These letters contain messages on a variety of subjects to churches he had founded or was about to visit. Thus they were not originally intended to be Holy Scripture but occasional correspondence with Christian communities around the eastern Mediterranean Sea.

The wisdom of Paul's missionary strategy is apparent in the places that he chose to establish churches; each was a natural center from which the good news could spread to the surrounding territory. His first letter was to the church in Thessalonica, the important seaport and capital of Macedonia and still the second largest city in Greece. Corinth, from which he wrote Thessalonians, was also a major port, governing as it did the narrow isthmus that attaches the southern part of Greece to the mainland; at the time it was the capital of Achaia, the southern province of Greece. Galatia was the name of one of the Roman provinces of central Asia Minor (modern Turkey). Other letters were addressed to Ephesus, just across the Aegean Sea from Corinth, and Colossae, a little inland from Ephesus. One letter was addressed to Rome, the capital of the civilized world.

These letters were written in the 50s and perhaps early 60s of the first Christian century. They show both the vitality and the growing pains of the post-resurrection community. The church had emerged as a result of the resurrection's impact on the followers of Jesus and it was now spreading among both Jews and Gentiles throughout the Roman empire. Paul's letters were addressed to new converts to the faith and touched a wide variety of topics. They begin with profound theological analysis and then go on to make application of that theology to the practical problems in the life of that local church that caused Paul thus to intervene.

THE SYNOPTIC GOSPELS

The English word *gospel* is derived from an old Anglo-Saxon term *Godspell* which meant "good tidings." Gospel, then, means "good news," the glad tidings that in Jesus God has acted finally and decisively for the reclamation of a lost world. Gospel is used to translate into English the Greek word *euangelion*, which also means "good news." The Latin transliteration is *evangelium*. We see the Greek root drawn on for our word *evangelist*, by which we mean either the writer of a Gospel or anyone who tries to convert others to Christianity.

Traditionally it has been believed that the writers of the four Gospels included two disciples of Jesus (Matthew the tax collector and John the son of Zebedee) and two companions of apostles (John Mark, the companion first of Paul and later of Peter, and Luke "the beloved physician" who was a companion of Paul). Scholars have now recognized, however, that the process behind the writing of the Gospels took longer and was more complex than is suggested by the traditional theory that the Gospels are memoirs of Jesus written either by his immediate followers or by their assistants to whom they told their stories.

Much of this insight is the result of the discovery that the first three Gospels—Matthew, Mark, and Luke—can be set down in parallel columns and compared to one another. When this is done, startling results occur. We see that almost every word in Mark recurs in Matthew and half recur in Luke. In addition, Matthew and Luke share another large body of material, mostly sayings of Jesus, that Mark does not have. Finally, Matthew has some material that Luke does not have, and vice versa.

This capacity of Matthew, Mark, and Luke to be studied together in parallel columns causes us to refer to them as the Synoptic Gospels. This term is derived from a Greek word that means "capable of being seen together." John does not

have either the outline or the content that makes such comparisons with other Gospels very profitable. The results of the
comparison of the Synoptic Gospels, however, creates what
is known as "the synoptic problem." By this we mean the
question of how Matthew, Mark, and Luke are related to one
another so that they can be compared in the way that we have
described with the results that we have reported.

The detailed similarity of Matthew and Luke to Mark,
alongside Mark's not having large blocks of material that the
other two share is explained by saying that Matthew and
Luke used Mark for a source, that they each had copies of
Mark open before them when they wrote. The other shared
material of Matthew and Luke, which consists largely of sayings of Jesus, suggests that they had another source in common in addition to Mark. The German scholars who first
noticed this did not know what to call the source except
"source," which in German is *Quelle*. From that it has come
to be called the Q document. The material that Matthew has
that is not duplicated in Luke is referred to as M and that
which is peculiar to Luke is known as L. The pattern of
synoptic relations may thus be diagramed as follows:

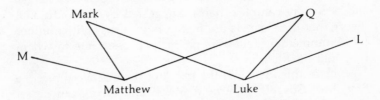

Knowing how these Gospels are interrelated, however,
does not tell us anything about when they were written.
There are reasons for believing that Mark was written near
the time of the death of Peter and that of the destruction of
the Temple at Jerusalem by the Romans. Thus we have a date
in the late 60s or early 70s A.D. Since Matthew and Luke both
use Mark for a source, they must have come later, probably as
much as twenty years later.

This late dating of the earliest Gospel means that at least a
generation elapsed between the time of the crucifixion, usu-

ally dated around A.D. 30–33, and the writing of the earliest
Gospel. That brings into question whether any of the Gospels
is the work of an apostle or apostle's companion, or even of
an eyewitness of any sort. How was information about the
life and teaching of Jesus preserved and passed down during
that thirty or forty years? A close study of the Gospels shows
that the material in them was passed down by word of mouth
in the form of single stories or sayings. It was in the preaching and teaching of the church that the memories of Jesus
were kept alive until Mark began to write. Thus there is a
period of oral transmission of tradition behind the New Testament as well as behind the Old.

THE FOURTH GOSPEL

Anyone who has read the Synoptic Gospels and then turns
to the Gospel attributed to John has a sense of having moved
into a different world. As early as the third century it was
being observed that while the other Gospels give us the story
of Jesus' life, John gives us the spiritual interpretation of it.

This difference is felt partly in the prologue (1:1–18) with
which the Gospel of John begins. It speaks of our Lord as the
Word and tells of his existence before the creation of the
world—a very different beginning from the stories of his infancy in Matthew and Luke. The story is told differently: only
about seven miracles of Jesus are reported, but these stories
heighten rather than diminish the supernatural atmosphere
of the Gospel. Furthermore, while the stories are obviously
intended to narrate real events, it is also clear that the events
have a symbolic meaning. Then too, Jesus talks in a different
way in this Gospel from the way he speaks in the others:
instead of giving a series of pithy "one liners," he presents his
thought in long and orderly discourses with carefully developed points.

All of this leads scholars to conclude that the author drew
on oral tradition about Jesus in a form similar to but independent of that followed by the synoptics. He was not content merely to pass this information along, but he meditated
on it and thus presents it in the perspective of a unified

vision. Some even think that Jesus' speeches in John were used as sermons by the evangelist before they were incorporated into the Gospel. The long period of reflection presupposed by this interpretation had led to the conclusion that the Gospel was not written down until the last decade of the first century A.D.; although some scholars now tend to date it much earlier.

ACTS

The author of this history of the expansion of the early church from Jerusalem to Rome makes it clear that he is also the author of the Gospel according to Luke and that he intends his two books to be taken as the unified parts of a larger work. He did not have the sources for this later work, however, that he had for his Gospel. The early church did not believe that the proclamation of salvation depended on the memory of the apostles the way it did on the memory of their Lord. He did have a list of the stops that Paul made as he toured the northeastern Mediterranean in his missionary activity and of his hosts along the way.

Then, too, there were stories connected with these various places as there were also stories that had been passed down about Peter. The account does not record the acts or deeds of all the apostles; the first half of the book centers around Peter and the second half around Paul. In a real sense, the main character of the book is the Holy Spirit who was guiding the church into its mission to the Gentile world. From these sources Luke was able to put together a series of vivid scenes that record the important early expansion of this community that was guided and filled by the Holy Spirit.

LATER EPISTLES

The influence of the example of Paul was so powerful in the early church that for a time it seemed to be thought that the only form other than a Gospel that Christian literature could take was that of a letter. Thus we have documents that employ the convention of appearing to be letters addressed by

Paul to his assistants, Timothy and Titus. Since they give instructions for the pastoral oversight of congregations, they are known as the Pastoral Epistles. These letters reflect a situation so different from that of the authentic letters of Paul, and they are written in such a different style, that they are not thought to be the work of Paul himself. They are not addressed to new missionary churches, as Paul's letters are, but to a second generation of Christians concerned about internal structures for maintaining the now established life of the church. Since these letters show a familiarity with the life of Paul and great admiration for him, they are thought to be the work of those who wanted to tell a later generation what they thought Paul would have said. Some scholars also doubt the Pauline authorship of 2 Thessalonians, Colossians, and Ephesians, believing them to be later and more highly developed statements of Paul's thought by some of his theological heirs.

Other epistles addressed to the church at large rather than to an individual congregation and thus called Catholic or General Epistles are 1 and 2 Peter, James, Jude, and 1, 2, and 3 John. These letters deal with the problems of a developing church institution: persecution, false teachers, ministerial authority, biblical interpretation and the delay of Jesus' second coming.

Some persons today may be shocked or offended that the traditional authorship of biblical books is questioned. They need not be. In ancient times a famous name was often attached to a given work to insure its wider acceptance. Thus the name of an apostle might be given to a work that actually came from the followers of that apostle. As with the Old Testament prophets, words were thought to be so vital that they could be reapplied to later situations and could also be added to in order to show what the great leader would have said in the new circumstances. These writers thought that they spoke in the spirit of their esteemed predecessor and that in a very real sense he continued to speak through them. There was no sense of plagiarism or of stealing another's ideas, as we would expect today. Rather, the name of the prominent person was used to make sure that the writing would be given the reading it deserved.

THE REVELATION

Just as Daniel, the last book of the Old Testament to be written, was an apocalyptic vision, so the last book in order of appearance in the New Testament, Revelation, is the only book in the Christian section of the Bible in that literary form. In some ways it is related to the epistles because near its beginning it has what appear to be letters to seven churches on the western coast of Asia Minor. The basic literary pattern, however, is that of a series of heavenly visions that reveal the future. Although the message in Revelation is stated in highly symbolic language that is difficult to interpret, it appears to be a message of consolation to these churches just before a great persecution broke out against Christians for refusing to participate in the worship of Roman emperors that began in that area.

The Validation of the Word of God

THE CONCEPT OF A CANON

Knowing how the books of the Bible were written and how they came to be translated into English still does not touch on the heart of the matter. The crucial question is: What makes these books different from any others? The answer sketched in our first chapter is that it is through these books that the church has heard and continues to hear God speaking. But that raises a further question: why do we hear him speaking through these and not through others? It would be foolhardy or dishonest to say that he has never been known to speak through any others. The real claim of the church is that God may be relied on to speak through these books and that these books are reliable in what they treat as the word of God. This implies what is true: these books have been certified by the church, and by Israel before her, as dependable channels of the word of God.

The list of certified books is called the *canon* of Scripture and the process by which books were included on the list is known as *canonization*. The term canon comes from a Greek word that means cane or rod, and thus, by extension, standard, rule, or guide. In the same way, church law is known as canon law and the canonization of a saint is the church's official recognition of the exemplary witness of that person.

THE OLD TESTAMENT AND APOCRYPHA

As we have already seen, the Torah or Pentateuch was already recognized as authoritative by the time of Ezra. The Prophets and the Writings appear to have been accepted no later than 132 B.C., when a Jew had moved to Egypt, as many did during that period, and taught his faith down there. As a means of instruction, he wished to use a book that his grandfather had written in Hebrew. In order to make use of it, he had to translate it into Greek. This book appears in our Apocrypha as Ecclesiasticus. In his prologue to the book, the grandson tells us that his grandfather devoted himself especially "to the reading of the Law and the Prophets and the other books of our fathers." Thus we hear the Prophets and the Writings referred to in a manner that suggests that they were regarded as a part of the Bible.

This does not mean, however, that the list was exact. The process of specifying exactly which books constituted the Writings took at least until A.D. 90. The Jews made a desperate, futile, and heroic effort to throw out their Roman invaders between A.D. 66 and 70. Before the final destruction of Jerusalem, a group of rabbis got the permission of the Romans to leave the city and found a rabbinical college and council in the little coastal town of Jabneh, or Jamnia. By the last decade of the century, Christianity was already recognized as a religion distinct from Judaism. While trying to pull their religious community together in a tight unit that could hold fast in the trials ahead, the rabbis defined their faith in a way that explicitly excluded the Christians. One of the ways they did that was to draw up their list of biblical books in a way that would exclude anything that might furnish support for Christianity.

To understand that, we have to go back a little and notice that the books that are listed in our Old Testament are by no means the only religious works written by Jews. We have already mentioned the Septuagint, the translation of the Old Testament into Greek that was made in Egypt. This Greek translation of the Old Testament became the first Bible of Christians. It contained, in addition to the original Hebrew Torah, Prophets, and Writings, a number of other religous writings, many of which had originally appeared in Greek. These extra books were excluded from the list of canonical books drawn up by the rabbis in Jamnia. They were kept in the Christian Old Testament, however, both in its Greek Septuagint form and in its Latin translation known as the Vulgate.

By the time of the Reformation, Christian scholars had learned about the shorter Hebrew canon of Jamnia. The Calvinists said the books in the Septuagint that were not in the Hebrew canon were uninspired, and they left them out of their Bibles. Lutherans and Anglicans, however, decided that, while no doctrine of the faith could be based on a teaching that appeared in one of these books but nowhere else in the Bible, the books were nevertheless worth reading. They published these additional "hidden" books between the Old and New Testaments as the Apocrypha. Roman Catholics and the Eastern Orthodox continued to publish them as part of the Old Testament as they had always done. The different reactions of the different churches at the time of the Reformation accounts for the different number of books in Catholic and Protestant Old Testaments and for the inclusion of the Apocrypha in some Bibles and not in others.

THE NEW TESTAMENT

Just as not all Jewish religious books are included in the Old Testament, so not all early Christian writings are included in the New Testament. Some of them, especially additional Gospels and acts of individual apostles, were produced by heretical groups as propaganda for their own tenets. Others, while perfectly orthodox, do not represent the earliest impact of the life and teaching of Jesus on the Christian community. Many of these books were valued very highly though and some were treated for a while as though they belonged to the canon.

The fluid situation in which a wide range of literature was used in the early years of the church came to an end with the increasing pressure of heresies within the church. The first person ever to draw up a list of Christian books as canonical was in fact a heretic named Marcion who arrived in Rome from Asia Minor about A.D. 140. Marcion's views led him to reject the Old Testament and many of the Christian writings with which he did not agree. His Bible consisted exclusively of the letters of Paul and the Gospel of Luke. The fourfold Gospel idea was developed in reaction to this narrow, exclusivistic viewpoint and it was well established in the church by the time of early Church Fathers like Irenaeus (A.D. 183) and Tertullian (A.D. 200).

By this time the letters of Paul were also recognized as authoritative. The later epistles and Revelation took longer to be recognized and for a while it was uncertain which books were accepted, which disputed, and which rejected. By the time of Athanasius (A.D. 367) and the councils of the church in North Africa, held in Hippo in 393 and in Carthage in 397, our list of twenty-seven books of the New Testament was established as canonical and authoritative for the whole church.

Appendix I

Order of Books in the Hebrew Bible*

LAW

1. Genesis (*Bereshith* = "In the beginning")
2. Exodus (*Shemoth* = "Names")
3. Leviticus (*Wayiqra* = "And he called")
4. Numbers (*Bemidbar* = "In the wilderness")
5. Deuteronomy (*Debarim* = "Words")

---

* The italicized words following the English names of the books are the Hebrew names. The words in quotation marks are the translation of the Hebrew when that differs from the English. Most Hebrew names of books that are not names of the author are the initial words of the book.

PROPHETS

Early Prophets
6. Joshua (*Yehoshua*)
7. Judges (*Shophetim*)
8. Samuel (*Shemuel*)
9. Kings (*Melakim*)

Later Prophets
10. Isaiah (*Yeshayahu*)
11. Jeremiah (*Yirmeyahu*)
12. Ezekiel (*Yehezkel*)
13. The Twelve Prophets (*Shenem Asar*)

Hosea	Nahum
Joel	Habakkuk
Amos	Zephaniah
Obadiah	Haggai
Jonah	Zechariah
Micah	Malachi

WRITINGS
14. Psalms (*Tehellim* = "Praises")
15. Job (*Iyyob*)
16. Proverbs (*Mishle*)
17. Ruth (*Ruth*)
18. Song of Solomon (*Shir Hashirim* = "Song of Songs")
19. Ecclesiastes (*Qoheleth* = "Preacher")
20. Lamentations (*Ekah* = "How")
21. Esther (*Ester*)
22. Daniel (*Daniel*)
23. Ezra-Nehemiah (*Ezra-Nehemyah*)
24. Chronicles (*Dibre Hayamim*)

Appendix II

Relative Order of Books in Anglican/Protestant and Roman Catholic Editions of the Old Testament and Apocrypha

Anglican/Protestant	*Roman Catholic*
I. LAW	
1. Genesis	1. Genesis
2. Exodus	2. Exodus

3. Leviticus
4. Numbers
5. Deuteronomy

II. HISTORY
6. Joshua
7. Judges
8. Ruth
9. I Samuel
10. 2 Samuel
11. 1 Kings
12. 2 Kings
13. 1 Chronicles
14. 2 Chronicles
15. Ezra
16. Nehemiah

17. Esther

III. POETRY
18. Job
19. Psalms
20. Proverbs
21. Ecclesiastes
22. Song of Solomon

IV. PROPHETS
23. Isaiah
24. Jeremiah
25. Lamentations

26. Ezekiel
27. Daniel

The Twelve Prophets
28. Hosea
29. Joel
30. Amos
31. Obadiah
32. Jonah

3. Leviticus
4. Numbers
5. Deuternomy

6. Joshua
7. Judges
8. Ruth
9. I Samuel
10. 2 Samuel
11. 1 Kings
12. 2 Kings
13. 1 Chronicles
14. 2 Chronicles
15. Ezra
16. Nehemiah
17. Tobit
18. Judith
19. Esther

20. Job
21. Psalms
22. Proverbs
23. Ecclesiastes
24. Song of Solomon
25. Wisdom of Solomon
26. Ecclesiasticus

27. Isaiah
28. Jeremiah
29. Lamentations
30. Baruch
31. Ezekiel
32. Daniel

33. Hosea
34. Joel
35. Amos
36. Obadiah
37. Jonah

33. Micah	38. Micah
34. Nahum	39. Nahum
35. Habakkuk	40. Habakkuk
36. Zephaniah	41. Zephaniah
37. Haggai	42. Haggai
38. Zechariah	43. Zechariah
39. Malachi	44. Malachi
	45. 1 Maccabees
	46. 2 Maccabees

THE APOCRYPHA*

1. 1 Esdras
2. 2 Esdras
3. Tobit
4. Judith
5. Additions to Esther
6. Wisdom of Solomon
7. Ecclesiasticus (Wisdom of Jesus Ben Sirach)
8. Baruch
9. Letter of Jeremiah
10. Prayer of Azariah and Song of Three Young Men
11. Susanna
12. Bel and the Dragon
13. Prayer of Manasseh
14. 1 Maccabees
15. 2 Maccabees

---

* There is no Apocrypha column on the Roman Catholic side because the books of the Apocrypha accepted as canonical by Roman Catholics are integrated into the Old Testament. Many Protestant editions of the Bible do not contain the Apocrypha. The order of books in the New Testament is the same in both Anglican/Protestant and Roman Catholic editions.

· 3 ·

How the Bible Has Been Interpreted

The Need for Interpretation

A priest from overseas comes to an American seminary to do further study in theology. His native culture is one in which gradations in social rank are sharply distinguished so that each person knows exactly what his position is in relation to anyone else. He is either a subordinate or a superior. Subordinates can earn honor by being deferential to superiors and by giving them costly gifts.

When the priest arrives at the American seminary, such patterns of behavior are the only ways that he knows to function in society. He probably assumes unconsciously that they are built into the structure of the universe. Yet they do not succeed in his new environment. The faculty who receive his deference and gifts have difficulty in not regarding them as efforts to curry favor. His fellow students, on the other hand, do not assume that they should treat him with a great deal more respect and formality than they treat one another merely because he has already been ordained and they have not. The American faculty and students assume as readily as the overseas priest that the social patterns to which they are accustomed are built into the structure of the universe.

Because the priest and the American faculty and students did not make the same cultural assumptions, communication between them was impeded and the behavior of each needed

41

to be interpreted to the other. Much greater than these cultural differences are those that separate modern Christians from the world of the Bible. The thought world of ancient, oriental, primitive people is very different from that of modern, occidental, technological people. Since the Bible is a product of that ancient world, it does not have the immediate accessibility of understanding to people today that writings of their own time have. A prerequisite for understanding much of the Bible is familiarity with the cultural assumptions that lie behind its stories. In short, the Bible needs to be interpreted.

Cultural differences alone, however, do not account for the need for interpretation. Interpretation is inevitable, even when people are dealing with their own experience. To cite a common example, three witnesses to an automobile accident will give three varying descriptions of it, not because anyone is trying to deceive anyone else but because each person perceived the event differently. The mind receives far more sensations than it can possibly process, so it has developed sorting techniques that select which sensations will rise to the conscious level. An interpretive process has already begun in the selection of just those sensations. Further organization of the material occurs when the subject of the experience tells anyone else about it; that organization—the decision to tell the story one way and not another—is a form of interpretation, even when the decision is about no more than the order in which to report the events.

Memory continues to shape awareness of what has happened as time passes. Stories told over and over tend to settle into fixed patterns of recitation. In time the story is remembered better than the event it records. Favorite stories get to be like trips home in horse-and-buggy days. The wheels of the buggy were set into the ruts of the road and the horse then pulled the buggy safely all the way with no signals on the reins for guidance. This settling of memory is also a form of interpretation.

The recognition that interpretation is inevitable leads to an insight of the first magnitude: in any discussion about the meaning of a passage in a book—from a biblical text to a comic strip—there is no "natural" meaning that is objectively there and independent of any subjective interpretation. Rather, meaning occurs when a mind seeks to understand a passage. This means that there is no single, original, only valid meaning to a text from Holy Scripture. It is not necessary to invoke the doctrine of the inspiration of the Bible by God in order to be able to say that the Scriptures have meaning beyond anything that their authors were aware of when they wrote. No writer ever comprehends all that she or he wrote. To read the Bible, then, or any other book, is to engage in interpretation.

If we remember that to read the Bible is to engage in interpretation, we will be protected against reading our own cultural attitudes into the text. The more we are conscious of the fact that we are "doing" interpretation, the more adequate our interpretation is likely to be.

Even though there is no one single objective meaning to a biblical passage, there is something about human nature that wishes there were such a meaning. People want meaning to be something that is hard and fast, something they can readily detect. If they are to build their faith on it, they want it to be firm and steadfast. Such aspirations, however, are doomed to disappointment. If there were any such objective, obvious, easily ascertainable single meaning of a passage, different Christian bodies would not disagree so vigorously over the interpretation of particular passages. Since it cannot be assumed that those who disagree with one's own interpretation do so because they are either ignorant or evil, it must be recognized that disagreements occur because no single meaning is obvious to all fair-minded readers. Manifold meaning is a fact of life that must be lived with. Living with it may be made a little easier with the recognition that the multiplicity of meaning to a biblical passage is not a recent discovery or invention; it has always existed. An appreciation of that historical truth can make the lack of a clear, single meaning today more palatable. In fact, such historical study can show that the manifold meaning of biblical passages is an enrichment of them rather than an impoverishment. Thus a short look at the history of biblical interpretation is called for.

The History of Biblical Interpretation

THE OLD TESTAMENT

The history of the interpretation of biblical tradition actually began before any of the traditions had been written down. This history thus begins with the oral transmission of narratives that were later to be incorporated into biblical books. The interpretation of the Old Testament that will be discussed in this section, then, is the interpretation that occurs within the Old Testament itself. The principles to be observed may all be noted in the Pentateuch.

The stories in Genesis about the patriarchs Abraham, Isaac, Jacob, and Joseph reflect a time in the land of Canaan long before the Exodus, as Chapter 2 showed. Many of these stories were passed down to account for practices of worship performed at places mentioned in the stories such as Bethel, Beersheba, and Hebron—or Beer-la-hai-roi, the spot of Hagar's vision.

These traditions about the patriarchs were reinterpreted in the light of all the later crises of Israel. The J writer interpreted the patriarchal narratives and the stories that followed in terms of the establishment of the monarchy under David in the tenth century. The E writer understood them from the perspective of the breakaway of the northern kingdom in the ninth century. The Deuteronomist (D) saw it all in terms of the teaching of the prophets who had lately appeared and the Priestly (P) writers drew strength from these stories after the exile.

The same stories, then, were not tied forever to their original association with particular places of worship. Instead they were used and reused from a number of different perspectives over a period that spanned more than fifteen centuries before they were finally crystallized in the written form in which they are known today. The same story was applied to succesive events in the nation's life; it was understood within the context of those new events and it, in turn, lent understanding to those events.

We may see this process of constant reinterpretation at work in the story of Isaac and Ishmael. As we noted in Chapter 2, the purpose of this story in its original patriarchal form was to explain the shrine at Beer-la-hai-roi and to account for the wild manner of life of the Ishmaelites to the south. The point was shifted in the J version of the story. The main effect of the story when it is incorporated into the J narrative is to slow down the action and to heighten suspense. In the previous chapter, God's promise that Abraham would be the ancestor of a great nation had been narrated. This story of the effort to make the promise come true through the son of a slave rather than through the son of the wife has the effect of stretching out the time between the promise and its fulfillment, raising doubts about whether the promise will be kept. There is also a comment on human nature that is almost a moral: our faith is sometimes so fainthearted that we take things into our own hands rather than leave them in the hands of God. Yet the meaning comes through clearly that God does not need our help; he is capable of bringing his own plans to completion without our assistance and in spite of our interference. In addition, the J writer affirms that, while the promise lies with Abraham and his family, God also cares for the family of Hagar. A theory of the election of Israel is combined with a universalism of God's love for all nations.

In the E account there is no longer any recollection of the original purposes of the patriarchal stories: not only has the name of Beer-la-hai-roi dropped out, but even Ishmael is not mentioned by name. There is, however, a new moral and theological sensitivity. The characters have changed. In J Abraham was a passive character who submitted without thought to the cruel requests of his wife. In E, however, Abraham was upset by Sarah's demand and did not go along with it until God told him in a vision that her callous plan was to be used by him to accomplish his divine purpose. Hagar, too, is different; in J she was proud and contemptuous and had brought her fate on herself, but here she is innocent. In addition, there is in the E narrative a recognition that the sacred history of Israel has byways in which other nations are blessed by God, even if they do not belong to the people to whom salvation is promised.

The P writer has dropped the story altogether and is concerned with nothing but vital statistics: Abraham had two sons, one by his wife Sarah and the other by her maid Hagar.

From this reconstruction we see that the same event was reported four times over a period of twelve to thirteen hundred years, each time with different emphases and even with differences in plot. The final editor of Genesis, then, did not think there was only one way to tell the story or that it had one, single, clear, objective meaning. He was content to permit the multiplicity of meanings to remain. The story had been enriched by each retelling. And the enrichment did not stop there. The story originally came to our attention in the form in which St. Paul used it. He was writing to the Galatians, Gentiles who had been converted directly to Christianity without becoming Jews first. Now some of them thought that they needed to add to their Christian faith such Jewish practices as circumcision. Paul wants to warn them that trying to satisfy God by the correct observance of religious regulations commits a person to such perfect obedience that one *deserves* God's approval—an impossible accomplishment. To make his point he compares the relation of Christians to Jews with that of the descendants of Isaac to those of Ishmael. His logic here may seem very artificial to us (although we will have an opportunity to study it more closely later on), but in one very clear way his analysis penetrated to the heart of the story in Genesis. He understood the story to be about the relation of two groups of people to God. At the earliest patriarchal stage which dealt with the relation of the Ishmaelites to the Israelites, exactly that question was the issue.

To continue briefly this extension of our study of the history of the interpretation of the Isaac and Ishmael story beyond the Old Testament period, we may note that the church calendar also furnishes a context in which biblical stories may be reinterpreted. The Galatians passage just discussed is the traditional epistle for the Fourth Sunday in Lent. Because

Paul speaks there of the church as our mother, the medieval church made this a special occasion for visiting the cathedral, the mother church of a diocese; the day even came to be called Mothering Sunday. A later English development was to set this day aside for servants and apprentices to visit their parents and take them a *simnel* or "mothering" cake. Thus the story of Hagar, originally told to account for liturgical observances at Beer-la-hai-roi, came finally to be the occasion for the development of new liturgical observances.

From this historical survey we may conclude that there never was at any stage of the biblical tradition a biblical passage that had an objective meaning that was its "real" meaning and which was maintained unaltered through the ages. Rather, meaning has been appropriated by each new generation and that has added to the field of meaning of the original event. The biblical narrative is heard as a living dialogue between the remembered tradition and the ongoing life of the religious community. There was never a situation in which the tradition did all the talking and the community did all the listening. The biblical narrative was constantly reinterpreted in the light of the new situation. At the same time, every new interpretation added new meaning to the original story. As we have received them, the stories are clothed with many layers of such added meaning. This is to say that interpretation is not only inevitable, it is also immensely valuable for its additions to our storehouse of meaning.

It is possible to show how such continuous reinterpretation led to a build-up of meaning throughout the rest of the Old Testament after the Pentateuch. For instance, the process can be traced in the historical books from the original court records in the time of David through the work of the Deuteronomist and Chronicler or in the connections between sections of the Book of Isaiah. These examples are enough to show, though, that the need for interpretation of the Bible today is documented and justified by the fact that each story began as an interpretation of events long before it was ever written down, and that it has been reinterpreted at each new stage of biblical tradition. To read it now is to add to that ongoing interpretive process.

THE NEW TESTAMENT

Having seen that biblical interpretation is inevitable and desirable, we now examine the interpretation of the Old Testament by New Testament writers. This serves four purposes: First, it illustrates what is meant by interpretation. Next, it promotes better understanding of many New Testament passages by showing the logic behind them. Then, since some of these methods of interpretation were in common use up until the modern period and continue in use in some circles even today, gaining familiarity with them assists one in understanding biblical interpretation throughout the premodern period. Finally, the study of particular methods of interpretation enables one to form important conclusions about all interpretation.

The Bible of Jesus and his first followers was our Old Testament. Much of the theology of the writers of the New Testament is an outgrowth of their efforts to understand Jesus in terms of the Old Testament. In these efforts they used four methods of interpreting that Bible: apocalyptic, allegorical, typological, and rabbinic.

Apocalyptic

The name for this kind of interpretation is derived, as we have seen, from a Greek word for a revelation, an unveiling of hidden truth. Apocalyptic thought, so far as we know, first appeared in the Book of Daniel in the Old Testament, and it was characteristic of much Jewish thought in the intertestamental period.

Basic to apocalyptic thought is a time scheme of two ages: the present age, understood to be an evil age under the control of demonic powers; and the age to come, considered to be a good age in which God rules over history. This age to come is in the future and is to be ushered in by a cosmic war in which the powers of evil will be defeated and God's reign or kingdom will be inaugurated. Since the principal message of Jesus was that "the kingdom of God is at hand," it is obvious that his role, ministry, and message were understood from this perspective by his contemporaries.

What the apocalyptic method reveals is a scheme of history in which it is believed that the historic moment has arrived for the shift from the present age to the age to come. Such a scheme may be seen in Daniel 7:23–24 where the prophet has a dream about four beasts, the last of which has ten horns. It is made clear that the four beasts refer to four empires and that the horns of the fourth beast refer to the ten kings who have ruled the last empire. Thus the people of the time knew that this dream culminated in their own time when Antiochus IV Epiphanes was the tenth ruler of the Seleucid empire. He had conquered Israel and defiled the Temple, but this vision promised that God was going to intervene in history on behalf of his people. The book is written as though Daniel lived 400 years before the time of Antiochus, so the story is understood as a prediction that had been made centuries before the events of 167 B.C. that it describes.

The existence of a book like Daniel, which purports to be a prediction of the future course of history written in a symbolic way, led to the conclusion that other books were to be understood in the same way. They, too, were to be decoded in the light of current events. There is a major difference, however, between books that were originally written as apocalyptic predictions and those that were only interpreted that way: the books written as apocalypses were written in highly symbolic language, but the fulfillment of prophesy discovered by the apocalyptic interpretation of nonapocalyptic books usually turned on a literal rather than a symbolic detail. In Daniel, the horn of a beast could refer to an emperor, but, as we shall see, Matthew thought Isaiah predicted the virgin birth of Jesus because he talked about a virgin. This apocalyptic interpretation of nonapocalyptic books goes back at least as far as a commentary on the Book of the Prophet Habakkuk that was discovered among the Dead Sea Scrolls, but it still goes on in the work of such contemporary Christian writers as Hal Lindsey, whose book *The Late Great Planet Earth* has sold in the millions of copies.

While innumerable examples of apocalyptic interpretation could be cited from the New Testament, some of the clearest examples appear in the Gospel according to Matthew. Eleven of the many quotations from the Old Testament that the author of the first Gospel applies to Jesus are introduced by a formula such as: "All of this took place to fulfill what the Lord had spoken by the prophet." This shows that he thought that the Old Testament books were not written for their own times, but as a series of veiled predictions of the coming of Jesus.

A good example is in Matthew 1:22–23. After the author has told of the virginal conception of Jesus, he goes on to say:

> All this took place to fulfil what the Lord had spoken by the prophet: "Behold, a virgin shall conceive and bear a son, and his name shall be called Emmanuel" (which means God with us).

The quotation is from Isaiah 7:14.[1] Isaiah himself had used these words to reassure the king of Judah that he need not fear the hostile coalition of kingdoms to the North, because the Assyrians would conquer both countries within the period that it takes a child to grow to the age of discretion. In making an apocalyptic interpretation, however, Matthew assumed that Isaiah was not writing about his own time, but was prophesying about the time of Jesus instead.

Other examples of apocalyptic interpretation are spread throughout the New Testament. For example, the story of the crucifixion in Mark is clearly built around allusions to Psalms 22 and 69 and Isaiah 53. In all of these passages the presupposition is that Christ is the key that unlocks the veiled meaning of the Old Testament. Underlying this concept are several assumptions. The first is that the Father planned the Son's work on earth before the beginning of time and that he had caused the Holy Spirit to inspire the prophets to insert into their writings some indications of this divine plan.[2] Furthermore, it was believed that this same Spirit of God was needed to guide Christian readers in their interpretation of the Old Testament so that they would discover this christological meaning there.

Allegorical

This method of interpretation treats Old Testament stories as though they had been written in code so that every character or thing stands for something else. The reader who learns what each item stands for is able to decode the story and discover its Christian meaning. This allegorical method of interpretation had been devised originally by Stoic philosophers who, on the one hand, assumed that Homer's Iliad and Odyssey were in some sense inspired Scriptures, and on the other, were frankly shocked by some of the immoral goings-on of the gods that are reported in these two epics. The way they reconciled these two beliefs was to suppose that anything unedifying was not intended to be interpreted literally, but instead was about something other than its apparent subject.

In the same way, New Testament writers knew that there were no explicit predictions of Jesus in the Old Testament, but they were incapable of imagining that God's revelation failed to mention his greatest gift to humanity. The explanation had to be that the references to Jesus in the Old Testament were veiled and meant to be decoded allegorically. This may sound very much like apocalyptic interpretation, but there are important distinctions. Apocalyptic interpretation always treats a passage in an inspired text as a prediction of the future, but allegory can be without any time reference. Further, apocalyptic interpretation, as opposed to apocalyptic composition, depends on a literal rather than a symbolic connection.

A clear example of allegorical interpretation in the New Testament is the passage in which Paul tries to show that the story about Abraham's sons by his slave woman and his wife has as its true subject the relation of Christianity to Judaism. The lack of familiarity with allegorical interpretation among modern Christians is responsible for the difficulty they have in understanding this passage. It would never occur to them that the author of Genesis meant for Isaac to stand for Christianity and Ishmael for Judaism. Some books are written that way, however. Most people think that Jonathan Swift wrote *Gulliver's Travels* as a delightful children's story, but English scholars recognize that it is a biting social and political satire. The two political parties in Lilliput are the Big-endians and the Little-endians; their dispute is over which end of the boiled egg should be broken. In this passage Swift was poking fun at the differences between Roman Catholics and Anglicans. The question then is not whether allegorical interpretation is ever appropriate, but whether it is appropriate for a particular book.

Another example of allegorical interpretation follows the Parable of the Sower. The different kinds of soil into which the seed in the parable fell are understood as different personality types who respond to Christian preaching in different ways.

Typological

This kind of interpretation sees a common principle operating between the Old Testament event and the New Testament event. The relation of the events in the two testaments is not that of a veiled prediction and its fulfillment, as it would be in apocalyptic interpretation; nor is it that of a coded message to its decipherment, as it would be with allegorical interpretation. Both the Old Testament event and the New Testament event are actual events and each has its own importance. There is a relation between them, however: The same principle operates in both, but to a different degree. The redemptive event in the Old Testament, while considered to be a real event that is important in its own right, is to be understood as a promise of the New Testament event. The most pervasive typology in the New Testament is the interpretation of the exodus of the children of Israel from bondage in Egypt as a foreshadowing of the salvation that Jesus brought. The Exodus promised what Christ delivered.

Many scholars think that Matthew makes extensive use of this typology. He sets the body of his Gospel off into five sections, each containing long passages of narrative and teaching. Each of these five sections is concluded with the same formula, "when Jesus finished these sayings." The use of this formula in only those five places indicates that Matthew wanted to use it to divide his Gospel into five parts. (Remember that the Bible was not divided into chapters until the Middle Ages and into verses until the Renaissance; thus such internal indicators were the only way that Matthew had to show the structure of his book.) By treating the Gospel as five books corresponding to the Pentateuch, Matthew shows that Jesus was the fulfillment of what was begun in Moses. He is understood to be the "prophet like Moses" who was promised in Deuteronomy 18:17ff and elsewhere.

This Mosaic typology is also strong in Matthew's version of the stories of Jesus' infancy. The slaughter of the Holy Innocents by Herod recalls the slaughter of the male Hebrew children by the pharaoh which Moses escaped. Joseph's taking the Holy Family into Egypt to escape persecution makes it possible for salvation in Jesus to come out of Egypt just as the salvation of the Exodus did. These examples could be multiplied, but the point is clear: one way of suggesting the importance of Jesus was to interpret him as the one for whom Moses was a "preview of coming attractions."

The most thoroughgoing typological interpretation in the New Testament is given by the Epistle to the Hebrews. There Jesus' work is understood in terms of the sacrificial system of the Temple. Jesus, our great high priest, is the perfect priest and also himself the perfect sacrificial victim; he offers his sacrifice, not in the earthly sanctuary of the Temple at Jerusalem, nor in the tent of meeting during the Exodus, but in the heavenly sanctuary where he makes intercession for Christians.

Rabbinic

This method of interpretation must be defined very carefully. It is typical of the interpretation performed by rabbis who functioned quite differently from contemporary pastors. These rabbis were not Jewish clergymen, a misunderstanding that many contemporary Christians have. Nor were they the great scholars of the postbiblical age who assembled such collections of interpretations as the Mishnah or Talmud, or who spent their lives studying these collections. They may not have even been called rabbi, but scholars refer to their interpretation as rabbinic because it is the sort of interpretation that appears in the rabbinic collections mentioned above. These interpreters are the scholars around the time of Jesus who understood the Old Testament chiefly as a code of religious law or instruction that gives precise directions for the conduct of life according to the will of God. The Pharisees, from whose party most of the rabbis came, thought that God wanted his people to be "a kingdom of priests and a holy nation." The way that could happen was for all of the people to follow at every moment the regulations for purity which the Old Testament gives for priests while they are actually officiating at the Temple. It was the job of the rabbis to spell out how these regulations would work when applied to the conditions of daily life.

This application of priestly regulations to the daily life of all religious people constitutes a type of biblical interpretation. It is essentially legal interpretation. There is little rabbinic interpretation in the New Testament in the sense that it is used to establish the regulations for religious living, but there are some places where the rules of logic used by the rabbis were adopted by Christians in their effort to interpret the Old Testament. For example, in Deuteronomy 30:11–14 the reader is told that it is easy to obey the Torah. St. Paul, however, quotes that passage in Romans 10:5–9 and intersperses into it a number of explanatory comments according to the rules of rabbinic interpretation. The effect of these interpretive comments is to change the meaning of the passage entirely and make it agree with Paul's doctrine of justification by faith in Christ rather than by works of the Law. Needless to say, there is more to this than rhetorical trickery. Paul sincerely believed that was what the passage meant. Christ was still the key to interpreting the Old Testament.

The rabbis used another method of interpretation when their task was to develop moral homilies rather than to give judgments about religious regulations. They retold Old Testament stories with additional details that are mentioned nowhere in the biblical text. An example of this is seen in The Epistle to the Hebrews when reference is made to Melchizedek, a priest who is mentioned briefly in Genesis 14:18–20. The whole seventh chapter of Hebrews is an expansion of the brief note in Genesis that Abraham paid his tithe to Melchizedek. The author of Hebrews deduced that Melchizedek was without father or mother or genealogy simply from the failure of Genesis to mention his parents.

In our survey of the four methods by which New Testament writers interpreted the Old Testament, one concluding comment is called for: None of these methods deals with what we would consider to be the natural sense of the passages interpreted. All begin with the assumption that the Old Testament was about Jesus Christ. It is hard for contemporary Christians to assume that any Old Testament writers thought this way. To this extent, these methods appear to force an unnatural meaning onto the text.

Yet being a Christian involves at least the assumption that these interpretations expressed a fundamental and necessary truth, however foreign the paths of reasoning leading to that conclusion may appear to us. There is a real sense in which St. Paul is correct in seeing that Christ has been a part of God's plan for the world from its inception. The mystery of God has always included the work of Christ and everything that came before in the Old Testament pointed to this ultimate meeting of God and human life. It seems unlikely that the Old Testament writers thought they were predicting Jesus, but he did come as the satisfaction of all their highest yearnings. That was no accident. In addition, it is clear once again that the meaning of the tradition is increased by the very act of its application to a new situation.

CHURCH HISTORY BEFORE THE MODERN PERIOD

In this section the task will be to look very briefly at the methods of interpretation that were used between New Testament times and the modern period. From this one can both learn more about techniques of interpretation and also lay a foundation for understanding the revolution of method in biblical interpretation that is characteristic of the modern period.

Of the four methods that were used in the New Testament, three continued to be used widely: apocalyptic, allegorical, and typological. Only the rabbinic method ceased to be employed as the church moved out of a Hebraic culture and into a Greco-Roman one. By the Middle Ages, the types of interpretation came to be referred to as the "senses" of Scripture. Four main senses in which the Bible was to be understood were recognized: the literal, the allegorical, the moral (also called the tropological), and the anagogical (which deals with the "last things": death, judgment, heaven, and hell). These senses and their uses were summarized in a Latin verse that has been translated as follows:

> The letter shows us what God and our fathers did;
> The allegory shows us where our faith is hid;
> The moral meaning gives us rules of daily life;
> The anagogy shows us where we end our strife.

By the end of the second Christian century, the church was so threatened by heretical movements that its very survival was at stake. Many of the heretical teachers said that the doctrines of their particular sect were not derived from written records of Jesus in the Gospels but from secret tradition given by Jesus to the apostles and passed on by word of mouth within the sect.

Orthodox writers at the time claimed that no such secret tradition existed. They asserted that the New Testament was the only authoritative record. Furthermore, since the church had preserved these written records, the church was more likely than any outside group to have information on how Jesus intended his words to be understood. Today it can be recognized that such a claim was the only historical appeal available at the time. It was also a natural extension of the principle that Christ is the key to biblical interpretation, which was so important to New Testament writers.

By this time there had also arisen a question about the status of Jesus; it was the focus of much of the heresy. That question had to be answered prior to any effort to use him as the key to the interpretation of the Bible. The early defenders of orthodoxy said that the guide to understanding the Bible was the *regula fidei,* the rule of faith. By this they meant short summary statements of Christian belief that share most of their content with the creeds. (These do not appear, however, to have had any direct influence on the history of creed making.) This attitude toward Scripture, which was developed in the late second and early third centuries, came to a full and classic expression in A.D. 434 when St. Vincent of Lerins gave his famous dictum that "the line of the interpretation of the prophets and apostles must be directed according to the norm of the ecclesiastical and catholic sense." That catholic sense consists of *quod ubique, quod semper, quod ab omnibus creditum est* ("what has always been believed by everyone everywhere"). This "ecclesiastical and catholic sense" may be spoken of as the authoritative interpretation of the Bible.

Another trend in biblical interpretation during this time was toward literal, historical interpretation. As noted above, the literal sense was one of the four senses recognized in the Middle Ages, as, indeed, it had been all along. What is at stake here is a matter of emphasis. In contrast to the great interest in allegorical interpretation that was characteristic of the theologians of Alexandria, Egypt, there was an emphasis on literal interpretation in the rival city of Antioch. Church Fathers who made this emphasis include Theodore of Mopsuestia, St. John Chrysostom, and St. Jerome in his later days.

In the Middle Ages St. Thomas Aquinas was a lone voice in the defense of literal interpretation, but the great theologians of the Protestant Reformation, Luther and Calvin, called for the literal, historical, and grammatical interpretation of the Bible. Neither of them had the same views as people of today, however. Luther was convinced that in order to understand the Bible one had to be guided by the Holy Spirit and to have experienced justification by faith. Calvin made a similar point but phrased it differently: he said that in order to recognize the Bible as God's word, one had to be predestined by God to election to salvation. Luther and Calvin thus combined the literal and the authoritative interpretations of the Bible.

· 4 ·

How the Bible Is Interpreted[1]

The Historical-Critical Method

BACKGROUND

The book in its tooled calf binding now scuffed with age, metal clasps retaining its bulk of pages, looks so ancient, ponderous, and authoritative that it could pass for the magician's tome of spells in a horror movie. The title page, ornamented with a view of London that shows Shakespeare's Globe Theatre and old St. Paul's before they were destroyed by the fire, reveals that the book is a Bible printed in 1679. On almost every other page there is a steel engraving of a painting of a biblical scene by Rubens or one of the other masters of the Lowlands Renaissance. Part of the charm of those pictures is that they make all the events in the Bible from 2000 B.C. to A.D. 150—events that occurred anywhere from ancient Babylon to classical Rome—look as though they had taken place in Belgium or the Netherlands at the time those great masters were painting. The modern recognition of the differences between the customs, thoughts, social structures, and artifacts of different societies makes it impossible for anyone to paint that way anymore, unless they do so in a spirit of self-conscious primitivism. By the same token, no one can think of biblical history in that naïve way either.

The change of attitude, by which the painting of historical subjects can no longer be attempted in an anachronistic way, represents the revolution in thought that distinguishes modern from premodern thought, a revolution that was already beginning when the pictures in the old Bible were being painted. This revolution has affected scientific investigations, philosophical thought, the way that history is written, and the way that Christians think theologically. Modern science made possible the Industrial Revolution and, with it, modern technology and the modern way of life. A key factor in the rise of science was the scientific method of investigation, which does not make presuppositions about what is true in the world of nature, but instead conducts experiments under controlled conditions, observes the results, and draws conclusions from these observations. Inevitably, theories about natural phenomena that grew out of scientific experimentation were in conflict with some views of nature that were thought to be revealed in the Bible.

Related changes took place at the same time in the work of philosophers. From the time of the early Christians through the period of the Reformation, philosophers assumed that the Bible revealed truths about God and the universe that should be taken into account in any adequate philosophy. From the seventeenth century onwards, however, it was assumed that human reason alone was needed for the philosophical task. Many philosophers came to assume that miracles do not happen and that God had not revealed the truth about himself and the universe in the Bible.

Similar changes were taking place in the field of history. Historians recognized that many accounts of past events were simply not reliable, even if some of them were contemporaneous with the events they reported or if people had assumed them to be true for centuries. Techniques for assessing the reliability of ancient records were confined at first to the investigation of the history of Greece and Rome, where they raised doubt about whether the Trojan horse had ever existed or Rome had been founded by Romulus and Remus. It was inevitable that in time the same techniques would be applied to stories in the Bible. History as we know it is thus a modern invention. Only in recent times have people become aware that it is inappropriate to paint biblical events as though they occurred in seventeenth-century Holland.

These changes have had profound effects on Christian theology. When conflicts appeared to arise between scientific theories about the origin of the universe and the story of creation as told in Genesis, for example, Christian thinkers had to decide how to deal with these conflicts. Some wanted to excommunicate science and say, "Don't confuse me with the facts. My mind is made up." Others were willing to capitulate completely and say that the Bible is nothing but a pack of lies and superstition. Others thankfully decided to seek some way to be both honest and intellectually integrated, embracing both the scientific world view and the Christian faith.

Many people have accepted each of these alternatives. It would be impossible to estimate how many people have been lost to the church because of the inroads of secular thought, but it is common to refer to contemporary society as "post-Christian." Yet a Gallup poll taken in 1976 showed that 46 percent of American Protestants and 31 percent of American Roman Catholics still believe that the Bible is "to be taken literally, word for word." The overwhelming majority of theologians and biblical scholars, however, are committed to the task of showing that it is possible both to be a convinced Christian and to accept the scientific view of the physical universe.

The biblical scholar who combines Christian belief with the scientific world view employs the historical-critical method of interpreting the Bible. In many ways its goals are the same as those of the literal interpretation that was done throughout church history. The main difference is that the historical aspect of the historical-critical method is the kind of history writing that grew out of the revolution separating modern from premodern thought. No assumption is made, therefore, that all events reported in the Bible are historical.

The description of this method as critical is a source of confusion to many people. Another source is the designation of many of the techniques of the historical-critical method as a kind of criticism, such as form criticism, textual criticism, redaction criticism. The popular use of the verb *to criticize* conveys the sense of making an adverse judgment. Even when this word is used in a technical sense, such as in the designation of a "movie critic," we usually think of someone who pans the films we like. Another word, *discriminate*, is derived from the same root and is closer to the sense of the word *criticism* as it is used in relation to biblical studies. *Discriminate* means to make distinctions, to analyze. That is what is meant when a method of biblical study is called "criticism."

The purpose of the historical-critical method is to discover what a biblical writer intended his first readers to understand. The practice of this method is called *exegesis*. The literal derivation of this word suggests the meaning of "leading out," but even in Greek its primary sense is "explanation" or "interpretation." This explanation, however, is not in terms of what the biblical passage means for people today but of what it meant originally. This is to say that exegesis is a historical discipline. It should thus be possible, at least in theory, for scholars with different religious commitments or with none at all to come to the same decision about what a biblical writer wanted his intended audience to understand.

Does this mean that our faith makes no difference in our understanding of the Bible? Even more seriously: Does it mean that all our study of the Bible can be expected to produce is information about the religious opinions of ancient people, and that it cannot supply illumination to the lives of present-day Christians? The answer is an emphatic no. What it does mean is that the process of applying the Bible to our lives is broken down into two steps. The first step is historical reconstruction; in this step the religious commitment of the interpreter should make little difference. The next step, though, is to ask what difference the communications of biblical writers to their first audiences makes to us today. In this phase our own religious commitment makes all the difference.

The historical-critical method, which is used to accomplish the first step in applying the Bible to our lives, consists of a number of operations that scholars go through in trying to discover what the biblical writer wanted his first audience to understand. These operations, often referred to as one kind of criticism or another, each elicit certain kinds of information that are helpful in recovering what the biblical writer intended to convey. Understanding what each of these operations is supposed to accomplish and how it goes about it can be of enormous help in seeing why scholars think a particular passage is about one thing instead of another.

TEXTUAL CRITICISM

There are slight variations between any two manuscripts of the same work, as there are between any two pieces of handwork. These variations are so numerous that it is difficult to decide what words the ancient author actually wrote. Textual criticism, then, is the effort to reconstruct the exact wording of the author and to account for all the changes in wording that occur in later copies of the work.

Textual criticism is concerned with the language in which the biblical book was originally written—Hebrew, Aramaic, or Greek. Translations into other languages are of interest to the textual critic, but only because they may preserve original wordings that somehow have dropped out of the manuscripts we have in the original language.

Oddly enough, even though the Old Testament was written before the New, until recently our best manuscripts of the New Testament were centuries older than any extensive Old Testament manuscripts we had. The most ancient Hebrew manuscripts we had went back only to between the late ninth and early eleventh centuries. The great care that was given to the production of Hebrew biblical scrolls for use in the synagogue, however, gave good grounds to believe that the text preserved in these medieval manuscripts was very close to what the text had been early in the Christian era when the control processes were set up that made such accurate copying possible.

We could not be sure, however, of the degree of variation before those controls were set up. Part of the little evidence we had, such as the translation of the Old Testament into Greek in the last two centuries B.C., suggested that it was considerable. With the discovery of the Dead Sea Scrolls in

1947, though, our knowledge of the pre-Christian transmission of the text of the Old Testament has taken dramatic steps forward. Many of the scrolls and fragments found at Qumran were of books or parts of the Old Testament. The most impressive find was a copy of the entire book of Isaiah from the last two centuries B.C., almost 1,000 years older than any other Old Testament manuscript in Hebrew that we had.

These Dead Sea biblical manuscripts indicate that rather than just the old textual tradition we find in the medieval manuscripts, there were four or five main traditions before the control processes were instituted. We are not yet in position, however, to say that any one of these is more likely than another to be original, nor does it appear probable that we will ever be able to. Besides, we fall far short of having a complete text of the Old Testament in all of these traditions.

We are in a very different position when we come to the New Testament. We have about 5,000 Greek manuscripts in whole or in part, although it must be admitted that over four-fifths of these are relatively late and many of them are not arranged as complete books in the familiar order, but are passages arranged to be read in church through the liturgical year. For some time, however, we have had several very good copies of the entire New Testament that go back to the fourth or fifth century, and at one time it was thought that the original text of the New Testament could be reconstructed from these. For instance, in 1885 two great English scholars, Westcott and Hort, published an edition that they optimistically titled *The New Testament in the Original Greek*.

Since then many older manuscripts and fragments written on papyrus have been discovered. These manuscripts were written on a paperlike substance made from the pulp of a certain reed. Papyrus was in use as writing material until it was replaced by parchment or vellum, the genuine "sheepskin" from which we get our slang expression for diplomas. Just under ninety papyri have been recorded. Some of these go back very close to what is called the "autograph," the author's own original copy. A fragment of several verses of John is from within twenty-five to fifty years of the time the Gospel was probably written. Another papyrus from A.D. 200

or before has the first fourteen chapters of John. Still another, containing much of John and Luke, comes from about the same period.

Unfortunately, here too there is no confidence that any copy we have is exactly what a sacred writer wrote, or even close to it. The time between when the books were written and even our earliest papyri were copied was a period when the church was small, poor, and persecuted. The leisure to copy books carefully and well did not exist. Most of the variations in the text crept in during that period and, while different collections of variants have since settled into four main text types, there is no reason to assume that any of these is usually the correct one. The decision of what an original reading was has to be made on the basis of what the author probably wrote rather than on that of how many manuscripts contain it.

This pessimistic judgment raises the question of whether we really know what the Bible says. It can be answered quickly by saying that the overwhelming majority of variations make very little difference, no more than it makes if we say "a history" instead of "an history." But if the aim of exegesis is to discover what the sacred writer meant his first audience to understand, we need to try as hard as we can to find out exactly which words he wrote.

While none of the variants brings into question a major Christian doctrine, some are quite interesting. No early Greek manuscript of Mark, for instance, has verses 16:9–20. They have the Gospel end with the women rushing from the empty tomb in a state of great fright; no resurrection appearance is related, although there are indications that one will occur. The story of the woman taken in adultery in John 7:53–8:11 is also not in our oldest manuscripts, although the story may well be true. These variants do not change doctrine but some are important for interpretation.

An example of the problems faced by textual critics may be seen in the now familiar Galatians passage about Isaac and Ishmael. The RSV translation of 4:28 reads: "Now we, brethren, like Isaac, are children of promise." There is a footnote to the verse, however, that says that other ancient authorities (manuscripts) say *you* instead of *we*. The difference could not change the meaning of the passage; verse 26 used the first person plural, so Paul is obviously including both the Galatian Christians and himself in the category of the children of promise. Many scholars, however, do believe that Paul wrote "you" (*hymeis*) instead of "we" (*hēmeis*). They reason that later copyists could very easily have changed verse 28 to make it agree with 26, since in Greek there is a difference of only one letter. It is much less likely that a copyist would have taken something that was originally consistent and turned it into something that was inconsistent but which clearly meant the same thing. This particular variation is unimportant, but the textual critic has to examine all variations to make certain that he has not overlooked something that radically affects the meaning of a passage.

SOURCE CRITICISM

We are dealing here with phenomena with which we have already become familiar even though we have not said that their study goes under this designation. The division of the Pentateuch into J, E, D, and P sources is source criticism. The same is true of the separation of Isaiah into different parts, each coming from a prophet who lived at a different time from the others.

The intention here is not to report every effort to parcel out biblical books into constituent sources, but to come to understand one technique that scholars use in studying the Bible. There is need, therefore, for only a couple of New Testament examples. The most familiar and most important to understand occurs in the Synoptic Gospels. Their sources were discussed in Chapter 2.

A kind of source criticism in which the sources are different writings by the same author is seen in the study of Paul's Second Letter to the Corinthians. Chapters 1–7 have a pleasant and conciliating tone, while chapters 10–13 sound angry and threatening. The topic of chapters 8–9 is the offering that Paul has been collecting for the poor Christians in Jerusalem and does not appear closely related to either what comes

before or what comes afterward. The obvious question is:
What caused Paul to change his attitude toward his flock at
Corinth between chapters 7 and 10? In 2:1, 4 he refers to both
a "painful visit" and to a letter that he had written them "out
of much affliction and anguish of heart and with many tears,
not to cause you pain but to let you know the abundant love
that I have for you." That letter sounds like an accurate description of chapters 10–13.

Perhaps, then, 2 Corinthians is not one letter but several.
Chapters 10–13 would thus have been written after a painful
visit and then efforts at peacemaking would make it possible
for Paul to write Chapters 1–7 as a conciliatory letter. Chapters 8–9 may have been added on to the conciliatory letter or
have been a third letter.

Dividing a biblical book into its component sources is not
an end in itself. Rather, it is a means of tracing the development of thought. This should be clear from the analysis in
Chapter 2 of the different meaning of the story of Isaac and
Ishmael in the patriarchal traditions and in the J, E, and P
sources. It can be further illustrated in relation to the Synoptic
Gospels: when Matthew, for instance, uses Mark as a source,
and changes something that Mark said, the change is an indication of something that Matthew himself thought. Knowledge of his sources, then, alerts us to his special emphases.
More will be said of this in the discussion of tradition and
redaction criticism.

FORM CRITICISM

An additional method of literary analysis is known as form
criticism. It seeks to discover the pattern into which the literary units of a biblical book fall. Various types of literature are
recognized by their structure or their pattern. When, for example, we read a poem that is fourteen lines long and the
lines are in iambic pentameter and the final syllables of each
line fall into a certain rhyme scheme, we know that the poem
is a sonnet. While we would find it a little more difficult to
state the specifications of a novel, we generally know when
we have read one.

Oral literature falls into similar patterns. The easiest way to demonstrate this in our society is to look at one of our largest bodies of oral literature, jokes. We could easily draw up the specifications of elephant jokes, shaggy dog stories, "some good news and some bad news" gags, "knock-knock" jokes and so on. The person trained to do so can do equally well in describing and recognizing the forms of literature appearing in the Bible, many of which were oral forms before they were written down.

The identification of the form of a biblical story is not just an interesting intellectual exercise; it is an important guide to the purpose of the author. Form is also one of our best indicators of the situation in which a story has been used. This was seen in the discussion of the patriarchal narratives in Genesis. Most of them purport to tell a story of how some practice of worship came to be associated with a particular locality. Such stories were used to justify the continuation of that practice there. This was seen to be the case in the story of Hagar at the well Beer-la-hai-roi. The story was told as an explanation of how the well got its name (Gen. 16:13, 14). Form critics call such stories aetiologies, derived from the Greek word for "a statement of a cause." The great pioneers in the use of form criticism with biblical literature first identified these sagas. They also used form analysis on the psalms, dividing them into hymns, hymns of Zion, enthronement psalms, community laments, individual laments, songs of confidence, thanksgiving psalms, royal psalms, wisdom psalms, liturgies, pilgrim psalms, and mixed types. Since then form criticism has been an extremely valuable tool, not just for literary analysis but for historical reconstruction and theological interpretation as well.

In New Testament studies, form criticism has been of use mainly in the study of the Gospels. The Gospel itself is a unique literary form invented by St. Mark for spreading the Christian message, but the stories that make up a Gospel employ a wide variety of subforms. They too indicate to us the situation in the early church to which that particular sort of story was applied. These subforms include stories that lead us to an authoritative statement by Jesus as the dramatic "punch line," stories that relate some miracle performed by Jesus either in healing or over nature, parables, or many others. Most of these have as their basic purpose the proclamation of salvation in Jesus, but there are variations in the way they express it.

By and large the use of form criticism in dealing with the Gospels is limited to the individual story. This focus on the individual unit is appropriate because of the way that the Gospels came into existence. Long before they were incorporated into written accounts of the life of Jesus, the individual stories were passed down separately by word of mouth in the Christian community. The work of the Gospel writers, then, was to string the separate stories together into a continuous narrative. Mark, of course, took his stories over from oral tradition, but Matthew and Luke drew on their sources of Mark, Q, and their own special material.

SUBJECT AND CONCEPT EXEGESIS

At some point biblical scholars have to look up everything mentioned in the passage they are working on and with which they are not familiar. If a character is mentioned, they find out what else is known about that character and how it squares with what is said about him or her in the passage. If a place is mentioned, they learn about it. Obviously, they will know a good bit about most of these things already if they are experienced scholars, but it is always good to check one's memory. The fact that was forgotten may be the one that will cause everything to fall into place. Units of measurement and amounts of money need to be checked. Translating ancient coinage into contemporary buying power is a challenge. Checking references to living conditions is often very illuminating; for example, the Parable of the Sower makes little sense unless you know that in ancient Palestine, sowing was done before plowing.

The scholar needs not only to check out persons, places, and things, but also to check out theological vocabulary. Many key words are used differently by different writers and none of their meanings is likely to be precisely the same as the modern use of the same word. St. Paul and the author of the Letter of James do not mean the same thing by "faith," for instance, and neither of them means by it what the author of Hebrews means.

A number of things to be looked up can be spotted in the two versions of the story of Isaac and Ishmael in Genesis 16 and 21: Shur, Kadesh, Bered, Beer-la-hai-roi, Beer-sheba, and Paran should be located on a map; the changes in the spelling of Abram/Abraham and Sarai/Sarah bear looking into; and the history of the practice of circumcision ought to be checked—to list but a few.

TRADITION AND REDACTION CRITICISM

These two terms are very closely related, but tradition criticism is normally used in relation to the study of the Old Testament and redaction criticism is usually confined to New Testament scholarship. Both concern the different uses that are made of the same material. The Old Testament, especially the Pentateuch, represents a process of assembly that took almost a thousand years, while the time from the death of Jesus to the writing of the last canonical Gospel is only about sixty years. The first Gospel was written about midway between these two events. The passing down and reactualization of material through a millennium is a process of tradition, while the restatement of stories in Gospels that were written a generation apart is a matter of editing or, to give it a latinized name, redaction.

To illustrate the complex history of a tradition in the Pentateuch we can recall some of the things we said about the patriarchal narratives. Often they go back to the association of a particular act of worship with a given locality. They may also be offered to account for the relations of one tribe to another. The story, then, goes back to some original event, the establishment of a practice or relation. It is passed down for centuries by word of mouth to account for the continuing situation.

As the situation changes, the story is modified. Stories that perhaps were originally told about different people will cluster around the same tribal ancestor. A number of shrines will be connected with the same figure. The collection of stories will have developed one way in the north and another way in the south.

When the J writer edits the southern collection he gives it a comprehensive theological vision. The E writer has different interests in his editing and still other purposes are served by the merging of the two. The P editor goes back over the whole thing to make it support contemporary practice at the Temple, and the Deuteronomist fits it into his philosophy of history. Thus the treatment in Chapter 2 of the meaning of the story of Isaac and Ishmael in the different pentateuchal sources is an example of tradition criticism at work.

When we talked about the form criticism of the Gospels, we said that the work of the individual evangelist was to string together the stories that had been passed down separately in the oral tradition. These writers of the Gospels did not put together only what had been passed down to them so that their assembled Gospels show no personal contributions. This "untouched by human hands" view of the construction of a Gospel is quite misleading. To begin with, the order and the context in which they put the stories together make some differences in the meaning of the whole. Not only that, but when we do source analysis, we see that there are changes in the way a story is told that do not suggest so much that the Gospel writer is drawing on fresh outside information as that he is deliberately writing to express a point of view.

The study of this sort of editing is what we call redaction criticism. This editing is our guide to the Gospel writer's attitude toward the situation for which he is writing. We ask why he changed this detail and that one and why he put this story where he did, and we begin to get some idea of his purpose in writing.

The process of redaction can be illustrated in the story of the baptism of Jesus. Even though Mark's is the first written account we have, it is still late enough for the emphasis to have shifted from the baptism itself to the miracle following in which the Father reveals the role of Jesus (1:9–11). Both Matthew (3:13–17) and Luke (3:21–22) take pains to make the revelation from heaven seem more objective than it appears to be in Mark, where the opening of the heavens and the voice of God are observed by Jesus alone. To protect Jesus from the charge that his baptism indicated that he was either a sinner in need of repentance or inferior to John the Baptist, Matthew inserts John's protest of his unworthiness to baptize Jesus. Luke is far more interested in the descent of the Spirit on Jesus than he is in the baptism itself and so the baptism is relegated to what in English is an adverbial clause but in Greek is a participial phrase.

A visit to an English cathedral may show that it includes in its structure almost the entire history of English architecture. The crypt may be Saxon and the nave Norman, the choir Decorated and the sanctuary Perpendicular, while the rood screen is Jacobite and the baptistry Victorian. The same kind of indications of period in a biblical story are obvious to a trained eye. In the Gospels one may detect which elements go back to the ministry of Jesus, which were added during the time the story was handed down by word of mouth, which came from the hand of Mark, and which from a later Gospel writer. When we have done all that, we ought to be in position to reconstruct the historical situation of each of these stages and thus be able to understand what that passage meant in each stage. Thus we will have completed the task of exegesis; we will have arrived at our conclusions about what the original author wanted his first readers to understand.

Applying the Bible to Our Thought and Lives

THE BIBLE AND THE CHURCH

Up to this point, the work of religious and nonreligious biblical scholars will have been much the same. Both intended to discover what the biblical writer wanted his first readers to understand. The work of nonreligious scholars stops here, but that of the religious scholars has just begun. The religious scholars' purpose in studying the Bible is not just to satisfy historical curiosity. They expect far, far more: through their study of the Bible they expect to come to see their lives and the lives of those about them from God's point of view. More than that, they expect to encounter God himself in their study and to hear him speaking to them and to the church.

The basis for their expectation is that they belong to a religious community that has had many of its deepest and most powerful experiences of God mediated through the Bible. Even if they have not often been conscious of this presence and this power themselves, they know that the community to which they belong has had this experience. Since it has been in the fellowship of the church that they have come to their own deepest experience of meaning in life and since the church corporately claims that its awareness of meaning has been mediated through Bible reading and study, Christians expect that God will continue to make his presence felt and his will known through the Bible.

In all of the activities that make up the life of the church—preaching the Gospel, celebrating the liturgy, administering the sacraments, teaching the doctrine and lore of the faith, giving pastoral care, offering service to the world's needy, making prophetic judgment on immorality both in the lives of individual members of the church and in society at large—the church has experienced God and come to an understanding of life, the world, and God's will for his people through Bible reading and study.

As a way of testifying to this experience of the presence of God mediated through the Bible, Christians have developed a special vocabulary for talking about the Bible. They call it *Scripture*, for instance, even though the derived meaning of this word is nothing more than "writing." These are writings in a special sense; they are said to have *authority*. What we mean by calling the Scriptures authoritative is simply that we know that the church has experienced the presence and power of God through the Bible and that we rely on its being able to do so in the future. The list of books that may be thus relied on is called the biblical *canon*, as noted in Chapter 2. The notion of canon, however, is not limited to the claim that God speaks through each of the books on the list; it includes the further assumption that it takes all of the books on the list to constitute the full medium through which God speaks to his people.

The terms already noticed focus on the experience of people, they emphasize the receiving end of this communication between God and creatures. Two other terms concentrate on God's role in this process. To say that God *inspired* the Bible is to offer an explanation of why the church experiences the presence and power of God when reading the Bible: God intended us to receive his power this way and he caused the Bible to be written in such a way that we could. A closely related term is *revelation*. By derivation it means an unveiling: God discloses himself to his people. One may thus speak of the Bible as a record of past revelations, when God made himself known to Abraham and Moses, to Peter and Paul. One may also speak of the Bible as a channel of ongoing revelation since God continues to make his presence and power felt when it is read.

THE ELABORATION OF BIBLICAL TEACHINGS

A great student of the law has said that the quality of a law that makes it a good law is its capacity to be extended to circumstances for which it was never envisioned. This means that a law should not be overly specific, so confined to a certain set of circumstances that it applies only rarely. Our national Constitution meets the standard of good law. Having been designed for a sparsely populated nation dispersed through villages, farms, and wilderness on the rim of a continent and before the Industrial Revolution, it has proven adequate to shape our existence when we have spread from coast to coast, number more than two hundred million persons, and live in a technocracy. Since the Bill of Rights was appended immediately after its adoption, it has required little other amendment, and what there is may be thought in most cases to be merely a working out of the implications of what was already there—such as the amendments related to former slaves and to women.

The potential of a good law for extension to new situations is similar to the quality of biblical passages that makes it possible for God to speak through them to men and women of every generation. The story of Isaac and Ishmael, for instance, had its original meaning in relation to the shrine at Beer-la-hai-roi. It was extended by the J writer to illuminate the situation in Israel after the foundation of the monarchy under David. The E writer was able to extend it further to the time when the northern kingdom had broken off from the southern kingdom. The P writers saw it as relevant to the worship of the Temple in Jerusalem after the exile in Babylon. St. Paul extended it further to make it apply to the situation of the early church in relation to Judaism. This story, then, is capable of extension to many situations for which it was not originally intended.

It is worth noting that the meaning of this story did not remain the same in all of these applications. Part of what permits it to be extended to so many situations is the fact that it does not have one simple meaning, but rather has a rich diversity of meanings, some of which could not have been anticipated until the story was understood in the light of the new situation to which it was being applied. Thus one thing that Christians claim when they say that God inspired the Bible is that he caused it to be written in such a manner that it could be applied to a variety of new situations, in each of which a new facet of its meaning would be revealed.

Proposing applications of biblical passages to new situations is the task of theology. The population explosion, for instance, is a new situation; for the first time in history human reproduction does not appear to be an unmixed good. To the contrary, if it is unchecked, human life on this planet will become impossible. This new situation raises important moral questions about such matters as the legitimacy of artificial birth control, the permissibility of abortion, the purpose of sexual intercourse, the acceptability of extramarital intercourse, and the morality of homosexual relations, to name but a few. On most of these questions the Bible either has explicit teaching or its teaching has been extended to apply to them. Those teachings and their applications, however, date back to a situation in which no one questioned the value of abundant human fertility. How can teaching that originated in such a situation be legitimately extended to a new situation in which it is clear that childbearing must be curtailed? The task of theology is to propose ways in which biblical teaching may be extended to cover new situations such as this.

The proposals made by different theologians do not and will not all agree. Thus the various proposals must be evaluated and the yardstick by which they are evaluated is their consistency with the biblical teaching extended to cover the new situation. This consistency of the extension with what it extends may be called the *aptness* of the theological proposal. Similar questions come up in law: the issue at stake in the Equal Rights amendment is its consistency with what the Constitution already teaches about the rights of human beings and the equal humanity of men and women. Those who believe that the amendment would be consistent with what is already in the Constitution consider it to be an apt proposal.

Just as lawyers do not always agree on which extensions of legal principles are valid, so theologians are not of one mind on how to extend and apply biblical teaching. The variety of methods of biblical interpretation that have been used through the centuries is one evidence of this lack of agreement. The aptness of contemporary proposals or the lack of it is not always evident. It takes time to discover if a particular proposal is a valid extension of a biblical teaching.

Beyond that, it cannot be assumed that there is only one apt proposal. Since biblical stories do not have one simple meaning, but have instead a rich diversity of meaning, extensions of that meaning may be equally diverse. Deciding upon the relative aptness of proposals that are such different but valid extensions is a difficult but necessary task of the church.

SYMBOL AND MYTH

Interpreters of the Bible in the eighteenth and nineteenth centuries thought that the meaning of biblical passages lay in their reference to something outside the passages themselves. The passages were thought either to refer to historical events or to be narrative ways of stating concepts. In either case the Bible came to be undervalued. If the value of the Bible lay in its accuracy as a historical record, its value was well short of absolute, because the historical record could be shown to be inaccurate in a number of respects. If, on the other hand, the value of the Bible was in its statement of concepts in a narrative form, those concepts could be stated more concisely and accurately in a nonnarrative form.

A third possibility exists, though, as to the element of biblical passages in which meaning resides and through which, therefore, we receive God's messages to us. That element is the story itself, since the meaning of a story is not reducible to a concept or anything else. The meaning of a story is the story itself.

Until recently it was assumed that the nearer a statement approached the shape of a mathematical formula, the greater its accuracy and truth would be. In time, though, it was realized that all of the subjects that are most important for human beings—such as life, death, love, and beauty—could not be dealt with adequately in the literal language of analytical concepts. Poetry is a more adequate way of talking about such things than formulas. This realization focused attention on the importance of symbols and it came to be seen that symbols furnish us with an access to depths of thought of which literal language is incapable.

That this is so should surprise no one in an age whose thought has been so shaped by the thought of Sigmund Freud as ours has been. We know that our deepest thoughts and feelings are stored in our subconscious mind in a tightly compressed symbolic form and that they emerge into our dreams in this form. The academic disciplines of anthropology and the history of religions have demonstrated that the minds of primitive people express themselves in the same kind of symbolic vocabulary. At least one school of modern painting draws on these symbols for its subject matter.

Symbols, then, give us access to a reality from which the literal language of analytical thought is blocked. In order to see how this is so, it is necessary to distinguish between several meanings of the word *symbol*. In the widest sense, a symbol is something that stands for something else. The various categories of symbols differ from one another in the way that the symbol stands for what it symbolizes. Some symbols, for instance, are completely arbitrary and have no connection with what they stand for. An example of such an arbitrary symbol is a dollar sign, which is connected with money only by our decision to let it stand for one of our monetary units. Other symbols have some connection with what they stand for, but the connection is not self-evident; it has to be pointed out. When the poet says that his girl friend's eyes are like stars, we can recognize what he is talking about, but we would not have noticed it if he had not pointed it out.

The symbols that give an access to reality that is unavailable to literal language, however, are symbols of a much more restricted category. Not only is there an analogy with what they symbolize, but that analogy is recognized spontaneously and is seen to be significant. Such a symbol is not made but discovered. An example of a symbol of this sort is thinking of a human shortcoming or failure as a defilement, a blot, a stain. Thus, when we ask to be cleansed from our sins, there is an implied assumption that our sin has something in common with a stain that can be washed away. What the sin has touched has been rendered impure. Most of our vocabulary about evil has this basic symbol behind it.

Some symbols are not static; they are extended narratively into stories. Even though they are like other stories in the sense that they are set at a certain place and occupy a certain time, they cannot be located in either history or geography. This is not to say merely that they are fictional, but that they function as symbols that have been extended into stories without losing their quality of spontaneousness and significance. In this book these narratively extended symbols will be called *myths*. There are many other definitions of myth, definitions that range all the way from "antique lies" to "stories in which supernatural beings function as characters in human history." When the term is used here, however, its meaning will be a symbol that has been extended narratively.

Exile, for example, is a symbol for alienation. The story of the expulsion of Adam and Eve from the Garden of Eden is this symbol narratively extended into a myth. Not all stories of exile are myths of alienation, however. Myths, like other symbols, cannot have their meaning reduced to literal language. One reason this is so is that symbols by their very nature have a diversity of meanings. Water, for instance, symbolizes both life and death; the mother symbol suggests both nurturing and devouring.

Naïve, primitive persons were unaware that their symbolic world was not the literal world. Thus they had an immediate access to realities from which modern persons are blocked. The revolution of consciousness separating modern from premodern times that was discussed in the last chapter is the reason why. Just as we could not paint scenes of biblical events as though they happened in seventeenth-century Holland or twentieth-century America without being aware of the anachronism involved, so we cannot hear a myth without knowing that it is a myth. We could never assume that it was a literal picture of reality. Our minds are too critical and analytical for that.

Thus we are caught in a dilemma: we know that the symbolic offers an access to reality that the analytic does not, but we have no way of ceasing to have analytical minds and of reentering the world of the symbolic as primitive persons. We need a way of recognizing the access that symbols give to reality and of proceeding through that access, not with the naïve literalism of the primitive, but by means of critical, analytical thought. By interpreting the meaning of myths analytically, we can hear their meaning again.

This rehearing of myths has been called a "second naïvete." Just as myths were the means by which primitive people encountered the sacred, so this second naïvete allows postcritical persons such as ourselves to approach the sacred through myths also, even though it is never easy and it is never achieved perfectly. The task, then, is to start with symbols and elaborate them into existential concepts; that is, concepts about what it means to be human. This could sound like a repetition of the error of the eighteenth- and nineteenth-century scholars who wanted to say that the meaning of a biblical story is a concept that can be stated more precisely in a nonnarrative, abstract form. There is, however, quite a crucial difference. The earlier scholars thought that the biblical narratives were an inefficient way of saying something that they in their sophistication could say much more accurately. The stance of the interpreters of myths who seek to achieve the second naïvete is far humbler. They feel more like the blind trying to learn to walk with a cane. The report of a dream is very short, but a psychoanalyst's interpretation of it may go on for pages and still not exhaust the richness of the dream's compressed meaning. The analyst is engaged in an effort to achieve a second naïvete. A similar effort is required of the one who would interpret myths.

MYTH AND HISTORY IN THE BIBLE

Some stories in the Bible are unquestionably myths in the sense that they are symbols that have been extended into stories without losing their qualities of spontaneousness and significance. The story of the expulsion of Adam and Eve from the Garden of Eden is such a myth. This event cannot be located geographically or historically, but it still is our most satisfactory means of accounting for the existence of evil in the world. One does not have to believe that Adam and Eve were historical figures to know that people universally find it easier to do wrong than right, think they know better than God, and prefer their own will to his.

By the same token, there are sections of the Bible that are clearly intended to be history. The sections of 2 Samuel and 1 Kings that deal with the choice of David's successor on the throne, for example, have been labeled above as an effort to write history centuries before Herodotus and Thucydides did. History and myth are not incompatible categories, however. The Davidic succession narrative, for instance, does give an accurate report of what actually happened in such a way that it becomes clear that Solomon was the right successor to his father although he was one of David's younger children. The individual stories that make up this account often have a theological dimension that gives them a universality. There are, then, mythic aspects to this history.

Most of the Bible is historylike in the sense that it consists of realistic narrative. The narratives are never reported merely for the sake of conveying accurate information about past events. The stories are always told from a theological perspective. Events are judged from the point of view of whether the participants obeyed God or disobeyed him. Each character is a model to be imitated or to be avoided. Thus the stories all take on a mythic quality. The meaning of these stories cannot be reduced to an abstract concept; it takes the entire story to express the meaning of the story. That meaning may be explicated through the exercise of a second naïvete and it thus becomes available to be applied to our lives.

Even the parts of the Bible that are not narrative imply narrative because they are addressed to particular historical situations. Such works are the writings of the prophets in the Old Testament and the letters of St. Paul in the New. Even when the real historical situation of a biblical writing is not what it appears to be—for example, Daniel, which comes from the time of Antiochus Epiphanes rather than the time of Nebuchadnezzar; the Proverbs, or Ecclesiastes, which are not the work of Solomon; or the epistles to Timothy and Titus, which are not the work of Paul—they do nevertheless accurately reflect *some* particular situation in the history of Israel or the early church. Thus their meaning also occurs in the context of a story.

The quality that makes it possible for these mythically understood stories to give meaning to our lives is, as we saw above, that they have the capacity to be extended to apply to our situations. Our attitude toward these stories then has been appropriately described as that of a wager, as betting that their use will give us a more direct access to reality than abstract thought alone would. The wager goes even further than that: it bets that in extending these stories to apply to our situations, we will experience God himself speaking to us. Christians make that wager when they approach biblical stories with the second naïvete. After all, some three centuries ago Blaise Pascal described Christianity as a wager, as betting your life that God exists. We can also bet that God will continue to speak to us through the stories by which he has spoken to his people over the ages.

The process by which the meaning of a biblical story is extended to our situation needs to be illustrated, but before that can be attempted it is necessary to say a word about historical accuracy. The first point to be made is that there is no question that the Bible records a great deal of history reliably. A more important point is that the ability of biblical stories to function mythically does not ordinarily require that the stories be historically accurate. The one important exception to this will be discussed below. If the myth is true, if it correctly symbolizes some aspect of the relations of human beings to God, it does not matter whether the story which it shaped is a correct report of a historical event or not. The myth can still reveal the shape and meaning of events in our lives.

It should be obvious, furthermore, that the recognition that biblical stories have been passed down over many centuries, that they have been applied to many different situations, and that in each application the stories have been modified (all of this is exemplified in the history of the story of Isaac and Ishmael) is a far more historical point of view than that of the biblical literalists. Every reapplication of the story represented an additional historical moment that was preserved and passed down with all later retellings of the story. Not one but many historical situations are made present to us when we tell the story again.

Yet there remains the question of whether there is some point at which one has to be certain of the connections between the biblical narrative and a concrete event that actually happened in history. There are at least two minimal claims that Christians have to make. One is historical as such and the other is about the meaning of history. First is the necessary minimal historical statement for Christians. It has been said that the great Christian addition to man's understanding of God has been that it has taken the problem of human suffering and evil up into the Godhead. The question of why pain and sin exist is the crucial one for any religion. Christianity alone has dealt with it adequately. It has done so, not by some elaborate philosophical explanation, but with the affirmation that pain and evil are finally dealt with by God himself. By becoming a man in Jesus Christ God bore their whole weight himself.

The Christian claim, then, is that Jesus embodied this solution to the problem of suffering and evil. For that claim to be true requires the minimum historical statement that Jesus' death actually occurred in the manner in which it is reported in the Gospels. This is not to say that all of the details were reported accurately but rather that he went to the cross on his own accord. In free obedience to the will of the Father, he offered himself to make it possible for the Father's reign to be inaugurated. The Christian claim is that our salvation was accomplished in Jesus' death on the cross. That teaching is noble, but if in fact Jesus had been dragged kicking and screaming to his death, the teaching would have been insignificant. Jesus would not have embodied the myth. The myth of vicarious suffering is either attached to accurate history or Christianity is a fraud and a farce. The historical claim that Christians have to make, then, is that Jesus' death was consistent with his own teaching and the teaching of the church about him.

The other necessary claim has to do with the significance of the first one. Merely to stop with the first claim would leave us with no more than the understanding of God held by a noble man who manifested in his own life the qualities that he considered to be most characteristic of God. It would tell us nothing about God as he is in himself, but only about Jesus' opinions about God.

In order to validate the statement that the problem of human suffering and evil is resolved by being taken up into the Godhead, there must be some way of accepting the death of Jesus as a statement by God about his own nature. This is to say that it must be seen that in Jesus God became man.

With these two claims and a second naïvete as a means of interpreting the biblical tradition, the modern Christian can discover that the belief of the church that God is present to his people in the reading of the Bible can become a matter of personal experience.

PUTTING THE THEORY TO WORK

An elaborate method and its theoretical justification have been spelled out, but, as the saying goes, the proof of the pudding is in the eating. A demonstration of the method at work is called for. Again, the story of Isaac and Ishamel lies ready at hand. The historical-critical method showed that the story as found in Genesis 16 and 21 began as an aetiology for the shrine at Beer-la-hai-roi and to account for the relations of the Israelites with the Ishmaelites. The J, E, and P writers each made use of it in their presentations of the traditions about the patriarchs. Paul used it in Galatians for purposes of his own.

While the J writer used this story as a part of his thesis that the promises to the patriarchs achieved its fulfillment under the Davidic monarchy (to be discussed in a later chapter), and while the immediate effect of the story's appearing where it does is to heighten suspense about whether God's promise of many descendants to Abraham will be kept, the story has its own internal moral that when God promises something, he does not need human assistance to accomplish his purposes. In this story Abraham comes off as the man who prayed: "Use me, Lord, use even me (in an advisory capacity, of course)." The historical-critical method was probably not necessary to discover this. It has been clear to many generations of Bible readers. The purpose of the method is to remove any barriers to understanding the story so that the story can make its own point.

The second naïvete leads us to expect that Abraham's experience is a warning to us. There are many situations in modern life in which Christians may be tempted to take things into their own hands, fearing that God cannot be relied upon to accomplish his purposes. Biblical criticism is one such situation, and it is a particularly apt one for the purposes of this test case. (There are other situations in which he expects our cooperation, but that is another story.)

The promise to Abraham was that of a land and descendants to live in the land. The modern world, separated from the premodern world by the revolution of consciousness discussed earlier, has many analogies with the land promised to Abraham. The land has many blessings, but it also has many dangers. The spies sent out by Moses, when the children of Israel returned centuries later to take possession of this promised land, discovered that it was both a land flowing with milk and honey and one inhabited by giants. All the blessings of modern science and technology belong to this land of modern thought. There are also blessings in critical study of the Bible.

A danger in discussing the second naïvete is that one might praise the first naïvete too highly. While it is true that in taking myths literally, premodern persons were in contact with realities that modern persons have to approach laboriously, that is not the whole story. Because of that very literalness, the world of primitive people was often fear-ridden. Furthermore, the myths are not literally true, and it is better to know that than not to know it. The God of truth is not served by having people kept in ignorance. It is better to know the difference between literal and nonliteral truth.

Yet there are dangers. Many people have been lost to the church as a result of this revolution of consciousness. Some are still being lost and among those are some biblical scholars. Anyone who has spent much time around graduate schools of theology has seen one scenario replayed a number of times. A young scholar comes to do graduate work in Bible. His motive for coming is that he has had an experience of meaning to life in some Christian body, usually a conservative one. In that church he was told that the life and the power with which he was in contact were mediated through the Bible. His own efforts at studying the Bible had convinced him that was so and he decided to dedicate his life to helping others share his experience; he would become a Bible teacher. In his study, though, he loses his first naïvete and no one helps him acquire the second. He has learned to interpret the Bible through the use of the historical-critical method, but he no longer expects to hear God speaking through it. He is too sophisticated to believe "all that" anymore. Yet he is unwilling to think of his subject as an academic discipline like any other. If he had studied Ancient Egyptology he may not have expected his scholarship to have any implications for contemporary living, but he does expect the Bible to. He begins to ask what sort of meaning that might be. Since he no longer believes in religious meaning, he begins to look for some other kind: psychological, sociological, literary, what have you.

He is like Abraham in that he still expects the promise to be kept. He continues to look for meaning in the Bible. But he no longer has confidence in God's power to keep the promise so he sets out to keep God's promise for him. He arranges for the meaning that the Bible will display, just as Abraham arranged for the son that God promised him.

This young scholar is a composite figure drawn from a number of real persons. He is also an allegory of a church in which the Bible has become silent.

The promised land is dangerous, then, and full of giants. Many will thus hold back and refuse to enter. There are a lot of people who don't know anything about J, E, D, and P and who really believe the Bible, and they constantly find inspiration and guidance from it. "It would be better to ignore biblical criticism than to lose our faith!" they will say. There is also a story that speaks to them. It says that when the children of Israel were frightened by the reports of giants and refused to enter the promised land, they were turned back into the wilderness and forced to wander for forty years until all the doubters had died out before they were allowed to enter the promised land. We cannot let fear hold us back from going in the direction in which God is leading us.

In the second naïvete, however, in which we combine an approach to the Bible that is fully critical with an expectation that God makes himself present and known to his people through the Bible, we will hear him speaking to us, giving us his perspective on this complex world in which we live and showing us how we can serve him in it.

· 5 ·

The Story of the
Old Testament I

Story and History

When the great Rabbi Israel Baal Shem-Tov saw misfortune threatening the Jews, it was his custom to go into a certain part of the forest to meditate. There he would light a fire, say a special prayer, and the miracle would be accomplished and the misfortune averted.

Later, when his disciple, the celebrated Magid of Mezritch, had occasion, for the same reason, to intercede with heaven, he would go to the same place in the forest and say: "Master of the Universe, listen! I do not know how to light the fire, but I am able to say the prayer." And again the miracle would be accomplished.

Still later, Rabbi Moshe-Leib of Sasov, in order to save his people once more, would go into the forest and say: "I do not know how to light the fire, I do not know the prayer, but I know the place and that must be sufficient." It was sufficient and the miracle was accomplished.

Then it fell to Rabbi Israel of Rizhyn to overcome misfortune. Sitting in his armchair, his head in his hands, he spoke to God: "I am unable to light the fire and I do not know the prayer; I cannot even find the place in the forest. All I can do is to tell the story, and that must be sufficient." And it was sufficient.

The process begun in Elie Wiesel's tale[1] could be completed soon: the story itself may be forgotten. The assumption of the eighteenth and nineteenth centuries, that the value of biblical stories was either in their being accurate historical records or in their being awkward narrative statements of concepts that could be better stated abstractly, has resulted in a devaluation of these stories so that they are no longer learned as a matter of course. Christians have become illiterate in their faith. Education may be defined as initiation into a community of allusion; most allusions to biblical stories have become unrecognizable to contemporary church people. Far from helping people understand their lives in terms of the biblical stories, the allusions themselves are not understood. The purpose of this chapter and the two following is to retell these stories concisely.

The words *story* and *history* have the same derivation, and in practice the two are often difficult to distinguish. In the account that follows, the story line of the Bible will be set in the context of what modern archaeology and biblical scholarship have been able to learn about the world and the time to which the stories belong. At the beginning, the stories will be vivid and the history vague, since we know only the most general things about the world of the patriarchs. Toward the end, the pattern will be reversed, because we know a good bit about the history of the prophetic period, but we do not have many lively anecdotes about them and their times.

The Prehistory (Gen. 1–11)

The Bible begins with two accounts of the creation set side by side. In the first, God began by creating day and night, and went on to devote successive days to creating heaven; the land with its vegetation and the seas; the sun, moon, and stars; the birds and fish; the land animals; and man, in an ascending order of creation. In the second, God set man in the Garden of Eden and then created other animals as candidates to be his helper. None was an adequate helper until God created woman out of man's rib. The man and woman were Adam and Eve. God had provided for all their needs to be met in the Garden of Eden, but had forbidden them to eat of the fruit of the tree of knowledge of good and evil. Tempted by a serpent, Eve tried the forbidden fruit and persuaded Adam to taste it too. God expelled them from Eden, cursing Adam with the necessity to work for food and Eve with the pains of childbirth.

Their sons Cain and Abel followed competitive ways of life: the settled life of a farmer, and the nomadic life of a shepherd. In their rivalry Cain killed Abel. From there things went from bad to worse so that by the time of Noah, God was sorry that he had ever created human beings. He decided to destroy all of them except the righteous Noah and his family, with whom he would begin the human race over again. He commanded Noah to build a giant ark that would hold a pair of all living creatures. When the survival cargo was loaded, rains began that lasted for forty days. When a dove that Noah released from the ark failed to return, he knew that it had found land, and he prepared to debark. God then set a rainbow in the heavens as a sign that he would never destroy the earth with water again.

Even the new race of Noah's descendants did not permanently solve the problem of evil. At Babel they had so mastered the art of building that they thought they could build a tower that would reach to heaven. To keep them from accomplishing this, God confused their tongues. Before they had spoken only one language, but now no one could understand anyone else. Further work on the tower was impossible. Men were spread over the face of the earth, carrying different languages with them.

The Patriarchs

ABRAHAM (Gen. 12:1–25:18)

Since the whole human race could not be depended upon to serve him, God decided to create his own chosen people. He called Abraham, who lived in the Chaldean city of Ur, to leave his father's house and go out to become the ancestor of a new nation. Abraham's father lived until they arrived in Haran, but there he died. Abraham had taken his nephew Lot along with him, but eventually their flocks became too large to graze together. Abraham gave Lot his choice of land. Lot chose the beautiful land around Sodom, leaving his uncle land that was apparently less desirable. Soon though he was captured and his uncle had to rescue him.

Many things happened during these years. In a time of famine Abraham went to Egypt. His wife Sarah was so beautiful that he said that she was his sister rather than take the risk of defending her honor as his wife. The pharaoh added her to his harem until God sent plagues on him and warned him to return her to Abraham. On another occasion Abraham met the priest-king Melchizedek and gave him a tenth of all that he possessed.

Abraham was getting old and he began to wonder when he would become the father of one child, much less a mighty nation. In a vision God promised him that his descendants would be as numerous as the stars in the sky. He also promised them land that would reach from Egypt to Mesopotamia. It was about that time that Sarah and Abraham decided to give God a helping hand by letting Abraham have a son by Hagar. Abraham was ninety-nine years old when God made his covenant with him, obligating Abraham to see that all his male descendants were circumcized. The Lord appeared to Abraham at the oaks of Mamre, manifesting himself as three men. After Abraham had extended to them the hospitality of the desert, they promised that Sarah would have a son by the next spring. Sarah, listening outside the tent door, laughed at the idea that she would have a child after her menopause. For this reason, the son when he came was named Isaac, which is derived from the verb meaning "laugh." After he came, Sarah's jealousy caused her to have Abraham send Hagar and her son Ishmael out into the desert.

Lot, meanwhile, was in trouble again. God had decided to destroy Sodom, the city where he lived, for its wickedness. Concerned for Lot, Abraham asked God if he would destroy the city if there were fifty righteous persons in it. God would not. Forty-five? No. Forty, thirty, twenty, ten? No. It was too late for the city to be saved, however. The Sodomites had tried to attack two angels sent to Lot, and Lot was lucky to get out with his wife and two daughters before God destroyed the city with fire and brimstone. Lot's wife, however, looked back on the sinful city with longing eyes and was turned into a pillar of salt.

Abraham had shown great faith in leaving his home and family to go to a new land. That faith was severely tested by the delay of the birth of Isaac. Its hardest test came when Abraham believed that God had asked him to offer his son Isaac as a sacrifice. Abraham, however, set out for Mount Moriah to do what he thought was commanded. When he had built the altar, laid Isaac on it, and raised the sacrificial knife to slay him, an angel came and showed him a ram that was caught in a thicket by its horns. Abraham named the mountain, "The Lord will provide."

When Sarah eventually died, Abraham bought the cave of Macpelah to be her tomb. This was the first piece of land in Canaan that Abraham owned. The promise of the land was to be fulfilled in the future.

ISAAC AND JACOB (Gen. 25:19–36:43)

In his old age, Abraham sent his servant back to his own people to secure a bride for Isaac. When he arrived in the city of the kinsmen, he asked God to indicate which young woman it should be: let her be the one who offered water to him and the camels. In this way, the servant found Rebekah, the daughter of Abraham's nephew.

Rebekah bore Isaac twin sons, Esau and Jacob, whose rivalry had a prenatal beginning. Esau, the firstborn, became an outdoorsman, while Jacob was a quiet type, and very envious of his brother's right of succession. Once when Esau came in exhausted from the hunt, he asked Jacob for some red lentil soup. Jacob offered to trade him the soup for his right of inheritance, to which Esau readily consented. Being promised the inheritance was one thing; collecting it was another. When Isaac was old, near death, and almost blind, he sent Esau out to kill some game and prepare a last meal for him. After the meal he would confer the inheritance blessing. Rebekah, who was partial to Jacob, told him of his father's plans, and helped him to circumvent them. They covered Jacob's arms with the skins of young goats so that he would feel as hairy as Esau. Jacob gave his father a stew made from goat meat rather than wild game, but the spices disguised the flavor. Isaac, then, blessed Jacob, thinking he was Esau.

When Esau discovered what had happened, Jacob had to flee for his life. Rebekah sent him to stay with her brother Laban in Haran. On the way he camped one night at a place where he used a stone for a pillow. In his sleep he had a vision of a ladder that reached to heaven, on which angels were ascending and descending. Then God repeated to him the promise to Abraham: he would be the ancestor of a nation whose inhabitants would be as numerous as particles of dust and all the families of the earth would be blessed by them.

Laban had two daughters. Jacob immediately fell in love with Rachel, the younger, and promised to work seven years for her hand. On the wedding night, though, Laban substituted his older daughter Leah. Jacob thus had to agree to work another seven years for Rachel. Leah, however, had six sons and a daughter before Rachel's first son, Joseph, was born.

Laban's business ethics were about as good with his flocks as they were with his daughters. He had prospered so with Jacob that he wanted to keep him in his employ. However, ten times he changed his wages and finally Jacob became disgusted and planned his revenge. He said his own share would be only the relatively rare sheep and goats that were speckled or spotted. That would have been a very satisfactory arrangement for Laban if Jacob had not been so crafty. On the primitive assumption that mothers were influenced by what they saw at the time of conception, Jacob arranged to have spotted sticks held before strong animals that were breeding. In this way his animals got to be stronger and more numerous than those of Laban. The business came to be risky, however, and so Jacob packed up his belongings, herded up his animals, took his wives and children, and headed back to his homeland.

Returning to his homeland meant that Jacob would have to deal with Esau, the brother whom he had defrauded of his birthright. He sent peaceful messages ahead, however, and when he learned that Esau was coming with a large force, he sent him rich gifts and, to be on the safe side, divided his retinue into two groups, so that at least one could survive. While he waited alone on the banks of the Jabbok, a man appeared to him with whom he wrestled all night. Jacob knew that his foe was no ordinary mortal, so he refused to let him go without his blessing. Jacob was amazed that he had seen God face to face and survived. His name from then on was Israel, "He who strives with God." Then Jacob went on to meet his brother Esau, discovering to his immense relief that Esau welcomed him. Still cautious, however, Jacob settled in Shechem, a safe distance from Esau.

JOSEPH (Gen. 37–50)

Jacob had twelve sons: six by Leah, two by Rachel, and two each by the maids of his wives (a custom of the times, as the story of Isaac ahd Ishmael showed). His favorite was Joseph, to whom he gave a long-sleeved coat that would be useless to anyone expected to do any manual labor (Joseph's "Amazing Technicolored Dream Coat" is the product of a mistranslation). The jealousy of Joseph's brothers was further kindled by two dreams he had and talked about: one in which the sheaves of wheat bound by his brothers bowed down to the one bound by him, and another in which eleven stars and the moon and sun bowed down to him. Not surprisingly, the brothers threw him into a pit until they could kill him, planning to soak his coat in the blood of a goat and tell his father that he had been killed by a lion. His oldest brother Reuben talked them into selling him as a slave instead, and he was taken to Egypt by traders.

In Egypt he was bought by Potiphar, the captain of the pharaoh's guard. Joseph impressed his master very favorably and rose rapidly in his service, but unfortunately he impressed his master's wife too. When her efforts at seduction failed, she told Potiphar that Jacob had made advances to her, and Jacob was thrown into prison. While there he met two members of the pharaoh's staff; he correctly interpreted their dreams to mean that one would be executed and the other would be restored to duty. The one who was restored forgot his promise to put in a good word for Joseph until the pharaoh was troubled with dreams. Then, on his recommendation, Joseph was brought in to interpret them. Their meaning, he said, was that Egypt would have seven years of abundant crops followed by seven years of famine. The pharaoh decided that no one could be so effective in dealing with this situation as the one who had predicted it, so he appointed Joseph to be his second in command and to supervise the storing of the surplus during the years of plenty so that it could be drawn on in the years of famine.

The famine extended into Canaan where Joseph's father and brothers were. When Jacob heard there was grain in Egypt, he sent all of his sons except Benjamin to get some. Benjamin was the other son of his beloved wife Rachel, who had died giving birth to him. Joseph arranged for a special audience with his brothers, not revealing himself to them. He accused them of being spies and said that they could not return for more grain unless they brought their younger brother to confirm their story. When the intensity of the famine convinced even Jacob that he should send Benjamin with them, they returned to Egypt. Joseph gave orders that his gold cup was to be secreted in one of Benjamin's sacks, and then sent an official to search their baggage and accuse them of theft. He said that the rest could return home, but Benjamin would have to stay as his slave. The oldest son, Judah (called Reuben in another source), begged to be allowed to stay in Benjamin's place so that their father would not suffer the loss of his second favorite son. At that Joseph could contain himself no longer. In tears of joy he told his brothers who he was and was reconciled with them. They returned to bring their father and all the family to Egypt to benefit from the powerful position of their brother whom they had sold into slavery.

These stories of the patriarchs that make up the Book of Genesis fit into a historical context that is known to us through the work of archaeologists. Abraham and his family migrated from Haran near the Euphrates River in the northeastern section of Mesopotamia into Palestine and southward to the edge of the African continent in Egypt during the period known to archaeologists as the Middle Bronze Age. These closing centuries of the second millennium B.C. saw movements of many peoples and much caravan trade between the great cultural centers of Babylon and Egypt. The pyramids of Egypt had already been standing for almost a thousand years and the great cities of Babylon such as Ur and Haran were already ancient. The Palestinian religious sites of Shechem, Bethel, and Hebron that Genesis mentions had long been in existence. Customs illustrated in the patriarchal narratives, such as having children by slave women or stopping at way-station oases, are well documented archaeologically. The names of biblical heroes were common to the region and period. Even though these stories are legendary in form and come from the threshold of history, they fit comfortably into what is known of their period. They fit the cultural situation of the time and place.

Just as the patriarchs are contemporaneous with Near Eastern movements between 2000 and 1700 B.C., so the stories of Joseph and the sojourn of the Hebrews in Egypt can be fitted into the period of foreign domination in Egypt from 1700 to 1500 B.C. The success of Joseph at the pharaoh's court is quite plausible against the background of the invasion of Egypt by the Hyksos ("foreign people") during that time. The Genesis account contains a number of Egyptian words and refers to Egyptian customs like embalming (Gen. 50:26), all of which lend verisimilitude to the idea that the Hebrews were welcome guests in Egypt before the oppression that came under a pharaoh who "did not know Joseph" (Ex. 1:8).

The Exodus

MOSES (Ex. 1-4)

After several centuries the descendants of Joseph and his brothers became so numerous that each of the twelve was the ancestor of a tribe that bore his name. Their increase in number was threatening to the current pharaoh and his people;

they did not remember Joseph and his contributions; they were aware only of an alien people that threatened to gain control over them. Various expedients were employed to deal with this threat, including a command that all Hebrew male children should be thrown into the Nile. One Hebrew mother arranged to save her son by putting him in a floating basket near where the pharaoh's daughter bathed in the river. When the princess discovered him and decided to keep him, the baby's sister stepped from behind the reeds and offered to find a Hebrew nurse for the baby. Thus the baby, who was Moses, was brought up in the pharaoh's palace by his own mother.

After he had grown up, Moses became aware of the plight of his people when he saw an Egyptian beating a Hebrew. In his anger he killed the Egyptian. Then, when it became apparent that his crime was known, he fled across the Red Sea into Midian in Arabia where he assisted the shepherd Jethro and eventually married one of his daughters. Once, while he was tending the flock of Jethro, Moses saw a bush that was aflame but did not burn up. When he stepped aside to inspect it, God revealed himself to Moses and called him to deliver the Hebrews from their slavery to the Egyptians. At last God was going to give to his people the land flowing with milk and honey that had been promised to Abraham. Moses was intimidated by what was expected of him. First he asked God's name and learned that it was Yahweh, "I Am Who I Am." Then he complained that he was not a gifted public speaker and God said that his brother Aaron could speak for him.

RELEASE FROM BONDAGE (Ex. 5–18)

After telling the Hebrew people of this revelation, Moses took Aaron and went before the pharaoh to request that his people be allowed to take a three-day trip into the wilderness to sacrifice to their God. The pharaoh's reaction was to increase the work load of the Hebrews, compelling them to make twice the bricks they had previously been expected to make and to do so without the straw that held the clay together. Even though Moses performed miracles, the pharaoh did not change his mind. God sent nine plagues to persuade him: turning the Nile into blood, sending overwhelming numbers of frogs, gnats, and flies, smiting the cattle with disease, causing people and animals to suffer from boils, pounding the country with lethally sized hailstones, devastating their crops with locusts, and covering the land with darkness. Still the pharaoh did not relent. The tenth plague succeeded where the others had failed: when the firstborn male children and animals died within a night, the pharaoh called Moses and urged him to take his people and leave. The Hebrews had escaped having their sons die because God had commanded Moses to have them cover their doorposts with the blood of a lamb so that the angel of death would pass over their doors. The meal they made from the slain lambs, bitter herbs, and unleavened bread was the institution of the Passover feast.

When the Hebrew people left, the pharaoh regretted his decision and ordered his army to pursue the slaves and bring them back. The chariots of the Egyptians overtook Moses and his followers on the banks of the Red Sea, but Moses held up his miraculous rod and the seas parted to permit the Hebrews to cross on dry land. When the pursuing Egyptian chariots and cavalry were in the middle of the sea, however, the waters closed in on them and they drowned. Moses' sister Miriam sang in joy:

> Sing to the Lord, for he has
> triumphed gloriously;
> the horse and his rider he has thrown
> into the sea. (Ex. 15:21)[2]

In spite of their marvellous deliverance from slavery in Egypt, the Hebrew people were not satisfied and continuously grumbled and murmured their dissatisfaction. God fed them by sending a fine flakelike food, which they called manna, that they could gather each morning. In the evening he sent them quails so that they could have meat. When they needed water Moses would strike a rock with his rod and it would come forth. When an army came against them, the Hebrews won as long as Moses held up his rod; when his arms got tired, Aaron and Hur held them up. Moses was visited by his father-in-law Jethro who helped him to organize the people for effective administration.

THE GIFT OF THE LAW (Ex. 19–40 and Lev.)

When their migration brought the people to the desert of the Sinai peninsula, God appeared to the people through fire and smoke. On Mt. Sinai God revealed the Ten Commandments to Moses, as well as many other religious regulations. The commandments were to be engraved in stone and carried in a special box called the Ark of the Covenant. It was to be carried before the people when they were on the move and to rest in a special tent or tabernacle when they stopped. The top of the box was thought of as God's throne and was thus called "the mercy seat." The tent was to serve as the Temple of the people in their journey, and Aaron and his sons were to be the priests.

While Moses was on the mountain receiving the commandments and regulations, the people grew impatient and had Aaron make them an idol in the shape of a calf out of their gold jewelry; then they proceeded to engage in the licentious rites usually performed for such fertility gods. When Moses came down and saw what was happening, he was so angry that he broke the stone tablets on which the commandments were written and melted the golden calf and ground it to powder. Then he ordered the slaughter of the 3,000 people responsible. After that Moses had to go back up the mountain to receive the Ten Commandments again.

WANDERING IN THE WILDERNESS (Num. and Dt.)

When all of the provisions for worship commanded at Sinai had been made, Moses and the people set out, the ark going before them. God's presence and direction was manifested in a pillar of cloud during the day and in fire at night. As they went, there continued to be trouble, with the people mur-

muring about this and that. Even Miriam and Aaron spoke against Moses once. When they arrived at the boundary of Canaan, Moses sent in spies (see page 84). Because the reports of the spies frightened the people, and they were unwilling to take possession of the land that God was to give them, they were condemned to wander in the wilderness for forty years until all of the fainthearted had died out.

The people were not more contented in this phase of their travel than they had been before, but they did have other things to think about. Many of the kings through whose land they travelled objected to their passing through, but God always protected the Hebrews when they were attacked. Balak, the king of Moab, sought supernatural aid against them by trying to bribe Balaam, a Mesopotamian priest and prophet, to curse them. Balaam did his best, but the odds were against him. His donkey balked three times when he saw an angel of God blocking his way. When Balaam tried to whip him, the donkey talked and spoke out in his own defense. Three times and in three different places Balaam tried to pronounce the curse for which Balak was paying him, but he could only speak the word that God put in his mouth, so each time he wound up blessing Israel instead of Moab.

When the wandering in the wilderness was completed and the people had come to the area just across the Jordan River from Jericho in the promised land, neither Moses nor Aaron was with them. Aaron had already died on Mount Hor because he had criticized Moses. Moses was not to be allowed to cross over into Canaan because he had apparently lacked faith when God commanded him to bring forth water from the rock of Meribah. After giving a final blessing to Israel, Moses ascended Mount Pisgah in the mountains of Moab and looked down on the land across the river that had been promised to Abraham. There on the mountain he died, secure in the knowledge that the promise of the land was on the brink of fulfillment. The people mourned a month for Moses, but the command had already passed to Joshua.

In the story of Moses we come closer to a historical personage than we did with Abraham, Isaac, Jacob, or Joseph. Even though we have not reached the point of having hard historical data connected to the story, the religious texts and legal documents that form the core of Exodus, Leviticus, Numbers, and Deuteronomy bring us closer to the events reported than the legends that link us with the more distant patriarchs.

The time and place of the events from the call and commissioning of Moses up to his death just before the entry into Canaan can be set within narrower limits than those given to the patriarchs. Our first solid historical anchor for this story is a stone monument set up by Pharaoh Merneptah in 1220 B.C. which mentions Israel as a seminomadic tribe in Palestine and is thus the first nonbiblical reference to the Hebrew people. With this fixed point of reference establishing the presence of Israel in Canaan, the history of the events of the Exodus may be reconstructed: (a) the Exodus itself took place around 1280 B.C., (b) the pharaoh of the Exodus was Ramses II (1290–40 B.C.), and (c) the pharaoh of the oppression, who "did not know Joseph," was Seti I (1305–1290). The events reported in the Bible took place in the easternmost region of the Nile delta and in the Sinai peninsula that links Africa and Palestine. Archaeological data shows that the pharaohs were engaged in enormous building efforts in the delta area after the expulsion of the Hyksos invaders, undoubtedly the explanation of the need for the bricks the Hebrews made. Moses is an Egyptian name. Other elements in the story, such as the use of forced labor for these projects, reflect the conditions that existed there at the time and thus confirm the essential historicity of the account.

The covenant or legal pact between God and his people established through the mediation of Moses at Sinai resembled the form of treaties used in the ancient Near East to link a vassal with a powerful overlord. In such treaties the continued well-being and even existence of the obligated party depends upon the faithfulness of that party in fulfilling the stipulations of the treaty. Thus Israel is shown to stand in the same relation to God as a vassal people stood toward their overlord. When they were in bondage in Egypt, the Hebrew people were landless and thus not many rungs higher on the social ladder than their ancestors who were "wandering Arameans." Thus they resemble the landless wanderers we know from archaeological sources, the Habiru or Apiru (note the similarity of these names to "Hebrew"), who existed on the fringes of Near Eastern society. The Sinai covenant gave them a new status that was symbolized by the name Israel. With the name they now had the heritage of the promised land of Canaan.

The Occupation of the Land

JOSHUA (Jos.)

The books of Joshua and Judges give quite different impressions of the conquest of Canaan. Joshua depicts the conquest as one campaign under Joshua that takes place quickly and is followed immediately by a division of the conquered territory among the twelve tribes. Judges, on the other hand, conveys an impression of sporadic local campaigns under the leadership of men especially inspired by God for the task; these charismatic leaders were the judges.

Joshua began his invasion by sending two spies into the city of Jericho, just across the Jordan from where Israel was camped. A report of the presence of the spies in the city came to the king of Jericho, but they were hidden by a prostitute named Rahab who had living quarters in the wall of the city and who credited the previous victories of the Hebrews along their route to divine assistance. For this help, Rahab was the only inhabitant of Jericho whose life was spared.

The campaign began when Joshua ordered priests to carry the Ark of the Covenant before the people into the Jordan River. When the feet of the priests carrying the ark touched the river, its waters parted and permitted the Hebrews to cross over on dry land. A monument of twelve stones was set up to commemorate the event. Jericho itself was taken in a manner no less miraculous. After all of the Israelite males had been circumcised, a daily procession around the city walls took place which was led by the Ark of the Covenant and seven priests blowing ram's horns. The soldiers of Israel thus made one circuit of the city each day. On the seventh day, however, the procession circled the city seven times. On the seventh time around, the horns blew, the people shouted, and the walls of the city came tumbling down. All living creatures in it were put to death, but the gold and other metals were taken for the treasury of the Lord.

Initial efforts to take Ai, the next city, were frustrated until a man who had tried to take booty for himself had been discovered and punished. Then God revealed to Joshua a plan to take the city by ambush. This time the Israelites were allowed to take spoils, and the city was left a ruin. The citizens of Gibeon, fearing they would be next, put on clothing that made them look as though they had come on a journey of many days. The Israelites, taken in by this ruse when the Gibeonites appeared to them, made a peaceful settlement with them. The kings of the five Amorite cities in the hill country and on the coastal plain, however, allied themselves to meet the invaders with a united front. Joshua surprised them by an all-night-march, however, and put them to flight. In their headlong retreat they were bombarded by hailstones that killed more of their soldiers than the Israelites did. In order to complete his victory in one day Joshua commanded the sun and moon to stand still until the battle was over. From then on it was just a mopping-up campaign until Joshua completed his conquest first of the south and then of the north of Palestine. Then the land was divided between the twelve tribes.

Years later, when peace had long been established and Joshua was an old man, he called the people together at Shechem. He gave them the choice of serving the gods of their ancestors, the gods of the Canaanites, or Yahweh. When the people joined him in swearing allegiance to Yahweh who had brought them out of Egypt into their own land, Joshua set up a stone monument to this covenant under the oak tree in the sanctuary at Shechem. The bones of Joseph, which had been brought along on the Exodus, were buried there. Then Joshua died and he was buried on his own property in the land of promise.

JUDGES (Jg.)

The beginning of Judges gives quite a different picture, suggesting that the conquest of the land was piecemeal and that each tribe entered the land separately and conquered its own territory. The conquest was not always accomplished immediately, because the inhabitants of the cities of the land were better armed and had chariots. This picture is quickly replaced with another that depicts an equally gradual occupation of the land, but one that has been harmonized with the story of Joshua: the land was indeed conquered by Joshua, but after occupying their territory, the people began to go over to the religion of the local people. When they fell away from the worship of Yahweh, they got into trouble. If they called upon God in their distress, he sent them judges to lead them. After the judge had restored their prosperity, however, they fell away from God again.

Some of the judges are barely more than names to us. Of Othniel we know that he defeated a Mesopotamian king and thus provided Israel with forty years of peace. Eglon of Moab then conquered the country for eighteen years until he was assassinated by the judge Ehud. Ehud was left-handed and succeeded in concealing an eighteen-inch sword under the right side of his clothing when he had an audience with the king. Eglon was so fat that the sword sank into him up to the hilt. Ehud was able to escape because the courtiers thought the king was answering a call of nature. The great accomplishment of the judge Shamgar was that he killed 600 Philistines with an ox goad.

One judge was a woman: Deborah. She called Barak to join her in leading the forces of Israel against those of Canaan, even though Sisera, the general of the enemy, had 900 iron chariots under his command. The greatly outclassed and outnumbered Israelites scored a great victory and Sisera had to flee on foot. He managed to get to the tent of Jael, the wife of Heber the Kenite, and asked her to give him a drink of water and to hide him. When he fell asleep from exhaustion, she drove a tent peg through his head and made the Israelite victory total.

A contemporary ballad commemorating the event achieves great artistry by depicting the impact of Sisera's death through the eyes of his mother:

> Sisera's mother looked out of the window;
>> she gazed from behind the lattice.
>
> "Why is his chariot so late in coming?" she asked.
> "Why are his horses so slow to return?"
> Her wisest ladies answered her,
>> and she told herself over and over,
>
> "They are only finding things to capture and divide,
>> a girl or two for every soldier,
>
> rich cloth for Sisera,
>> embroidered pieces for the neck of the queen."
>
> (Jg. 5:28–30, Today's English Version)

By the time of Gideon, the Israelites had made the transition from a seminomadic life to one of settled farming. Thus they were vulnerable to the migrations of the Midianites whose flocks destroyed their crops. God gave Gideon a miraculous call to judge his people, and Gideon responded by tearing down a sanctuary of the local fertility cult. When called to lead Israel against the Midianites, Gideon asked God for two signs to make certain that the call was real: on the first night dew would appear on a sheepskin but not on the grass around it; on the second night the process would be reversed. When Gideon issued his call to arms, too many responded. By various tests he pared his force down from 32,000 to 300 men. He gave each of them a torch, a trumpet, and a pottery jar. During the night he placed them around the Midianite camp and at a signal they blew their trumpets, smashed their jars, and held their torches aloft. The Midianites were so frightened that they fell over themselves and killed one another in their panic-stricken flight.

Gideon's son Abimelech took advantage of his position and made himself king, even though violence was required in obtaining and keeping his throne. So unfit for rule was he that the situation was compared to the effort of the trees to get a king: since the olive and fig trees and the grape vine all were too busy with productive activity to be king, only the bramble bush had the leisure and inclination for the job.

After the long and uneventful judgeships of Tola and Jair, Jephthah, an outlaw chieftain, was called to lead Israel against the Ammonites. To secure victory, he resorted to a vow of human sacrifice and promised that he would offer up the first person who came from his house to greet him when he returned victorious. That person was his only child, a daughter.

The last judge mentioned in the book was Samson, who came after Ibzan, Elon, and Abdon. His birth was in answer to the prayers of his barren mother, but she was told that he would be called by God to lead his people against the Philistines. Because of his holy vocation, he was to abstain from intoxicating beverages and ritually impure food, and he was never to cut his hair. Samson's life, however, was one of selfish indulgence rather than heroic leadership. At an early age he wished to marry a Philistine woman. On the way to see her, he killed a lion with his bare hands. He bet thirty Philistine men a suit of clothes each that they could not guess a riddle he made up about the lion. When they bribed his fiancée to wheedle the answer out of him, he procured the thirty suits he owed by killing thirty Philistines and taking their clothes.

Later when Samson went back to see the woman he had intended to marry, he discovered that she had been married to someone else. In vengeance he caught 300 foxes, set their tails afire, and sent them running through the grain fields of the Philistines. On another occasion, when he stayed with a Philistine prostitute until late at night, the inhabitants closed the city gates, hoping to have him at their mercy in the morning. Samson, however, simply tore down the gates, tossed them over his shoulder and walked off with them.

In Delilah, Samson finally met his Waterloo. She promised the Philistines that she would learn the secret of his great strength. Even after she brought them in to bind him twice when he gave her wrong answers, he still told her that if his hair was cut, he would be as weak as any other man. When he was overpowered, his eyes were put out and he was set to turning a mill in prison. After some time had gone by and his hair had grown back out, he was brought out to be ridiculed at a festival of the Philistine god Dagon. In the temple he was allowed to stand between the two main pillars that supported the roof. Placing a hand against each, he pushed them apart so that the building caved in and killed him and 3,000 of his enemies.

HISTORICAL BACKGROUND

As suggested above, the conquest was a complicated and extended process as suggested by Judges, rather than a whirlwind campaign such as Joshua describes. This segment of the story of redemption brings us from the threshold of world history into its arena. The thirteenth century B.C. saw the movement of many peoples in the area of the eastern coast of the Mediterranean both into Egypt and along the Palestinian coast east of the Jordan River. On the stone monument that he erected in 1220 B.C., Pharaoh Merneptah tells of his conquest of some of these groups and he includes the Israelites in Palestine among his victims. The occupation of Palestine is thus to be understood as a part of a wider movement of peoples, as the patriarchs before them had been.

The twelve tribes probably moved in one by one rather than as a united migration, but some time in the middle of the thirteenth century B.C. Israel moved from across the Jordan River into Canaan. Archaeological evidence supports the essential historicity of the stories of the conquest of some of the cities, but brings others into question. Jericho and Ai, for instance, were destroyed long before the conquest, but Hazor and Lachish seem to have fallen at that time. Other sites that are not listed as captured, such as Shechem, do not show damage. The picture of the occupation that emerges is that some land was taken by armed conquest, some acquired through treaties, and some by joining with peoples who gave the Israelites a friendly reception.

Israel functioned during this period as a confederation of tribes who shared a common religious tradition and cultic

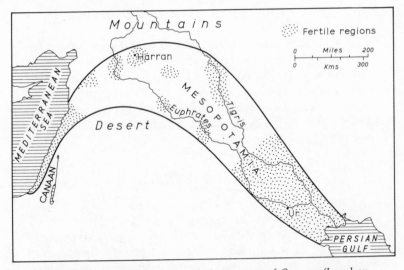

The Fertile Crescent. *The strategic importance of Canaan (Israel or Palestine) in the ancient world may be seen in this map of what is called "The Fertile Crescent," the only land in that area that is suitable for human habitation. Canaan thus was the land bridge between Egypt and Europe and Mesopotamia, the region between the Tigris and Euphrates rivers where the Assyrian, Babylonian, and Persian empires arose.*

shrine. Joshua ends with an account of the establishment of a ceremony at Shechem by which the covenant with Yahweh was to be renewed (see page 101). In this covenant ceremony groups that had not been among the original invaders were incorporated into the people of God. Among these were both Hebrews who had remained in Palestine from the time of the patriarchs, and who thus had not been a part of the Exodus, and Canaanites who were willing to unite with their invaders. The covenant ceremony thus reinforced the faith of some and brought others to it for the first time.

The Song of Deborah in Judges 5, which we saw to be the oldest long poem in the Bible, illustrates the tribal structure during this early period in Canaan. The twelve tribes had been alloted segments of the land (Jos. 13–21), although their boundaries seem to have shifted from time to time. The new homeland extended from the region around the lake of Galilee in the north to the desert of the Negev in the south,

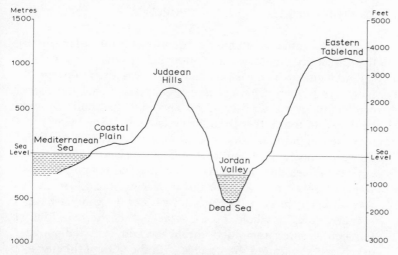

Cross-section of Palestine. *The Palestinian land bridge between Egypt and Europe and Mesopotamia varies considerably in terrain. The landscape consists of four north-south bands that are represented schematically above. The coastal plain is the easiest band for travel. The Judean hills are very fertile on their western slope in the South, although they rise to high mountains in the North. The Lake of Galilee, Jordan River, and Dead Sea lie in a geological fault that is 6–1200 feet below sea level. The eastern tableland is not the scene of many biblical events. The vertical scale on the diagram is very different from the horizontal one so that differences in elevation can be emphasized. Knowing that the Holy Land is divided into these topographical bands facilitates our understanding of biblical history.*

and from the mountain range just east of the Jordan in the east to the Mediterranean coast in the west. Certain Canaanite enclaves remained in the central hill country, along the southern coastal plain, and in the north. The Song of Deborah reflects the situation when the focus of the biblical story is shifting from the conquest to the consolidation of the Israelite holdings.

The fragile unity of the widely scattered Israelite holdings was threatened by Canaanite culture. As the seminomadic Israelites became settled farmers, the fertility religion of the Canaanites proved very alluring, as did also their advanced urban culture and Iron Age technology. That tribal bands, even after being welded together through the long wilderness experience, could overcome the superior culture and might of the Canaanite city-states was an amazing achievement.

One element in the Israelite victory was their concept of holy war (*herem*). This concept presupposed that the chief combatant in the war was God and that the spoils of war belonged to him rather than to the Israelites. The belief that they were fighting on God's side and with his aid gave them the vigor and commitment that made victory possible against superior forces. In a holy war the enemy and his possessions were destroyed as a form of burnt offering to God, so there was no personal gain for the soldiers. Yet the conquest was not genocide, a whole people was not destroyed. Many Canaanite centers remained untouched and, as noted above, others actually united themselves with the faith of the invaders. Indeed, most of the Israelite settlements in the central hill country are revealed by archaeology to have been new settlements that were not built on the ruins of captured towns. Enough of the Canaanite population and religion remained, therefore, to pose a threat to the seminomadic Israelites as they made the adjustment to settled farm and urban life.

The period of consolidation and confrontation with Canaanite culture that constituted the period of the judges lasted from around 1200 to 1050 B.C. and archaeologically it marks the transition from the Bronze to the Iron Age. The Hebrews, and other groups now joined together in the faith of Yahweh, were still learning to think of themselves as the united people of Israel. During this century and a half, while individual tribes were responding to various internal and external crises, the people were strengthening their hold on the land of promise and upon the covenant bond that existed between them and the God of Sinai.

Many of these crises were the efforts of other peoples to invade Canaan. The tribe of Dan, for instance, was dislodged by the sea people who gave their name to Palestine, the Philistines. Their threat sets the stage for the events which finally led Israel to replace the tribal league system with a monarchy.

· 6 ·

The Story of the
Old Testament II

The Beginnings of the Monarchy

SAMUEL (1 Sam. 1–8)

The Ark of the Covenant was at the sanctuary of Shiloh, and Hannah, a barren woman, went up with her husband to pray there for a son; if her prayer was answered, she would give him to God. When he found her praying alone, the priest Eli thought she was drunk, but when he learned the truth, he promised that her prayer would be answered. When the baby Samuel was weaned, Hannah presented him to Eli and sang a song of thanksgiving that resembles Mary's Magnificat (Lk. 1:46–55).

Eli had already been informed by God that his self-indulgent sons would not succeed him, so he was pleased to have Samuel with him. Once when the boy was lying at night in the sanctuary, he thought he heard his name called and rushed to Eli. The old priest said that he had not called him and sent him back to bed. The same thing happened a second time and then a third, but the third time Eli recognized what was happening and instructed Samuel on what to do. When the voice came again, Samuel replied, "Speak, Lord, for your servant hears." Then Samuel learned that he was to succeed Eli as God's priest and prophet.

After Samuel had grown up, the Israelites were hard

pressed in battle by the Philistines and decided to take the ark into battle as divine aid against their enemies. Much to their dismay the ark was captured, and Eli's two sons who had been responsible for it were killed. Upon learning the news, Eli himself fell dead. Possession of the ark did the Philistines little good though: when they put it into their temple, the image of their god Dagon fell apart, and a pestilence of tumors and a plague of mice afflicted them. They hastily returned the ark to Israel along with golden offerings for reparation. Then Samuel offered sacrifice to God and the Israelites gained a victory over the Philistines.

Samuel's own sons proved in time to be no better than those of Eli, and the people came to him and asked him to give them a king like the surrounding nations had to rule over them. Samuel tried to warn them of the dangers, but they were insistent, so God told Samuel to do as they requested.

SAUL (1 Sam. 9–15)

A young man of the tribe of Benjamin was head and shoulders taller than anyone else; his name was Saul. Once when he and a slave had journeyed some distance to find his father's lost donkeys, they decided to enlist divine aid in their search by asking Samuel to discover the location of the animals by his prophetic power. Samuel recognized Saul as the one God had chosen and anointed him king. His selection was later made public when Samuel called all the twelve tribes together and let God reveal his will by having lots drawn to show from which tribe the king was to come, then from which family, and finally which member of the family.

Saul began to exercise his leadership after the Ammonites attacked Jabesh-gilead. When the besieged people were offered no terms but unconditional surrender, they sent out messages for help. Threatening them if they refused, Saul called the twelve tribes to follow him in an expedition to relieve Jabesh-gilead. The response was immediate and unanimous and their victory was complete. Afterwards Saul was crowned.

Samuel still warned the people about the dangers of having a king, and events soon proved him right. After one great triumph, when Samuel was late in arriving to offer sacrifice, Saul presumed to offer it himself. After another victory that was supposed to have been a *herem*, in which all the enemy and their livestock were killed, Saul did not destroy the king and the choicest animals. When Samuel learned of it and demanded an explanation, Saul said the animals were being kept for sacrifice. Samuel replied, "To obey is better than sacrifice." On another occasion, Saul had vowed that any soldier who ate before victory was complete would be put to death. His son Jonathan was off on a scouting expedition that led to the victory and he did not know of his father's vow. When he unwittingly took a taste of wild honey and it was later revealed to Saul that he had, the army would not allow the hero of the day to be put to death.

The House of David

DAVID'S INTRODUCTION TO THE KING'S COURT
(1 Sam. 16–20)

God told Samuel that he would find the man to be anointed as Saul's successor among the sons of Jesse. Although the seven older sons were all outstanding specimens of manhood, Samuel was directed to anoint the youngest, David, who had to be called in from tending the sheep. By this time Saul was subject to spells of deep depression and David was introduced to his court to play the lyre as music therapy for the king. David's entry into public prominence came when his brothers were off with Saul's army doing battle against the Philistines. Sent by his father to take food to his brothers, David discovered that the battle had been held up for weeks by a Philistine champion who challenged the Israelites to settle the war by single combat. Since he was a ten-foot tall giant named Goliath, no Israelite was willing to take the challenge. David, however, who had killed bears and lions in protecting his father's sheep, thought that he could manage. Saul wanted to give him his own weapons and armor, but they were too large and heavy for the boy. When Goliath saw the boy who was sent against him, he snorted in contempt; "Am I a dog, that you come to me with sticks?" What David had brought, however, was rocks and, putting one of these into his sling, he twirled it and let fly. The rock sank into the giant's forehead and ended his threat.

David quickly became a leader of the king's armies. Soon, in fact, Saul became jealous of his prowess and renown, for he heard the Israelite women cheer a victory by singing, "Saul has slain his thousands, and David his ten thousands." Even though Saul gave David his daughter Michal in marriage, he began to plot against David's life. Occasionally his anger became so great that he would fling his spear at him, but David was always able to dodge. On another occasion Michal saved David's life by letting him out through a window and placing a dummy in his bed. David had won the friendship of Saul's son Jonathan and Jonathan arranged to signal David that he should flee for his life by directions that he gave to his caddy in archery practice.

DAVID ON THE RUN (1 Sam. 21–30)

In his haste to get provisions, David stopped by a sanctuary and took the holy bread there and also Goliath's sword. The priest and his family forfeited their lives for this assistance to David, even though they did not know that he was running from Saul. After a short campaign against the Philistines, David and his followers went to live in the wilderness of Ziph. Several times when Saul was chasing David, David came close enough to him to take his life, but he still considered Saul to be the Lord's anointed king and would not kill him even to protect himself. When David asked the assistance of a rich man and he refused, the man's wife Abigail, aware of the damage that David could do them, took him abundant provisions. When the rich man died shortly afterwards, David married Abigail. He also soon added a third wife to his harem.

Eventually David decided that the only way he could protect himself was to enter the service of the Philistines. He and his band of 600 followers entered into the service of Achish of Gath and used Ziklag as a base from which to attack native Canaanite peoples who were enemies to both the Israelites and the Philistines. When the Philistines leagued together to make war on Saul, David was not trusted by the allies of Achish and did not participate in the war. Saul was so terrified by the prospect of the war that he used a witch to summon up the soul of the deceased Samuel to advise him. Samuel told him, however, that the Philistines would win, Saul and his sons would die, and the kingdom would go to David. At the battle of Gilboa Samuel's prophecy came true and in his despair Saul committed suicide.

DAVID THE KING (2 Sam.)

The Amalekite who brought news of Israel's defeat to David at Ziklag claimed to have administered the *coup de grâce* to Saul's suicide attempt. David had him executed for killing the Lord's anointed and lamented the death of Saul and Jonathan in the Song of the Bow:

Thy glory, O Israel, is slain upon thy high places!
How are the mighty fallen!

David then went up to Judah where he was made king of the southern tribes, but Saul's general, Abner, made the king's son, Ish-bosheth, king over the northern tribes of Israel. For six years Abner led Ish-bosheth's army against David's army under Joab. Eventually Abner decided to sue for peace, but Joab killed him for personal vengeance. Two foreigners slipped into Ish-bosheth's palace and killed him, and David rewarded them as he had the Amalekite who had killed Saul. The Israelites asked David to reign over them as well as Judah and the kingdom was united. Then David, at the age of thirty-six, took Jerusalem from the Jebusites and made it the capital of his country from which he ruled for thirty-four more years.

David wanted to bring the Ark of the Covenant to Jerusalem and went to do so with great solemnity. When they had gone a certain distance, though, a man named Uzzah touched the ark and died. This made David afraid to take it any farther. When, however, David discovered that Obededom, the man at whose house he had left it, prospered, he again went to bring it to Jerusalem. He led the procession into the city himself, and he danced to celebrate the presence of the ark in his city, much to the shock of his wife Michal. David wanted to build a temple to house the ark, but God told him that was an honor reserved for his son.

David was successful in subduing all the enemies of Israel, but he did not succeed in ruling his own household or even in controlling his own passion. He did win favor, however, by inviting the one remaining son of Saul, the cripple Mephibosheth, to come into his household and live like one of his own sons.

When David saw Bathsheba stripped to perform her postmenstrual purification, he was inflamed with lust and had her brought to him. After she was discovered to be pregnant, David tried at first to arrange for her husband Uriah to think that he was responsible, but this plot failed because Uriah preserved the continence that was expected of a soldier on duty during time of war. David then instructed Joab to place Uriah in the center of danger in battle. After Uriah's death, David added Bathsheba to his harem. The prophet Nathan came to David, though, and told him a parable about a rich man who had many sheep, but who had taken a poor man's only ewe lamb to feed a guest. When David was filled with indignation and wanted to punish the offender, Nathan said, "You are the man." In spite of David's repentance, Bathsheba's child died. Later, however, she gave birth to Solomon.

David's eldest son Amnon became obsessed with the beauty of his half sister Tamar and succeeded in raping her. When she reported to her full brother, Absalom, what he had done, Absalom said nothing but plotted his revenge for two years. Finally, during festivities at the time of sheepshearing, Absalom had Amnon killed while he was drunk. Absalom then fled for his life, but in time David accepted the loss of Amnon and longed to be reconciled with Absalom. When

Joab saw this he arranged for David to pronounce forgiveness of a murderer in a similar situation. When the analogy was pointed out to David, he permitted Absalom to come home, although he was not to be allowed in the king's presence.

In two years Absalom was restored to favor. Then he began systematically to undermine the popularity of the king. He told everyone who had a case to be decided by the king that his cause was right and that, were Absalom in a position to do so, he would certainly decide the case in that person's favor. In this way the handsome Absalom built up a constituency and, when he knew the time was right, he called those on his side to join him in a revolt against David. David and the minority loyal to him had to flee Jerusalem for their lives. Only David's arrangement for Absalom to receive bad advice prevented his being chased down and killed that night. As it was, David had time to get his forces organized and in the field.

Absalom had long beautiful hair about which he was very vain. When he rode into a thick forest to avoid pursuit, his hair caught on an oak branch and his mule ran out from under him, leaving him suspended in mid-air. When Joab heard about it, he took three darts and went to kill him, even though David had given orders that his son was to be dealt with gently. When David received the news, he was more grieved over the death of Absalom than he was joyful over the victory, until Joab remonstrated with him for this ingratitude to the people who had supported him. David concluded a generous peace settlement with those who had revolted. A small group that wished to continue in rebellion was quickly defeated.

In spite of his domestic difficulties, David was very successful in his campaigns against the enemies of Israel, especially the Philistines. The greatest threat to Israel's hold on the promised land was posed by the Philistines, recent arrivals in the country themselves. The judges of the tribal league system had been able to meet the sporadic crises of the twelfth century, but the league was not equal in the eleventh century B.C. to the steadily growing power of this people that had entered Canaan from the Mediterranean Sea and the Nile delta. The Philistines had established themselves in the city-states along the southern coastal plain, but they also had garrisons within Israelite territory and were able to influence the twelve tribes, as the stories of Samson show.

A major reason for the ascendancy of the Philistines over Israel was their monopoly on iron weapons and implements that had been recently developed. The onset of the Iron Age is set at 1200 B.C. by archaeologists. At this time the Philistine sea people introduced into Palestine this metal that had been found superior to bronze for farm tools and weapons. They had acquired the secret of its manufacture in Asia Minor and they kept it to themselves, allowing no iron-working among the Hebrews (1 Sam. 13:19–20).

The inability of a loose confederation of tribes to meet the onslaught of these more heavily armed people from the sea was painfully evident in a disastrous series of battles around 1150 B.C., just a generation after the Philistines had settled in Palestine. Their league of city-states dominated the region of Judah and began to make inroads into the territory of Israel to the north. It was at this time that the Ark of the Covenant was captured and the central sanctuary of the tribal confederation was destroyed.

As judges no longer provided leadership adequate for the times, two new institutions developed: prophecy and the monarchy. Prophets were persons who were especially conscious of being chosen by God to proclaim his word on a given historical situation such as the Philistine crisis. The concept of prophecy was borrowed from Israel's neighbors, but was an appropriate expression of the relation in which Israel stood to God.

In the introduction of the institution of monarchy, Saul was a transitional figure. As king—more technically prince or commander—he had a standing army and established a court at Gibeah in the central part of the country. Archaeological excavations show it to have been a rather modest and rustic complex, a far cry from the opulence of the kings of Israel's neighbors. Saul's rule lasted from around 1020 to 1000 B.C. David, who reigned from 1000 to 962 B.C., turned the greatest threat against Israel, that of the Philistines, into the shining hour of the people. He created what had never existed before in Palestine, a single autonomous kingdom throughout the area. This golden age of Israel took place at a time when the superpowers of Asia and Africa were unable to interfere in the affairs of this landbridge between their continents.

THE MAGNIFICENCE OF SOLOMON (1 Kg. 1–11)

When David had grown so old that he took his last wife to be not a sexual partner but a nursemaid, his eldest surviving son Adonijah began to take active steps to occupy the throne immediately. When news of the feasts he was holding prior to taking over reached Bathsheba and the prophet Nathan, they reminded David that he had promised the throne to Solomon, his son by Bathsheba. David arranged to have Solomon crowned instantly, even before Adonijah's feast was over. Solomon spared Adonijah's life until after the death of David, but then had him killed when he asked to be allowed to inherit Abishag, David's last wife, since this request implied a claim of right to succession. Joab, the general who had sided with Adonijah, was also put to death and Solomon's throne was secure.

In order to seek an oracle from God about his reign, the king went to the hilltop sanctuary ("high place") at Gibeon and offered abundant sacrifices. While he was there he had a dream in which God appeared to him and told him: "Ask what I shall give you." Solomon did not ask for long life, riches, or revenge against his enemies, but asked instead for an understanding mind to govern God's people. God promised to give him not only what he asked for but also the lesser things he had not requested. In this way Solomon's name became synonymous with wisdom. When two prostitutes asked him to settle a dispute between them over which was the mother of a baby, he learned the truth by threatening to split the baby in two, thus forcing the real mother to withdraw her claim in order to preserve her baby's life. Solomon's fame for wisdom reached so far that the Queen of Sheba in Arabia came to test him and found that the reports were understated rather than hyperbolic. In time Solomon's name was associated with most of the Wisdom books of the Old Testament and Apocrypha.

As God had promised David, Solomon was allowed to build the first Temple in Israel, locating it in his capital city of Jerusalem. There he also built for himself an even more magnificent palace. Solomon's reign was characterized by many building projects. In order to carry these out he had both to extort heavy taxes from the people and to force them into labor crews. Thus he transformed the Israelite monarchy into the sort of institution of conspicuous consumption that the monarchy was in surrounding kingdoms. Solomon, indeed, entered into alliances with these foreign kings. He married one of the daughters of the Egyptian pharaoh and received much help from Hiram of Tyre in the construction of the Temple. His harem is said to have consisted of 700 wives and 300 female slaves. The wives were princesses and were married for purposes of diplomacy. While the numbers may well be inflated, there is no reason to doubt that his harem was quite large. His foreign wives are blamed for inducing him to permit the introduction of the worship of foreign gods into the Temple. All he did displayed the opulence of an oriental potentate; he had mines and a navy to provide him with luxury goods from all over the known world. He also had a large standing army that included many horses and chariots, by no means the least expensive luxuries that he enjoyed.

In view of the self-indulgence of his reign, there is reason to doubt Solomon's reputation for wisdom. Certainly there were several efforts to rebel against him and to remove the yoke of his oppression. One of those who attempted an uprising was Jeroboam, whom Solomon had placed in charge of one of his forced labor units. The prophet Ahijah, who was walking with him one day, tore his new robe into twelve pieces and gave ten of them to Jeroboam, saying that God was going to give him ten of the twelve tribes of Israel to rule over.

The Divided Kingdom

REHOBOAM AND JEROBOAM (1 Kg. 12–16)

The prophecy of Ahijah was not fulfilled in Solomon's lifetime. When, however, Solomon's son Rehoboam came to be crowned at the ancient shrine of Shechem, Jeroboam appeared with all the elders of Israel to ask Rehoboam not to be as harsh and demanding a ruler as his father had been. Rehoboam took three days to reply, consulting with both his father's elderly advisers and with his own young friends. Rehoboam made the mistake of taking the arrogant advice of his friends rather than the conciliatory advice of the aged; he told the people: "My father made your yoke heavy, but I will add to your yoke; my father chastised you with whips, but I will chastise you with scorpions." When this happened, the people of the northern ten tribes sounded the ancient cry of rebellion, "To your tents, O Israel!" Only the tribes of Judah and Benjamin remained loyal to Rehoboam and the Davidic dynasty.

Jeroboam was made king of the northern tribes. During the time of the divided kingdom the northern kingdom was called Israel and the southern one was called Judah. This is a little confusing because before the division the united tribes were known as Israel. Israel, of course, was the name given to Jacob after he wrestled with the angel (see page 92). The twelve tribes were understood to be the descendants of his twelve sons. Since ten of the tribes were in the northern kingdom under Jeroboam, it is no surprise that they were called by the name that had previously been applied to the entire nation. After the northern kingdom was captured by the Assyrians, led away into captivity, and lost from view as a nation, it became common to refer to the remaining kingdom in the south as Israel (e.g., Is. 5:7; Mic. 1:5).

The Deuteronomist who put together 1 and 2 Kings was more concerned with the limitation of sacrifice to the Temple at Jerusalem than anything else, and the value judgments that he made on the various kings of Israel and Judah are based exclusively on their attitudes toward that central sanctuary. For that reason, he leaves out many of the things that would interest us and includes a large number which it is difficult for most of us to get excited about. The summary of the story of that period will therefore be less complete than what has been attempted up to this point.

In order to keep the Israelites from having to go to Jerusalem to worship at the Temple, Jeroboam built temples at Dan and Bethel where he erected golden calves that were probably intended to represent Yahweh's throne, even though later influence of foreign religions caused them to be considered as idols. The sin of Jeroboam in doing this was confirmed by miracles. Even Ahijah, who had prophesied that Jeroboam would reign over the ten tribes, denounced him and prophesied the eventual disappearance of Israel into captivity. The disinterest of the Deuteronomist in every other aspect of Jeroboam's reign is expressed in a formula that recurs often in the records of the later kings:

> Now the rest of the acts of Jeroboam, how he warred and how he reigned, behold, they are written in the Book of the Chronicles of the Kings of Israel. (1 Kg. 14:19)

The only event of any importance that is reported of the reign of Rehoboam in Judah is that the king of Egypt invaded the country and took all the Temple treasure as booty.

Eventually there came to Israel's throne a king who was relatively important on the international scene at that time, Omri. He established a capital city at Samaria, defeated Moab, entered into alliance with the Phoenicians, and even married his son Ahab to Jezebel, daughter of the king of Tyre. Almost two centuries later the Assyrian emperor still referred to Israel as the land of Omri. Since, however, "Omri did what was evil in the sight of the Lord, and did more evil than all who were before him" (1 Kg. 16:25), only a few verses are devoted to his story.

ELIJAH VS. AHAB AND JEZEBEL (1 Kg. 17–22)

From the Books of Kings one would gather that the most important king of Israel or Judah after Solomon was Ahab. There are two reasons why he is assigned such significance: (1) by importing into Samaria the worship of Baal, the god of his Phoenician wife Jezebel, he committed the worst sin against the Temple of any of the kings, and (2) during his reign there appeared Elijah and Elisha, two of a new breed of prophet. They were more than the ecstatic seers who had been designated prophets before. In their willingness to pronounce to the king himself their oracles about the will of God for the life of the nation, they were harbingers of the great writing prophets who were to come, such as Amos, Hosea, Isaiah, and Jeremiah.

Elijah began his prophetic activity by telling Ahab that God was going to send three years of drought when there would be neither rain nor dew. Fleeing from the drought, Elijah was directed first to the side of the brook Cherith where he was fed by the ravens. Then he was sent to Zarephath where God had provided for a Phoenician widow to take care of him. When Elijah arrived, the widow had left only a handful of flour and a little olive oil in a jar and she was preparing what she expected to be a final meal for her child and herself. Elijah asked her to feed him first, and her faith was rewarded by having the flour and the oil stay at a constant amount through the rest of the famine. Elijah was also able to heal the woman's son miraculously when he suddenly came down with a mysterious disease.

After the three years of drought Elijah returned to Ahab and through him extended a challenge to the prophets of Baal to join him in a contest to see whose god was more powerful. On Mt. Carmel they built two altars, one to Baal and one to Yahweh, piled up wood on them, and laid slaughtered sacrificial bulls on them. Even though the 450 prophets of Baal lacerated themselves and did everything else in their power to call down fire from heaven, they spent a whole day and received nothing for their pains except the merciless teasing of Elijah. Elijah then had his altar drenched three times in water, but when he called upon the Lord the effect was instantaneous: fire immediately came down and consumed not only the bull but even the altar of stone as well, and turned the water into steam. After that Elijah had all the prophets of Baal killed. Then he waited for the rain to start.

When Jezebel learned of this she threatened to give Elijah the fate that he had conferred on the prophets of Baal. He fled for his life again and, although he received divine protection all along the way, he began to feel very sorry for himself and to think that he was the only godly man left. While he was busy with that, a cyclone came, followed by an earthquake, which was in turn followed by a fire. God, however, was in none of these. He came instead as a still small voice. The voice commanded him to anoint Hazael to be king of Syria and Jehu to succeed Ahab. Then God told him that he was by no means unique in his faithfulness: there were 7,000 who had not bowed their knees to Baal.

When Ahab wanted the vineyard of a man named Naboth who would not sell it to him, Jezebel arranged for Naboth to be killed so that Ahab could have the vineyard. Elijah went to Ahab and predicted that the dogs would lick up his blood where they had licked up the blood of Naboth and that they would eat the body of Jezebel by the wall of Jezreel. Several years later Ahab allied himself with the king of Judah to seize Ramoth-gilead from the king of Syria. They consulted with the prophets, 400 of whom said they would be successful, but Micaiah, the son of Imlah, predicted that Ahab would die in the battle. In order to escape his fate, Ahab disguised himself for the battle, but an arrow shot at random struck him in a gap between sections of armor. His body was taken back to Samaria and buried, but the chariot in which he had ridden was washed and the dogs drank the blood that ran off.

ELISHA (2 Kg. 1–13)

After Elijah had successfully prophesied the death of Ahab's son and called fire down from heaven on the soldiers sent to arrest him, the time for his own death came. He had already indicated that his successor was to be Elisha by coming up to him while he was plowing and placing his cloak on Elisha's shoulders. As a sign of his break with his former occupation of farming, Elisha killed the oxen with which he plowed, cooked the meat, and distributed it to his neighbors. On the day that Elijah's life on earth was to end, he and Elisha were walking from town to town. In each place they were met by a band of the "sons of the prophets," wandering ecstatics similar to the modern dervishes of Islam, who told Elisha that the Lord would take his master that day. Finally, after Elijah had made the waters of the river part by striking them with his cloak, they crossed over the Jordan. There Elisha asked that he might inherit Elijah's full power. Elijah was one of three men whom the Old Testament says were privileged to be taken alive into heaven. He told Elisha that if he saw him departing, his request would be granted. When Elisha saw his master taken into heaven by a chariot and horses of fire, he tore up his old clothes and put on Elijah's cloak, having used it first to separate the waters of the Jordan for his return trip.

Many miraculous deeds are attributed to Elisha, a number of which were done in the presence of the sons of the prophets. He purified the water supply of Jericho, called bears out of the forest to maul forty-two boys who teased him about his bald head, caused a poisoned pot of stew to become safe for eating, fed a hundred people with food adequate for twenty, caused an axe head that had fallen into the Jordan to float so that it could be recovered, performed for two women miracles similar to those performed by Elijah for the Phoenician widow, healed the leprosy of the Syrian general Naaman, blinded soldiers who came out to arrest him, and participated in the overthrow of kings.

Elisha had a part in the deaths of king Ahaziah of Judah and Jehoram or Joram, the son of Ahab, who was king of Israel. He sent one of the sons of the prophets to the garrison of Ramoth-gilead to anoint Jehu to be king instead of Jehoram. When Jehu told his fellow officers what had occurred, they joined with him in rebellion. Jehu set out in his chariot in which he had a reputation for driving furiously. He went to Jezreel where Jehoram had gone to recover from wounds. There he killed Jehoram and caused Ahaziah, his ally, to be shot as well. Then he went to the wall of Jezreel where Jezebel, who had heard that he was coming, was looking out of a window. When she yelled at him, he had some of the eunuchs who were harem attendants throw her out the window. He went inside to eat and, when he thought to have something done with her corpse, discovered that Elijah's prophecy that dogs would eat her body had been fulfilled.

The Kingdoms Come to an End

POLITICAL EVENTS

The Davidic monarchy lasted from 1000 to 587 B.C., when Jerusalem was destroyed by Babylon. The rival northern kingdom of Israel lasted only two centuries after the break away in 922 B.C. to the destruction of Samaria by the Assyrians in 721. During the ninth century, the period in which Elijah and Elisha flourished, the southern kingdom of Judah played a role that was secondary to that of the more prosperous and populous Israel in the north. For a while Judah was Israel's vassal and gave aid against her enemies. The most dangerous enemy at first was Israel's northern neighbor Damascus, but the rise of the Assyrian empire spelled even greater danger to both Judah and Israel. The famous Black Obelisk of king Shalmaneser III of Assyria, which was erected in 853 B.C., shows Jehu paying tribute to the Assyrians. For a while the Assyrians subdued Damascus and helped bring peace to Israel. Before they went on to destroy Israel and humble Judah in the middle of the ninth century, each of those kingdoms had strong rulers for a time whose cooperation brought prosperity to their people. The reign of Jeroboam II in Israel (786–46 B.C.) and that of Uzziah or Azariah in Judah (783–42 B.C.) represented something of a return to the good old days of the united monarchy under David and Solomon.

AMOS AND HOSEA

During these declining years of the divided kingdom, an imposing succession of prophets helped the people of God to interpret their fate upon the stage of international history. Amos and Hosea, the first of the writing prophets, chided the northern kingdom for its complacency and warned that divine judgment was coming as punishment for the superficiality of Israelite religion. Amos attacked the social injustices in that prosperous land which had led to social stratification in a country where there had been none before. He said that God was not so interested in having many elaborate ceremonies performed in his worship as he was in having "justice roll down like waters, and righteousness like an ever-flowing stream" (Am. 5:24).

Hosea placed the blame for Israel's approaching eclipse on her failure to live up to the obligations she had in her covenant with God. To depict God as both loving and just, Hosea used the striking image of Israel as an unfaithful wife whom God divorces and remarries. This love of God for his chosen people is also expressed in other vivid images:

> When Israel was a child, I loved him, and out of Egypt I called my son. . . . I led them with cords of compassion, with bands of love, . . . How can I give you up, O Ephraim! How can I hand you over, O Israel! (Hos. 11:1, 4, 8)

These warnings of coming destruction were to show the people that Israel's downfall was not due to the weakness of God, but to the failure of the people to abide by the pact that God had made with them on Mt. Sinai during the time of Moses.

Israel fell to Assyria in 721 B.C. The northern kingdom and its tribes disappeared from history. The capital was razed and its population was deported, being replaced with colonists from other sections of the Assyrian empire—a method of keeping the peace in conquered territory that was common in ancient empires. The total destruction of Israel had a traumatic effect on Judah to the south. This effect may be studied in two kings and two prophets.

HEZEKIAH AND ISAIAH (2 Kg. 18–20 and Is.)

Isaiah, whose collected oracles introduce the books of the writing prophets, and who is the prophet most quoted in the New Testament, tells us how his ministry began at a dramatic turning point in the history of the times:

> In the year that King Uzziah died I saw the Lord sitting upon a throne, high and lifted up; and his train filled the temple. Above him stood the seraphim, . . . And one called to another

and said: "Holy, holy, holy is the lord of hosts; the whole earth is full of his glory." (Is. 6:1–3)

Isaiah thus began his ministry during the rapid turn of events which saw the total destruction of Israel by the Assyrians and the threatened subjugation of Judah. The golden age of Jeroboam and Uzziah had passed as Amos and Hosea had warned, and now the remaining kingdom of Judah had to receive the message of impending doom.

Toward the end of the eighth century kings Ahaz and Hezekiah of Judah tried to save their nation by playing in the high-stake game of international politics. Ahaz had been so hard-pressed by Israel in its declining days for aid against the Assyrians that he actually invited the Assyrians to come to his defense. Their doing so not only hastened their conquest of Israel but also enabled them to require tribute money of Judah. King Hezekiah (715–687 B.C.) is remembered for his loyalty to the Lord in his efforts to regain control over the northern region that had been Israel and to establish religious reforms throughout Judah. Many of the religious traditions of the northern kingdom were brought into Judah at that time and incorporated into the traditions of the south. We know from Assyrian sources, as well as from the Old Testament, that Hezekiah even went so far as to attempt an alliance with Egypt to prevent the Assyrians Ahaz had invited in as protection against Israel from conquering Judah too. Sennacherib the Assyrian laid siege to Jerusalem, but the city was miraculously spared destruction, even though the land came under foreign domination. A tunnel still survives that Hezekiah had constructed in those days to give the city a secret access to its water supply outside the city walls. The preservation of Jerusalem led to a later belief that the city was a sign of God's unfailing good will toward his people and strengthened the messianic hope that God would send a ruler to restore his reign over his people.

During this time when the king was involved in the dangerous game of playing one world leader off against another, Isaiah warned him and the people that Assyria was the instrument of God's righteous anger. Thus he prophesied doom and destruction, but did leave a hope that a remnant of God's people would be preserved and would have a glorious future. His main advice to Hezekiah was to trust in the Lord rather than to place his reliance on anything so undependable as foreign military alliances:

> If you do not believe, surely you shall not be established. (Is. 7:9)
> In returning and rest you shall be saved: in quietness and trust shall be your strength. (Is. 30:15)

JOSIAH AND JEREMIAH (2 Kg. 22–25 and Jer.)

A century after the death of Hezekiah the Assyrian empire had waned and its threat had been replaced by that of Babylon. Judah was to succumb to Babylon and to be taken into captivity there. In the last days of Jerusalem the most important figures were the king Josiah and the prophet Jeremiah. The events of these last days moved so rapidly that it is difficult to keep track of them. Judah was caught in the cross fire of great world powers because she occupied the land bridge that connected and was a buffer between Asia and Africa. During this difficult time Josiah tried to reform the Temple and its religious practices from the corruption of Assyrian influence. A book had been discovered in the Temple that contained a blueprint for such reform. This book is identified with chapters 12–26 of our present Book of Deuteronomy and the movement is thus known as the Deuteronomic Reform.

Chief among these reforms was the confinement of sacrifice to the Temple of Jerusalem instead of allowing it to be offered at hilltop shrines throughout the country, and the reinstitution of the Passover celebration. Passover commemorates the Exodus and the establishment of the covenant on Mt. Sinai. The traditions about it had been more important in Israel than in Judah, and the prophets had brought these and other northern traditions south during the time of Hezekiah and incorporated them into the traditions there, which had emphasized David and Jerusalem more than the events of the time of Moses. These sectional differences of emphasis within the common tradition had developed during the centuries and the destruction of Israel had made their reintegration possible. Thus the various elements of belief in Yahweh were drawn together and codified in the scroll that was discovered in the Temple in 621 B.C., and were made the religious constitution of the people by Josiah.

The prophet Jeremiah lived through the days of reform and of final decline and defeat. He saw the original enthusiasm of the reform fade into lifeless legalistic observance. His preaching took on the style of the exhortation of the Book of Deuteronomy as he urged the people to renew their obedience to their covenant with God. Josiah's tragic death at the hands of the Egyptians in 609 B.C. brought an end to the spirit of reform and its attendant receptiveness to the message of Jeremiah. Like his predecessors, Jeremiah warned the people that the coming destruction was God's will and therefore unavoidable. They should, therefore, repent and accept the Babylonian aggressors as agents of God, and trust that there would be survivors for a better age to come.

The successors of Josiah were not ready for such a message. Instead they placed their hopes for survival on international intrigue, now allying with Egypt, now with Babylon. They put Jeremiah in jail. Jerusalem was besieged first in 597 B.C. and exiles were taken into Babylon. Judah continued to engage in intrigue until the Babylonians finally destroyed the city in 587 and carried off its remaining leading citizens. King Jehoichim and another great prophet, Ezekiel, had already been carried off to Babylon, but Jeremiah was spared and was eventually taken to Egypt by refugees from Jerusalem who were fleeing a yet more destructive Babylonian attack on its rebellious provinces. Thus it was that the throne of David and the Temple of Solomon ceased to exist in 587 B.C. Jerusalem was destroyed and its leading citizens deported.

Exile and Restoration

The Babylonians did not follow the destructive Assyrian policy of repopulating land vacated by conquered people who were deported. The Assyrian policy had caused Israel to become the "ten lost tribes," and its land to be occupied by people imported from various parts of the Assyrian empire whose descendants became the Samaritans so despised in New Testament times. The Judean captives, however, could look forward to returning to the Holy Land. A Davidic king, the Temple priests, the prophets, and the other deported leaders awaited the time when they could return and rebuild the kingdom.

LITERARY ACTIVITY DURING THE EXILE

Surprisingly, the period of the exile, which lasted from 587 to 538 B.C., was literarily one of the most productive ages of the people of God. Other crises before had been the occasion for the writing, collecting, and editing of other parts of the Old Testament and this crisis had even more remarkable results. The first two major sections of the Hebrew canon, the Torah and the Prophets, took the shape in which we know them during the exile. The preservation of their sacred literature was a matter of life and death to the exiles during that trying time: the survival of their identity as the people of God depended more on that literature than on such former symbols of their national identity and their covenant bond with God as the land, the monarchy, and the Temple.

The three main contributions to the Old Testament that were made during this time were: (a) the collection of the oracles of the writing prophets into books, (b) the completion of the Deuteronomic history, and (c) the Priestly additions to the Pentateuch.

Two prophets were active during the exile, Ezekiel and the one who is known as the Second Isaiah. Ezekiel, one of the early deportees, saw in his visions that, while God had left the Temple, he would return when the community had been purified and made fit for the divine presence again. Chapters 40 to 48 of his book are his blueprint of what the community had to do if it was to remain the people of God. In his vision of dry bones coming to life again (chapter 37), he gave hope to a people who had little of it.

The prophet who is called Second Isaiah is thus designated because we know nothing about him except that his oracles from the time of the exile have been added to those of Isaiah. His work commences with chapter 40. He proclaimed the hope of an imminent end to the exile. His prophecy came true after the Babylonian empire fell in 539 B.C. under the onslaught of the Persians, whose empire would last until the time of Alexander the Great. His words promising release from captivity in Babylon were later picked up as a promise of Christ. They are familiar to many English-speaking Christians as part of the text of Handel's *Messiah:*

> Comfort ye, comfort ye my people, saith your God. Speak ye comfortably to Jerusalem, and cry unto her, that her warfare is accomplished, that her iniquity is pardoned: for she hath received of the Lord's hand double for all her sins. The voice of him that crieth in the wilderness, Prepare ye the way of the Lord, make straight in the desert a highway for our God. (Is. 40:1–3, KJV)

RETURN AND REBUILDING (Ezra and Neh.)

The Second Isaiah considered the Persian emperor Cyrus to have been chosen by God as the liberator of his people and went so far as to call him God's "anointed," which in Hebrew is the word that we transliterate as "Messiah." This confidence was well placed since Cyrus did indeed practice a policy of religious toleration. In 538 B.C. he made a decree that permitted the Jewish people to return to their homeland, and he supported the rebuilding of their Temple. While many of the deportees remained in Babylon and formed the nucleus of what would become the center of Jewish life after the destruction of the second Temple by the Romans, others did return. They were led home by Zerubbabel, a royal prince. By this time there was also a substantial Jewish colony in Egypt. One result of the exile, then, was that from that time on Jews made up a significant portion of the population of countries outside of Palestine. By New Testament times this proportion was to increase to the point that about one-seventh of the population of the Roman empire was Jewish.

Jerusalem, however, remained as the center of the people of God, even though for some time after the exile the city retained but a shadow of its former glory. After an abortive attempt at an uprising under Zerubbabel, who was serving as Persian governor, the monarchy was lost. Except for a brief time under the Maccabees, the Jews no longer had any national existence except as a province of someone else's empire. They existed chiefly as a religious community whose priests were their leaders. Those who returned from captivity in Babylon were so impoverished, and they found the land to which they returned so devastated that all of their energies were required at first merely to maintain existence; rebuilding would take a long time. The prophets Haggai and Zechariah, however, did shame the people into making the efforts to rebuild a temple of sorts. The story of that time is a record of a long struggle and many hardships. Those who returned from exile were met with hostility and opposition from neighbors who in their absence had laid claims to their land.

Our records of this period are sparse. We do know, though, of two heroes in this struggle, Ezra and Nehemiah. Nehemiah, one of the great lay leaders in the Bible, held the exalted position of cup bearer to the Persian monarch. The king gave him leave of absence to restore the physical fabric of Jerusalem, especially its city walls. The spiritual fabric was restored through the efforts of Ezra, who was an emissary of the Persian government and one of the first examples of a religious type that was to become very familiar by New Testament times: a scribe, a scholar of the religious law of the sacred writings of the Jews. He strengthened the morale of the people by recalling them to the distinctive religious heritage set forth in the Torah. There is an account in Nehemiah 8–9 of how Ezra read the Torah of God to the people in the city square by the Water Gate and how the people accepted it as their law with tears of joy.

This event symbolizes a remarkable transition that was taking place in the religion of the people. The Bible story which saw the wandering Hebrews become the nation of Israel in its opening pages, now at the close of the Old Testament shows the origins of the Jewish faith. In place of the older symbols of national unity we now see new emphases such as the rite of circumcision, dietary rules, strict observance of the Sabbath, and study of the Torah in the new synagogues that were developing. During the exile, the preservation of the sacred writings of the people together with the impossibility of Temple worship in Babylon had meant a subtle shift in emphasis that was to increase dramatically with time, a shift from having a religion of the Temple cult to having a religion of the book of religious law, the Torah. The history of the period from the exile to the end of the Old Testament is not well known. Much literature in the Old Testament comes from this time, but it is the Wisdom literature which deals with timeless truths rather than the concrete events of history. Old Testament history as such is now over.

· 7 ·

The Story of the
Apocrypha

Since most Bibles printed in America do not contain the Apocrypha, its story is even less familiar than that of the rest of the Bible. This unfamiliarity is unfortunate, not just because the books of the Apocrypha may be read "for example of life and instruction of manners," if not "to establish any doctrine," as the Articles of Religion say. The most important reason for studying the Apocrypha is that without knowledge of its period no one can understand the historical context in which Jesus appeared. One must know the Apocrypha, then, to understand the New Testament.

After the work of Ezra in the late fifth century B.C., the people of God fashioned their lives according to the Torah. Under the Persians, with their policy of religious toleration, that was relatively simple. Persian rule was brought to an end, however, by the conquests of Alexander the Great. Alexander had been tutored by the philosopher Aristotle and he understood his campaigns as missionary activity in behalf of Greek culture. To be more exact, his goal was to unify the culture of the Greeks with that of the Middle East. This merger of cultures is known as Hellenistic culture.

When Alexander died, his empire was divided among his three generals, each of whom established a dynasty that ruled its section of the empire for several centuries. At first Palestine was a part of the empire of the Ptolemys in Egypt. After

133

that it passed into the hands of the Seleucids in Syria to the north and east of Israel. During all of this time there was a certain impetus to accept Greek culture, but by and large the Jews were able to resist it. When Antiochus IV came to the Seleucid throne, though, things began to change. He believed that he was the Greek high god Zeus manifest in human form and therefore was called *Epiphanes* ("Manifest"). Thus he insisted that the Jews live as Greeks and worship the Greek gods. In 167 B.C. he defiled the Temple at Jerusalem by turning it into a temple of the Olympian Zeus, erecting a statue of himself in it, and having swine offered as sacrificial animals. He forbade the observance of the Sabbath, the offering of the sacrifices commanded in the Torah, and the circumcision by which infant males were initiated into the Jewish religious community. His efforts to enforce these laws was the world's first example of religious persecution. It is against the background of his reign that the Book of Daniel in the Old Testament and 1 and 2 Maccabees are to be understood.

DANIEL

Although Daniel was written in reaction to the persecution under Antiochus Epiphanes, it is set in the time of the exile in Babylon in order to disguise its attack on the Seleucids. Because of its setting it is included in the Old Testament, but the situation to which it was addressed is more easily discussed in connection with apocryphal works. It gives the story of Daniel, a pious Jew, and his companions who tried to remain faithful to their religious obligations under the adverse circumstances of captivity in Babylon.

The first half of the book consists of stories that show Daniel and his companions reacting to pressures in Babylon similar to those the Jews were under in Israel at the time of Antiochus Epiphanes. They maintained their observance of the dietary laws rather than enjoy the delicacies of the king's table and grew healthy from doing so. The companions did not kneel to a colossal statue of King Nebuchadnezzar when the musical signal was given, and were thrown into a fiery furnace as punishment, but not a hair of their heads was singed nor was their clothing scorched.

Daniel interpreted two dreams of the king, one that had to do with the fall of his kingdom and the other of which predicted accurately that he would go through a period of insanity when he would eat grass like an ox. When King Belshazzar used vessels stolen from the Temple for a feast, a hand came and wrote on the wall words the Daniel interpreted to mean that God was bringing Belshazzar's kingdom to an end. That very night Belshazzar died and his kingdom was taken over by Darius the Mede. The rest of the book is taken up by elaborate dreams and visions of Daniel that are clearly symbolic predictions of God's judgment on Antiochus Epiphanes.

1 AND 2 MACCABEES

The books of the Maccabees tell of the persecution by Antiochus Epiphanes and the revolt against him led by Judas Maccabeus. By the time Seleucid rule was established there were already Hellenized Jews who were taking on such external manifestations of Greek culture as participating in Greek schools (called *gymnasia*) and the nude exercises and games from which the schools derived their name. The efforts of Antiochus to unify his empire by imposing Greek standards meant that not only cultural conformity was called for, but religious as well. Many Jews succumbed, but others resisted fiercely and showed their willingness to die for their religion. Being threatened by pressure from the Romans, Antiochus increased his efforts to unify his empire against his enemies by the imposition of a common culture and religion. The ban on Jewish practices mentioned above went into effect. One group of loyal Jews, called the *Hasidim* or "pious," went so far as to refuse to break the Sabbath even by defending themselves militarily on it. Thus they sealed their witness with their blood.

In the hill-country village of Modein there was a priest called Mattathias who not only refused to participate in the pagan sacrifices demanded by the officers of Antiochus but also killed anyone else who tried. He and his sons were quickly joined in revolt by the Hasidim and others. The leadership of this guerilla army was undertaken by Mattathias' son Judas, who was called *Maccabeus*, "the Hammer." Despite incredible odds, Judas and his followers won significant victories outside the urban area of Jerusalem. Eventually he was able even to retake the Temple and it was cleansed and rededicated in 164 B.C., just three years after its desecration by Antiochus. The Jewish festival of Hanukkah continues the celebration of this rededication down to the present day. This success inspired the people so much that they were not content with religious liberation; they went on to achieve full independence. Some of the Jews, however, had fought only for freedom of worship, and there was division afterwards between those whose motives and goals were exclusively religious and those who fought for political goals as well.

2 Maccabees, which is motivated by a particular religious outlook and concerned only with religious freedom, ends with the victories of Judas shortly after the rededication of the Temple. 1 Maccabees, on the other hand, which is concerned with political freedom as well and is much more reliable historically, carries the story to the point where independence has been achieved under Simon and he passes the reign to his son John Hyrcanus. After the death of Judas, first his brother Jonathan and then his brother Simon succeeded him in the leadership of the revolt against the Seleucids. Although Simon was ultimately slain like his brothers before him, he won impressive military victories, not the least of which was the removal of the Seleucid garrison from Jerusalem. Simon was even able to compel the Seleucids, who were being pressed by other forces, to recognize him as high priest of the Temple, commander of the armies, and governor of the territory. Although the status of Israel became that of a client kingdom within the Seleucid empire, the distraction of the Seleucids with the breaking up of their empire meant that the Jews became virtually independent and the Maccabean leaders became kings whose heirs had the right of succession to the high priesthood and throne.

The Maccabees, who were called the Hasmoneans after

their ancestor Hasmon, were able to extend their control eventually to most of the territory that David had ruled by the time of Alexander Janneus, the first of the Hasmoneans actually to take the title of king. Seleucid power was at a low point by then, but so was respect for the rulers at Jerusalem. Although their rule had begun with the religious fervor of the Maccabean rebellion, the Hasmoneans became corrupt and deteriorated morally. Thus, by the last days of the dynasty, the people were so fed up with oppressive rule and internal strife that they sent a delegation to Pompey, a Roman general on campaign in Syria, to intervene. He captured Jerusalem in 63 B.C. and Israel became a part of the Roman empire. The next time Jews were to have political independence was when the United Nations established the Israeli state in 1948.

OTHER STORIES IN THE APOCRYPHA

1 and 2 Esdras

Not all of the books of the Apocrypha are narrative and not all of the narratives need to be summarized here. First Esdras, for instance, recounts history from the time of Josiah to that of Ezra, largely on the basis of Old Testament sources. The only part of this work that is unique is the story of the three bodyguards in the court of King Darius (3:1–5:6). The bodyguards had a contest to see who could name the strongest thing in the world. They gave answers such as wine, the king, and women, but the final answer was: "Truth endures and is strong forever, and lives and prevails forever and ever" (4:38). The man who said that was Zerubbabel, who became the royal governor of the Jews who returned from exile. His reward from the king for winning the contest was support in rebuilding Jerusalem and its Temple. Second Esdras has very little story line since it is an apocalypse (see p. 48).

Tobit

Tobit was a pious Jew living in Nineveh who became blind and poor even though his piety and charity were exemplary. His prayer to God for help was heard, however, as was also that of Sarah, the daughter of his cousin Raguel. Sarah was plagued by the demon Asmodeus who had killed the seven men to whom she had been married. Tobit remembered that he had left a considerable sum of money on deposit in another city and sent his son Tobias to collect it. God arranged for Tobias to hire the archangel Raphael as his guide for the journey under the impression that he was a man. On the trip Raphael arranged for Tobias to catch a man-eating fish and to keep its vital organs. Then Raphael took Tobias to the home of Sarah so that he could marry her. When Asmodeus came to kill him Tobias set the fish's organs on fire and the smoke drove the demon away permanently. Tobias sent Raphael to collect the money that his father had on deposit. He then returned to his parents and used some more of the fish organs to cure his father's blindness.

Judith and Esther

In a story in which there is more patriotism than piety—or, rather, piety takes the form of patriotism—Holofernes, one of Nebachadnezzar's generals, laid siege to the Jewish town of Bethulia. In the city there lived a beautiful, rich, and very devout widow named Judith (which means "Jewess"). In order to protect her town, Judith put on her most gorgeous clothes, made herself up to look her best, and had herself admitted to the tent of Holofernes. When he passed out from drinking too much wine in celebration of her arrival, she took his own sword and cut his head off. When his death was discovered, the Assyrians fled in panic, leaving their possessions behind for the Jews to plunder.

The Book of Esther in the Old Testament is very similar in theme to that of Judith. Indeed, the patriotic element is so strong that God is not even mentioned. The book was probably written to justify the celebration of the festival of Purim, which was acquired by the Jews somewhere in the Persian empire and brought back to Palestine. The book tells how Esther, a Jew, was taken by the Persian king Ahasuerus to be his queen after he deposed her predecessor for disobedience. The king's vizier or prime minister, Haman, plotted to have the king order the slaughter of all Jews because of Haman's jealousy of Mordecai, Esther's cousin and guardian. Esther, however, invited Ahasuerus and Haman to a dinner at Mordecai's suggestion, and there she persuaded the king to spare her people. A significant ingredient of the plot is the assumption that the law of the Medes and the Persians is unalterable. The decree for the attack on the Jews had to stand, but another was made that permitted the Jews to defend themselves. Haman was executed, Mordecai succeeded him, and the Jews lived happily ever after. The Additions to the Book of Esther in the Apocrypha supply vivid details and also introduce an element of piety, the lack of which in the canonical version must have been sorely felt by the Jews of the time.

The Additions to Daniel

The Additions to Esther are followed in the Apocrypha by the Wisdom of Solomon and Sirach (also called Ecclesiasticus), two long books in the Wisdom tradition of Proverbs, Ecclesiastes, and Job. These are followed in turn by what purport to be two supplements to Jeremiah: a confession of sins to be read on feast days that claims to be written by the prophet's secretary Baruch, and a letter supposedly written by the prophet to those taken into captivity in Babylon. Next come three additions to the text of Daniel. The first is reported to be the prayer of Sharach, Meshach, and Abednego while they were in the fiery furnace. Two canticles for Morning Prayer in the Book of Common Prayer, *Benedictus es, Domine* and *Benedicite, omnia opera Domini,* are taken from this prayer.

The other two additions to Daniel, however, are among the most delightful stories in the Bible. Furthermore, historians of crime fiction consider them to be among the first mystery stories ever written. Susanna and the Elders concerns the beautiful wife of a very upright Jew. Two elders tried to blackmail her into having intercourse with them by threatening to accuse her of adultery. When she resisted, they had her brought into court and condemned to death until a young man named Daniel stood up and defended her. He questioned the elders separately in the presence of the people, thus demonstrating publicly the inconsistency between their stories. The elders were executed and Susanna was praised.

Bel and the Dragon tells two stories about the relations of Daniel with his friend the king. The king provided immense quantities of food and wine every day for the statue of the god Bel-Marduk in the temple of Babylon. He claimed that the disappearance of the food each day was a demonstration that the idol was a real god. By sprinkling ashes on the floor of the temple, however, Daniel showed by footprints that the food was consumed every night by the priests and their families. When the king claimed that a dragon was a living god, Daniel fed it some cakes made of pitch, fat, and hair that killed it. The priests had Daniel thrown into the lions' den for killing their god, but the prophet Habakkuk was miraculously transported from Judea to Babylon to share Daniel's dinner with him in the lions' den. When the king learned that seven days with the lions had not resulted in the death of Daniel, he pulled him out and threw the priests in. The last book in the Apocrypha before the two books of Maccabees is The Prayer of Manasseh, which the wicked king of Judah is supposed to have prayed in repentance while he was in exile.

· 8 ·

The Story of the
New Testament

At a feast celebrated in the north of England in the year
A.D. 708 some of the diners (who also had been busy wining)
began to shout that a monk at a nearby monastery, a famous
scholar, was a heretic. The basis of their charge—to the extent
that it had any basis—had to do with a recent book of his
about time, an important subject for monks who had to figure
the date of Easter and other feasts without the help of printed
calendars or mechanical clocks. The scholar's book had assumed that history was divided into six ages, five of which
were inaugurated by such Old Testament events as the creation, the flood, and the time of Abraham, and the sixth of
which began with the birth of Christ.

The doctrine of the six ages was familiar enough and was
not in itself a topic of controversy. What had shocked the
people at the feast was that the scholar had not accepted the
judgment of previous authorities about the length of the ages,
but had himself computed Old Testament chronology on the
basis of the Old Testament itself. With Eusebius, Jerome, and
Isidore of Seville, he assumed that each age was roughly a
thousand years, but his exact count made the period from the
creation to the birth of Christ last only 3,952 years. Those
whom he scandalized said that he put the birth of Christ at
the beginning of the fifth age rather than the sixth age, thus
denying that the Lord came in the flesh in the sixth age of the
world.

Whatever modern Christians will think about the gravity of such heresy, the scholar was so horrified at the folly or ignorance of his accusers that he dropped the habit of dating events from creation and followed the suggestion made a century and a half earlier by Dionysius Exiguus of dating all events by the number of years they fell before or after the birth of Christ. The scholar's name was Bede and later centuries have given him the title of Venerable. In addition to being holy, he was one of the last polymaths in the history of Western civilization; he was one of the last masters of all knowledge available to his age. He used his new dating system in the work for which he is best known, his *Ecclesiastical History of the English Nation*. It was the first major historical work that employed this system of dating and its influence was responsible for the widespread adoption of a usage that has become universal.

This method of dating has become so familiar to us that we hardly think of it. The article on chronology in the fourteenth edition of the *Encyclopaedia Britannica*, for instance, occupies twenty-one columns and has full and accurate information about ways of dating events of which one has never heard. But it makes only a passing reference to the origin of the B.C./A.D. distinction, saying in a participial phrase that this base of dating replaced that of reckoning events in relation to the founding of Rome. Yet all of the dates given in the article are identified as being either B.C., before Christ, or A.D., *Anno Domini*, in the year of our Lord.

Even though our age has thus become unaware of them, the theological implications of dating all historical events in relation to the birth of Jesus are astounding. Such a method of locating events in time proclaims that time has never been the same since Jesus came. Humanity and the universe were re-created by his life, death, and resurrection, the world had a new beginning, a second change. To the extent that our lives, or the lives of anyone who ever might live, have meaning, they have that meaning in relation to Christ. When we get to the story of the New Testament, then, we get to what Christians must regard as the heart of the matter.

Jesus' Story in the Synoptic Gospels

The narrative parts of the New Testament, with the exception of the autobiographical sections of Paul's letters, are the four Gospels, which recount the life of Jesus, and the Acts of the Apostles, the story of the expansion of the early church from Jerusalem to Rome. Since Matthew and Luke follow the chronology of Mark, inserting material from Q and their own private sources within this framework, it is easy to harmonize these synoptic accounts into a single story line. Even though the emphases of each of these evangelists get skewed in the process, the overall picture is accurate enough for our purposes here. John's Gospel, however, has a different outline, and thus should be looked at separately.[1]

JESUS' BIRTH AND CHILDHOOD

Mark says nothing about the early period of Jesus' life, beginning his account with Jesus' baptism at the start of his ministry. Although we are accustomed to blending what Matthew and Luke report about this time, the two accounts are not completely consistent and should be summarized separately. After recording the genealogy of Jesus in a way that divides Old Testament history into three ages rather than Bede's six, Matthew tells how Joseph became engaged to Mary and then discovered that she was pregnant. The visit of an angel convinced him that divine plans rather than human sin were responsible and so he went on with the wedding.

When the baby was born in their home in Bethlehem, they were visited by astrologers who brought gifts to the newborn king. They had been delayed on their journey, however, because they assumed that the baby would be born in the palace and had stopped to see King Herod. Anxious to eliminate a potential rival, Herod had all the baby boys in Bethlehem killed, much as the pharaoh had ordered all the Hebrew boys slain in the time of Moses. Jesus escaped, though, because Joseph had been warned in a dream to flee to Egypt. After the death of Herod, Joseph took his family back to Israel, but to be on the safe side, settled at Nazareth, up north near the Lake of Galilee, rather than return to Bethlehem so near to Jerusalem.

Luke intertwines the story of Jesus' birth with that of his cousin John who grew up to be called "the Baptizer." Like many famous Old Testament mothers, Elizabeth was barren. When her husband Zechariah was taking his rare turn as a priest to offer the incense in the Temple, an angel announced to him that his wife was going to have a son in her old age and that he should be named John. When Zechariah could not believe his luck, he was rendered speechless for his lack of faith.

Later the angel announced to Mary that she would become the mother of the Son of God without the intervention of a biological father. Her response was to say that she was God's serving girl and that she would do as he wished. Mary then went to visit her cousin Elizabeth in the hill country where the infant John in Elizabeth's womb leapt for joy at the presence of his Lord in Mary's womb. When Elizabeth's son was born, Zechariah wrote that he should be called John; then his speech returned to him.

Luke understands Nazareth to have been the home of Mary and Joseph before the birth of Jesus. Thus a census for Roman taxation is given as the reason for their trip to Bethlehem where the only lodging they could find was in a stable. Their visitors were shepherds who had been instructed by an angel. When Mary had finished the time that a woman is considered ritually unclean after childbirth, they stopped in Jerusalem to offer the thanksgiving for a firstborn son required by the Torah, and then went back to Nazareth. At the Temple the holy child was recognized by the holy Simeon and a prophetess named Anna. Luke's birth stories contain several hymns of thanksgiving that are included in the Prayer Book as canticles: the *Magnificat, Benedictus,* and *Nunc dimittis.*

Mary and Joseph made one of the three pilgrimages to the Temple for a festival each year, that for the Passover. When Jesus was twelve, they took him along for the first time. They discovered at the end of the first day of the trip back home that he was not with their party and they hurried back to the city to find him. Eventually they discovered him in the Temple engaged in a precocious discussion of the Torah with the rabbis. His parents were shocked and amazed, but to him it seemed very natural that he should be in his Father's house. The only other report that Luke or any New Testament writer gives of his childhood is that "Jesus increased in wisdom and stature and in favor with God and man" (Lk. 2:52).[2]

JESUS' BAPTISM AND TEMPTATION

When John the Baptist grew up and began his ministry, he lived in the wilderness territory of the geological fault where the Jordan River runs into the Dead Sea. His clothing was made of animal skins and his diet consisted of anything edible that could be found in that desert country. Yet he preached the apocalyptic message that God's reign was about to break into history, and many flocked to him for baptism, which would demonstrate their sorrow for their sins so that the coming day of the Lord would not be a day of wrath for them.

One day when John was preaching and baptizing, Jesus came and asked to be baptized. To show that Jesus had no sins from which he needed to be cleansed and that he was not John's inferior, Matthew reports John as saying that it would be more appropriate for Jesus to baptize him. When Jesus was baptized, the heavens were opened in a vision and the Holy Spirit hovered dovelike over his head. A voice from heaven said to Jesus, "You are my beloved son in whom I take delight."

After Jesus was baptized and received the Holy Spirit for his mission, the Spirit drove him out into the wilderness to be tested by the devil for forty days. Mark does not divide this experience into separate temptations, but both Matthew and Luke do. They picture Jesus as tempted to use his power for his own welfare by turning rocks into bread, to attract the attention of people by a display of miraculous power such as being rescued by angels when he threw himself off the high wall surrounding the Temple precincts, or to gain power over the people through a pact with the devil. When Jesus resisted

all of these temptations, the devil left him and angels came
and waited on him.

THE BEGINNING OF JESUS' MINISTRY

According to the Synoptic Gospels all of Jesus' ministry,
except for the journey to Jerusalem where he was to die, was
spent in the region surrounding the Lake of Galilee. It does
not appear to have lasted for more than a year or so. The
purpose of the evangelists was not to give a historical reconstruction but to propagate a religion, so the sequence of
events is not always chronological. Mark's sequence of
events, more or less followed by Matthew and Luke, begins
Jesus' ministry with a day in the port town of Capernaum. It
seems to be a typical day in the life of Jesus, one on which he
engaged in his characteristic activities. He went to the
synagogue and preached there, where he was recognized as
the Holy One of God by a demon that he then expelled. He
went home for lunch with his new follower, the fisherman
Peter, and cured Peter's mother-in-law of a fever. That evening everyone who had family or friends who were sick
gathered around Peter's door while Jesus healed them and
expelled unclean spirits. The next morning Jesus arose early
and went off alone to pray. His followers found him and
urged him to come back and capitalize on his auspicious
beginning, but he told them that he would go to the surrounding towns to preach there, since preaching was what he
had come to do.

At about this point Matthew inserted the block of Q material known as the Sermon on the Mount, which Luke fits in as
either the Sermon on the Plain or as part of the discourses by
which he expands the account of the journey to Jerusalem so
that it makes up one third of his total Gospel. Mark, however, is still dealing with introductory material. Just as the
day at Capernaum listed typical activities of Jesus, so now
comes a group of stories of Jesus' controversies with the religious authorities that typify the issues between them and
him.

In healing a lame man who was let down to him through a

hole in the roof because of the crowd, Jesus forgave the man's sins, which shocked members of the religious establishment. He broke dietary laws by eating at the home of a ritually impure tax collector who collaborated with the Roman invaders, thus stirring up more indignation. Not only did his disciples not fast, but when they technically broke the Sabbath by plucking grain to munch as they walked through a wheat field (thus reaping, and therefore working, on the Sabbath), he said that he was superior to the Sabbath. Then he broke the Sabbath himself by healing a man's withered arm.

THE CALLING OF THE TWELVE

Jesus' preaching attracted great crowds who came from some distance to hear him and be healed by him. Once when his hearers had come from all over the territory occupied by the twelve tribes of Israel during the reign of David, Jesus took twelve people from the crowd up into the hills and appointed them to have the special task of staying with him until they were ready to go out and extend his ministry by proclaiming that the reign of God was breaking into history through his ministry and documenting that fact by their power to cast out evil spirits.

By this time the friends and relatives of Jesus tried to persuade him to come home and stop his preaching because they thought he was insane. Their interpretation of his behavior was very similar to that of the religious establishment, which attributed his ability to cast out demons to his being in league with the devil. Jesus replied, however, that the devil does not set his troops to fighting each other. He also said that the unforgivable sin was to say that he was insane; the ability to look goodness square in the face and call it evil precludes any receptivity to goodness. Thus when his mother, brothers, and sisters came to see him, he said that his true family consisted of his followers who did the will of God.

THE PARABLES OF JESUS

Mark has very little of the teaching of Jesus, confining his record to his deeds. The two exceptions are chapter 4, which tells how Jesus used parables for his main teaching device, and chapter 13, which talks about the time of the end. By the time the Gospels were written, the early church had forgotten the original setting of the parables and had reapplied them to suit its own time and needs. Like all of the preaching of Jesus, their subject is the reign of God that is breaking into history through his proclamation of it. Rather than being addressed to Christians, the parables were addressed to Jesus' opponents to convince them that the kingdom really was being inaugurated. Parables are not simply sermon illustrations; they are a kind of argument. By offering an analogy that his opponents are able to accept as valid, Jesus is able then to get them to look at the situation from a different angle and they then must choose between continuing to view it as they had before or accepting Jesus' view of it. In a parable Jesus affords his hearers an opportunity to see things from the perspective of God. To be able to do that is already to be able to enjoy the reign of God.

Something so abstract must be illustrated. In Mark 4 the Parable of the Sower comes equipped with an interpretation that makes the different kinds of soil on which the seed fell symbolic of different personality types who respond to the preaching of the Gospel in characteristic ways. That is the way the early church reapplied the parable. When Jesus spoke the parable, he intended to make the point that in spite of inevitable waste, the harvest is abundant. He meant this to show that his proclamation of the kingdom was really going to inaugurate it, even if it met at first with a poor response. The unreceptivity of the first kinds of soil could be accepted by his opponents as a valid analogy to his preaching; the rich harvest of his ministry then must be considered by them as a real possibility.

THE MINISTRY OF JESUS

The Synoptic Gospels tell of a number of miracles performed by Jesus. After his day of teaching in parables he went across the lake with his followers. While he slept in the boat, a sudden storm arose, but he rebuked the wind and the storm died down. Across the lake he found a man possessed by unclean spirits who wandered tormented among the tombs, crying out and injuring himself on the stones. When Jesus asked the man his name, the demons replied, "My name is Legion, for we are many." Jesus expelled the demons from the man and forced them into a nearby herd of pigs that went rushing headlong down a steep bank into the lake where they drowned. When the herdsmen returned and found the man cured and their pigs gone, they begged Jesus to leave. A woman who had suffered from a hemorrhage for twelve years was cured just by touching the hem of Jesus' robe. Jesus raised the twelve-year-old daughter of Jairus from the dead.

When Jesus returned to his home town of Nazareth to preach in the synagogue, the people there did not think that anything special could be done by anyone who had grown up there, so he was not able to do much in Nazareth. He sent the Twelve out to extend his mission, giving them instructions to travel light so they could spread the word before it was too late. Meanwhile word of Jesus' activity had come to Herod Antipas, son of Herod the Great and heir of a third of his kingdom. Herod Antipas had imprisoned John the Baptist some time before because John had condemned him for taking the wife of his brother. The wife hated John and had persuaded her daughter Salome to dance sensuously before Herod, to make the king promise to kill John the Baptist and give her his head on a platter. When Antipas heard about Jesus, he imagined that John the Baptist had come back to life.

After the Twelve returned, Jesus tried to spend most of his remaining time with them, but the crowds would not let him. Wherever he went, they would find him and go to him. Once he was preaching to 5,000 people who had followed him to a remote place. When it grew late and they had nothing to eat, Jesus fed them all with a young boy's lunch of five rolls and two fishes. After that he sent the disciples back across the lake while he dismissed the crowd and prayed for a while in the hills. That night while the disciples were having a hard time rowing against the wind, they saw Jesus walking to them on the water. When they landed on the other side, Jesus healed many people and engaged in a controversy with theological scholars from Jerusalem, telling them that the moral law is more important than all of their ceremonial regulations.

After this Jesus began to venture into non-Jewish territory. When a foreign woman asked him to heal her daughter, he said that it is not right to give children's bread to dogs. When the woman replied that dogs eat the crumbs that fall from the table, he complimented her on her faith and healed her child.[3] Next he healed a deaf mute in another section of gentile territory. Mark then records a sequence of events like the feeding of the 5,000 and those that follow it, but set this time among non-Jews. Matthew and Luke appear to treat these as duplicates of the earlier stories and do not repeat them.

The climax of Jesus' retreats away from the crowds with his disciples occurred near Caesarea Philippi, some distance north of the Lake of Galilee. There he asked his followers who people thought he was. They supplied various answers: John the Baptist come back to life, the prophet Elijah whom the prophet Malachi said would return on the day of the Lord (Mal. 4:5), or one of the other prophets from Old Testament times. Those were all overwhelming claims, but when Jesus asked who they thought he was, Peter said that he was the Messiah, God's anointed, whom some expected to inaugurate the reign of God. Even this answer fell short of the truth, though, as soon became clear. Jesus said that the Son of Man was going to be persecuted and put to death by the religious establishment. When Peter tried to talk him out of this fate, Jesus said, "Get behind me, Satan! For you are not on the side of God, but of men." He went on to tell his followers that the only way to save their lives was to be willing to lose them for him and the Gospel.

Six days later Jesus took Peter, James, and John with him up a very high mountain. While they were there his appearance changed so that he became white and shining all over. Moses and Elijah came and talked to him. Peter was so excited that he wanted to erect three booths there, one in honor of each of the three great men of God. A cloud covered them and a voice out of the cloud said, "This is my beloved Son; listen to him."

When they got back down the mountain they found a large crowd. A man was there with a demon-possessed son that the disciples who had been left behind were trying unsuccessfully to heal. When Jesus told him that his son could be healed if he believed, he said, "I believe; help my unbelief!" Then Jesus cured the boy.

By now Jesus' predictions of his coming death and the concern of his disciples for their own recognition were beginning to come between them. John reported that he had rebuked someone who expelled demons in the name of Jesus, but Jesus said that anyone not against him was for him and that anyone who gave so much as a cup of cold water in his name would be rewarded. He then warned his followers that the crisis before them was radical: it would be better to lose a hand, foot, or eye than to miss out on the kingdom for the sake of that part of one's body.

After that he began the journey down the Jordan valley that would take him to Jerusalem and the cross. Along the way he spoke to the crowds. In one place he objected to the ease of divorce under the Torah, saying that human beings should not divide those whom God had joined together. He compared those who receive the reign of God to little children. When a rich young man came and asked what he should do to inherit eternal life, Jesus told him to obey the commandments, but the young man said that he had obeyed them all his life. Jesus then told him to sell all that he had and give it to the poor and follow him. The young man went away sorrowful; he was one of the rich for whom getting into heaven is more difficult than passing through a needle's eye is for a camel. Still, with God anything is possible.

Walking along the road, Jesus prophesied his death again. James and John still did not get the point and asked to be appointed as his two chief assistants when he entered into his glory. He asked if they were able to endure what he had to go through and they naïvely said they could. When the others heard of their outrageous request there was much indignation, but Jesus explained that leadership in the kingdom is

not a matter of lording it over anyone, but is rather a leadership in service of others. From Jesus it would require his life
as ransom for many.

As Jesus and his companions reached Jericho at the head of
the Dead Sea and began the twelve-mile walk up the mountains to Jerusalem, a blind beggar named Bartimaeus called
out for Jesus to have mercy on him. The crowd tried to shut
him up until Jesus called him and healed him. In Jericho too
Jesus saw Zacchaeus, a corrupt collector of Roman taxes who
had climbed a tree in order to get a look at Jesus. Jesus called
him down and said that he would dine with him. The self-
righteous were shocked, but Zacchaeus responded with a
promise to pay back four times over everything he had ever
gained by fraudulence.

THE LAST WEEK IN JERUSALEM

When Jesus and his followers approached Jerusalem, he
sent two of them into a nearby village to get a donkey colt
that was waiting for his use. He rode into the city on the colt,
reminding people of the words of the prophet: "Your king is
coming to you, humble, and mounted on an ass" (Zech. 9:9).
Some people spread their clothing in his path and others
waved branches and shouted, "Blessed is he who comes in
the name of the Lord." The Gospels are not consistent about
what happened next. According to Mark, Jesus merely looked
around the Temple area that evening and did not drive out
those involved in currency exchange and the sale of sacrificial
animals until the next day. Matthew and Luke, however,
make this cleansing of the Temple the climax of Jesus' messianic entry into the holy city. Matthew and Luke seem likely
to be right, since Mark appears to have held the event over in
order to sandwich it between Jesus' cursing of the fig tree the
next day and the discovery of its withered condition later in
the day. There are a number of indications, however, that the
confinement of Jesus' ministry in Jerusalem to one week is for
editorial rather than historical purposes.

The picture we get of Jesus' activity during that Holy Week
is that he spent his days discussing theological issues in one

of the colonnades in the Temple precincts and his nights on the Mount of Olives across the Kidron valley from the city and the Temple. The religious leaders asked him what his authority was for his messianic entry and cleansing of the Temple. He asked them about the authority of John the Baptist and, when they could not agree on an answer to his question, refused to answer theirs. He told them a parable about tenants who refused to send a landlord his profits. When he sent messengers to them, they beat them up and even killed some. As a last resort he sent his son, but they killed him, hoping to inherit the estate under the local law. Jesus said that the landlord will then come and destroy the tenants and let out the vineyard to someone else. The leaders, recognizing that Jesus referred to them, wanted to arrest him, but were afraid to try.

Others tried to trap Jesus into some damaging admission. They asked him if they should pay taxes to the Roman emperor, knowing that if he said no, the Romans would get him for fomenting rebellion. If he said yes, he would lose the support of all those who wished to throw off Roman rule and expected the Messiah to lead them in doing so. Jesus borrowed a coin from one of them, though, and pointed to the emperor's image on it and said, "Render to Caesar the things that are Caesar's, and to God the things that are God's." Representatives of another group, the Sadducees, tried to catch him out on a question about the resurrection (in which they did not believe), but he showed them the superficiality of both their question and their attitude. When someone asked him to give a succinct summary of the entire Torah, he said: "You shall love the Lord your God with all your heart, soul, mind, and strength, and love your neighbor as you love yourself."

Jesus then turned the tables and asked them a question about the ancestor of the Messiah. They said the Messiah was to be a descendant of David. On the basis of their methods of biblical interpretation Jesus showed that such a nationalistic, military Messiah would be inferior to David and thus less than the Messiah. Then going out among the people, Jesus pointed out the hypocrisy of the religious leaders. Even the offering of a poor widow was greater in the sight of God than the large gifts of the rich and powerful. He prophesied the destruction of the Temple and made a long talk about the terrors of the coming day of the Lord.

All that Jesus did—especially his messianic entry, the cleansing of the Temple, and the prophecy of the destruction of the Temple—convinced the religious leaders that he was a serious threat to the entire religious system that they held sacred. In order to protect it, they must put him to death. Originally they had thought it best to wait until the Passover was over and the many pilgrims—around 100,000—had left the city before they attacked this popular figure. When one of his Twelve, Judas Iscariot, offered to betray him, however, the time seemed ripe. Meanwhile Jesus had been unintentionally and symbolically anointed for his burial by a woman who came and poured a bottle of precious perfumed ointment on his head.

The night on which Jesus was to be betrayed was the night of the Passover meal (since a day began at one sundown and ended at the next according to the local method of reckoning). At the meal Jesus predicted that one of the Twelve would betray him, and each one seemed to think that he was capable of doing so. Then Jesus gave a new meaning to the breaking of bread at the beginning of the meal and the blessing of the cup of wine at the end: when the Twelve continued to have fellowship meals together in the future, they would do so in order to recall Jesus' presence into their midst. The bread was his body that would be broken the next day and the wine was his blood that would be spilled.

After dinner they walked to the Mount of Olives. On the way Jesus told Peter that before the rooster crowed the next morning he would deny his Master three times. Stopping at the bottom of the Mount of Olives at a place called Gethsemane, Jesus asked his followers to wait while he prayed for the ordeal ahead. He asked God to take away his cup of suffering if possible, but went on to say, "Yet not what I wish, but what you wish." Three times during his long vigil of prayer he went back to check on his followers, but each time found them asleep.

The last time he returned to them, those sent to arrest him were already approaching. They had been led by Judas who identified Jesus to them by greeting him with a kiss. When he was arrested, all of his followers fled in fear. Peter, however, followed Jesus and his captors from a safe distance as Jesus was taken to the home of the high priest. The members of the religious establishment were gathered there trying to think up some charge against Jesus that would make the Romans willing to execute him. Upon being asked by the high priest, Jesus admitted that he was the Messiah. This was the first time that he had accepted the term as a designation of himself, usually referring to himself in the ambiguous term Son of Man. Since the usual expectation of the Messiah was for a military leader like David, Jesus' acceptance of the term was thought to be an adequate indictment: the Romans would treat him as a potential leader of an insurrection. They would know what to do with him. While all of this was going on, Peter was trying to sit unobtrusively in the courtyard below so that he could know what was happening to his master. His appearance and his accent gave him away, though, and three times he was accused of being a follower of Jesus. His response to each accusation was a vehement denial; after the third denial, a rooster greeted the dawn with its crow.

The religious authorities took Jesus to Pontius Pilate, the Roman governor, to get him executed for insurrection. The Synoptic Gospels give the impression that Pilate had no desire to execute Jesus and tried to make him the prisoner that was released annually at Passover; the crowd, however, were incited by their spiritual leaders to request instead the release of Barabbas, a real insurrectionary. After being beaten, Jesus was led away by the Roman soldiers to their guardhouse where they ridiculed him with mock regal honors.

The soldiers forced a passerby, Simon of Cyrene, to help Jesus bear the crossbar of the cross on which he was to be executed. The Gospel writers depict Jesus' crucifixion with details that remind us of three passages from the Old Testament: Isaiah 53 and Psalms 22 and 69. These details include the soldiers gambling for Jesus' clothing, his hanging between two thieves, the vinegar he was given to drink, and his reciting in Aramaic the opening words of Psalm 22: "My God, my God, why have you forsaken me?" His crucifixion began at nine o'clock in the morning. At noon the sky became dark until three, when he died. At that moment, the curtain in the Temple that separated the Holy Place from the Most Holy Place was torn in two from top to bottom. Previously only the high priest had gone into the Most Holy Place and he went there only on the Day of Atonement (*Yom Kippur*). With the death of Jesus, the Father had made a new provision for the restoration of his people to At-one-ment with himself. The Roman officer in charge of the execution squad looked on Jesus at the moment of death and said, "Truly this man was the son of God."

After sundown a member of the ruling council of Israel who also shared in the expectation of the Messiah, Joseph of Arimathea, asked Pilate for permission to bury Jesus in the new tomb that he had had carved out of the rock in his garden for his own future use.

THE RESURRECTION

There are some differences between the three synoptic accounts of the resurrection appearances of Jesus to his followers. These inconsistencies are not to be attributed so much to conflicting historical sources as to the ways in which each of the Gospel writers wanted to highlight what they saw as the meaning of the event by the way they told the story of it. All begin with the distress of some of Jesus' women followers that they had not been able to render him the last respects of preparing his body with aromatic spices for burial. Since the Sabbath, when such activities were unlawful, had begun on the evening after the crucifixion, they had to wait until Sunday morning to rush to the tomb, hoping that someone would be there to roll away the stone that sealed the tomb. When they arrived, though, they found the tomb open and empty except for Jesus' graveclothes. An angel told them that Jesus had risen from the dead.

The oldest form of Mark that has been preserved (which many think is the original form) has the Gospel end with the women leaving the tomb in a state of fright. At that point Matthew has Jesus meet the women and ask them to inform his followers that he will meet them up north in the region of the Lake of Galilee. When the leaders of the religious establishment discovered that Jesus was not in the tomb, they gave orders for the report to be circulated that the body had been stolen by Jesus' followers. Jesus met the eleven apostles on a mountain in Galilee, although some of them doubted that it was Jesus. He gave them the Great Commission:

> Go therefore and make disciples of all nations, baptizing them in the name of the Father and of the Son and of the Holy Spirit, teaching them to observe all that I have commanded you; and lo, I am with you always, to the close of the age. (Mt. 28:19–20)

After telling about the empty tomb, Luke continues with the story of two followers of Jesus who were going to the village of Emmaus about seven miles from Jerusalem. As they walked along they talked about their great disappointment. Jesus fell in with them and walked along the road with them, but they did not recognize him. When they explained their sorrow to him, he proved to them from the Old Testament that the Messiah was supposed to die and be raised from the dead. When they stopped for the night, they asked Jesus to stay and eat with them. When he broke bread in blessing the food, they recognized him. Then he disappeared and they rushed back to Jerusalem to take the good news of the resurrection to the apostles. While they were telling their story, Jesus appeared in the group, proving his identity by showing them his wounds and proving that he was no ghost by eating food. After commissioning them to spread his Gospel, he led them out to Bethany and from there ascended into heaven.

HISTORICAL SETTING OF THE GOSPELS

It is very easy to read the Gospels as though the story of Jesus occurred in a historical vacuum, as though nothing else going on at the time had anything to do with what Jesus did. Much insight into the events of Jesus' life, however, is lost when that approach is taken. Christians, for instance, are apt to think that the title Messiah, which was translated into Greek as *Christos,* refers only to Jesus and was coined to refer to him. The long history of the use of the term will be studied in the section on New Testament theology. Meanwhile, however, a look at the messianic expectation that existed at the time of Jesus will help to show how he was viewed by his contemporaries and thus will assist modern readers in coming to understand Jesus in the context of the history of his own times.

Since the Babylonian captivity, Israel had spent most of its time as a part of someone else's empire, being reduced to the status of a pawn in the hands of the great powers of the day. Such a situation was hard for people to take who believed that they were God's chosen people and that they should have no king but God. By the time of Daniel, however, it began to look to some pious Israelites as though their beloved people would never have the military might to resist alien empires on their own terms. The people would have to depend upon God to intervene miraculously in history in order to restore to them the privileged position they were entitled to. This was the situation in which apocalyptic thought developed. Apocalyptic thought conceives of history as divided into two ages: the present age, an evil age dominated by the powers of evil, and the age to come, in which God will rule over history. In many expressions of this apocalyptic hope it was believed that the reign or kingdom of God would be inaugurated by a special agent of God to be known as his anointed (classically transliterated as *Messiah*).

The empire in which Israel was currently a province was the Roman. This had come to pass, as noted above (see p. 137), when the Maccabean rulers had become so oppressive that the Israelites invited Pompey, the Roman general in Syria to the North, to intervene. Rome itself was going through a considerable transition at the time, having its republican constitution mask the emergence of an emperor. Julius Caesar had almost assumed kingly power when he was assassinated by Brutus and Cassius. Mark Anthony was assisted in defeating the murderers by Caesar's nephew and adopted son, Octavius. Eventually Anthony and Octavius fought it out between themselves for control of Rome. Octavius won and served his term as the first emperor with the title of "the august person," which in Latin is *Augustus*. Jesus was born during his reign.

For local rulers in Israel, Rome began by leaving the tag end of the Maccabean family in office, but they were quickly supplanted by their enterprising allies from nearby Idumea. From them came Herod the Great who ruled as client king over most of the territory of David's kingdom from 37 to 4 B.C. His kingdom was divided after his death among three of his sons. Archelaus did so poorly in Jerusalem and the surrounding area of Judea that he was replaced after ten years in office by a Roman governor. At the time of the crucifixion the situation was still that Herod's sons ruled two-thirds of Israel with the remaining section under the Roman governor. A grandson of Herod, Herod Agrippa I, succeeded to these three sections one by one so that from A.D. 41 to 44 he ruled all of the former kingdom of Herod the Great. After his death the Romans sent governors to rule over the whole territory. Each was worse than his predecessor so that in 66 the rebellion that had smoldered so long finally erupted. By 70 the Temple was destroyed and the Romans were firmly in control. Another abortive uprising took place 132–35 under Bar-Kochba, but for all practical purposes the history of Israel was over. Bar-Kochba was regarded by many at the time as the Messiah. Jesus, in fact, was one among many who were so identified during the troubled time of Roman rule.

The Jews of Jesus' time were divided into religious parties that had very different ideas about what obligations their religion committed them to. The vast majority of the people did not belong to any of these parties and were patronizingly dismissed as "the people of the land" (Hebrew: *Am ha-aretz*). The priestly aristocracy, by no means the most religious section of the population, were conservative and believed in nothing not explicitly taught in the Torah. For instance, they doubted the existence of evil spirits and did not believe in resurrection.

The other three parties were rigorists in one way or another. The Pharisees considered the Old Testament to be essentially a code of religious law that needed to be interpreted so that all its ritual provisions could be observed. The rabbis who later produced the Mishnah and Talmud were the spiritual heirs of the Pharisees. This movement seems to have begun near the time of the Babylonian captivity when pious Israelites were not able to participate in the worship of the Temple. The nonsacrificial worship of Torah study offered Judaism a way to survive after the destruction of the Temple.

If anything, the Essenes and the Zealots were even more rigorous than the Pharisees. The Essenes were a group who decided that the Maccabean high priests were not lawful because they did not come from the valid priestly family. Thus the Essenes withdrew from the worship of the Temple and formed religious communities in remote places. The community at Qumran, which produced the Dead Sea Scrolls, is generally believed to have been Essene, for instance. Not all Essenes withdrew from society completely, though; some lived in the world and were married, but tried to follow a community rule. The Zealots believed that Israel should have no king but God and were committed to armed rebellion against the Romans. Most of the people described in the Gospels as robbers or bandits were probably Zealots engaged in guerilla warfare against the Romans. They especially would think of the Messiah in terms of a descendant of David who would lead them in driving out the Romans. Those who tried to trip Jesus up by asking if tribute should be paid to the emperor knew that he would lose the support of the Zealots if he said yes.

To complete this section of historical background something should be said about dates. Not much can be said with any assurance, however. Neither Jesus' birth nor his death can be dated with any certainty. Both Matthew and Luke place the birth within the reign of Herod the Great who died in 4 B.C. Luke also says that a census was being conducted at the time by the Roman governor of Syria, Quirinius. Since, however, the census of Quirinius was not taken until A.D. 6, Luke's information appears to be incorrect. Most scholars are content to place the birth a year or so before the death of Herod and say that Jesus was born around 6 B.C. That means, of course, that something was wrong with the arithmetic of Dionysius Exiguus, the Syrian monk upon whose reckoning our current calendars are based. The only New Testament information that would help establish the year of Jesus' death is Luke's statement that Jesus began his ministry when he was about thirty years old. We do not know, though, whether the ministry lasted only a little over a year or lasted three or four. For Jesus to have died before he was near his mid-thirties would require that he be crucified before Pilate was governor. A date between A.D. 29 and 33 seems as close as we can get.

The Acts of the Apostles

The Book of Acts was not at first a separate volume but was the second section of a two-part work, Luke-Acts. Thus the name did not come from the author and does not describe the contents of the work. Acts is not a record of "the Deeds of the Twelve" as its title implies, since the Twelve as a group are not mentioned after chapter 6. The only two major characters are Peter and Paul; and Paul, of course, was not one of the Twelve. In a sense, the main character of Acts is not an individual but the church; the story of Acts is the story of the expansion of the Spirit-filled community throughout the northeastern area of the Mediterranean. More precisely, it is the story of the transfer of the center of the movement from Jerusalem to Rome. We could push the question of main character even further and say, as someone has said, that Acts is "the Gospel of the Holy Spirit" since the author makes it very clear that the motive power behind the expansion of the church was not human but divine.

Acts begins with the Ascension, which does not occur on Easter as most of the rest of the New Testament implies, but comes forty days later. The Eleven asked Jesus if he were going to restore the kingdom to Israel at that time. He replied in effect that the answer was none of their business. What did concern them was that God had something for them to do. Soon they were to receive the Holy Spirit. When they did he would empower them to be Jesus' witnesses in Jerusalem, all

Judea, Samaria, and to the end of the earth. This sentence furnishes an outline of Acts, which tells of the expansion of the church in Jerusalem, Judea, Samaria, and to Rome, "the end of the earth." Then Jesus ascended while two angels promised his followers that he would come again.

Since Judas had died (Matthew says that he committed suicide), Peter felt that Old Testament prophecy required that they find someone to take his place in giving an eye-witness account of Jesus' resurrection. Matthias was chosen by lot to fill the vacancy since the church had not yet received the Spirit to guide its decisions.

The Holy Spirit descended on the church on the Feast of Pentecost, fifty days after Passover. The Spirit came like a roaring wind and settled on Jesus' followers like fire. They rushed into the streets and began to preach the good news about Jesus. The author of Acts knew that ecstatic utterance had been a part of the experience of the apostolic generation and he uses the concept here in two ways: speaking in tongues is regarded, on the one hand, as incomprehensible speech, and, on the other, as the ability to be understood by those whose native language is other than one's own. Thus the gift of tongues is both a sign of the powerful presence of God and is also a missionary gift. Jews who have come to Jerusalem from all parts of the Roman empire hear and understand the Gospel. When they treat it as drunken babbling, Peter is able to defend Jesus' followers in a speech that has the same outline as most of the speeches that make up fully a third of the Book of Acts: (a) events were prophesied in the Old Testament, (b) those prophecies were fulfilled by Jesus, (c) the Twelve saw them happen, and (d) therefore their hearers should repent and be baptized. Three thousand responded to that invitation and became sharers in "the Apostles' teaching and fellowship, . . . the breaking of bread and the prayers." Their early existence was a communal one in which all material goods were used in common.

It was to be some time before Christianity was recognized as a religion separate from Judaism, and the early church in Jerusalem participated fully in the worship at the Temple. When Peter and John healed a beggar lame from birth at one of the Temple gates and told the crowd that they had been able to do so because of Jesus, the leaders of the religious establishment had them arrested; in spite of that, five thousand were converted by their preaching that day. When Peter and John defended themselves in court with divinely inspired eloquence, the religious leaders decided that it was dangerous to provide them with such a platform and released them.

Luke looks back on the time of the Twelve as a golden age when the Spirit bound Christians together in harmony and led the church triumphantly on its march through the ancient world. Thus the picture one gets is quite different, for instance, from that in Paul's correspondence with the church at Corinth where the all-too-human actions of people had split the congregation into a number of factions. Occasionally, though, Luke does allow human foibles to show, as in the case of Ananias and his wife Sapphira. They had sold their property and tried to hold part of the proceeds back from the church while claiming that they were contributing all. Divine retribution was swift, with both husband and wife being struck dead for their sins.

When Peter's fame for miracles of healing proved a threat to the establishment, he was placed in prison. He was miraculously released, though, and was soon back preaching in the precincts of the Temple. The leaders reminded Peter that they had told him to stop preaching about Jesus, but he told them that he had to obey God rather than men. When they wanted to kill him, one of them, Gamaliel, suggested a policy of wait and see toward the Christian movement so that they would not be found opposing God if the movement came from him.

There were some complaints that the widows of Jewish Christians from the Greek-speaking world were not treated as well as those from Israel in the distribution of community alms. Since the Twelve had all they could do in preaching the word of God, they asked that seven assistants be appointed to look after such administrative matters. Although these assistants are not explicitly called deacons in Acts, they have been identified as the first members of that order for a number of reasons. Although they were set aside to free the Twelve for preaching, the only two of whom we hear more, Stephen and Philip, preached too. In fact, Stephen's preaching so infuriated the religious leaders that they stoned him, making him the first Christian martyr. A bystander and "coatholder" for this mob violence was Saul of Tarsus, of whom we will hear much more later.

After the death of Stephen, real persecution of the Christians began in Jerusalem, so most of them scattered to other places where they began preaching the Gospel. Philip went to Samaria where, since he was able to perform more miracles than the local wonder-worker, many were baptized. Peter and John came down to lay hands on the Samaritans. When the Holy Spirit descended upon the Samaritans in visible power, the wonder-worker tried to purchase the power of the bestowal of the Spirit. Since his name was Simon, the effort to purchase church office is now known as simony. Meanwhile, Philip found himself on a road in the Gaza strip when a eunuch from the court of the Ethiopian queen came by. He was a non-Jew attracted to the religion of Israel and had been to Jerusalem on a pilgrimage. On his return trip he was reading about the Suffering Servant in Isaiah 53. When Philip explained that the passage was a prophecy about Jesus, he asked to be baptized at a stream along the way.

The coat-holder at Stephen's stoning, Saul (called Paul by those who spoke Greek) had begun to take a position of leadership in the persecution of Christians. After the raids in Jerusalem he began to look further afield. The high priest gave him authority to go into Syria to the north and bring back Christians who had fled to such cities as Damascus and were preaching the Gospel there. While in the caravan on the way, however, Paul was blinded by a vision of Christ and had to be led to Damascus. There a Christian by the name of Ananias had been instructed in a revelation to go to Paul, heal him, baptize him, and tell him that he had a special mission to the Gentiles. After overcoming the suspicion of Christians in Antioch, Paul preached there until the threat of his own capture forced him to escape the city in a basket lowered over the city wall. Acts next outlines Paul's movements in a way that does not entirely agree with Paul's own account in Galatians 1:11–2:14.

Meanwhile Peter had been preaching in Judea and had healed a paralyzed man in Lydda and raised a woman from the dead in Joppa. While he was in Joppa he had a vision one day in which animals were let down from heaven on a sheet. When a voice told him to kill and eat, he replied that he never ate anything that was not kosher, not ritually pure. The voice then told him that he should not call anything impure that God had cleansed. When the same event had been repeated three times, messengers came to him from Cornelius, a Roman officer in Caesarea, the seaport that was the administrative capital of the province. Cornelius, who had a deep attachment to the religion of Israel, had been instructed in a vision to send for Peter. Peter went to Caesarea and preached Christ to Cornelius and his family and friends. While he was preaching, the Holy Spirit came upon his audience and Peter understood his vision: Gentiles could become Christians directly without having to become Jews first. When Peter returned to Jerusalem he discovered that word had already reached there of his activities, and many opposed his eating with Gentiles who did not keep a kosher kitchen. When Peter justified his action by telling his story, his opponents were convinced and said: "Then to the Gentiles also God has granted repentance unto life."

Meanwhile the Christians who had been scattered by the persecution began to make converts in such places as the island of Cyprus and in Antioch, capitol of Syria and the third largest city of the Roman empire. The church at Jerusalem sent Barnabas to Antioch when they heard of the converts there and he in turn went to get Paul to help him in his work. It was in Antioch that the followers of Jesus were first called Christians.

Things continued to go badly for the church in Jerusalem: Herod Agrippa I had James the son of Zebedee killed and Peter arrested. Peter was again released by an angel at night and went to the home of Mark's mother to bid farewell to the congregation meeting there before he moved on to a safer place. Acts attributes the painful death of the king to divine retribution.

After Barnabas and Paul returned to Antioch from taking money to relieve the Christians in Jerusalem from the famine there, the Holy Spirit instructed the church in Antioch to send Barnabas and Paul to preach the Gospel on Cyprus and in the cities near the coast on the mainland to the North (the southern coast of modern Turkey). A magician who opposed them at the court of a Roman proconsul was blinded temporarily. Paul and Barnabas attended a synagogue service in the Pisidian city called Antioch (not to be confused with their home base). This was to be their usual strategy in beginning a Christian mission in a new place. As a visitor, Paul was asked to preach and he proclaimed Christ as the fulfillment of prophecy. The synagogue congregation was split over this new belief. When not all of the Jews would accept the Gospel, Paul and Barnabas went to the Gentiles. Many people in the area accepted Christ before persecution drove the Apostles on. Much the same story was repeated at Iconium. When they healed a congenitally lame man in Lystra, however, the people there took them to be the pagan gods Zeus and Hermes (Jupiter and Mercury in Roman religion). Then, after they explained that they were mortal, messengers arrived from Antioch and Iconium, and Paul who received divine honors so shortly before was stoned. Going on to Derbe, they preached there and then retraced their steps, organizing the congregations in each town and appointing elders.

When they got back to Antioch, Paul and Barnabas found that conservatives in Jerusalem opposed them as they had Peter when he baptized Cornelius and the others in Caesarea. Their contention was that no man could be a Christian without being circumcized and observing the Torah. Paul and Barnabas, therefore, took their case to the apostles and elders in Jerusalem. Peter defended them and they stated their own case by reporting the success of their efforts. James, the brother of Jesus, who had led the Jerusalem community since the departure of Peter, told the group that he thought that Gentile converts to Christianity should be required to obey only the parts of the Torah that were directed to all of Noah's sons and were thus binding on all mankind: not eating food offered to idols, not being unchaste, not eating meat from strangled animals from which the blood had not been drained. No decision made by the early church was more significant for the future than this decision that the Gospel was open to Gentiles on an equal basis with Jews.

After returning to Antioch, Paul and Barnabas decided to visit the congregations they had founded. In Cyprus they fell out over whether they should take Mark with them, and Paul went on, taking Silas as his companion. At Derbe Paul and Silas were joined by Timothy. After visiting the churches already started, they wandered around over most of what is now Turkey, not knowing where to go. When they arrived at Troas, the site of the Trojan war, which was just across the Aegean from Greece, Paul saw someone in a vision who said, "Come over to Macedonia and help us." This made it clear that the Spirit had been directing them to move into Europe and begin the proclamation of the Gospel there.

Macedonia, the northern part of Greece and the home of Alexander the Great, had as its major city Philippi, built by Alexander's father, Philip of Macedon. In Philippi Paul healed a slave girl from possession by a demon that gave her psychic powers. Her owners, who had profited from her fortune-telling, had Paul and his friends beaten and thrown into jail. They were freed that night by a miraculous earthquake and, when they did not take advantage of this opportunity to break jail, their jailer was converted. Then Paul reminded the judge that a Roman citizen such as himself could not be subjected to such arbitrary treatment. Moving on to Thessalonica, the capital of the province, Paul and Barnabas preached for three weeks before persecution was stirred up against them there. From there they went on to Beroea where they had a similar experience.

In Athens Paul is depicted in a situation that many modern readers have understood in a way different from what Luke intended. There he is shown proclaiming the Gospel to the intellectual capital of the ancient world in the vocabulary of pagan philosophy. Since nothing is said about the foundation of a church there, many have thought that Paul had his greatest failure when he tried to depend on the persuasive power of human reason. Luke, however, clearly wants to show that the apostle par excellence is able to take on the intellectual aristocracy of his time and beat them at their own game.

From Athens Paul went to Corinth, the city that dominated the narrow isthmus that connected the Peloponnesus, the southern part of Greece, to the mainland. Since ancient sailors transshipped most of their cargoes there rather than venturing into the open sea, the city was of immense importance as a crossroads of the world. The mission was begun there in the synagogue in the usual fashion, but Paul had the advantage there of finding Christians already in the city: Acquila and his wife Priscilla had fled there when Claudius drove the Jews out of Rome in A.D. 49 and they shared Paul's profession of tentmaking. Paul was able to spend eighteen months there before the Jews tried unsuccessfully to take legal action against him. Sometime later, though, he returned to Antioch, stopping at Ephesus, across the Aegean from Corinth, long enough to promise to return and preach there. He left Priscilla and Acquila there as a nucleus for the congregation.

Before Paul returned to Ephesus, Apollos, an imperfectly catechized Jewish Christian preacher of great ability, stopped there. Priscilla and Acquila were able to complete his instruction and he went on to Corinth to preach there. When Paul arrived in Ephesus he found that he still had to teach about such elementary matters as the Holy Spirit. Taking a group from the synagogue, he preached in a public hall for two years so that the entire area knew about Christ. Indeed, Paul's preaching became so popular that some wonderworkers tried to cash in on Christianity to their own great discomfort. Many other magicians were converted and burned their books of spells for which Ephesus was well known.

When the church in Ephesus was well founded, Paul felt called by God to move on to Rome. Before he could leave, however, there was a riot in Ephesus stirred up by those who had profited by the presence in Ephesus of one of the Seven Wonders of the Ancient World, the temple of Artemis (equivalent of the Roman goddess Diana). The riot was quelled by a high local official, however, who exonerated the Christians of all wrongdoing. Before returning to Antioch, Paul made a circuit of the churches he had founded in Greece. In Troas he healed a young man who had fallen asleep while Paul was preaching and fell out of a window. After a farewell visit with the elders of the church at Ephesus, he sailed for Israel.

Upon landing Paul received several supernatural warnings about danger in Jerusalem, but he went on anyway, saying, "The will of the Lord be done." In Jerusalem James and the leaders of the church informed him that his work among the Gentiles made many devout Jews think that he despised the Torah. They suggested that he relieve their doubts by going through a purification ceremony at the Temple. This scheme backfired, though, for Paul was then falsely accused of taking Gentiles into the Court of Israel where they were not allowed. He would have been killed by mob violence if he had not been rescued by Roman soldiers. Identifying himself to their officer, Paul asked permission to address the crowd in an attempt to establish his innocence. His Christian preaching, however, stirred them up even more and Paul had to be taken into protective custody by the soldiers.

When the officer asked the Jewish council to help him understand what the crowd was angry about and Paul said that the real issue was belief in resurrection, the Pharisees sided with him and the Sadducees opposed him and the meeting broke up in a fight.[4] After that some of the more fanatical of Paul's opponents conspired to ambush him. Paul's nephew got wind of that, though, and the Romans transported Paul to Caesarea in order to protect him. The Roman governor at Caesarea, Felix, kept Paul in prison, hoping for a bribe. When his successor Festus tried to inquire into the case, Paul exercised his right as a citizen and appealed to Caesar to be tried by him in Rome. Before sending Paul on, though, Festus let him plead his case before Herod Agrippa II in order to understand what this question of Jewish law was about. Agrippa confirmed the universal opinion of those in authority that Paul had done nothing that merited death.

Paul was sent to Rome by ship. Off the coast of Crete they ran into a storm that almost wrecked the ship. After a couple of weeks, however, they finally drove the vessel aground on Malta. While Paul was gathering wood for a fire, a very poisonous snake struck his hand and held on. The Maltese who saw this thought at first that he must be guilty of some terrible crime for which retribution was catching up with him. When he did not die, though, they decided he must be a god. Paul also healed the father of the chief local official. It was three months before they could sail again. When they landed at Puteoli in Italy, Paul was able to stay with local Christians. Nearing Rome, he was met by Christians from the city who had heard of his arrival and come out to meet him. Once in the city he called together the leaders of the local Jewish community who had heard nothing against him and who were anxious to learn his beliefs. As in other places, some believed and some did not. He stayed two years in Rome under house arrest, free to preach the Gospel to all who were interested.

For many centuries the ending of Acts was a mystery. Why did it not say how Paul's trial came out? Was he released so that he was able to go on and engage in the events mentioned in the pastoral epistles that do not fit into the chronology of Acts? Was Acts itself a brief for his defense at the trial? Most scholars are now agreed that these considerations grow out of our own biographical interpretation of the purpose of Acts. Yet if the real subject of Acts is not Peter and Paul but the expansion of the church, having Paul preach the Gospel openly in Rome is a natural and triumphant ending. Paul's fate is incidental when compared to such an accomplishment. That fate is almost certainly implied in chapters 20 and 21 when he is warned about what awaits him in Jerusalem. His response was to say: "What are you doing, weeping and breaking my heart? For I am ready not only to be imprisoned but even to die at Jerusalem for the name of the Lord Jesus" (21:13).

THE CONTEXT OF ACTS

Jesus died a little before or after A.D. 30. Just over thirty years later, when the city of Rome burned and the emperor Nero was widely believed to have set it afire himself, he looked around for the most obvious bugbear or scapegoat on which to place the blame. That Christians were his best bet meant that some extraordinarily successful religious propagation must have occurred in that one short generation. The majority of Jesus' ministry had taken place in a remote section of a peripheral province of the Roman empire. Only the closing weeks or months of his life had been spent at the major city of the province. And by the time he died he had been deserted by most or all of his followers. Those followers so increased in number during the intervening thirty years that 1200 miles away, at the heart of the empire, popular anxiety focused on them as the most dangerous threat to society around. This means that their movement must have grown with phenomenal success. Indeed, their fame may have so spread in about half this time. The Roman historian—court gossip may be a more accurate designation—Suetonius, said: "Because the Jews at Rome caused continuous disturbances at the instigation of Chrestus, [Claudius] expelled them from the City."[5] Most scholars believe that "Chrestus" is Suetonius' garbling of "Christus." The date usually assigned to this event is A.D. 49.

In order for the Christian movement to have spread fast enough to come to the attention of an emperor so soon, there had to be conditions very favorable to its growth. Among these were the dispersion of the Jews throughout the Roman empire and beyond. This *Diaspora* (to call it by its Greek name) began when the Assyrian empire took the northern kingdom of Israel into captivity in 722 B.C. The Babylonian Captivity, a little over a century later, left some more permanent Jewish residents in Mesopotamia. In the days of the successors of Alexander the Great, large Jewish colonies were established in Egypt. Rome also attracted many. The Jews of the dispersion present in Jerusalem on Pentecost included "Parthians, Medes, and Elamites; residents of Mesopotamia,

Judea, and Cappadocia; Pontus and Asia; Phrygia and Pamphylia; Egypt and the parts of Libya belonging to Cyrene; and visitors from Rome, both Jews and proselytes, Cretans and Arabians." That is to say they came from most of what was regarded as *oikumene*, the inhabited universe. Estimates place Jewish population as a seventh or eighth of that of the Roman empire.

This presence of Jews throughout the empire meant that everywhere people had heard of Judaism with its worship of one God who was invisible, omnipotent, and righteous, and many had heard of their expectations of a Messiah. As we shall see later, many dissatisfactions were felt with pagan religion, and many devout pagans attached themselves to the synagogues, attracted by the monotheism and high moral standards of the Jews. Some of these became converts or proselytes to Judaism, but many more held back because of their unwillingness to undergo circumcision, the withdrawal from pagan society that the dietary laws required, and relegation to the inferior status within Judaism that proselytes had. These were called "God-fearers" and included such persons as Cornelius and the Ethiopian eunuch (Acts 8:26–40; 10:1–11:18).

Other conditions propitious to the spread of Christianity relate to situations in the Greco-Roman world. Alexander the Great had conquered the known world with a missionary commitment to merge Greek and Near Eastern cultures. Greek had remained the international language of government, business, and culture down into Roman times. Furthermore, Greek philosophy and the popular thought forms in which it was disseminated furnished the intellectual categories in which all cultivated people thought. Nothing is so important for the spread of ideas as a common language and shared concepts.

Some of the Greek thoughts that circulated widely were a criticism of traditional religion that considered the myths told in Homer's Iliad and Odyssey to be immoral and absurd. An inclination toward monotheism and high ethical standards was characteristic of many philosophical trends of the times. The main religious expressions in the territory that was the scene of Acts were civic or state cults in which the patron deities of a city, state, or the empire were offered worship in the expectation that they in turn would give to their people prosperity and victory in war. Their worship, therefore, was far more a matter of patriotic duty than of personal devotion. In fact, many enlightened pagans felt obliged to continue to participate in this civic cult even though they did not believe in the gods to whom its worship was addressed.

Thus there was very little of what we would recognize as personal religion in the Greco-Roman world. The Romans did have their household gods, but these were hardly personal and they were cultivated more for the luck of the family than from any sense of devotion to a supreme good. There had come in from the East a number of ecstatic cults that did give some personal involvement in religion. These are called mystery cults because they centered around rites of initiation designed to convey enlightenment through drama, much in the manner of the Masonic orders or fraternities and sororities. Christianity must have looked much like a mystery religion to people at the time. Astrology and magic were also quite popular as we see from the birth stories in Matthew and the magicians that Philip met in Samaria and Paul met in Cyprus and Ephesus.

The Roman empire took an attitude toward the state religions of the various countries very different from the one they took to mystery religions and other private religious groups. A civic cult had the status of a *religio licita,* the lawful religion of a country, while a private group was designated as a *superstitio,* a private belief entitled to no protection of the law and perhaps suspect for a number of reasons. As Christianity was at first considered to be a sect of Judaism, it enjoyed the status of *religio licita,* but when it was perceived to be a separate religion it was demoted to the status of *superstitio.*

Not only did the new Christian proclamation appear in what was in many ways a religious vacuum, it also had other advantages for its rapid propagation. The silent transformation of the Roman republic into an empire under Augustus left a world at peace for the first time in many centuries. While we might wonder at the value of peace that was purchased at the price of independence, few people in the ancient world did. An era of unparalleled prosperity, ushered in by the *pax Romana*, caused grateful citizens throughout the empire to erect monuments in praise of Augustus as their savior. The famous Roman road system was both a result of and necessary to this peace. Paul's easy travel from one end of the empire to the other would not have been possible before Augustus.

By the same token, Christianity could not have started so successfully much later than it did. The religion of Israel furnished the context in which Jesus appeared; by A.D. 70 the Temple was destroyed and the Jews no longer existed as a people living in their own land. The religious success story recorded by Acts was thus made possible by what the fourth-century church historian Eusebius called *praeparatio evangelica*, the preparation for the Gospel. As St. Paul said:

> When the fulness of the time was come, God sent forth his Son, made of a woman, made under the law, to redeem them that were under the law, that we might receive the adoption of sons. And, because ye are sons, God hath sent forth the Spirit of his Son into your hearts, crying, Abba, Father. (Gal. 4:4–6, KJV)

What the Bible Teaches: Old Testament[1]

The apocryphal gospels told the story of Jesus from the point of view of pious imagination rather than from any historical reminiscences. The stories they contain tend to emphasize the miraculous power of Jesus hidden within his human boyhood rather than his example of self-giving love. Thus, on one occasion, Jesus had spoken disrespectfully to Joseph.

Now a certain teacher, Zacchaeus by name, who was standing there, heard in part Jesus saying these things to his father, and marvelled greatly that, being a child, he said such things. And after a few days he came near to Joseph and said to him: "You have a clever child, and he has understanding. Come, hand him over to me that he may learn letters, and I will teach him with the letters all knowledge, and to salute all older people and honour them as grandfathers and fathers, and to love those of his own age." And he told him all the letters from Alpha to Omega clearly, with much questioning. But he looked at Zacchaeus the teacher and said to him: "How do you, who do not know the Alpha according to its nature, teach others the Beta? Hypocrite, first, if you know it, teach the Alpha and we shall believe you concerning the Beta." Then he began to question the teacher about the first letter, and he was unable to answer him. And in the hearing of many the child said to Zacchaeus: "Hear, teacher, the arrangement of the first letter and pay heed to this, how it has lines and a middle mark that goes through the pair of lines which you see, how these lines converge, rise, turn in the dance, three signs of the same kind, subject to and supporting one another, of equal proportions; here you have the lines of the Alpha!"[2]

The surprising thing about the rest of this story is that Zacchaeus praised Jesus for this behavior instead of striking him, as another teacher did on a similar occasion later in the book. Even more surprising for people today, though, must be the assumption underlying the story that there is a mystical significance to the letters of the alphabet that is open only to the initiated. The assumption that letters can have meaning independent of their function in the spelling of words is foreign to contemporary culture.

Yet there is a tendency among many who attempt to tell what the Bible teaches to abstract the meaning of biblical stories from the stories themselves in much the way that Jesus in the Infancy Gospel abstracted the meaning of Alpha from its use in a word. Biblical theologies are written in which the teaching of the Bible on various subjects is set out systematically in a series of abstract statements. Thus it might be said that the biblical teaching about God is such and such, and the biblical teaching about Jesus is something else, all neatly set out in paragraphs that follow an outline arranged in terms of logical sequence.

The approach taken thus far in this book, however, calls for a different approach. Having said that the meaning of a story is the story itself, it would be inconsistent now to begin an exposition of meaning that was abstracted from the stories. Thus where possible we will state each of the basic biblical doctrines first in terms of the narrative in which it appeared.

How God Has Acted in Israel's Past (Historical Books)

OLD TESTAMENT CREEDS

The English word "creed" is derived from the Latin *credo*, "I believe." Thus a creed is a statement of belief. Most Americans, if asked to state their basic beliefs, would probably make a list of abstract statements. The main creeds of the

Christian church, however, contain a number of historical statements or at least references to events, especially in their second paragraph which deals with faith in Jesus Christ:

I believe in Jesus Christ, his only Son, our Lord.
He was conceived by the power of the Holy Spirit
    and born of the Virgin Mary.
He suffered under Pontius Pilate,
    was crucified, died, and was buried.
He descended to the dead.
On the third day he rose again.
He ascended into heaven.
    and is seated at the right hand of the Father.
He will come again to judge the living and the dead.

One of the major observations of modern biblical scholarship is that the Old Testament contains a number of short summary statements of historical events that also sound like confessions of faith. One of the clearest examples is Deuteronomy 26:5–9:

A wandering Aramean was my father; and he went down into Egypt and sojourned there, few in number; and there he became a nation, great, mighty, and populous. And the Egyptians treated us harshly, and afflicted us, and laid upon us hard bondage. Then we cried to the Lord the God of our fathers, and the Lord heard our voice, and saw our affliction, our toil, and our oppression; and the Lord brought us out of Egypt with a mighty hand and an outstretched arm, with great terror, with signs and wonders; and he brought us into this place and gave us this land, a land flowing with milk and honey.

The wandering Aramean was the patriarch Jacob, who followed his son Joseph into sojourn in Egypt. The events of the creed thus stretch back into the time of the patriarchs. The degeneration of that sojourn into slavery is recorded. Deliverance from that slavery in the Exodus comes next and the recitation concludes with the occupation of the promised land under Joshua and the judges.

Similar summaries occur elsewhere in the Old Testament, most of which are much longer. A taste of these can be derived from Psalm 136. This psalm exhorts the people to give thanks to the Lord whose enduring mercy has been manifested in many interventions in history in behalf of Israel. Verses 10–16 tell of the Exodus:

> Who struck down the firstborn of Egypt,
>   for his mercy endures forever;
> And brought out Israel from among them,
>   for his mercy endures forever;
> With a mighty hand and a stretched-out arm,
>   for his mercy endures forever;
> Who divided the Red Sea in two,
>   for his mercy endures forever;
> And made Israel to pass through the midst of it,
>   for his mercy endures forever;
> But swept Pharaoh and his army into the Red Sea,
>   for his mercy endures forever;
> Who led his people through the wilderness,
>   for his mercy endures forever.

Scholars may argue about whether these confessions of faith about God's shaping of the history of Israel are early creeds that shaped the development of the Pentateuch or merely summaries that were constructed later, but the indisputable point is that when the Old Testament wishes to express belief in God, the statement of that belief does not take the form of an abstract list of his qualities and characteristics, but takes instead the form of a list of his actions in history.

THE PEOPLE OF GOD

For God to have acted in history, he must have acted in the history of human beings, whether in the lives of individual persons or in the history of the whole human race. In the Old Testament, though, it is neither individuals nor all of humanity in whose history the hand of God is seen to move; it is rather in the history of Israel. One could say that the Old Testament has two main characters: God and Israel. As has been said, "Israel, the people of God, . . . always acts as a unit, . . . with which God always deals as a unit."

One of the main concepts used in expressing God's relating to Israel as a unit is that of a covenant, a solemn oath that provides a new basis for the relation of two parties. This term became so basic for later thought that it furnished the terminology for the distinction between the major divisions of the Bible, the Old and New Testaments. The Latin, *testamentum*, was used to translate a Greek word for a will (as in "last will and testament"), *diathēkē*, which had been used in the LXX, the Greek Old Testament, to translate *berith*, the Hebrew word that we render into English as "covenant."

Recent scholarship has done much to illuminate our understanding of the concept of covenant by studying the pattern of treaties made by ancient Near East peoples, especially those made by Hittite kings with their vassals. Many forms have been discovered. Treaties made by a superior with an inferior would furnish an appropriate form to express the relation between God and Israel. Some of the forms spoke only of the obligation of the superior, some only of the duties of the inferior, and others of the reciprocal and conditional obligations undertaken between the two parties. All of these are used in one place or another in the Bible to express the relation between God and Israel.

By the time the Torah was in the state in which we now find it, it was unified by the theme of various covenants that God had made with Israel under her leader at the time. The first covenant was with Noah and was God's promise that he would not destroy the earth by water again. In the covenant with Abraham God promised the land of Canaan to him and his descendants and, more importantly, a unique relation with himself. The promise of the land was not fulfilled until the conquest under Joshua. Meanwhile, a new covenant had been entered into at Mt. Sinai when Moses was given the Law that would be the basis of Israel's faithfulness to God. Thus the concepts of covenant and Torah are closely interrelated.

The concept of covenant continued to be very important. David was understood to have been promised in a covenant that his descendants would sit on the throne of Israel forever.

The prophets were to frame their messages in terms of covenants that Israel had broken. When King Josiah found the book in the Temple, he and all the people made a covenant to follow all the words that were written there. Then, after the return from exile in Babylon, Ezra the scribe read to the people the book of the Law of Moses and he and the people made a covenant to obey it. Finally, of course, Jesus spoke at the Last Supper of instituting a new covenant in his blood.

The vocabulary of covenant is by no means the only language that is used to express the concept of the people of God. Other examples will be brought in as appropriate.

CREATION, MAN AND SIN

The Christian creeds begin with a first paragraph or article that proclaims God the Father as Creator of the universe. The creeds of the Old Testament do not list creation as one of the mighty acts of God, though, and the doctrine of creation seems to appear rather late in the history of Israel and receives relatively little attention. The first two chapters of Genesis and passages in Second Isaiah furnish the most important treatments of the theme. Although Israel undoubtedly had some beliefs about how the world came into existence from very early days, there are two reasons why she was slow in integrating those beliefs into her major confessions of faith. The first is that all of the other articles in the Israelite creeds were events in history through which God's action for the benefit of his people shone with particular clarity. It was not until creation could be understood as the first of these acts for God's people that it could be fitted into the scheme of Israel's proclamation of faith.

Furthermore, the religions of Israel's neighbors were all centered on the role of their gods in the fertility of their fields and flocks. Thus creation in those religions had an orgiastic sexual emphasis that Israel would have considered blasphemous if it were associated with Yahweh. Besides, these religions related creation to the annual cycle of seasons that was so important for agriculture. It was treated as a mythical event that occurred before time began and to which one could return annually in the festivals of the religious cult. The timelessness of this "eternal return" was hard to fit in with Israel's understanding of the events of history as the arena of God's action.

The older creation story in Genesis is the second, which begins at 2:4. Here, as elsewhere in the Bible, the picture of the world is the one common throughout ancient times, which sees the universe as being constructed like a super-dome erected on pillars over water. The earth is the playing field, a flat surface that is nevertheless corrugated with mountains, rivers, and seas. The dome is called the "firmament" and both keeps out the heavenly ocean and functions as the foundation for the dwelling place of supernatural beings (God and his angels in the Bible, gods in pagan versions). The waters under the building are chaotic (as are also those above it) and Sheol, the place where the dead carried on their shadowy existence, is located in their depths.

This J version of the creation story has God begin by making the flat earth and the dome of the firmament above it as a sort of bare-walled building in which vegetation and rain had not yet been installed. God moulded some of the earth's soil like a potter, and then animated his mud doll by breathing into it the breath of his own life. Then God planted the earth and set rivers in it to make a habitation for man. Birds and animals were created to furnish man with a proper companion, but all were inadequate until God anesthetized the man, removed one of his ribs, and made a woman out of it. This version of the creation story shows the kindliness of God to man and also shows man in relation to his environment. It connects very naturally with the history of Israel because it is clear that creation centers around man and it will become clear that mankind finds its center and meaning in Israel. In fact, the prohibition against eating the fruit of the tree of the knowledge of good and evil is built into the creation story and history is ready to begin with the fall in the next chapter.

Although the P account of creation that occupies Genesis 1:1–2:3 was written down a number of centuries later than the J story, it is in some ways more closely connected with the myths of creation from surrounding cultures, such as the

Babylonian myth. In the Gilgamesh epic, the god Marduk creates the world out of the body of his rival Tiamat, and there are reminiscences of that idea in the P narrative, but they are only obvious from the Hebrew text. In this account there are six days of creation and things are created in an ascending order. Creation begins as far away from God as possible, with the watery chaos, and moves through inanimate objects to plants and then to animals before it climaxes in the creation of human beings, who are created in the very image of God. This image is conceived as a physical form but the point is not that God is anthropomorphic (imagined to be like a man), but that man is theomorphic, he has the very shape of God. Or, more precisely, he *and she* have the shape of God, since in this story it is clear that God transcends the polarity of the sexes and the image of God is manifested in women and men equally.

The Old Testament uses a special verb for creation by God. That verb is never employed with a being less than God as its grammatical subject. Thus God's creative activity is not treated as being in the same category with the creative acts of people. God's manner of creation is *fiat* (from the Latin for "let there be"). God has only to speak the word and what he wishes comes into existence. His creation, then, is effortless. It cannot be said, however, that Genesis has a doctrine of creation out of nothing (Latin: *ex nihilo*) because such a concept is far too abstract for early Hebrew thought. Chaos existed before creation and the creative word of God brought order out of chaos. Whether the chaos was a preexisting material from which the earth was created is a question that no Israelite got around to asking. Yet the chaos is still thought to reside in the waters above the firmament and below the earth and to pose a continual threat to creation, a threat that only the ordering power of God holds off. In other places in the Old Testament there are vestiges of the pagan belief in which the chaos was personified as an opposing supernatural being with whom God had to struggle in creation, but those concepts had long since ceased to have any meaning for Israel.

Second Isaiah furnishes an example of such thought which also shows that writer's general attitude toward creation.

Awake, awake, put on strength,
   O arm of the Lord;
awake, as in the days of old,
   the generations of long ago.
Was it not thou that didst cut Rahab [the chaos monster]
     in pieces,
   that didst pierce the dragon?
Was it not thou that didst dry up the sea,
   the waters of the great deep;
that didst make the depths of the sea a way
   for the redeemed to pass over? (Is. 51:9, 10)

Creation here is referred to as the slaughter of the chaos monster (Rahab), but it is closely connected with Israelites in the Exodus, for whom God parted the waters of the Red Sea. Creation is thus closely linked with God's efforts in history to save Israel. Creation is regarded by Second Isaiah as itself a saving event and also the basis for hope that God can act again in the prophet's time to bring the Israelites home from captivity in Babylon. The only other development of thought about creation in the Old Testament comes in the Wisdom literature, where the orderliness of creation, the regularity of the seasons or the planets in their courses, evokes awe and wonder before the God who brought it into existence. In the New Testament, as will be seen below, there are two major developments in thought about creation: (1) Christ is seen as the Father's agent of creation, and (2) redemption in Christ is regarded as a re-creation of humanity and the universe.

The Old Testament gives no more systematic consideration to human nature than it gives to other basic questions. What its writers teach about being human has to be inferred from statements on other subjects. Much of their whole view, though, is implied in the early chapters of Genesis which treat of creation and the fall. Since persons are created in the image of God, they have value and dignity, yet, since they are creatures and not the creator, there is an infinite difference between them and God. At times people are regarded as frail creatures who can get sick, grow old, and die. They are regarded as capable of falling into sin, although they are not thought of as having been created evil. All that exists, including humankind, was created by God and he looked on all that he had made and saw that it was very good. Sin, as we shall see, is usually the result of persons aspiring to the prerogatives of God.

One of the hardest things to remember for those who have grown up in the intellectual tradition of Western civilization is that even though the Old Testament and much of the New talk about the flesh, soul, and spirit of persons, there is no intention whatsoever to distinguish between a physical part of a human being that is mortal and a spiritual part that is immortal. Rather, a human being is thought of as a psychophysical organism that is made of many parts and that may have its unity viewed from several aspects. Flesh, soul, or spirit may refer to the entire person. And, although the heart may be treated as the seat of reason and the will, and the intestines, liver, or kidneys (King James: "reins") may be referred to as the seat of the emotions, there is no sense of a diffusion of the personality throughout the body. The human person always functions as a unit. That unit comes to life together and it dies together.

The basic biblical view of sin comes from the story of the Garden of Eden. Indeed, even though the existence of sin is assumed throughout the Old Testament and is referred to often, here it receives its most extensive investigation. (This is not to say that the story of the fall is widely alluded to elsewhere in the Old Testament, because it is not.) The story of the temptation of Adam and Eve is crowded with elements that are common to myths that were familiar throughout the ancient Near East, but they are widely separated here from those appearances. The story is told with such psychological realism that everyone who has ever been tempted can recognize his or her own experience in this story. The fruit of the tree in the midst of the garden was not an apple, of course, but was "knowledge of good and evil." This is not to say moral knowledge, but rather knowledge of all things. Our first parents wanted to pass beyond their creaturely limitations and share in the omniscience of God. The infinite difference between the creature and the creator was ignored and thus the relation between them was broken. Since Adam was dissatisfied with his place in the universe, he forfeited it and exchanged it for a life of physical toil.

It is often not realized that this theme of man's pride and his desire to usurp the prerogatives of God is the theme also of the next two major stories that follow it: Noah and the flood and the Tower of Babel. The climax of human wickedness that made God sorry he had created human beings was the intermarriage between angels and mortal women, which resulted in the birth of persons of gigantic size. This mixture of human beings with heavenly beings broke down one of the barriers of creation and seemed to open up to people the possibility of immortality before God put a stop to such goings-on with the flood. The Tower of Babel was intended to reach to the heavens and God felt that it would be only the beginning of human encroachments on divine territory unless he interfered with the human capacity for concerted action that one language permitted. Thus technical progress is seen here as progress away from God.

The stories of Noah and the Tower of Babel also have important implications for the relation of Israel to other nations. All nations of the earth are descended from the three sons of Noah, so that there is a unity and parity of humanity in creation. Israel is not even listed and thus derives her special place, not from a superior status of creation but from God's election, which comes in the story of Abraham. The Tower of Babel accounts for the diversity of the nations, not through a common descent from Noah but through the loss of a common language. Yet this story also points toward Abraham, through whom all the families of the earth are to be blessed.

THE PATRIARCHS

According to the Torah, the history of Israel began with the call of Abraham. The name Israel, however, belongs to Abraham's grandson Jacob. It was given to him by God when he wrestled with him all night by the Jabbok River, and it was interpreted to mean "He who strives with God" (Gen. 32:28). The twelve tribes were thought to be the descendants of Jacob's twelve sons. Only the first generation of these tribes went down into Egypt, but when they returned they were large tribes.

As the ancient confessions of faith show (see p. 176), the Torah is held together by the understanding that those who came out of Egypt under Moses and conquered the land under Joshua were the descendants of Abraham, Isaac, and Jacob and were finally inheriting the promise that God made to Abraham. The call that came to Abraham when he was still in Mesopotamia was that God was going to give him a land and make him the ancestor of a great nation. Even though, in the original story, the fulfillment of that promise seems to be expected in the immediate future, the J writer has unified all of the material of the Pentateuch around the assumption that the real fulfillment of the promise does not occur until the twelve tribes occupy the land under Joshua.

This overriding theme controls the way the stories about the individual patriarchs are to be understood. The story of Abraham is a story of continually delayed fulfillment of the promise, so Abraham is seen as the great exemplar of faith, who continued to trust God no matter how unlikely it seemed that God would be able to keep his promise. The faith required in the story of Jacob, however, is faith on the part of the reader that God could actually be achieving his purpose through such a shady character as Jacob. The hand of God behind the strange wanderings of Joseph comes out clearly in the last chapter of Genesis. When Jacob had died, Joseph's brothers were afraid that he would finally take revenge for their selling him into slavery. Joseph's response, however, was to say, "You meant evil against me, but God meant it for good" (50:20). Thus the ordering hand of God can be seen all through the story of the patriarchs, preparing all things for the achievement of his purpose centuries later in the Exodus and the occupation of the land.

The time spent in Egypt is not without theological significance. While God now had a people, they were a long way from being completely equipped to serve him. In Egypt they must increase in size. On the Exodus they must learn how to worship him and how he expected them to treat one another.

So far they did not even know the name of their God; that would be given to Moses at his call.

LEARNING GOD'S NAME

The editors of the Torah have done a skillful job of associating the patriarchs with the people of the Exodus, but it can still be seen through the seams of the text that the worship of Yahweh had not been the religion of Israel before the Exodus. Another way of saying that is that Israel as such did not exist until the tribes—each with its own separate history—had entered into the land and joined together to worship Yahweh, who prior to that had been worshiped by only some of the tribes. The story of Moses at the burning bush occurs when he was on the Sinai peninsula tending the flocks of his father-in-law, who was a priest of Midian. It seems overwhelmingly likely that it was from the Midianites or some other people in that area that the Hebrews acquired the worship of Yahweh. Thus there is a general historicity to the story of Moses learning the name of God. The identification of Yahweh with the God of the ancestors was the triumph of later theology.

The significance of the name of Yahweh, which means "I will be what I will be," is not just a philosophical statement about God's existence. Such concerns do not belong to that period. It rather is a promise much like the promise of Jesus in the final words of Matthew: "Lo, I am with you always, to the close of the age." Perhaps there is also an implied warning to Moses not to push too far. At any rate, the puns and etymologies so beloved by narrators of the Pentateuch are often on shaky ground as to the derivation of words and seldom furnish us with the main theological point of a story. The meaning of the name of Yahweh is not so important as the fact of the name.

In the ancient world, to invoke a name was to invoke the reality. "Speak of the devil and he appears" was no light thought then. By the same token, God could not be invoked unless one knew his name. Learning the name of Yahweh means essentially that Israel acquired a cult, a system of worship. The name of Yahweh is particularly important to his worshipers since they were not permitted to make images of him as other religious groups could of their gods. Thus the name of Yahweh had much the same significance for the worship of Israel that statues of the cult object had for other religions. The name of Yahweh came to be "hallowed," to be protected from any profane or "vain" use. This is to say that it was to be used only in worship. In time it was pronounced only once a year by the high priest on the Day of Atonement, and, the word "Lord" was substituted for it when the Old Testament was read aloud. This cult made Israel into a religious community. Now she only needed to know that Yahweh was righteous and expected righteousness of his people.

THE GIVING OF THE TORAH

There are three forms in which the story of the giving of the Torah to Moses on Mt. Sinai has come down to us. The JE version, which treats the Ten Commandments as what Moses received, appears in Exodus 19–24 and 32–34. The P account, in which directions for the worship of the Temple are what Moses receives, is intermixed with JE and occupies Exodus 25–31, 35–Numbers 10:10. The D version is set in the context of the speech that Moses makes to Israel on the banks of the Jordan River before the entry into the promised land. In it he alludes to the giving of the Ten Commandments which follow immediately: "The Lord our God made a covenant with us in Horeb [Sinai]. Not with our fathers did the Lord make this covenant, but with us, who are all here alive today. The Lord spoke with you face to face at the mountain, out of the midst of the fire, while I stood between the Lord and you at that time, to declare to you the word of the Lord" (Dt. 5:2–5). Here Moses associates with the Decalogue all the "commandments and statutes and ordinances" that the people are to live by in the land that God was giving them.

The Ten Commandments in JE are a concise way of summarizing all of Israel's duty toward God (1–4) and fellow human beings (5–10). They are stated in an absolute form ("thou shalt not") rather than in a conditional form in which the punishment for that particular sin is spelled out ("if you do _____, then _____ will happen to you"). This short summary of the total obligation to God and neighbor was probably used every seven years when the tribes gathered at Shechem to renew their covenant with Yahweh. The covenant was not thought of as a reward for obeying the commandments, but rather the commandments were seen to grow out of the covenant. This early form of the statement of Israel's obligations saw God as interested in every aspect of human life, the secular as well as the sacred, but did not make any effort to lay down a regulation to govern every situation. The legalism into which Israel was to fall by the time of the New Testament was still a long way off.

Deuteronomy, which is treated as a speech by Moses, is in fact a work that incorporates a number of sermons preached by Levites during the liturgical reform movement culminating in the legislation by King Josiah that restricted the offering of sacrifice to the Temple at Jerusalem. These sermons intend to spell out in some detail how the Ten Commandments are to be applied. Although the Old Testament never calls the commandments Torah, it does call these applications by that term. The term does not mean "law" in any English sense, but instead means the total revelation of God's will for his people. The threat perceived in Deuteronomy is from the orgiastic nature cults of surrounding peoples. The purpose of all the regulations is to safeguard Israel's exclusive allegiance to Yahweh. Such an allegiance is the only appropriate response to Yahweh's gift to Israel of the land of promise.

The P document is part of the historical work that makes up the Torah. It too is historical in its intention, seeking to account historically for elements of the worship of Israel, especially circumcision, Passover, and the status of Aaron and the Levites. The creation story in P implies that the worship of Israel was the reason why the world was called into existence. Much of the cult of the Temple is read back into the time of the Exodus; indeed, the law received by Moses at Sinai was cultic regulations. Thus the Tent of Meeting, where Moses received revelation from God, and the Ark of the Covenant, which came to contain the tablets of the Torah but which was basically the throne of God, were blended together into a mobile temple anachronistically operating during the Exodus.

The regulations that the P document says Moses received on Sinai have to do largely with priesthood and sacrifice. The most frequently offered sacrifice was for expiation or atonement. Understanding such sacrifices requires a deeper penetration into the Israelite approach to sin. Our modern distinction between ritual and moral law would have been meaningless to the ancient Israelites and they would have been equally hard put to comprehend our preoccupation with the motive of the sinner. Sin was thought of chiefly as a violation of sacred law, a turning of the clean into the unclean, that had punishment as its inevitable result and implied danger for the community as a whole as well as for the sinner. Modern reactions to the exposure of a live wire or the onset of an epidemic have more in common with the Israelite attitude toward sin than modern moral attitudes have. The attitude toward sin, then, is more materialistic than spiritual. Yet the mercy of God is seen in the fact that it is he who provides the remedy in the rites for expiation.

Each of these three understandings of what Moses received from God at Sinai expresses the attitude of its age toward what God expects of his people. The wandering tribes of Israel were thought to have everything they needed to be ready to enter into the land that God had promised to the patriarchs and to live there as his people. They looked back to their release from slavery in Egypt as their redemption by God. They looked forward to the conquest of the land under Joshua as the fulfillment of God's promise.

THE ADOPTED SON OF YAHWEH

Up to this point the history that has been discussed has been that summarized in the ancient creeds of Israel and narrated in the historical work comprised of the Pentateuch plus Joshua. The remaining historical works in the Old Testament have to do with the period after the entry into the land, the period of the judges and that of the kings. It is recorded in two sets of writings, the historical works of the Deuteronomist and of the Chronicler. The first deals with both judges and kings, while the latter is concerned only with kings.

The main article of belief for these later works picks up after the ancient creeds left off and has to do with a theological understanding of the monarchy. This understanding is stated most explicitly in the world of God that came to the prophet Nathan on the night after David said that he wanted to build a Temple for God. God told Nathan that another would build the Temple, but he went on to make a promise about the descendants of David.

> When your days are fulfilled and you lie down with your fathers, I will raise up your offspring after you, who shall come forth from your body, and I will establish his kingdom. He shall build a house for my name, and I will establish the throne of his kingdom forever. I will be his father, and he shall be my son. When he commits iniquity, I will chasten him with the rod of men, with the stripes of the sons of men; but I will not take my steadfast love from him, as I took it from Saul, whom I put away from before you. And your house and your kingdom shall be made sure forever before me; your throne shall be established forever. (2 Sam. 7:12–16)

There are two main themes to this promise: that David and his descendants will be adopted by God as his sons and maintained upon their throne forever and that they will also fall into sin and be punished by God.

The paradox of these two points—that the adopted son of Yahweh will be a sinner—is the theme of the Deuteronomist and makes possible the theological interpretation of the extraordinary documents he had to work with, especially the record of David's declining years and the provisions made for him to be succeeded. The "warts and all" portraiture of kings that occurs in the Deuteronomist history demands that the hand of God in history be shown in a new way. In this narrative it is impossible to recognize the "good guy" simply because he wears a white hat. God's providential shaping of events is not displayed through overt miracles. No, "the special field where this control of history operates is the human heart, whose impulses and resolves Yahweh in sovereign fashion makes subservient to his plan for history," as one writer put it.

Yet, since the sinful mortal on the throne is also the adopted son of God, his sinfulness will not cause his adoption to be revoked. God will keep him and his heirs on the throne of Israel forever. Thus the line of David is a new object of faith for Israel. On this article of faith all of the messianic hope of both Testaments will be erected.

THE THEOLOGY OF THE DEUTERONOMIST

This work, which relates the promise that David's heirs will be on the throne of Israel forever, ends with the destruction of Jerusalem and the king taken into captivity in Babylon. Thus the total work is constructed on the irony of what appears to be an unfulfilled promise. It can be understood as the effort of someone who believed the promise implicitly to come to terms with an overwhelming threat to its fulfillment.

The basic pattern that the Deuteronomist sees in history is more easily discernible in Judges than in Samuel and Kings. That pattern was that God would intervene in the history of his people to save them from a calamity. (In Judges the usual form of intervention was to send a charismatic leader who dealt with the immediate crisis and then retreated into the background.) For a while the people would be loyal to God and everything would go well for them. With the sense of emergency lost, however, they would fall into their old ways. Immediately they would find themselves in hot water again and cry to the Lord for help. He would then send another judge and the cycle would start all over.

The leadership of the judges was intermittent, while that of the kings was continuous. The cycle of apostasy, calamity, repentance, and redemption, therefore, is not limited to the time of one crisis, but is spread over several generations. The same pattern, however, does continue to operate; the only difference is that the cycle is longer. The Deuteronomist wrote during the Babylonian Captivity and was very much under the influence of Josiah's reform that dealt with the tendency of the people to participate in the orgiastic fertility cults of the Canaanites by restricting the offering of sacrifice to the Temple at Jerusalem. The apostasy into which the people fell, then, was always that of pagan worship. The sole criterion by which the Deuteronomist evaluated the kings of Judah and Israel, therefore, was their loyalty to the Temple at Jerusalem as the sole place of worship. This standard resulted in a very low rate of approval of the kings, with only Hezekiah and Josiah getting good marks, but the Deuteronomist had an ideal of David as the perfect king who was passionately devoted to the Torah. From this perspective the Babylonian Captivity could be seen, not as a revocation of the promise to David but as a disaster that Israel had brought upon herself, and from which she could still save herself if she would only repent and call upon God again.

THE THEOLOGY OF THE CHRONICLER

The Books of Chronicles, Ezra, and Nehemiah cover the time from David to the restoration of worship in Israel after the Babylonian Captivity. They were written near the time of the Priestly writer and share something of his preoccupation with the cult of the Temple. Their writer seeks to justify the role in the liturgy of the Temple of certain bodies who traced their institution to David, especially the Levitical Temple singers, of which the writer was a member. His treatment of history is very moralistic, devoted to showing that each generation will receive the punishment for its own guilt and that of its king. This focus on the "trees" of the guilt of the various generations leaves little sense of the shape of the "forest" of the entire history of Israel. The king is understood to have both royal and sacred responsibilities, and guilt in relation to Temple worship brought quick retribution. Yet David has been whitewashed into the ideal king and no embarrassing reminiscences remain of his treatment of Uriah or his inability to discipline his children. The Chronicler fell into the temptation of many religious educators since: to be so preoccupied with edifying that one loses contact with the life that the community of faith and its members have actually lived. The Chronicler preferred plaster saints to those of flesh and blood. Yet given this failing, the Chronicler helped downcast post-exilic Israel survive the trauma of exile and the uncertainties of return. We may question Ezra's policy of rejecting contact with foreigners as a sign of siege mentality, an all-too-human reaction of a people pressed by their neighbors. Yet there is a ray of hoped-for openness to God's Spirit in the stories of Jonah and Ruth, which come from this same period. Jonah is a parable with God's forgiveness of repentant foreigners, while Ruth, among other things, is a reminder that David's ancestor was herself a foreigner.

How God Is About to Act in Israel's Present (Prophets)

While the prophetic movement can be traced further back and has parallels with phenomena in other religions, the particular sort of prophecy normally associated with the Old Testament emerges on the scene during the reign of David. Nathan received the word of God and spoke it to David, at times in condemnation of David's sin. During the reign of Ahab and Jezebel in the northern kingdom, Elijah and Elisha were active. None of these earlier prophets wrote their oracles down, however. Thus the literature of classical prophecy did not begin until Amos began to preserve in writing the words that God had given him to say.

Two temptations need to be avoided if one is to understand the prophetic movement. The first comes from popular culture and is the temptation to regard prophets essentially as prognosticators, predictors of the future, whether in the personal sense of a fortune teller or in the long range sense of someone like Nostradamus. The other temptation comes from the biblical scholarship of the late nineteenth century, when evolutionary views dominated the study of history. This temptation is to regard the religion of the prophets as being very ethical and spiritual, in contrast to what was considered to be the materialistic preoccupation with cult in an earlier period.

Both views are mistaken. Prophets did speak of the future, but it was the immediate future of the nation that was considered. The prediction did not result from some special ability of the prophet but was given to him as God's judgment on the current situation against which he would take action. A decision of God to intervene is what is reported. Thus prophets were not engaging in extrasensory perception, but were serving as message carriers for God. The word they spoke was God's, although they were expected to supply in their own words the context in which the message was to be spoken. The message was not to individuals but to the nation, and it was about the immediate rather than the indefinite future.

While some prophetic oracles were against injustice, the reason they were was not to state general religious principles that are valid in all times and places but to report the judgment that God had revealed to the prophet about the particular situation. Furthermore, some prophets hardly referred to ethical shortcomings at all, but confined the abuses that they condemned to failures with regard to the cult.

Like the editors and writers of the historical books, the prophets saw the history of Israel to be the arena of God's action and revelation. Under divine inspiration, their work was to show the hand of God at work in the midst of contemporary events. Not surprisingly, the periods of their greatest activity are clustered around three major turning points in the life of the chosen people: the Assyrian conquest of Israel in the late eighth century, the Babylonian conquest of Judah in the early sixth century, and the return from the Babylonian Captivity in the fifth century. (It is instructive to compare the periods of prophetic activity with the the times when various layers of the historical books were being composed. See the chart on page 196.)

It is impossible to abstract a "theology of the prophets" or a "teaching on the prophets" that depicts a system of thought developed and shared by the prophets. While the prophets certainly share some common points of view about their own

	POLITICAL EVENT	HISTORICAL WORKS	PROPHETS
1300	Exodus	Pentateuchal traditions and poetic fragments	
1200			
1100			
1000	David	J Source Royal records begin on which Samuel and Kings are based	Nathan
900	Divided Kingdom	E source	Elijah, Elisha
800			Amos, Hosea, Isaiah, Micah
	Assyrian Conquest		
700		D Source (most of Deuteronomy)	Zephaniah, Habbakuk, Nahum
	Reform of Josiah		

	POLITICAL EVENT	HISTORICAL WORKS	PROPHETS
600			
	Babylonian Conquest		Jeremiah, Ezekiel
		Deuteronomist History (Judges, Kings, Samuel)	2 Isaiah
	End of Captivity		
500			
			Haggai, Zechariah Malachai, 3 Isaiah
	Nehemiah		
		P Source	
400	Ezra		
			Jonah
		Ezra, Nehemiah, Chronicles	
300			

role, the word of God, and other matters, almost the only attitude they consistently have in common is toward the covenants that God established with his people in the past. There is remarkable unanimity among the prophets that Israel can no longer depend on her election by God in the past because she has violated the covenant and thus abrogated the status with God that it gave her. The covenant to which northern prophets usually referred was the Sinai covenant of the Exodus, while southern prophets would refer instead to either the promise to David or the establishment of Jerusalem, built on Mt. Zion, as the holy place. Whichever former election was referred to, however, it was now considered to be no longer in effect. Usually, however, the prophets foresaw a new blessing of God in the future, which would be on a par with his mighty acts of the past, and that would restore Israel after she has been punished. Since a theology of the prophets in general cannot be written, it will be necessary to look at the teaching of at least the major figures to see how they advanced Israel's understanding of God.

First, though, it is helpful to remember the way in which the oracles of the prophets were put into the form in which we have them. Even though disciples of the prophets wrote their oracles down to be able to say "He told you so" when the prediction came true, very few of the predictions came true literally. Either the nation did not respond to the prophet's warning or something else happened that kept what the prophet had predicted from occurring. The response of later generations, however, was not to abandon the oracles as untrue. Rather, they were edited slightly and thus transposed from words about a particular situation in the past into words that have an enduring validity, words that say how God always views certain kinds of situations. The church still uses them to see how contemporary situations look from the perspective of God.

PROPHECY DURING
THE ASSYRIAN CONQUEST OF ISRAEL

The first prophet whose oracles were written down was Amos. Although the Assyrians were just beginning to move into the vicinity when Amos spoke, he could already anticipate the captivity of Israel. His concern, though, was not international so much as it was internal. He had come from the southern kingdom to speak God's word against Israel's disregard for the commandments. Seldom has righteousness been so indignant:

Hear this, you who trample upon the needy,
    and bring the poor of the land to an end,
saying, "When will the new moon be over,
    that we may sell grain?
And the sabbath, that we may offer wheat for sale,
    that we may make the ephah small and the shekel great,

and deal deceitfully with false balances,
    that we may buy the poor for silver
and the needy for a pair of sandals,
    and sell the refuse for wheat?" (Am. 8:4–6)

Amos saw visions of locusts and fire, two means of destruction that God would not use on Israel. A plumb line indicated that Israel did not measure up and was to be destroyed, and summer fruit signified that the time was ripe. Only at the end is there allowed a ray of hope that God will raise up the kingdom of David that has fallen.

A romantic tradition has interpreted Hosea's oracles to mean that his experience of forgiving a grossly unfaithful wife taught him about God's forgiving attitude toward Israel. The expression that was thought to mean "an immoral woman," however, only refers to a woman who participated in the fertility cult of the Canaanite god Baal, and thus could apply to most Israelite women of the time. It is this religious disloyalty (which Hosea understands as adultery on the part of Yahweh's bride Israel) that will bring destruction upon the country. Hosea did predict, however, that, deprived of all that made social and religious life possible, Israel would eventually repent and be restored by God.

The prophet regarded as the greatest theologian of the Old Testament was Isaiah. Coming from the court circle in Jerusalem, he prophesied in Judah during the period when Assyria conquered Israel to the north and became a next door neighbor just a few miles away. Isaiah upheld the law much as Amos had done, but he also saw the political implications of disobedience. The kingdom of Judah did not extend far beyond the boundaries of Jerusalem in his time and the election tradition on which he based his proclamation was that of the Holy City. God complained about Jerusalem in the way that a father complains of a disobedient son.

Isaiah did not assume that his message would be listened to. He had a strong belief that God would "harden the hearts" of the people of Judah so that they would become incapable of response. (This concept of God's being responsible for the resistance of people to his word goes back much earlier than Isaiah and continued to be important down through the New Testament period when it was used to account for the failure of Israel to respond to the message of Christianity.) Another basic motif in Isaiah's thought was the holy war. He tells of several attempts in the past to lay siege to Jerusalem that proved futile, not because Jerusalem defended itself so valiantly but because God intervened directly and saved his city. On the basis of this record Isaiah recommends that Judah make no effort to participate in the political horse trading going on at the time in order to protect itself by strategy. No, Judah should put itself entirely into the hands of God and, far from taking any action in its own defense, rely completely on him for protection. Isaiah thus called for faith of the ultimate degree. But, Isaiah says, Yahweh has his purpose, his plan, to save Judah by a work of his own, and only that work can prove effective. Indeed, the Assyrians are only a razor that God has borrowed to shave with, to punish his disobedient child, but he plans not to let the punishment go too far. The one who provided the punishment will also provide the rescue from it.

Not surprisingly, Isaiah's election traditions included not only Jerusalem (Zion) but David as well. The Davidic tradition on which he draws is represented in such "royal" psalms as Psalm 45. These psalms speak of the current heir of David in almost supernatural terms, building on the theme of the promise to David. Isaiah, however, looks to a king of the future (even though it was the very near future). On him all the gifts of God would rest, but he was to be especially the one who provided justice for underdogs. His reign would be characterized by the peace and the material abundance of the Garden of Eden. Needless to say, Isaiah's beautiful oracles on this theme furnished much of the vocabulary in which the hope for a Messiah was to be stated later and much, too, of the language by which the early church interpreted the role of Jesus.

It is worth noting that neither of Isaiah's predictions—that of Yahweh's intervention to prevent the fall of Jerusalem and that of the coming of a new David in the near future—came to pass. This failure of fulfillment did not, however, cause Isaiah or his disciples to lose faith. The failure was not God's but Judah's. Somehow the failure of the prophecy to come true could almost be seen as a proof of its truth.

PROPHECY DURING
THE BABYLONIAN CONQUEST OF JUDAH

Although Nahum, Habakkuk, and Zephaniah prophesied during the time of the break up of the Assyrian empire and the formation of the Babylonian, they were completely overshadowed by the great prophets of their time: Jeremiah, Ezekiel, and, during the Babylonian Captivity, Second Isaiah. Jeremiah deals with the threat from Babylon in terms of the election traditions of the north which focused around the Exodus and the giving of the Law at Sinai rather than in terms of the Zion tradition of Jerusalem. He did draw on the tradition of the promise to David, however. In his reliance on the northern election traditions Jeremiah shows much similarity to Hosea, with whom he may have had some connection. Like the other prophets, Jeremiah uses the traditions of former covenants only to say that they are revoked and that God in his mercy will establish a new covenant after Judah has been punished.

> Therefore, behold, the days are coming, says the Lord, when it shall no longer be said, "As the Lord lives who brought up the people of Israel out of the land of Egypt," but, "As the Lord lives who brought up the people of Israel out of the north country and out of all the countries where he had driven them." (Jer. 16:14, 15; see also 31:31–34)

A major difference between the prophecy of Jeremiah and that of his predecessors is in the form in which his oracles are given. Earlier prophets had made a sharp distinction between the word that God gave them to say and the context of their own words in which they pronounced it. In Jeremiah's work this distinction is no longer clear. His oracles are more poetic than earlier ones and the personality of the prophet himself is allowed to appear to a greater degree. Jeremiah makes it clear that he did not enjoy the role of a prophet and he complains to the Lord about all his suffering. He does not go on, however, as Second Isaiah will do, to see any saving effect of his suffering.

Like Hosea, Jeremiah sees his country's sin to lie in forsaking the worship of Yahweh to participate in the fertility rites of Baal, and he speaks of this disloyalty metaphorically as adultery. God will punish his people for this adultery and for social injustices by conquest from the north. At first he hoped for remission after punishment, but then he went through a period of bleak depression when he saw only the finality of the conquest. He regained hope later during the last days of his activity. He used symbolic actions as well as words to convey his message, as when he wore first a wooden and then an iron yoke to proclaim the captivity to come, and when, in promise of the restoration to come, he bought land when the conquerors were already besieging the city.

The restoration would involve the Israelite captives in Assyria as well as the Judaean captives in Babylon. In the new covenant that would be in effect then, God would not depend on the ability of people to obey his written Torah, but would instead write his Torah in their hearts, thus changing human nature. In those days a "righteous branch" of David will sit on the throne as God's representative on earth. This passage contributes much to future messianic thought since it speaks of the personal risk taken by God's anointed:

> I will make him draw near, and he shall approach me, for who would dare of himself to approach me? says the Lord. (Jer. 30:21)

Ezekiel was a contemporary of Jeremiah in Jerusalem before it fell, and was also a member of a priestly family. While Jeremiah was taken into exile in Egypt, Ezekiel was one of the first deportees to Babylon in 598. His prophetic activity covered the first thirty years or so of the Babylonian Captivity. Like exiles of all periods, he made every effort to keep informed about what was happening back home.

The prophecy of Ezekiel is unique because of his use of

symbolism. It is not uncommon for him to open a chapter with a proverb that he then applies to the current situation. Or he may offer an allegory, such as when he speaks of the restoration of Israel in terms of a valley full of desiccated skeletons into which God breathes new life. Oracles are given to him directly by God, who addresses him as "Son of man," which is correctly rendered by the Good News Bible as "mortal man." These oracles are often precisely dated and some come to Ezekiel in the form of a vision; he may, for instance, be transported to Jerusalem in such a vision. The Book of Ezekiel is precisely arranged, with chapters that pronounce doom on Jerusalem and Judah collected together (1–24), those that are against foreign nations also assembled (25–32), and those that speak of the restoration and salvation of Israel grouped at the end (33–48). We cannot be sure how much this arrangement is the work of Ezekiel and how much that of a later hand.

In speaking of the sin of his people that brought the captivity on them, he refers mainly to forsaking Yahweh to worship other gods. He can describe this either in terms of a vision in which he is transported to Jerusalem and sees worship being offered to other gods in the very Temple itself; or, in a manner that is reminiscent of Hosea and Jeremiah but which goes into much more graphic detail, he can speak of Israel as the bride brought up and made beautiful by Yahweh who makes him a cuckold with anyone she can. The sin of the country is punished by the removal of God's glory from the Temple; the climax of the restoration, depicted in a vision of a rebuilt Temple, is the return of God's glory to the Temple and to Jerusalem. Ezekiel draws on a tradition of the history of Israel that is different from that in the Pentateuch. (He could not draw on the Deuteronomist history for the period of the monarchy because it had not yet been edited.) On his source he imposes an interpretative scheme not unlike that of Deuteronomy: (1) God reveals himself, (2) Israel disobeys, (3) God punishes Israel, (4) he then restores his people.

Ezekiel considers his task to be that of a watchman who informs the city of approaching danger; if he is responsible in making the danger known, then those who do not listen and get caught have only themselves to blame. In this way Ezekiel becomes more concerned with the variety of individual response than any of his predecessors. He can speak of the fate of individuals as independent of that of the nation: fathers can eat sour grapes without having the teeth of their children set on edge. He sees himself as set between the people and God to protect them from his wrath, thus anticipating something of the thought of Second Isaiah about the Suffering Servant (see below).

His view of the restoration of Israel involves a vision of the rebuilt city of Jerusalem, including a new Temple. The conditions of life there will be idyllic, but the prosperity of that time is not described in the mythological terms that Isaiah uses. The line of David will be restored to the throne. And, finally, the nations that have not known Yahweh will recognize him and come to worship him.

We know next to nothing about the person who wrote chapters 40–55 of Isaiah. Since prophets are persons to whom God has given words to pronounce in the concrete historical situations to which God directed them, one could quibble over whether Second Isaiah (as scholars call this author, having nothing else to call him) was a prophet in the strict sense or was merely a religious writer. Since he obviously thought of himself as a prophet and even gave an account of his call to be a prophet, there is no reason why he should not be accorded that title, especially since his fifty-third chapter approaches the Gospel more closely than any other Old Testament passage.

The historical situation in which he wrote is abundantly clear. Cyrus, the king of the Medes and Persians (whom Second Isaiah twice mentions by name), has already conquered the Lydian kingdom of Croesus, whose wealth was of legendary fame. It will be only a matter of time before he will also conquer Babylon and allow the exiles to return home. Second Isaiah, then, has no doom to proclaim, but only a release from captivity. No wonder then that the tradition on which he draws most heavily is that of the Exodus, since the return of the captives looks to him like a new redemption with close parallels to the earlier one. He also makes reference to the two other election traditions, those of David and Zion, on which the other prophets draw. Furthermore, as mentioned above, this writer also sees creation itself as God's first mighty act in history in behalf of his people Israel. Living and writing in Babylon undoubtedly gave him the more universal perspective that allowed him to think in terms of creation.

This new exodus will be more glorious than the first and Yahweh will lead it in person (52:12). Mountains will be cut down and valleys filled in to make a smooth highway for the return of the exiles. This new salvation will not be of significance for Israel alone, because it will make other nations realize that Israel's God is the only true one, and they will flock to Jerusalem to worship him. Indeed, they will bring Israel's exiles home. Never has such language been employed to describe the glory that God has in store for his people. Second Isaiah knew that his fellow deportees whom he addressed had lost hope of restoration, so he told them of God's unfailing love for his people:

But Zion said, "The Lord has forsaken me,
    my Lord has forgotten me."
"Can a woman forget her sucking child,
    that she should have no compassion on the son of her
    womb?"
Even these may forget,
    yet I will not forget you.
Behold, I have graven you on the palms on my hands.
                                                    (Is. 49:14–16a)

Appearing in Second Isaiah, and probably the work of the same author, are five poems that refer to "the servant of Yahweh," and thus have come to be called the Servant Songs (42:1–4; 49:1–6; 50:4–9; 52:13–53:12). The Servant is someone who is called by God not only to have a mission to Israel but also to be "a light to lighten the gentiles." There has been much discussion about the identity of this figure who will bring foreigners to participate in Israel's salvation. Since, however, the Servant is one who suffers for the salvation of the Gentiles, it seems likely that the Servant is thought of as a prophet rather than a king. Contemporary thought did speak of vicarious suffering by prophets but not by kings. And, although Second Isaiah undoubtedly drew on his own experience, the chances are that he was speaking of a future ideal prophet, very similar to the "prophet like Moses" spoken of by Deuteronomy, especially since this prophet was to lead the new exodus. There is also some sense in which all of Israel is "the Suffering Servant." What was prophesied of this Servant corresponds so closely to what Jesus actually did, that these songs were to furnish New Testament writers with much of their best language for interpreting the work of Christ. This is especially true of the last of the Servant Songs.

> Surely he has borne our griefs
>   and carried our sorrows;
> yet we esteemed him stricken,
>   smitten by God, and afflicted.
> But he was wounded for our transgressions,
>   he was bruised for our iniquities;
> upon him was the chastisement that made us whole,
>   and with his stripes we are healed.
> All we like sheep have gone astray;
>   we have turned every one to his own way;
> and the LORD has laid on him
>   the iniquity of us all. (Is. 53:4–6)

PROPHECY AFTER THE EXILE

The Old Testament has not preserved any account of the return of the exiles from captivity in Babylon, but what we are able to infer does not suggest that the return had any similarity to the triumphal march predicted by Second Isaiah. When Nehemiah came some time later he found Jerusalem without a city wall. The Temple that had been reerected on the urging of Haggai and Zechariah was no match in splendor for the one built by Solomon or that envisioned by Ezekiel. Non-Jews or persons of mixed blood had taken over much of the land during the exile and continued to be a threat to the returning deportees. The conditions of life fell far short of the paradisial glory that had been predicted.

The author of Isaiah 56–66 appears to have been a disciple of Second Isaiah and is thus referred to by scholars as Third Isaiah. (It is possible that several writers were involved in the production of these chapters.) Since the prophecy of Second Isaiah had not yet been fulfilled in its entirety, Third Isaiah tried to assure Israel that this long overdue promise was about to be fulfilled. He thus tried to "bind up the brokenhearted, to proclaim liberty to the captives" (61:1). He had to deal with the fear of the downhearted people that the arm of the Lord was "too short" to help them. The problem, he said, was not the ineffectiveness of God, but their own sins.

Haggai and Zechariah are also looking for the imminent approach of Yahweh and the establishment of his glorious reign. The reason he has not yet come, according to them, is that the Temple has not been rebuilt. The people had been too busy trying to eke a living out of the scorched soil to feel that they had time, energy, or resources to give to that work. Haggai disagreed completely. The people had their priorities wrong; when God had a Temple to return to, he would then give prosperity to the land. As he saw it, the Temple was to be rebuilt initially for Israel alone, but soon all nations would come to worship at the Temple and to enjoy the benefits of Yahweh's reign. The nations would first be engaged in a final war and then God's rule would be inaugurated, with his anointed upon Israel's throne. Haggai and Zechariah both identify this *mashiach* ("anointed"; transliterated Messiah) as Zerubbabel, the grandson of the last preexilic king, but he never came to the throne.

Zechariah agrees with Haggai that the glorious reign of God will begin when the Temple is rebuilt. He foresees that time in a series of seven visions in the night. In the first, heavenly messengers search the earth in vain for any sign of the coming events. In the second, however, the lines of battle between the forces of God and his opponents are seen to be already drawn up. Next a man measuring the city for new walls is told to stop because the new city of God is to have no defense except the glory of God. After that the high priest Joshua—and, by implication, all the community of faith—is tried in a heavenly court, but God dismisses the charge and sets Joshua over the Temple. In the following vision the high priest and the king are seen as the two "sons of oil," the two anointed ones (messiahs) who represent God on earth. Evil is then removed from the community and God reigns completely.

The short Book of Malachai deals mostly with the carelessness of the community about cultic matters, an indication itself that the reform of Haggai and Zechariah has been successful. Though it speaks only twice about God's reign, it ends with a prediction that Elijah will return just before the terrible day of the Lord. This prediction is associated with John the Baptist in the New Testament. Jonah does not preserve the oracles of a prophet, but instead tells the story of a legendary figure who flourished in the time of the divided kingdom. In this parable Jonah the prophet appears in a much less flattering light than the foreigners to whom he was sent to preach repentance. God rebukes his messenger for becoming angry when the hated Ninevites did repent and receive divine mercy. The Book of Ruth, though not prophetic, similarly tells a story teaching Israel about attitudes of and toward foreigners.

Israel's Response to God's Actions in Her History (Writings)

This chapter began with a recognition that it is inappropriate to separate the meaning of the narrative portions of the Old Testament from the stories themselves since the meaning of a story is the story itself. That principle was a helpful guide in the presentation of the theology of the historical books because they do tell a story. It was also valid for the study of the prophetic books since the oracles of the prophets were attempts to give the view of God on particular concrete historical situations that implied stories. It does not do at all for the books remaining to be discussed, though, since they contain little narrative material. These remaining books are not coextensive with the final section of the Hebrew canon, the Writings, since some of the books in that section have already been discussed as historical works (e.g., Ezra, Nehemiah, and Chronicles). Another, Daniel, has already been discussed adequately. Finally, some reference will need to be made here to works that lie outside not just the Writings but the entire Hebrew canon, such as Ecclesiasticus.

The Writings that will be considered are Psalms, Job, Proverbs, and Ecclesiastes. With the exception of Psalms, they constitute what is called "the Wisdom literature." What wisdom means in this context will be discussed later. First, though, the Psalms. An ancient Latin expression, *lex orandi, lex credendi*, means roughly that the theological concepts expressed in the prayers people pray come nearer than any other set of concepts to being what the people actually believe. The one exception to that rule is in the hymns they sing. Just as we today can often express our beliefs most readily by quoting well-loved hymns, so much of the theology of the people of Israel is expressed in their hymns, the psalms. While the historical books tell how God has acted in the history of Israel, and the prophetic books relate his word on particular historical situations, the books that we now come to discuss, including Psalms, tell of Israel's response to these actions and words. Thus, from their perspective, they tell much of what it means to be human, and especially of what it means to belong to God's people.

PSALMS

The basic response of Israel to God, especially in the psalms, was praise. In the ancient creeds that lie behind the Pentateuch there was an element of praise for God's actions in Israel's history; this element is expanded in numerous psalms. Another early form of praise is in acceptance of the justice of God's punishment. Thanksgivings for personal benefits are additional occasions of praise. God is also praised for his manifestations in nature, whether in terms of his miraculous disruptions of the order of creation or in terms of that very orderliness. Even nature itself is called upon to share in offering to God a hymn of praise, as in the *Benedicite, omnia opera Domini,* "O all ye works of the Lord, bless ye the Lord; praise him and magnify him forever." Some psalms, such as 97 and 99, speak of God as king over nature and were used on special festivals that celebrated his enthronement, festivals that got as near as Israel ever officially came to the fertility religions of the ancient Near East. It was in God's creation and his mighty acts in her history that Israel had her profoundest experience of beauty. These psalms of praise were not thought of as an alternative to sacrifice as a means of worship, but were designed primarily to accompany sacrifice. This offering of praise to God was considered to be so characteristic of life that death was understood partly as the end of opportunity for an Israelite to offer praise and for God to receive it from that person.

A different, related, but much more comprehensive term than praise in the Israelite's understanding of life is *zedaqah*, a term usually rendered in English as "righteousness," but misleadingly so. To Western minds, righteousness is in relation to a norm or code of what is right; it is thus closely linked with the concept of law. Indeed, the Latin translation is *justitia,* from which we derive "justice." The importance of this concept for later theology is seen in the Reformation watchword, "justification by faith alone," which means that one achieves the status of *zedaqah* through faith rather than through obedience of law. Many of our theological controversies could have been avoided if we had realized that Israel did not understand righteousness in terms of deeds in conformity with a code of law, but as fulfillment of the claims that a relationship makes, as satisfaction of the obligations of a relationship.

It was appropriate to speak both of the righteousness of God (in terms of his gracious acts in behalf of his people) and also of human righteousness. This human righteousness could be manifested either in one's relationship to God or in one's relationship with other persons. Thus righteousness is a concept that embraces every aspect of life. It is far more comprehensive than law, since no code could provide a regulation for every situation that relationships involve. We must not think, however, that righteousness toward God was religious while righteousness toward persons was secular. All human relationships and obligations grow out of Israel's relationship with God.

Righteousness was not thought of as an abstract set of principles that had been reasoned out, but was regarded in a quasi-spatial way as a sphere that one could enter, inhabit, or leave. Thus one's righteousness was always objectively ascertainable. Someone was either righteous or unrighteous, with no gradations between the two states. In Psalm 24 we have a rite for the admission of pilgrims to the Temple area. They ask, "Who can ascend the hill of the Lord?" The answer is, in effect, those who keep the commandments, that is, those who are willing to abide by the obligations of Israel's relationship with Yahweh. This corporate examination later became personal, and an individual could be thought of as having his own relationship with God. Since righteousness was regarded as such an "either/or" thing, it seemed natural for psalmists and for Job to insist on their own righteousness in a way that sounds strange to modern ears. This righteousness is essentially manifested in obeying the commandments, but that does not make it a legalism, because the righteous loved God's will as it had been revealed to his people. It was only toward the end of the Old Testament period that questions began to be raised about whether it was difficult, or even impossible, for Israelites to be righteous.

When an Israelite failed to be righteous, the ill effects of his deed were not thought of as punishment or retribution; indeed, Hebrew has no word for punishment. The Israelites considered the consequences of an act to be an inevitable result of the chain of events that was set in motion when the deed was performed; they saw an inevitable connection between an act and its effects. Thus God did not punish the evil deed. He was, however, the cause of all that exists, including this connection between act and effect, and he could, if he wished, break that connection. Some of the strength of Israel's conviction that this connection existed came from the deep involvement of the individual in the community. What each member did had inevitable impact on the welfare of the community. Private chickens came home to a corporate roost.

Even so, there were always many occasions on which Israel as a whole and her individual members had to ask, "Why?" This was especially true in relation to death. Death, like righteousness, was thought of as a sphere, but this state was not so much a matter of absolute alternatives as righteousness was. Death began any time that God forsook a man. God's authority extended into Sheol, the place of the dead, but he was not worshiped there and thus life there had no meaning. Even so, death was by no means always regarded as evil sent from God; sometimes it was seen as the fulfillment of life.

A particular time that many in Israel asked "Why?" was when Judah was in imminent danger of falling to Babylon. They complained that God was not just in allowing that to happen. This complaint presupposed that God dealt with Israel as a unit. Ezekiel's response was the thesis that God deals with each person individually. Thus he reestablished the connection between acts and their consequences that their complaint had sought to sever. A slightly different form of the question arose in the psalmists's wonderment at the prosperity of the godless.

After the introduction of the concept that God deals with individuals instead of with people as a whole, the blessings that had been expected from God—the promise of the land, victory over enemies—came to be more difficult to specify. This change of orientation from community to individual had immense implications for worship; instead of being thought of as a corporate obligation it now had to be considered in terms of the participation of the individual. And it was much easier to conceive of God's abandonment of an individual than of his forsaking the nation. In the psalms we find prayers to be spared such a fate. Such fears did not haunt the unrighteous alone; some of the most devout came to think of themselves as "poor" and "wretched" before God and, in fact, these terms came to serve as synonyms for the righteous.

It was hard for Israelites to deal with suffering since it was threatening to life and they were life-affirming. There are psalms in which there is a change of mood from complaint to rejoicing because the suffering has been removed. There is, however, little sense of any beneficial results of suffering beyond the occasional recognition that one has grown closer to God while suffering. Sometimes this is expressed through the analogy of the pursued person who relies on the ancient provision for asylum and seeks refuge in a temple. Another metaphor, that of God as one's portion or lot, comes from the apportionment of the land among the twelve tribes. Since the tribe of Levi was the priestly tribe and lived off offerings to God, it had no land. Thus it was said that Yahweh was their "portion" or "lot."

The devout came to feel that even death was no threat to such deep communion with God. At first this was probably only a confidence that the one who prayed would be snatched back from death, although later it became an expectation that one would be restored to life after death. There is very little expectation of life after death in the Old Testament; what there is often comes from this deep sense of communion with God. It is also the only consolation and justification for the prosperity of the wicked in this life. The conviction that such deep communion with God must last beyond the grave is very different from the expectation of the general resurrection expressed in apocalyptic literature. At times the apocalyptic hope extended only to a resurrection of the righteous, but in Daniel 12:1–3 there is a belief in a resurrection to punishment for the wicked.

JOB

While Job belongs to the Wisdom literature, it is wholly devoted to the question of the sufferings of the righteous and the implications of these sufferings for the assumption that the results of an act are inextricably involved in the act itself. The framework of the book is an ancient story of a righteous man whose loyalty God allowed Satan to test. Even though Satan took away all of Job's wealth, caused his children to die, and inflicted upon him intense physical pain, Job remained loyal to God. This old story was put to new use in an effort to deal with the problem of the sufferings of the righteous. The traditional view that would have made Job guilty of some sin that brought on all his suffering is vigorously put forward in long speeches by three of his friends. Job, however, contends that he is completely righteous, not in the sense that he is sinless, but in the sense that he implicitly accepts God's good will toward humanity and his own highest joy has been in responding to that good will.

Job thus deals with the dilemma that Israel had come to in trying to understand how the righteous could suffer: he could not admit that any fault of his was responsible for this suffering, yet he knew that God cannot be judged by any standard of goodness outside himself, since his sovereign will is the only criterion of what is good. Job thus sees himself as caught between two aspects of the nature of God, in one of which God is his only good and in the other of which God is the cause of all his suffering. Job frames the issue in terms of a legal contest in which God is, on one hand, the accused, and, on the other, Job's attorney. What is at stake here is not general reflections on the problem of evil and suffering, but an impassioned effort to deal with experience that has brought one's faith to the severest test: How can one go on maintaining trust when such things happen? God's answer to Job is to the effect that, since no human being can understand all of the purposes of God in their complexity and interdependence, no one is in a position to pass judgment on God. The way in which God says this is to list the wonders of creation, thus showing the care God has for even his smallest creatures. The real answer at which Job arrives then is this reassurance that God is turned toward his creation in good will, however much appearances may be to the contrary.

PROVERBS

Proverbs is essentially a collection of short pithy sayings that sum up experience of life. Such sayings were not originated by Israel. Indeed, the biblical collection includes material that was borrowed all the way from Egypt to Babylon over the course of many centuries. This epigrammatic sagacity was communicated by teachers to students, and some of it had its home in the training of princes for their future duties as kings. It was closely connected with the circle of court officials who were the only members of society trained in writing. The need for such officials only emerged in the time of Solomon so it is not surprising that this kind of wisdom is especially associated with the king who imported the purveyors of it. His name is connected with Proverbs, Ecclesiastes, the Song of Solomon, and the apocryphal Wisdom of Solomon. The biblical proverbs are by no means limited to knowledge that is appropriate for a king, but include observations on life relevant to the upper classes in Israel's villages, and folk sayings as well. Their subject matter ranges from the sublimity of God to so mundane a concern as table manners. They concern not only grave matters such as murder and adultery, but also such ordinary things as dealing with intelligent or foolish people, with those seeking favors, and with women; as how to manage one's money, one's body, and one's tongue.

Some scholars in the past wished to drive a wedge between the society that produced the Pentateuch and the prophets and that which produced the Wisdom literature on the assumption that the former was religious and the latter had become secularized. The situation is very different, however. The worship of Israel remained very much in force, even if it had come to be thought of as a subject that required technical expertise and which thus lay outside the competence of the sages. They dealt with the matters of everyday life, but they knew that "the fear of the Lord is the beginning of knowledge" (Pr. 1:7, 9:10, 15:33). Their words are not divine commandments but advice to be tested against experience. When ethical judgments are made, there is always the assumption that what is good is also useful, that goodness "works." God is not referred to except in statements declaring that he tests the hearts of people, that certain practices please or displease him, and that human freedom is always limited by the divine will—statements on the order of "man proposes, but God disposes." These latter statements are not made in a mood of despair, but rather in recognition of the practical limits imposed on life.

What has been said about Proverbs up to this point applies much more to chapters 10–29 than to chapters 1–9. The kind of reflection on experience that wisdom means throughout most of the book gets merged in the early part with an ancient understanding of wisdom as a gift from God to particular persons, such as Joseph, for instance, or the builders of the Tent of Meeting. In these early chapters wisdom is treated as a path that leads to God—or, rather, as *the* path, since it is in the call to wisdom that salvation is offered to someone. This in itself indicates a radical departure from earlier views since previously salvation was always thought to be offered to the nation as a whole instead of to individuals. Wisdom becomes a way of life that can be personified as a sister or intimate friend. Wisdom is thus the way in which God makes himself present to his followers, but it is not God himself, it is still a creature. It is not even recognized as being identical with the Torah; that connection is not made before Ecclesiasticus in the Apocrypha.

This personification of Wisdom reaches its Old Testament pinnacle in Proverbs 8:

> The Lord created me at the beginning of his work,
>   the first of his acts of old.
> Ages ago I was set up,
>   at the first, before the beginning of the earth.
> . . . .
> When he marked out the foundations of the earth,
>   then I was beside him, like a master workman;
> and I was daily his delight,
>   rejoicing before him always,
> rejoicing in his inhabited world
>   and delighting in the sons of men.
>   (vv. 22, 23, 29b–31)

This personification is still a figure of speech, although later Jewish speculation will treat this figure of speech literally enough for early Christians to build on this foundation for their understanding of Jesus as the Son and Word of God who was the Father's agent in creation. At the stage of Proverbs 8, though, while Wisdom was the first created thing, she was not yet seen to be an agent of creation (as she was to be treated in the apocryphal Wisdom of Solomon). In Proverbs the relation of Wisdom to creation is described in terms of play.

Creation is very important for all theological thought about Wisdom because Wisdom focuses much more upon empirical observation than upon God's revelation through history as understood in the Pentateuch. Thus the content of revelation came to be knowledge of God as creator. This revelation was totally unmythical and, indeed, had a strong rational and intellectual aspect, even though it could not be arrived at by the unaided human mind. Still it was a faith appropriate for an age when intellectual needs were strongly felt.

ECCLESIASTES

The movement which ceased to look for God in Israel's saving history but sought him instead in creation began as early as the monarchy when the recorder of the search for David's successor saw the purposes of God concealed deeply within the interactions of fallible men and women. The search for God in creation, however, proved as difficult as that in the saving history. Just as Job saw God's purposes to be concealed, so the Preacher of Ecclesiastes dealt with similar difficulties. He investigated life and discovered that the searches for wisdom, riches, work, or fame were equally pointless. He thus had no way to demonstrate that life was meaningful. That does not mean at all that he did not believe in God or that God had a purpose for the world. What he did believe was that God's action and purpose was completely hidden from him and that he thus had no access to the meaning he knew life had. His situation, then, was tragic, even though he did not resort either to self-destruction or oblivion through pleasure. He lives on, knowing that there is a meaning to life, but that he cannot find it.

· 10 ·

What the Bible Teaches:
New Testament

If an average Christian with no particular background in modern biblical study were to be asked, "What is the most important part of the Bible?," the reply would likely be, "The teaching of Jesus." This answer makes a lot of sense. Christians do believe that God the Son became the human being Jesus of Nazareth in order to reclaim a human race that had become alienated from the Father. The assumption, then, is that if God said it, it has to be so, and also that it has to be the most important thing to say. There are, however, at least two basic problems with that. The first is theological: classical Christian doctrine holds that our Lord's human consciousness did not have access to his divine omniscience. Thus, while his human words could be expected to be consistent with the Father's will, they were nevertheless human words, and thus conditioned by the limits of human knowing.

The other problem comes from an insight, achieved by recent scholarship, into how the Gospels were written. The Gospels were written between forty and seventy years after the resurrection, and thus they understand the ministry of Jesus in the light of the resurrection. This is to say that they read back into the ministry insights that no one had at that time, insights that came only after the resurrection. There are a number of indications in the Gospels that no one, not even his closest disciples, really understood Jesus during his ministry. This means that the Gospel records of the teaching of

Jesus have been filtered through the church's postresurrection insight and thus do not represent precisely the way his words were understood when they were originally spoken. A case in point is the assumption the Gospels make that these words were addressed to the church, which only came into existence after the resurrection, rather than to the opponents, potential followers, and poorly comprehending disciples who heard him originally.

This is to say that the identification of what Jesus actually said is a work of painstaking historical reconstruction. This does not mean that one has to be a scholar to gain from the Gospels the good news of salvation in Jesus Christ. It does mean that if we want to know as well as we can what Jesus himself said, we must depend on the work of scholars. As one of them pointed out, the content of the message of Jesus differed from that of the early church. The early church proclaimed Jesus Christ. Jesus himself proclaimed that the kingdom of God was breaking into history and had little to say about his own role in that event. Modern Christians assume that there is no basic inconsistency between these two messages; they see Jesus' role in the inauguration of the kingdom of God to be so necessary that we can only enter it through him. But the consistency of the two messages does not eliminate the difference in formulation. If, then, we want to know what Jesus taught, we must try to get behind the Gospel record.

The Teaching of Jesus

THE KINGDOM OF GOD

As already suggested, the one absolutely key concept in the teaching of Jesus is the kingdom of God. The importance of this term has been recognized only recently. In earlier times it was assumed that the kingdom of God was essentially the church and more recently it came to be thought that the kingdom was a perfect human society to be inaugurated on earth. Part of the difficulty in understanding this term for those who speak English is that in our language "kingdom" denotes a country, the realm of a monarch. The Greek word that the King James translators rendered as "kingdom," however, has more reference to a quality of God, his "kingship." While this kingship is a quality that God always has, its effectiveness in human history is more apparent at some times than others. When this effectiveness becomes inaugurated, God's kingship may then be spoken of from a human perspective as his reign or rule. When Jesus speaks of the kingdom of God, he refers to this reign or rule and his message about it is that at that moment, in his ministry, the inauguration of God's kingly rule is taking place.

The thought world against which this concept is to be understood is the apocalyptic movement that began with the writing of Daniel and continued in many of the apocryphal writings and Dead Sea Scrolls. As indicated above (see p. 48), the basic concept of apocalyptic is that of two ages. The present age is thought to be an evil age under the domination of the forces of evil, Satan and his unclean spirits or demons. Their control is to be broken, however, in a battle between the forces of good and evil that will involve angels and demons at a supernatural level and Israel and its enemies on a human one. The forces of good will win, they will judge and punish the forces of evil, and then history will be under the control of the forces of good. In this "age to come," God will be in obvious control of history. Thus that time can be referred to as the time of his reign or rule.

There are significant differences between Jesus' teaching about the age to come and that of apocalyptic. The first is that the apocalyptists always saw the inauguration of the kingdom to be something in the future, even if that future was considered to be just a few years away. Jesus, however, spoke of it as something that was already coming into effect. Later it will be necessary to consider the degree to which the kingdom was a present or future concept in the teaching of Jesus. Now it is enough to say that the change was already taking place and that the difference at most was only that between "in your midst" and "at hand" (right around the corner). In other words, what the apocalyptists promised, Jesus announced as being fulfilled.

Another difference between Jesus' teaching about the kingdom and that of the apocalyptists is that they saw it as having political implications in a way that he did not. Daniel, for instance, looked to a future deliverance in which the yoke of Syria would be removed from Israel's neck, a time when the control of Antiochus Epiphanes over the Temple would be at an end. Many of Jesus' contemporaries thought of the Romans as the forces of evil to be defeated. Since Jesus did not identify God's cause with the national cause, he did not use the vocabulary of warfare to describe the inauguration of the kingdom. The nearest to warfare he got was in curing the sick who were brought to him and, especially, casting out unclean spirits. It was in these expulsions that he demonstrated that their control over history had been broken and that of God was being instituted: "But if it is by the finger of God that I cast out demons, then the kingdom of God has come upon you" (Lk. 11:20). The only effect of these evil powers mentioned in the Gospels is to cause illnesses that from our point of view would be considered as both physical and emotional. Thus there is no identification of demons with the military invader as there was in apocalyptic, nor were they thought of as beings that tempt people to sin, as folk thought came to regard them.

THE AUDIENCE OF JESUS

Even a superficial reading of the Synoptic Gospels, however, shows that unclean spirits were by no means the only enemies of Jesus. Those who opposed him most bitterly, and who eventually conspired to have him killed, were not foreign invaders but the religious leaders of his own people. In the synoptics, this religious opposition to Jesus is usually referred to as "the scribes and Pharisees" before Holy Week when they were joined by the Temple hierarchy. They represented a religious movement that saw the main revelation of the Old Testament to be a system of commandments that covered every aspect of life. Essentially, the Pharisees felt obligated to obey at all times the rules for ceremonial purity observed by priests when they were officiating in the Temple.

Not surprisingly, they considered Jesus to be a serious threat to everything holy, and they devoted themselves to putting an end to him before he could put an end to their religion.

Jesus did not regard such punctilious ceremonial observance to be either what would bring in the kingdom or a sign that it had arrived. For him the essence of the kingdom was in relations: love of God and love of other persons. He recognized, therefore, that he would not find receptive ears among the members of the religious establishment. Instead, he directed his message to the outcasts of his society. Some of his followers were prostitutes and others were corrupt politicians who not only defrauded their own people but also broke all standards of ritual purity by defiling contact with the Roman invaders for whom they worked. He addressed himself principally, though, to the majority of the people who belonged to no religious party but who made up *Am-ha-aretz*, "the people of the land." To them in their suffering he proclaimed his words of consolation.

A NEW LAW

Some modern interpreters of Jesus' teaching have found this threatening instead of consoling. To them the ceremonial law of the Pharisees is far easier to keep than the radical demands of God revealed by Jesus. How can anyone turn the other cheek when struck, or love one's enemies, or go a second mile when asked to go one? How can one have the absolute trust in God that takes no thought for what one will eat or wear tomorrow? It was hard enough to be pure; how can one be perfect? This is to say that these interpreters understand the teaching of Jesus to be a new law that is impossible of fulfillment.

At any rate they take it more seriously than others who consider the Sermon on the Mount, for instance, to contain timeless religious and ethical principles that are always to be recommended as standards for human conduct. These latter miss the essential point that Jesus' teachings are rules for behavior *in the kingdom of God*. Obedience only becomes possible because God's rule over history is being inaugurated.

Thus Jesus' standards are not to be thought of as laws that must be obeyed, but as an invitation to experience what life can be like when it is lived in the kingdom. Such a way of life is not the way that one earns a reward, but is itself the reward. Jesus told his hearers, in effect, that they did not have to be content with the pettiness and futility of life as they were living it, they could move onto a whole new plane of the possibilities of human existence.

A PRESENT OR FUTURE KINGDOM?

Any such description of the blessings of the kingdom is bound to raise the question of when those blessings could be enjoyed. Was the kingdom already present during the ministry of Jesus or was it yet to come? Jesus used expressions that support both interpretations. He said, "the kingdom of God has come upon you," (Lk. 11:20) and "the kingdom of God is in the midst of you," (Lk. 17:21), but he also said that it is nearby (Mk. 1:15). What is nearby, of course, is not yet here.

Even though the editorial activity of the Gospel writers makes it impossible for us to be certain about the chronology of Jesus' ministry, the Gospel narrative does not completely obscure some evidence that makes this apparently contradictory usage comprehensible. Jesus is depicted as sending the Twelve out on an apparently urgent mission to extend his own proclamation of the kingdom. There is a strong sense of a race against the clock. Yet when they return, little is made of the results of their mission. There is, however, a change in activity. After that time Jesus drew apart from the crowds and tried to spend all of his time with the Twelve. Shortly afterwards, he predicts for the first time that he will go to Jerusalem and die. While this sequence undoubtedly reflects the evangelist's editorial hand, it still appears overwhelmingly likely that in the preaching of Jesus and the Twelve Israel had an opportunity to enter into the kingdom, an invitation that was declined. If Jesus' offer had been taken, the gap between the present and the future aspects of the kingdom would have been no longer than that between the issuance of the invitation and its acceptance.

As it was, Jesus was forced to another expedient in inaugurating the kingdom. He had to go up to Jerusalem. Scholars generally assume that the three predictions of his death that Jesus makes in Mark can be as detailed as they are because they are "prophecies after the event." That is, the early church, knowing what had happened, read foreknowledge of that back into Jesus' ministry. Yet this does not mean that Jesus did not know that going up to Jerusalem would result in his death. Supernatural knowledge would not be necessary to regard that as probable. What is less certain is how that knowledge was related to Jesus' conviction that he must go to Jerusalem.

Did he go up for some other purpose that made such a risk worth taking? Or did he believe that it would be through his death that his mission was accomplished? It is impossible to say.

Scholars have shown that the interpretation of Jesus' death in terms of the Suffering Servant of Second Isaiah occurs in the editorial passages of the Gospels rather than in the sayings of Jesus, but Jesus still could have believed that his death would inaugurate the kingdom. It seems unlikely that his own expectation was so detailed as to specify his resurrection. He probably knew only that through his death the Father would achieve his purpose and that his own ministry would thus be vindicated. That was enough. That was what could be done to bring in the kingdom. The idea that there would be a long interval between his resurrection and second coming during which the kingdom would be only partially in effect belongs to the reflection of a later age and would have no place in the thought of Jesus.

Yet even during the ministry the kingdom was already present to some degree. Knowing this is essential to understanding the miracles of Jesus, especially the expulsion of unclean spirits. Jesus' miraculous power was not understood as something that he possessed in his own right. He was no ancient equivalent of Captain Marvel. Rather, his miracles were the proof of his proclamation that the reign of God was breaking into history. His power over the demons was *prima facie* evidence that their control over history had been broken. The power of the kingdom was already present in the ministry of Jesus. It was displayed not only in his miracles but also in his ability to forgive sins. Thus there were both present and future aspects to the kingdom in the teaching of Jesus.

TEACHING BY PARABLES

Another way in which the presence of the kingdom was experienced was in some of the parables that Jesus used in his teaching. The rabbis before him had used parables of a sort to illustrate their thoughts, but no one else had used them in the way that Jesus did. All parables make use of an analogy between something that is well known with something that is less known. By pointing out the resemblance the parable allows the less known thing to be understood in terms of what it has in common with the better known thing and thus to become better known itself.

There are two ways in which Jesus' use of parables can be described. One is to say that he brought together elements that no one previously had thought could be associated with one another and thus opened up new vistas of thought. For example, in the Parable of the Good Samaritan he made a hero out of a member of a despised race. Before that it had not occurred to any of Jesus' hearers that goodness and Samaritans could be brought together in the same concept since Samaritans were bad by definition. Jesus' parable forced them to think what had previously been unthinkable for them.

The other way of describing Jesus' use of parables is to say that they functioned as arguments. Jesus began a parable by suggesting an analogy. For the parable to work, the analogy had to be recognizable to the hearer as accurate. Thus in offering an analogy, Jesus had to make an initial concession to the point of view of his hearers so that they could agree that he and they were talking about the same thing. In the Parable of the Prodigal Son, for instance, Jesus says, in effect, that the Am-ha-aretz, like the younger son, have received exactly what they deserved.

After the initial concession, however, Jesus calls on his

hearers to look at the same situation from a different perspective. He asks them to look at the prodigal, not in terms of what he deserved, but in terms of a father's love for a lost son. He was deprived of the joy he took in his child. God looks at the *Am-ha-aretz* in the same way. When his hearers do that, then they must choose whether in the future they will view them in the old way or in Jesus' way. Those who accept Jesus' perspective as more adequate have already experienced the presence of the kingdom, because they now see people the way that God sees them.

THE LORD'S PRAYER

Once someone is familiar with Jesus' teaching about the kingdom, it becomes obvious that the prayer that he taught his followers is to be understood in terms of that teaching. Scholars agree that the way it appears in Luke is most original. It can be translated as follows:

Father,
> May your name be held in reverence,
> May your kingdom come.
Give us this day the bread that belongs to it.
And forgive us our sins,
> for we also forgive everyone who is indebted to us.
And do not bring us to the last great trial.

The time when God's name will be revered will be when the kingdom has come. One of the most common ways of talking about the time of the kingdom was in terms of a great feast, since the joys of the fruitful earth and human conviviality are powerful metaphors of all that people long for. The petition for "daily bread" is one of the most difficult phrases to translate and understand in the Greek New Testament. Nevertheless, any reference to food in a passage so laden with language about the kingdom cannot escape association with the Messianic Banquet, as the feast is called. The forgiveness of sins was also associated with that time. In apocalyptic thinking generally, a last great trial was expected before the coming of the kingdom.

THE LAST SUPPER

One of the most scandalous activities of Jesus, from the perspective of his opponents, was that he often had meals with *Am-ha-aretz* and sinners, heedless of the risk of ritual impurity in eating nonkosher food. These meals also are to be understood in the light of the Messianic Banquet. Forgiveness of sins, one of the blessings of the kingdom, was being already enjoyed in the ministry of Jesus. The blessings of the kingdom were present in these meals and the kingdom was thus establishing a beachhead in history. These meals are part of the context in which we are to understand the Last Supper. Another part of that context is the Passover, the meal celebrated annually for the ritual recalling of release from bondage in Egypt at the Exodus. By the time of Jesus, Passover had come to take on a future reference to the Messianic Banquet in addition to its backward look at the Exodus. While many other things could be said about the institution of the Eucharist, these two points show that it derived part of its meaning from Jesus' teaching about the kingdom. In it Christians have a foretaste of the kingdom.

THE ROLE OF JESUS IN INAUGURATING THE KINGDOM

So far nothing has been said about how the ministry of Jesus was related to the inbreaking of the kingdom. The reason is that Jesus said very little about it. Mark does not portray Jesus as accepting the traditional title of Messiah until his trial (14:61, 62) and has him explicitly reject the title Son of David (12:35–37). Some special relation to the Father is indicated, however, in his unique habit of addressing him as *Abba,* an intimate Hebrew term that should almost be translated "Daddy." Furthermore, there are massive implications about his role in his assumption that it is through his proclamation of it that the kingdom breaks in.

If there is any special title that is a clue to Jesus' self-understanding it is *Son of Man.* In the Gospels it is virtually the only term that he uses in reference to himself, and only he uses it. Unfortunately, scholars are in utter disagreement about the meaning of this term. Some help might be expected from the way that the Old Testament uses the expression, but there it is used with at least three different meanings. By the rules for interpreting Hebrew poetry, its use in Psalm 8:4 means a human being. In Hebrew usage generally a "son of" something is a member of that category. In Ezekiel, though, Son of Man is the term by which the prophet is consistently addressed by God, and thus may be a technical term. In Daniel 7:13 "one like a son of man" comes with the clouds of heaven to the throne of God. There he is given "dominion and glory and kingdom" (7:14) over all people which will last forever. In verse 25 "the saints of the Most High" are those to whom kingdom is given. These saints seem to be the martyrs killed by Antiochus Epiphanes before the Maccabean rebellion. Thus Son of Man seems to refer here to a future, glorified figure but also to a group of slain heroes of the faith. A later work not included in the Apocrypha also makes much of a future, glorified Son of Man, but he is identified with one of the ancestors of Noah, Enoch (Gen. 5:24; the Similitudes of Enoch).

In the Synoptic Gospels Jesus is depicted as using the term Son of Man in three kinds of statements: (1) present tense statements in which the term means no more than "I," e.g., "the Son of Man has authority on earth to forgive sins" (Mk. 2:10), (2) predictions of his death and resurrection (Mk. 8:31), and (3) predictions of a future, glorified figure coming on the clouds (Mk. 13:26, 27). These have been interpreted in different ways by various scholars. Some assume that Daniel and the Similitudes of Enoch indicate that apocalyptic thought spoke of a future, glorified Son of Man. Jesus thus must have been alluding to that figure, so only the passages that refer to such a figure are genuine sayings of Jesus about the Son of Man. If only these are genuine, there is no indication that Jesus identifies himself as the Son of Man; he is only predicting someone in the future.

The interpretation just given was almost standard for a while, but it has been challenged by a variety of others. One is that the only guide to what Jesus meant by Son of Man is his own usage. By it he seems to mean the person who will keep the promises that he makes. Jesus did not identify himself as that person, but the early church soon did. Another view is that Jesus did not use the term at all; it comes from the early church's meditation on Daniel 7:13 after it had come to believe in the ascension through its interpretation of Psalm 110:1: "The Lord says to my Lord: 'Sit at my right hand till I make your enemies your footstool.' " Still another interpretation has it that Jesus' understanding of his mission was related to a widely circulated myth of the ancient Near East about the primeval man who was God's pattern for the creation of man.

All of these theories have serious shortcomings. When the Gospels are so careful to use Son of Man as Jesus' only self-designation and yet do not allow anyone else to refer to him by that term, it seems utterly unlikely that he did not use it. Also, Jesus' recognition that it is his preaching that will inaugurate the kingdom implies an awareness that he has a very exalted role. Since it is clear that people in the early church—and people today—had difficulty understanding the term, perhaps Jesus chose it for the very reason of its ambiguity. It forced on his hearers no interpretation of who he was; they had to make of him what they could. All of the traditional terms such as Messiah or Son of David fell so far short of what he was that they would have been misleading. He therefore refused to tell them who he was, forcing them to recognize for themselves the full reality of his being. Or, from their own inner lack to miss it. Such an approach would have been consistent for the one who taught in parables and, by doing so, made it possible for people to enter by anticipation into the kingdom.

St. Paul: The First Christian Theologian

At one time it was fashionable to make a distinction between the religion *of* Jesus and the religion *about* Jesus. Jesus was supposed to have taught a simple belief in the fatherhood of God and the brotherhood of man. Later theologians, especially St. Paul, were thought to have debased that into a complex creed in which Jesus was assigned divine status, and elaborate rituals were devised that transformed the loose fellowship of followers of Jesus into a religious institution. While it is true, as observed above, that Jesus proclaimed the kingdom of God while the early church proclaimed him, it is also true that Jesus' teachings implied his own unique status. It only took the resurrection to make it apparent to his followers that, since Jesus was the bringer of salvation, he was to be preached as the inaugurator of the kingdom.

Yet this emphasis on the bringer of the kingdom instead of the kingdom itself means that Paul's theology is framed differently from that of Jesus. Further, Paul gives little evidence of knowing much about Jesus' earthly life, writing as he did before the Gospels appeared. For him it was enough to know "Jesus Christ and him crucified" (1 Cor. 2:2). Two other characteristics of the thought of Paul also give a paradoxical appearance to his writings. On the one hand, he did not sit down to write systematic treatises, but intended instead to help his churches in dealing with problems that arose when he was not around. Thus we do not know how he related some of his thoughts to others. Yet he was the first Christian theologian in the sense that, believing as he did that even practical problems of the church are ultimately theological problems, he sat down and thought through the theoretical perspective from which a particular problem was to be viewed. In doing this, he did more to show the implications and interrelations of Christian affirmations than anyone before him. Indeed, all Christian theology since has been greatly in his debt.

Ideally, a study of St. Paul's theology would look at his formulations in relation to the practical situation that elicited such thought, but limitations of space require an effort to synthesize views stated in different letters.

THE HUMAN CONDITION

Since, before he was converted to Christ, Paul had been a Pharisee trying to observe all of the minutiae of the code for ritual purity, much of his understanding of the salvation that Jesus brings is stated in terms of what it means to have *zedaqah*, to be counted as righteous. He harks back to creation and the potentiality for righteousness that Adam enjoyed in the Garden of Eden. Adam, however, did not take advantage of his opportunity, but instead asserted his own will against that of God. Thus he fell, and all humanity since has been in sin, in the state of insisting on our own will in preference to the will of God.

When Paul was a Pharisee, he thought that the observance of the Torah could restrain his sin, save him from it, and show him what was good. After conversion, however, he saw it differently. Neither he nor anyone else could possibly obey the Law. All the Law could really do was to serve as a standard by which people could come to an awareness of their sin. The grip of sin on a person's soul was so strong, however, that even this awareness led one more deeply into sin rather than away from it. It did so by giving the impression that one could obey the Law and thus be saved. Thus, far from bringing righteousness, the practical effect of the Law was to inspire covetousness and a desire to trust in one's own capacities. While Israel alone had received the Law and had become conscious of sin through it, the Gentiles had received enough knowledge of God's requirements through creation to be held equally responsible for their failure to do his will. Thus all peoples were equally under sin before the coming of Christ.

In his discussions of the human condition, Paul uses many terms in a special way. Some definitions will assist anyone who reads his letters. He can use *world* to refer either to the stage on which human life is acted out or to humanity in general. As the scene of human sins, it can mean the realm of Satan. Paul has a number of terms that refer to human beings. When he says *body* or *spirit*, he does not imply a Greek understanding in which these are the two parts of one person; rather, each term means an entire human being viewed from one aspect. *Body* thus refers to an entire person seen from the perspective of always being under a master, whether it is sin, death, or the Lord. *Soul* denotes a person as one who has a manner of life, feeling, or disposition. *Spirit* focuses on a person as someone with consciousness, intelligence, and understanding. *Heart* refers to a person as a creature with a will.

Sin is to be distinguished from *sins,* wrongful acts. It is the inclination to perform such acts and, more basically, it is hostility to God. By the same token, *flesh* often refers to a person whose transience is in contrast with God's eternity. It can also refer to the powers under which the person has become captive—sin and death. Death is not just dying; its power over humanity is already felt in life. Sin and death have dominion over unredeemed humanity. The human condition, then, is a desperate, helpless state, a need for redemption.

The need of humankind is for righteousness. Only God has that trait and only he can make it available to men and women. God can attribute his righteousness to people and they become righteous. Their righteousness never becomes their possession because they are never the source of it, but they acquire it nevertheless. And they do so because God wants them to. God's wanting persons to share his righteousness and his conveying it to them is what is meant by *grace.* Paul gives no reason for the graciousness of God. He could have said that God is gracious because of his love for his children, but then Paul would have had to account for God's love. Why should God love such unrighteous creatures? Since there ultimately is no explanation for the grace of God, Paul gives none. It is just the way God is. The sin of Adam had created a breach between human beings and God. Human beings were incapable of healing it and so God healed it himself. This healing can be called *justification* (Latin: *justus* = righteous, *facio* = make), or it can be called *reconciliation* because of the healing of the breach. The means that God used to achieve this justification and reconciliation was the death of Jesus Christ.

The means by which people receive justification is faith. This does not mean that faith is a virtue that God rewards with justification. Paul never discusses what faith is like in abstraction. For him faith is always faith *that.* . . . Faith is always believing that something is so. And that something is that God has kept and will keep his promise to make his righteousness available to us, even though we have done absolutely nothing to deserve it and, in fact, are incapable of doing any such thing. Faith, then, is a radical trust in God. It thus is the abandonment of any claim of being able to save oneself or to be worthy of God's consideration. It is relying humbly upon God. It is believing that the Gospel is true.

Faith implies many things about the life of the Christian. It means that he or she is at peace with God. This peace does not imply that God never allows the faithful to suffer, but that faith gives them the perspective on their sufferings to know that such threats are never ultimate. Again, faith is death to sin; one continues to be tempted and to succumb; one no longer struggles against sin as a slave, but as one who has been set free. Thus there is freedom from the Law, because one no longer believes that one can or needs to earn acceptance by obeying its code. Faith does its work through love—although love does not become a new precondition for justification; it is rather a fruit of justification. This faith is always confidence in what God has done and is doing in Jesus Christ. Paul thus can speak of the state of justification as being "in Christ." This can mean no more than being a Christian or being a member of the church, or it can be the comprehensive term for describing what someone has called "the new basic and all-comprehending reality into which believers are transferred" once they accept justification.

THE GOSPEL

The way that all these blessings are made available is through the preaching of the Gospel. In one sense, the Gospel is the proclamation of something that happened in the past, the death of Christ on the cross. Yet, in another sense, it is the proclamation of a present possibility and a future hope, since it is by hearing what God did in Christ in the past that we are able now to lay hold on what he accomplished for us and to live in hope of its future completion. Thus what Jesus did then on the cross is made present in all its saving power when the word about it is proclaimed and believed. Paul knew how hard his contemporaries—Jewish and Greco-Roman—would find it to believe that it was actually through the execution of a criminal that the Father showed his grace and his power. Both alike wanted God to conform to their expectations before they would accept an action as his. But Paul knew that no one could ever receive God's gift who had not abandoned all such reliance on human standards of judgment and thrown himself completely upon God's mercy. This reliance is not a sacrifice of the intellect, but is instead a recognition of what it means for God to be God and a willingness to have it so.

THE CHURCH

The salvation that the Gospel proclaims is experienced as a present reality within the fellowship of the church. The Greek word that is translated as "church" was used in the Greek Old Testament to render a Hebrew word that referred to Israel when it was assembled before God—for instance, at Sinai. While St. Paul did not start the church, neither did Jesus during his ministry. The church as such could not exist before the resurrection because, from the human side, it is a response to the resurrection. It was not until after it became clear that someone could become a Christian without first becoming a Jew that the church saw itself as distinct from Judaism; Christians continued to participate in the Temple and synagogue worship for at least a generation after the crucifixion. While an individual congregation could be called a church, the term could also be used to refer to the whole body of Christians. The more inclusive usage pointed to the essential truth that there is one body of Christians throughout the world.

Paul saw the church as the inheritor of all God's promises to Israel. Thus it had access to God through his Spirit who dwells in the church. The impact that the indwelling Spirit has on the church was understood by Paul in a way that was consistent with the rest of this theology. As one writer put it: "For Paul God's Spirit is not the supernatural power that enables a man to transcend his earthly life and its limitations: instead, it is the power of God who shows himself mighty in lowliness and weakness." Paul had two groups of opponents: one that wanted Christianity to relapse into the legalistic piety of the scribes and Pharisees, and another that assigned status on the basis of religious experience. He saw both of these as efforts of people to make themselves independent of the mercy of God. The Spirit of God could not be behind any such movement.

Paul's attitudes toward worship, the principal activity of the church, had the same tendency to resist anything that gave Christians grounds for boasting, and to reinforce instead what turned them toward the needs of their brothers and sisters. This can be seen in what he says about baptism and the Eucharist. The word *sacrament* was not yet used to refer to these two actions of the church, but what it means was recognized from the beginning to be characteristic of them. In baptism someone really comes to belong to God, is forgiven of sins, receives the Spirit, and is joined to the church. It is through baptism that one dies and rises with Christ (Rom. 6:3), but while death to self occurs at the time of baptism, the resurrection will not occur until the end of time. Thus Paul's opponents who believed that they were already raised and therefore beyond the moral law were shown how perverted their doctrine was.

By the same token, the Eucharist made Christ's saving death a present reality to the church, but the effect of that presence was not to furnish an occasion for pride but rather to make Christians give themselves for others as Christ had given himself for them. The main gift that God has for anyone is to make that person like himself as he was revealed in Jesus, that is, willing to lay down his life that others might live. It was this understanding that made it possible for Paul to refer not only to the Eucharist but also to the church as the body of Christ. This body is only manifested as the body of Christ when it does what Christ did when he was in the body; he forgot self to serve others. Thus when the church calls itself the body of Christ, it does not brag, it proclaims its mission.

CHRISTIAN BEHAVIOR

We do not find anywhere in Paul's letters any effort to think through in a systematic way what patterns of human conduct work best. The basis of all his admonitions is what God has already done for us in Jesus. Through his death and resurrection we have been made righteous with the righteousness of God. We no longer have to prove ourselves or earn forgiveness. We are free to forget about ourselves and to give ourselves completely in the service of others. But St. Paul has very little to say about what that service involves in the way of ethical obligations. One reason why he says so little is that he expected the world to come to an end at any minute and Jesus to return and claim his own. Rules for a perfect society have no place in a world that is about to end. Paul is, therefore, willing to accept the current standards of behavior in regard to slavery or the status of women. Yet his understanding of Christian love transforms all the traditional moral teaching that he borrows either from the Old Testament or from Greek philosophers. His attitude can be summed up in the vocabulary of 1 John: Christians awaiting the imminent return of Christ should be in the world but not of the world.

CHRIST

Even though Paul knew little about the life and teaching of Jesus and focused instead on the simple facts of his death and resurrection as the means of our salvation, he did pick up and make his own one way of thinking about Jesus that had already become common before he wrote. Since the preaching of Jesus emphasized the kingdom of God, it was easy for the writers of the Synoptic Gospels to talk about his saving work in temporal terms: Jesus brought one age to an end by inaugurating another, the kingdom of God. In the thought world of the Mediterranean at that time, however, there was a spatial way of describing the work of a savior: a savior was one who came from the eternal world of the gods above to the transient world of humanity below in order to make it possible for humans to go from the world below to the world above. One characteristic of such a savior is his existence in heaven prior to his coming to earth.

In less than twenty years after the crucifixion, Christians had begun to appropriate this concept as a way of describing the work of Christ. They even incorporated it into their hymns. St. Paul accepted this as an adequate way of talking about Jesus and sometimes alluded to these hymns, as in Philippians 2:5–11:

> His state was divine,
> yet he did not cling
> to his equality with God
> but emptied himself
> to assume the condition of a slave,
> and became as men are;
> and being as all men are,
> he was humbler yet,
> even to accepting death,
> death on a cross.
> But God raised him high
> and gave him the name
> which is above all other names
> so that *all beings*
> in the heavens, on earth, and in the underworld,
> *should bend the knee* at the name of Jesus
> and that every tongue should acclaim
> Jesus Christ as Lord,
> to the glory of God the Father. (Jerusalem Bible)

Perspectives and Emphases of the Synoptic Writers

The discussion of redaction criticism above (see p. 69) showed that each of the Gospel writers put his story of Jesus together the way he did in order to bring out his own understanding of who Jesus was and what he means for the church. The perspectives and emphases of each evangelist can be seen when one studies the elements of each Gospel that are unique to it, those elements that the evangelist did not take over from previous tradition. Places to look for these individual contributions include the order in which stories appear, the transitions between stories and sayings taken over from tradition, the overall structure and shape of the Gospel, and, for Matthew and Luke, the way in which Q and Mark have been altered.

Q

Even though we do not possess a copy of Q, and we know it only because Matthew and Luke obviously draw on a common source in addition to Mark, it is important to have some idea of the theological approach that lay behind this collection of material about Jesus so that what is distinctive about Matthew and Luke may be distinguished from what they inherited from Q.

It is easy to discover what constitutes the Q material. One has only to take a book such as Burton Throckmorton's *Gospel Parallels,* in which the Synoptic Gospels have been arranged in parallel columns, and see what material is shared by Matthew and Luke and missing from Mark. When that is done it will be seen that Q consists almost exclusively of sayings of Jesus; there is almost no narrative material in Q. Particularly surprising is the absence of reference to Jesus' death and resurrection. An earlier generation of scholars that represented nineteenth-century liberalism took the content of Q as an indication that Jesus had been regarded as a great religious teacher before "the religion about Jesus" turned him into a savior. After the apocalyptic character of Jesus' teaching came to be recognized, however, Q came to be thought of as ethical teaching that was presented to Christians who had already been converted to belief in Jesus' saving death and resurrection.

Since then, however, closer attention has been paid to the actual kind of teaching that is attributed to Jesus in Q. It has been noticed that much of it sounds like the pronouncements of God's judgment on his people which occupy so many of the oracles of the Old Testament prophets. Other sayings take the form and share much of the content of wisdom literature: there are proverbs, admonitions, pronouncements of blessing and woe on certain categories of people, and comparisons of persons and things. The most distinctive set of teachings in

Q, though, is that which speaks of the imminent coming of the Son of Man. These, then, are references to the Son of Man as a future, glorified figure.

There is no doubt that the Son of Man is identified with Jesus in Q. If the reconstruction of Jesus' teaching about the Son of Man presented above is correct, then Jesus referred to himself as the Son of Man, but he did not explicitly predict his own second coming. He did predict that the kingdom of God was coming and, after the resurrection, it would have been seen that the kingdom would not be fully inaugurated until Jesus returned. In this case, his language about the coming of the kingdom was transferred by the community that produced Q to his coming again as the glorified Son of Man. This community, therefore, presented the message about Jesus in terms of getting ready for the second coming rather than in terms of dying and rising with Christ.

MARK

Mark is not only the first Gospel that we have, it is the first Gospel that was ever written. This does not mean just that Mark was the first Christian to write about the life of Jesus; he was the first to narrate someone's life for the purpose of offering readers the salvation that the subject of the narrative brought. It is not immediately apparent why Mark decided to present the Gospel about Jesus in the form of a connected life story. Prior to his time, as form criticism shows, the tradition about Jesus was usually passed down by word of mouth in units of single stories or sayings. Each of these stories contained the whole Gospel in a nut shell. For example, to say that Jesus has power to cast out unclean spirits, to calm a storm at sea, or that he is superior to the Sabbath or the Torah is to make claims about him that are ultimate. Why connect all of these into a consecutive narrative?

Mark himself does not say and, since his sources are not available for comparison, the only access to his purpose is in an analysis of his work. The Gospel falls naturally into divisions in which different stages of the work of Jesus are discussed. These divisions are often accompanied by a shift of scene from one locale to another. The sections may be set out like this:

I. 1:1–3:6. Jesus is brought on stage by John the Baptist. After he is identified as God's Son by the voice from heaven at his baptism, there is a series of events, especially on the day at Capernaum, in which Jesus engages in activities and teaching that will be typical of his ministry. This section is followed by a series of controversies in which Jesus becomes involved, each of which climaxes in a revelation about that time when the kingdom was breaking in or about the status of Jesus. This division ends with the Pharisees and Herodians already plotting to kill Jesus.

II. 3:7–6:6. When people come from the area of all twelve tribes to hear Jesus, he appoints the Twelve. He teaches in parables that the crowd does not understand, but which he explains to the Twelve. He performs miracles showing his power over the natural order, from calming a storm at sea to raising a girl from the dead. While doing this he is rejected by his friends, his family, and his home town.

III. 6:7–8:26. Jesus sends the Twelve out to extend his preaching of the kingdom. After they return he leaves the territory of Galilee where his ministry has been exercised up to that point and also tries to withdraw from the crowds. Since they have not accepted the message of the kingdom, he retreats into surrounding areas to concentrate on the Twelve. In spite of such overwhelming miracles as walking on the water and the feeding of the 5,000, the Twelve fail to comprehend.

IV. 8:27–10:52. On one of these retreats Jesus asks the Twelve who he is. Peter identifies him as the Messiah, but Jesus refers to himself as the Son of Man and predicts that he will go to Jerusalem to die and rise. Later he is transfigured before the eyes of three of the Twelve who thus see him as he will be at the second coming. The remainder of this section is occupied by the journey to Jerusalem on which Jesus twice more predicts his death and resurrection. Each time the Twelve misunderstand, respond inappropriately, and become more alienated from him.

V. 11:1–13:37. Jesus arrives in Jerusalem on Palm Sunday. His curse on a fig tree the next day is symbolic of God's rejection of the worship of Israel, which Jesus enacts in the cleansing of the Temple. These actions prompt reaction from the authorities and they engage Jesus in controversies. Besting them all, he predicts the coming in glory of the Son of Man at the time of the end.

VI. 14:1–16:8. There is a plot to kill Jesus in which one of the Twelve, Judas, agrees to betray him. At the Last Supper Jesus eats the Passover with the Twelve, institutes the eucharist, and predicts Peter's betrayal. Arrested afterwards in the garden and deserted by the Twelve, he is tried by the Council. In response to the high priest's question, he admits for the first time that he is the Messiah. During this time Peter is denying him. The Roman governor consents to his execution and he is led away and crucified. Two days later (three by the ancient way of counting), women followers come to the tomb to anoint his body for burial, but they find him gone and an angel tells them he is risen and will meet his disciples in Galilee. The women go away in fear.

When this structure is studied carefully, several points emerge. The first is that almost one-third of the entire Gospel is taken up by the last week of Jesus' life. A scholar at the turn of the century made this point vividly when he called Mark "a passion narrative with an extended introduction." What is more, all of the first two-thirds of the book points toward Jesus' death. There is already a plot to kill him by the end of the first section, and every other section ends with some form of rejection. The fourth section is built around three predictions of his death. Each time Jesus makes one of these predictions, the Twelve misunderstand it and he has to teach them that discipleship means that they must share their master's fate.

The misunderstanding of the Twelve is closely linked with other phenomena that the summary above does not show. One is that when Jesus encounters unclean spirits, they have supernatural knowledge of his identity and he forbids them to make him known. The other is when Jesus heals someone, he often tells that person to tell no one what he has done. Jesus, therefore, appears to have fostered a conspiracy of silence about his messianic identity until he revealed it to the high priest at the time of his trial.

In Mark, though, the reader is in on the secret of Jesus' identity and knows Jesus by several titles. One of these is

"Son of God," which appears to come from a Greco-Roman environment and links Jesus with the miracle workers and "divine men" who were so conspicuous a part of the life of the Roman empire at that time. In his astonishing miracles over nature Jesus most resembles such figures. The term *Messiah*, of course, comes from the promise to David in the Old Testament that his heirs would remain forever on the throne of Israel. This expectation was heightened by some of the oracles of the prophets about the glorious restoration of Israel after God's punishment. Apocalyptic thought sharpened this expectation and began to call the anticipated figure the anointed, *mashiach*. As we have seen, however, Mark does not show Jesus as accepting the title of Messiah until his trial. Furthermore, he recounts that Jesus rejected the claim that the Messiah was to be understood as the Son of David (12:35–37).

Mark, then, appears to have as one of his purposes the correction of two misunderstandings about Jesus, that of miracle man in the Hellenistic fashion and that of the warrior Messiah who would drive out the Romans. He allows both Son of God and Messiah as titles of Jesus, but insists that they always be understood in the light of the basic title, Son of Man. As Mark uses the term, Son of Man refers to the one with authority on earth during his lifetime who must suffer but who would come again in glory at the end of the world.

It is obvious that Mark expects that second coming to occur at any moment. He appears to have been writing at the time of the Jewish revolt against Rome in A.D. 66–70, although whether before or after the destruction of the Temple is not clear. Since Mark knows little about Palestinian geography, explains Jewish terms, and uses some Latin words in his Greek, it is apparent that he was writing in Rome or in some Roman territory. The war must have heightened his anticipation of Christ's return. While it does appear likely that he attached some special significance to Galilee, the contention of some contemporary scholars that the references to Jesus' meeting with the disciples in Galilee in 14:28 and 16:7 refers to the second coming rather than the resurrection appears unlikely.

The purpose for which Mark devised the Gospel form and wrote the first Gospel was undoubtedly related to his expectation that the second coming would soon occur. In part he probably wished to give some Christians a more adequate understanding of Christ so that they would be prepared as disciples to accept the fate of their master. The work also appears to be written to convince others who had not yet accepted Christ that he was indeed the Messiah, the Son of God, and the Son of Man who brings salvation.

MATTHEW

Matthew followed Mark very closely in composing his Gospel, fitting his additional material into the Markan outline. The first addition (which consists of the genealogy of Jesus, the stories of the annunciation to Joseph, the visit of the magi, the flight into Egypt, and the settlement in Nazareth) is made the preface. The Q material that Matthew uses is inserted in five long blocks as extended discourses: the Sermon on the Mount (5–7), instruction to the Twelve as they are sent on their missionary journey (10), an extension of Mark's section on parables (13), preaching about discipline within the Christian community (18), and an extension of the "little apocalypse" in Mark 13 (24–25). Matthew also uses eleven proof texts from the Old Testament that are not used elsewhere, introducing them with some variant of the formula: "This was to fulfill what the Lord had spoken by the prophet."

There are a number of indications that Matthew was written in a community in which there were many Jews. Matthew's congregation included many converts from Judaism and there was a constant effort to show that Christianity had become the true Israel. One indication of this Jewish milieu is Matthew's saying "kingdom of heaven" instead of "kingdom of God," displaying the Jewish reverence for the name of God. Much attention is given to questions of the interpretation of the Torah. Matthew takes the position that Jesus gave the key to the interpretation of the Torah in the Summary of the Law and the Golden Rule. Thus the ceremonial law is superseded by the law of love. Contemporary rabbis enjoyed giving succinct summaries of the law, but they would not have conceded that any of the explicit stipulations of the Torah could be overridden by an interpretive principle as Jesus urges in Matthew 5:17–48.

Matthew saw two major epochs, the time of Israel in the Old Testament and the time of Jesus, although, of course, he does not use those terms. He saw the age in which he was living to be a continuation of the new age that had been inaugurated by Jesus, an age that would be brought to an end by Jesus' second coming. This central place of Jesus in history implies what is true, that Matthew wrote primarily to make the significance of Jesus clear to Jews and non-Jews alike.

Although he uses many terms to refer to Jesus, his key concept is that Jesus is God's Son. This becomes clear from his application of Isaiah 7:14 to Jesus: " 'his name shall be called Emmanuel;' (which means, God with us)" (Mt. 1:23). It is reaffirmed by the Father himself when Jesus is baptized: "This is my beloved Son, with whom I am well pleased" (3:17). Obviously Matthew has no nuance of Hellenistic "divine man" such as Mark tried to avoid in his use of "Son of God." Rather, Matthew wishes to convey Jesus' unique relation with the Father; in Jesus the Father abides with his people to the end of time (28:20). The time of Jesus, then, is the time of salvation that is open to both Jews and Gentiles.

By the time Matthew wrote, the Jewish revolt against the Romans had failed, the Temple had been destroyed, and the danger of a militaristic, nationalistic interpretation of such terms as "Son of David" and "Messiah" had passed. Matthew could use them with impunity as terms to refer to Jesus, because they no longer had any content other than Jesus. Still, the overarching term under which all the others are to be comprehended is Son of God. However, Jesus continues to refer to himself in public as Son of Man. But this use is ironic since this ambiguous term will in the long run prove the more exalted: when Jesus comes again, he will come as the glorified Son of Man, and that will be his only title then.

Matthew refers a number of times to "the gospel of the

kingdom." As one writer has put it, Matthew means by that "the news, which saves or condemns, that is revealed in and through Jesus Messiah, the Son of God, and is proclaimed to Israel first and then the Gentiles to the effect that in him the dynamic Rule of God has in the 'last times' drawn near to mankind." The kingdom, in Matthew's thought, had been inaugurated in Jesus' ministry but would not be consummated until the second coming when the Son of Man will come and tell the sheep to enter into the kingdom that the Father had prepared for them, and the goats to depart into the eternal fire prepared for the devil and his angels. Between Jesus' ministry and his second coming the church will grow to the point that it will embrace the universe at the time of the consummation. Entrance into the kingdom will be on the basis of personal response to Christian proclamation: Matthew speaks of this response as either understanding or not understanding the "word of the kingdom" (e.g., 13:19, 23).

The kingdom of heaven is rivaled by the kingdom of Satan. Satan tries to resist the kingdom by tempting those in it to do something contrary to the will of God. He even tries to tempt Jesus. He cannot win, however, because Jesus has already resisted his temptations. At the second coming and the judgment he will be cast into eternal fire with all his angels. Israel, though, in its resistance to the message of Jesus, has succumbed to Satan's temptation and because of that the Temple has been destroyed and the status of being the true Israel of God has passed to the church. The church now does most of its proclamation of the kingdom to the Gentiles instead of to Israel, even though the Gentiles also resist.

The church is the sphere in which the kingdom of heaven is given effect by the presence of Jesus to the end of the age. In the church, though, there are false as well as true disciples, "tares" among the "wheat." Persecuted by Israel and tormented by the Gentiles, the church is experiencing the last great trial before the end. Life in the church is life in tension between this present age and the age to come. The disciples of Jesus have taken up the cross of Christ and salvation will be given to those who persevere to the end (10:22).

LUKE-ACTS

Luke added his special material to his Q material rather than mixing it in with what he inherited from Mark. In fact, he used only about half as much of Mark as Matthew did. He too prefaces his account of Jesus' ministry with stories about his infancy. Here the annunciation was to Mary. A census under Quirinius calls Mary and Joseph from Nazareth to Bethlehem. Shepherds from the fields come to see the newborn babe. After the presentation of Jesus in the Temple, the holy family returns to Nazareth. Only Luke tells of Jesus' visit to the Temple when he was twelve. Interspersed with these stories about the infancy of Jesus are others about that of John the Baptist. In the stories about the two of them appear the canticles the Prayer Book appoints for Morning and Evening Prayer.

Most of the Q material Luke uses, and most of his own special material, appears in Luke's expansion of Mark's account of Jesus' journey from the Mount of Transfiguration to Jerusalem. Taking less than two chapters in Mark, this journey occupies the middle third of Luke, stretching from 9:51 to 19:40. Luke's account of the passion and resurrection also varies from that of Mark, especially the resurrection. While Mark implied and Matthew narrated a resurrection appearance in Galilee, Luke had Jesus appear to two of his followers on the road to Emmaus and then to all of them back in Jerusalem.

Luke's confinement of resurrection appearances to the vicinity of Jerusalem made it possible for him to connect his Gospel to his history of the movement of the center of the church from Jerusalem to Rome, the Acts of the Apostles. It is obvious, in fact, that these two were originally conceived as a two-volume work and it was only when Luke came to be bound in a single volume with the other Gospels and the Acts bound in another volume as an introduction to the letters of St. Paul that they were separated.

The two volumes need to be studied together to gain a full understanding of the thought of their author. Thus joined they show that Luke conceived of time as divided into three ages: the time of Israel, the time of salvation, and the time of the church. The time of salvation is not the entire life of Jesus but extends from the end of his temptations, when we are told that the devil left him for awhile (4:14), to the temptation of Judas to betray him (22:3). Thus the time of salvation was the idyllic time when Jesus was engaged in his ministry and Satan was inactive. This was a foretaste of the kingdom. The time of Israel, then, lasted through the ministry of John the Baptist. The time of the church did not begin until the coming of the Holy Spirit on Pentecost. From the fact that the crucifixion occurred between the time of salvation and the time of the church, it should be obvious that the death of Jesus did not have the theological importance for Luke that it had for Paul and Mark. Luke's doctrine of Christ is much closer to that of the Q document.

Luke's understanding of the Holy Spirit is crucial to any effort to see how he organized his work as a whole. The Spirit had been given sporadically to prophets and other charismatic figures during the time of Israel. It belonged exclusively to Jesus during the time of salvation. His ascension makes it possible for the Holy Spirit to come upon the church so that the church is the Spirit-filled community. Every new place the church extends, which often includes groups among whom no one had thought previously the church could extend, the extension is validated by manifestations of the Spirit's presence, especially speaking in tongues—by far the most observable demonstration of the Spirit's activity. Thus it became obvious that the Spirit was responsible for the church's mission to the Gentiles and the transfer of its center from Jerusalem to Rome. All of this was also demonstrated to be in fulfillment of Old Testament prophecy.[1]

The effect of the addition of Acts to Luke with this emphasis on the prophesied and Spirit-inspired extension of the church is to show that God had a purpose for the delay of Jesus' second coming. He had intended all along that the church should come into existence and spread through the civilized world. The time spent waiting for the second coming, then, was not empty time, but time filled with divine purpose. In this way Luke wrote his two-volume work to console a church that was beginning to lose faith over the delay of the second coming. The wait of two generations since the resurrection had not been in vain; it had been a part of God's plan all along.

The Gospel According to John

The differences between the Fourth Gospel and the Synoptics have already been discussed (pp. 31). Those literary distinctions are accompanied by a variant way of talking about the difference that Jesus makes. It has long been recognized that this way of phrasing the Gospel is summarized in John 3:16 (one of the "comfortable words" in the Prayer Book liturgy):

> For God so loved the world that he gave his only Son, that whoever believed in him should not perish but have eternal life.

The thought of John can be presented as an expansion of the meaning of this one verse.

A good place to begin with is the way this evangelist uses the concept of "world." What did God love when he loved the world? There is a sense in which it means all of creation, the world that God made and looked on and saw to be good. It also has a narrower meaning of humanity. It was people that God loved. While John can use world in a neutral sense, it can also have the connotation of "humanity organized against God."

This becomes clear when one notices that this Gospel is filled with opposites that are constantly contrasted with one another: light/darkness, truth/falsehood, life/death, above/below, not of this world/of this world. Furthermore, all of the positive terms seem to refer to the same thing and the negative ones also have a common meaning. Life in this world is life in darkness, falsehood, bondage. It is, in short, death. Life that is not of this world, life from above, is life in light, truth, and freedom. It is, in fact, eternal life. The contrast is basically one of reality and appearances.

These alternatives are presented as options open to

people—the only choices there are. Ultimately one can only choose God and the real world that exists in him or the world of appearance that is the realm of death. In John 3:16 these alternatives are stated as "having eternal life" or "perishing." The one who receives eternal life is the one who believes in God's only begotten Son. Christ's coming into the world served to inform mankind that the options existed. Prior to his coming, all was darkness. No one could see. The response of a person to his message was a choice between the two worlds. One chose either to remain in darkness or to accept the light he brought.

If the world is God's creation, how did it come to be in darkness? God created human beings as good. Indeed, they have a natural longing for the good and for reality. They wish to look beyond the superficial, beyond good that is merely material. In this Gospel Jesus has a number of statements that begin: "I am." I am the true vine, the true bread from heaven, or the good shepherd. In all of these Jesus is claiming to satisfy all human longings. The trouble is that people want to discover for themselves what is good. They make themselves the final authority. When they wish to walk in their own light, they become blind, and the world is in darkness. The supreme example of this human tendency in the thought of John is the Jewish religion. He no longer speaks of Jesus' enemies as scribes and Pharisees, but simply as "the Jews." The Jews are so secure in their religion that they have closed their minds to new evidence of God's work. Thus they do not recognize Jesus as the Messiah they have been expecting; they have devised tests by which they can certify the Messiah and he does not pass them. Thus the very religion in which they take their pride (the true religion given by God that they misunderstand) is what stands between them and the life that Jesus offers.

To reclaim this world that he had created and still loves, God sent his Son. Like Paul, John speaks of the redeemer who came from above, from the divine world, down to the world of people in order to offer them salvation and life in the world above. As has been said, "in the person of Jesus the transcendent divine reality became audible, visible, and tangible in the realm of the earthly world." Jesus, like the divine wisdom in Proverbs, had existed eternally with the Father. Indeed, he was the Father's agent of creation. And he abased himself and became a man. To the mind of the fourth evangelist, becoming man was a greater act of condescension than even the crucifixion. It was the love of the Father for the world, however, which lay behind his own love, and in everything he was obedient to the Father and did the Father's will. His coming was to bring salvation but it also brought judgment, because some refused the salvation he brought. They refused to recognize him as its bringer. Their judgment, therefore, was not pronounced on them from the outside. It occurred when they rejected the salvation that Jesus brought. "This is the judgment, that the light has come into the world, and men loved darkness rather than the light, because their deeds were evil" (3:19).

The Fourth Gospel has something akin to Mark's understanding of the messianic secret. It does not appear in commands that Jesus' identity not be revealed. Rather, it appears in the contrast between the claims that are made about him and the reality of his appearance. The prologue says: "The Word became flesh and dwelt among us, full of grace and truth; we have beheld his glory, glory as of the only Son from the Father" (1:14). Yet the way in which that glory was seen is not made clear. It is true, as someone said, that John's Jesus appears to go around with his feet about eighteen inches off the ground. He is the Jesus of "religious" films, the one wearing a halo. Whenever he speaks, there is organ music in the background. He has supernatural knowledge and can see into the hearts of people and get out of tight places. He performs fewer miracles than the synoptic Jesus but they seem more miraculous. When all is said and done, however, he is still just a man and it is exceedingly difficult for anyone to take his claims seriously. The difficulty is not with him but with the world; it does not have eyes to see.

The relation of Jesus to the Father is a complex one. On the one hand he is equal to the Father. On the other, he is obedient to him and does nothing except what he says. What this means is that, although Jesus appears as only a human being, he actually speaks with the full authority of God. It is precisely that point that is so hard for his listeners to accept. This paradoxical revelation of the glory of Jesus in his ordinariness is taken to its ultimate manifestation in John's understanding that the death of Jesus was not his humiliation but his exaltation. This does not appear to be meant in a Suffering Servant way, but rather has to do with the assumption that, since Jesus came from the world above, his being lifted up on the cross is the beginning of his return to the status that he enjoyed before the incarnation. Because of this understanding of the crucifixion as glorification, the resurrection, for John, is almost a matter of dotting the *i* and crossing the *t*. The promise to send the Paraclete, the Comforter (John's term for the Holy Spirit), is essentially Jesus' promise to be with his followers in a very real way when he is no longer with them in the flesh.

Jesus' revelation in his teaching is about as paradoxical as his revelation in his life. What he reveals is simply and only that he is the Revealer. One looks in vain for more content to his revelation than that. It is he who makes it possible for people to pass from darkness into light, from death into life. The way they do that is to accept his message, to believe what he says. This believing is faith, and for John faith is knowing what the universe is really like because one has accepted Jesus' message that life and light are in him. Faith also implies that one keeps the commandments of Jesus; the new commandment that he gave was that his followers love one another. This love of the brethren was the validation of their discipleship. When those who hear become believers, they pass over right then from death to life. Eternal life is not something that begins after one has died and gone to heaven; for John it begins when one becomes a Christian. Death, then, is merely passing from one stage of eternal life to another.

The Faith of Emerging Catholicism

The last group of books in the New Testament to be written includes the Pastoral (1 and 2 Timothy, Titus) and Catholic

(James, 1 and 2 Peter, Jude) Epistles. The Catholic Epistles have been given that designation as a synonym for "General," another term by which they are called. It therefore means simply that these letters are not addressed to a single congregation but to the church as a whole. This is to say that they are not letters at all, but are essays that have the literary form of letters. Both the Pastoral and the Catholic Epistles come from the third or fourth generation of Christians. They were written at the time when the church was settling down to become an institution in society. While the second coming is still expected, it is recognized that the church may have to deal with a lot of practical problems before it does. Scholars have used several terms to refer to this institutionalization of the church; "emerging catholicism" will do as well as any other. In this literature we see the church settling down for the long haul of history.

The main thing we notice in this literature is the need to settle on an institutional identity. Adequate statements of Christian belief have to be distinguished from those that are less adequate. It has to be decided which earlier Christian writings are genuine and authoritative and which are not. What are the rites of Christian worship and how are they validly performed? Who may perform these rites and who may speak for the church officially? These are the questions that had to be settled; matters of creed, canon, sacraments, and ministers. None were settled in this period but the discussions did get underway.

The real problem was diversity. Many voices were being heard, each of which claimed to represent the authentic Christian message. How were such rival claims to be settled? The obvious way was to appeal to the apostles as those who had received straight from Jesus their ideas of what the church should be like. Thus the time of the apostles is looked upon as a golden age, while the time of writing was considered to be the last days before the end, a time when many were falling into sin and error. The only way to preserve true Christianity was to hold fast to "the faith once delivered to the saints" (Jude 3). "False teachers" appeared in great abundance. The strategy was no longer to refute them in detail as

Paul had done, but simply to identify them as false by showing how their teaching deviated from "the pattern of sound
words" (2 Tim. 1:13, 14).

By this time some Christian writings were coming to be
considered inspired, although it is not clear whether they
were yet thought to be on a par with the books of the Old
Testament. In 2 Peter problems of interpreting these are beginning to be dealt with. "No prophecy of scripture is a
matter of one's own interpretation" (1:20) but must be interpreted instead by those who were as much inspired by the
Holy Spirit as the original writers had been. The letters of St.
Paul especially gave problems:

> So also our beloved brother Paul wrote to you according to the
> wisdom given him, speaking of this as he does in all his letters.
> There are some things in them hard to understand, which the
> ignorant and unstable twist to their own destruction, as they do
> the other scriptures. (2 Pet. 3:15, 16)

In the Pastoral Epistles especially, a concern for orders of
ministry begins to express itself. Bishops, elders, and deacons
are discussed at length, but we learn much more about their
moral qualifications than about their duties. At this time the
church begins to take some notice of the world outside and is
thus concerned with such matters as the reputation of Christians among nonbelievers and the attitude of Christians toward pagan law and government.

It is easy to denigrate this literature as did the scholar of an
earlier generation who said that Paul was inspired while the
author of the Pastorals was only orthodox, but these authors
were responding to the challenge of their own times, times
when old ideas were being brought into question, times not
unlike our own. We may do well to listen to them.

The Epistle to the Hebrews

The Epistle to the Hebrews is unique in the New Testament.
It is like its own description of Melchizedek, the priest to
whom Abraham paid his tithe, "without father or mother or

genealogy" (7:3), since it not only was not written by any of
the major New Testament authors, it does not even resemble
any other writing in its basic thought world. That thought
world can be identified in a very general way as Hellenistic
Jewish Christianity. This is to say that its categories are those
of Jews who have learned to express their faith in the vocabulary of popular Greek philosophical thought, become Christians, and modified their earlier theological expressions in a
way that is at once thoroughly Christian yet unlike any other
phrasing of the faith in the New Testament.

This combination of Jewish, Greek, and Christian thought
is seen in the use that Hebrews makes of the basic metaphors
expressing the significance of Jesus. Apocalyptic Christianity, it will be remembered, used a temporal metaphor of
two ages; Jesus is the one who ushers in the "age to come."
Paul and John, on the other hand, used a spatial metaphor;
Jesus came to the world below to make it possible for persons
to go to the world above. Hebrews uses both metaphors. The
temporal metaphor is used in an apocalyptic interpretation of
the Old Testament in which Jesus is seen as the one who
fulfills everything that the Old Testament promised; Jesus
accomplishes in his perfect sacrifice what the cult of the Temple only promised. At the same time, the real world in heaven
has its shadowy manifestations in all that exists on earth;
Jesus has entered into the Most Holy Place of the heavenly
Temple, of which the Temple at Jerusalem (more precisely,
the tent of meeting during the Exodus) is merely a copy. As
our pioneer or trailblazer he makes it possible for us to enter
the heavenly sanctuary. Thus his significance is also expressed in a spatial metaphor.

This epistle (which has the form of a sermon to which a
letter has been added) begins by showing the superiority of
Jesus to the angels, to Moses, and to Joshua. Moses and
Joshua were supposed to have led Israel into God's promised
rest (Sabbath in Hebrew), but God's people chose to wander
in the wilderness rather than to enter into this rest. Thus they
were waiting for Jesus to usher them into God's real rest. His
obedience made up for their disobedience. For his obedience
Jesus was made a great high priest like Melchizedek (Ps.

110:4). His priesthood is vastly superior to that of the Temple because he was himself the sacrificial victim. Because the victim was perfect, unlike the animals offered at Jerusalem, the sacrifice of Jesus does not have to be repeated as Old Testament sacrifices did. Jesus thus initiated a new covenant with God and he has now entered into the heavenly Temple where he continually offers intercession for us. Our promised land of rest, therefore, is not an earthly land but is "the city which has foundations, whose builder and maker is God" (11:10).

The Revelation of John

The New Testament apocalypse is a paradoxical book in that it is almost impossible to interpret in detail, yet there is little doubt about its basic meaning. The major problem in interpreting details grows out of the structure of the book. After beginning with letters to seven churches of Asia Minor, the book relates a vision of the author in which appear seven seals on a book, seven trumpets sounded by seven angels, and seven bowls of wrath that are poured out. Inserted along the way are various other lists, some of which could have seven members, so that some scholars have thought that the intended structure is a scheme of seven sections each of which is divided into seven parts. Even if that were clear— which it is not—the significance of it would still be uncertain. Do the sevens represent weeks, that is, periods of time? If so, how are they interrelated? Are they sequential or concurrent or overlapping? Many theories have been advanced, some as bizarre as the imagery they seek to explicate, but none has found a wide agreement.

It is, nevertheless, agreed that the visions refer to a time when persecution was expected for the churches in Asia Minor because Christians would refuse to participate in the worship of the Roman emperor as a divine being, which was beginning to take hold there then. The time appears to have been the reign of the emperor Domitian in the closing years of the first Christian century. The author writes from imprisonment on the island of Patmos to urge the Christians to remain loyal in the hard times to come. The emperor is an agent of Satan and God is going to intervene in history to bring an end not only to the Roman empire but to history as such. The devil will be bound for a thousand years when Christian martyrs will be resurrected and reign with Christ. Then will come the last judgment after which the devil, the beast, and the false prophet would be thrown into eternal fire. After that heaven would descend to earth as the new Jerusalem.

Some sensitive Christians have been offended by the war-like tone of Revelation, considering it to be too vengeful to be associated with the God of love revealed in the New Testament. Such a position results from confusing the apparatus of apocalyptic too closely with the message of the book. On the latter topic Willi Marxsen undoubtedly had a proper perspective:

> The significant thing is that the One who will come in glory is identical with the Lamb that has been slain, was crucified outside the gates of the great city, and has redeemed with his blood those who believe in him. The Church therefore not only knows the one who is to come as present here and now: the Church is also his possession.[2]

Conclusion

Someone has pointed out that the Bible begins in a garden and ends in a city. That observation should be qualified with the realization that both the garden and the city were not the works of men. The one looks back to a time before human history began and the other looks forward to a time when God's purpose in history has been accomplished and this world is no more. We look back to the great things God has done in the past and ahead to what he will do in the future. The Bible reminds us more than anything else that the earth is the Lord's and we are the Lord's. Our life is about God. We are members of a people that began with Abraham and we look, as he did, for a city that has foundations, whose builder and maker is God.

The apocalyptic view of the New Testament saw God's reign on earth as inaugurated by the work of Christ but not to be fulfilled until his second coming. This accounts for the "already/not yet" character of human existence for those of us who live "between the ages." We know that in Christ a new quality of existence has become possible for us, but we do not live out that existence in its fullness yet. The New Testament consoles us for the ambiguity of our life now by assuring us that the future is in the hands of God and that he will bring his experiment in creation to a successful conclusion. Walking on in the path that was marked out for us by the patriarchs, prophets, and apostles, we live in hope of the vision of John:

> And I saw the holy city, new Jerusalem, coming down out of heaven from God, prepared as a bride adorned for her husband; and I heard a great voice from the throne saying, "Behold, the dwelling of God is with men. He will dwell with them, and they shall be his people, and God himself shall be with them; he will wipe away every tear from their eyes, and death shall be no more, neither shall there be mourning nor crying nor pain any more, for the former things have passed away. (Rev. 21:2–4)

· 11 ·

Ways We Hear the Bible Today

One the theories about the authorship of the Gospel according to Matthew is that it was written by a school of Christian rabbis who searched the Old Testament looking for verses that could be considered as prophecies of Jesus. The main evidence for this theory is Matthew's use of somewhere between ten and fifteen Old Testament quotations not used elsewhere in the New Testament as prooftexts that Jesus was the Messiah predicted in the Torah and Prophets. Each of these citations is introduced by a formula such as: "All this took place to fulfil what the Lord had spoken by the prophet" (1:22).

Whether there was one editor of Matthew or a school that cooperated in the work, there is little doubt that the ideal striven after in the Gospel is stated in 13:52: "Every scribe who has been trained for the kingdom of heaven is like a householder who brings out of his treasure what is new and what is old." A scribe trained for the kingdom of heaven is someone schooled in the rabbinical methods of biblical interpretation who has become a Christian. The old things that he brings out of his treasure are interpretations of the Torah and Prophets shared with the Pharisees. The new things are Christian interpretations of the Old Testament, either seeing passages as prophecies of Jesus or giving Christian rather than Jewish positions on the application of religious regulations about prayer, fasting, and so forth.

Up to this point this book, dealing as it has with what the Bible *meant* to its original readers, has been an effort to bring

258

old things out of the biblical treasury. This last chapter is devoted to a survey of ways in which the church discovers what the Bible *means* today. It is composed of short sections on the liturgical use of the Bible, biblical preaching, Bible study in Christian Education, personal study of the Bible, the use of the Bible in private devotions and in evangelism, and how the Bible is used authoritatively in deciding contemporary theological and moral questions. Needless to say, only the most rudimentary suggestions can be made in such short space. Those suggestions are supplemented, however, by short annotated bibliographies so that the reader will know where to go to learn more. The writers are under no illusion that these notes are exhaustive. The only reason for their appearance is that they document the overwhelming conviction that there are new treasures as well as old to be brought out of the storehouse of the Bible. It has as much meaning to give to the lives of Christian people today as it ever had.

The Liturgical Use of the Bible

The reading and interpretation of passages from the Bible has been a part of Christian public worship from the very beginning. This building of worship around Scripture is a Christian inheritance from the Jewish synagogue in which the services consisted of readings from the Torah and the prophets and comment on them. Jesus is seen participating in such synagogue worship in Luke 4:16, 17, and Paul is similarly depicted in Acts 13:15–16. Anyone familiar with the services of Morning and Evening Prayer in the Book of Common Prayer can readily see that they are essentially Christian versions of the old synagogue service. With a little more thought one can recognize that the same is true of the first half of the Holy Eucharist, the section designated The Word of God in the new Prayer Book.

The major Christian alteration of the synagogue rite was to add readings from the distinctively Christian Scriptures, the New Testament, to those from the earlier Jewish Scriptures, the Old Testament. This change had been made by the middle of the second Christian century, as may be seen from a description of a eucharistic celebration by a writer of that period, Justin Martyr:

> And on the day called Sunday there is a meeting in one place of those who live in the cities or the country, and the memoirs of the apostles or the writings of the prophets are read as long as time permits. When the reader has finished, the president in a discourse urges and invites us to the imitation of these noble things. (*First Apology* 67)

The reason that Jews and Christians have placed Bible reading, and preaching based on it, at the core of their worship is that by doing so they have experienced God and come to an understanding of life, the world, and God's will for his people (see p. 71). Such an experience of God's presence and understanding of his will, however, are by no means the inevitable result of such Bible reading in church, as many readers of this book can undoubtedly testify. What follows, therefore, is a series of practical suggestions about ways in which you can make more realistic the expectation that you will hear God speak to you when the Bible is read aloud at public worship.

The first way in which to make the Bible come alive is to see it as bearing a message for today and not simply as a word out of the past about the past. We must recognize it for what the first Christians took it to be, God's word for the present. While the books were written originally with the situations of their own times in mind, they nevertheless continue to serve as a mirror into which the faithful look for the image of their living Lord and of God's people Israel in order to understand who they are and what they must become. Just as the stories of the patriarchal tradition, such as that of Abraham's two sons, were retold many times to help Israel and the early church understand new situations in their history, so the biblical passages that we hear today can help us to understand the shape of our condition.

In addition to thinking of the Bible as God's word for us today, we must also think of it as his word to us corporately as well as (and perhaps more than) individually. The Bible is the record of the encounters of a people with their God rather than the spiritual pilgrimages of solitary individuals. Then, too, the setting of this Bible reading in the liturgy calls upon us to regard its implications for the community at that time just as its individual implications are more to the fore when one reads the Bible in private devotions. The Greek word from which *liturgy* is derived means "the work of the people." Thus it has a communal focus. Furthermore, the Bible was written, preserved, and transmitted by the community of the faithful and so it belongs to the community. The natural setting for hearing it and discussing it, then, is the community gathered for worship. One way of emphasizing liturgically this corporate character of the Bible is to involve lay people as well as clergy in reading it at services.

A third way to help the Bible come alive for us when it is read in church is to be conscious of the setting of that particular passage in the church year. We should ask ourselves why that selection was thought appropriate for the feast or season being celebrated at the time. The portions of the Bible to be read at worship on each day in the year and for special occasions are listed in the new Prayer Book in the section called The Lectionary. This lectionary ties readings to the life cycle of the church, which follows annually the sequence of the life of Jesus for half the year, with the long Pentecost period taking up the rest. Great persons in the history of the church are remembered on saints' days and provision is made for other special events in the life of the congregation, such as confirmation and ordination. The passages have been chosen because of their appropriateness for the occasions on which they are read. Associating them with the occasion fills them with additional meaning for us.

The new Book of Common Prayer does not print the text of the epistles and gospels for each Sunday and holy day as the 1928 Prayer Book did. The main reason is that, along with Roman Catholics, Lutherans, and many other denominations, Episcopalians no longer read the same passages for a given day in the church calendar year after year, but instead alternate the readings on a three-year cycle. This tripling of the amount of Scripture in the lectionary makes printing it out impractical. Besides, there are advantages to not having the lections printed in the Prayer Book. For one thing, having them read from a Bible instead of a service book is a reminder of how important we consider the Bible to be. Furthermore, we are not then confined to one translation but may use a variety of them. Since most denominational lectionary cycles are now nearly identical, one can gain a sense of the corporate nature of the Bible from the realization that other Christians are hearing the same passage that we are on a particular day.

A fourth way of insuring that the Bible receives a fuller hearing when it is read liturgically is to accent the readings with modern as well as traditional hymns on the same themes. Traditionally passages from the Psalms were used for this purpose, being designated as introits, graduals, or offertories because of the point in the liturgy at which they were used. The lectionary of the new Prayer Book provides for gradual psalms. Hymns from the hymnal or its modern supplements may be used for the same purpose, reinforcing what is read and adding their own nuances of interpretation. Creative use can also be made of modern songs with biblical themes and orientation, such as the spirituals and Gospel songs of the black church tradition or some of the popular music of today's youth. All of these make us conscious of the meaning of what is read.

There are many techniques by which the members of a congregation may participate actively as well as passively in the public reading of the Bible. They can, for instance, make a point of reading over the passages appointed for that day before they leave home so that they can anticipate what will be read in church. In some parishes the reading of the lessons from the Bible is prefaced by one or two sentence summaries of what will be read so that people will know what to listen for. Such summaries also may relate a given passage to what was read from the same biblical book the week before, thus giving a sense of continuity. Group discussion of the passage after it is read also helps to clarify the meaning. Or the lectionary can be the basis for continuing Bible study within the parochial Christian education program.

From these suggestions it can be seen that reading from the Bible is no mere appendage of the liturgy. The reading, hearing, and proclaiming of Scripture among the people of God is itself liturgy. The liturgy of the word and the liturgy of the sacrament are indispensable to one another. The lessons read from the Bible tell us why we have come together to worship and set forth the implications of our worship for our daily lives. The proclamation of the Word of God prepares us to experience our risen Lord in the breaking of bread, as it prepared the disciples on the way to Emmaus long ago. Having their eyes opened in the shared meal after the resurrection, the disciples remembered that as they had walked along the road with their unrecognized Lord, he had explained to them the meaning of the Bible. Then they said to each other, "Did not our hearts burn within us while he talked to us on the road, while he opened to us the scriptures?" (Lk. 24:32).

FOR FURTHER READING:

Borsch, Frederick H. *Introducing the Lessons of the Church Year: A Guide for Lay Readers and Congregations.* New York: Seabury Press, 1978. See the chapter on "Why We Read the Bible in Church," pp. 4–12.

Deiss, Lucien. *God's Word and God's People.* Collegeville, Minn.: Liturgical Press, 1976. An important—and somewhat technical—Roman Catholic work on the Bible in the liturgy.

Fuller, Reginald H. *Preaching the New Lectionary: The Word of God for the Church Today.* Collegeville, Minn.: Liturgical Press, 1974. Commentary on the lessons for the liturgy with emphasis on the preacher's use of them.

Interpretation (A Journal of Bible and Theology), vol. 31, no. 2 (April 1977). Richmond: Union Theological Seminary in Virginia. This issue of *Interpretation* has several useful essays on the rationale and thrust of the new lectionaries.

Micks, Marianne H. *The Future Present: The Phenomenon of Christian Worship,* New York: Seabury Press, 1970. A very fine, easily read book on the meaning of worship and the rationale behind the church's liturgy. Attention is given to the use of Scripture and preaching.

Shepherd, Massey H., Jr. *The Psalms in Christian Worship.* Minneapolis: Augsburg Publishing House, 1976. A short practical guide on the traditional and new uses of the Psalter in worship.

Biblical Preaching

The discussion of form criticism above (pp. 66–68) noted that all of the New Testament is preaching. Some of the preaching is aimed at persuading those who have not accepted Christ to do so, while the rest is directed toward Christians in an effort to urge them to bring their behavior into line with their profession. All Christian preaching since has served one of those two purposes, being devoted either to evangelism or exhortation. Indeed, during the period when the material that was later to be incorporated into the written Gospels was still being passed down by word of mouth with the individual story or saying as the unit of transmission, these stories or sayings were used as a point of departure for either sermons or the instruction of the faithful. Thus no activity has been more characteristic of the Christian church from its inception than oral preaching, which grew out of the preaching of the New Testament.

These two purposes are still what preaching is all about, even though appearances may sometimes be to the contrary. Since the historical-critical method became the basis of seminary instruction, however, many clergy have felt ill at ease in trying to preach from the Bible. Their training made them uncomfortable about preaching as though every word of the Bible were literal historical truth. However, it had not shown them what could and should be preached from the Bible. Thus, ironically, a tool that was intended to make it possible for clergy to understand the biblical proclamation more deeply has often impeded them from drawing on the Bible at all in their preaching.

Much of the blame for this must lie with seminary professors of the Bible who, on the one hand, have often forgotten that the purpose of their scholarship was not erudition in itself but to make the meaning of the Bible clearer to Christian people, and who, on the other, have neglected to teach their students how biblical criticism should be utilized as a resource for preaching. The development of redaction criticism, however, has proved a great corrective of these tendencies, since it has as one of its primary questions: "What proclamation is the biblical writer trying to make in this passage?"

Preachers should begin their sermon preparation with that question. When they find out what scriptural passages are to be read on the day they will preach, they begin to exegete them in the manner described in Chapter 3, beginning with textual criticism and going on through source, form, subject and object, and redaction or tradition criticism. While they will undoubtedly end by consulting commentaries and exegetical aids for preachers, they should begin by making their own efforts to discover what the biblical writers were trying to communicate to the original readers of those passages. When that answer has been established satisfactorily and checked in the appropriate reference books, the preacher then knows what to preach about, what proclamation to make in the sermon under consideration.

The next step of sermon preparation is to discover what situation in the congregation is analogous to the situation in the biblical passage that will be the sermon's text. Ascertaining this requires an interpretation of the congregation and the society in which it lives that is as thoroughgoing as the interpretation made of the biblical passage. The preacher who is to show parishioners how their lives are illuminated by the Bible must be as familiar with these lives as with the Bible. There are many ways of acquiring such familiarity: parish calling, hearing confessions, counseling, all of the pastoral contacts a priest makes. Since the preacher participates in the same culture as the congregation, no special effort is necessary to know what is going on in the culture. Newspapers, magazines, television, movies, bestsellers, and all the other media saturate us with information about current affairs as understood by what has been called the "knowledge industry." What is difficult for the preacher to acquire is some perspective on, some transcendence of the society's view of itself and its affairs. In order to hear what is really going on in the culture when it is viewed from a Christian perspective the preacher needs to acquire a theological equivalent of what the psychiatrist Theodore Reik called a "third ear."

By the use of free association the preacher discovers the

situation in the congregation that is analogous to the situation in the biblical text. When that is accomplished the construction of the sermon can begin. Although the preparation of the sermon began with the exegesis of the biblical passages to be read on the day of the sermon, the sermon itself should not begin with the text; it should instead begin where the people are. The first task of the preacher is to describe their situation in such a way that the people can recognize it as their own. Next the sermon should show that there is much in common between what is going on in the life of the parish and what was reported in the biblical passage that had been read at the service. The final task of the sermon is to apply the judgment passed on the situation in the text to the situation in the congregation. While, classically, sermons have begun with the Bible and only then moved on to deal with contemporary life, the preacher may no longer ccunt on a passionate curiosity among his hearers about what a particular portion of Scripture happens to be about. Attention can drift quickly from sermons that begin: "My text is taken from . . ." People are much more likely to follow the sermon through to the end when they are shown that matters directly relevant to themselves are to be discussed.

This method of biblical preaching is based on the assumption that, in spite of all of the changes in the material circumstances of human life since the last book of the Bible was written, the basic circumstances of what it means to be human have not changed. Thus God's perspective on recurring patterns of behavior remains constant. By finding out from the Bible what his attitude toward a pattern was revealed to be in the past, we may confidently know what it is in the present to the extent that other things are equal. Indeed such an assumption lies behind any interest in the Bible that is not merely antiquarian curiosity. The importance of biblical criticism is to make certain that cultural differences do not confuse us about what the situation in the past was like or what the divine perspective on it was. It is an insurance against misunderstanding. That is what makes it so important a part of preparation for preaching. It should give preachers confidence that their sermons can penetrate to the core of the lives of the people because they are drawn from the heart of the Word of God.

FOR FURTHER READING:

Edwards, O. C., Jr. *The Living and Active Word: One Way to Preach From the Bible Today*. New York: Seabury Press, 1975. The original book-length statement of the method described above.

Fuller, Reginald H. *Preaching the New Lectionary*. Collegeville, Minn.: The Liturgical Press, 1974. Short exegetical remarks on each of the lections for the three-year Roman Catholic lectionary cycle (very similar to the Episcopal) with suggestions for homiletical development by one of the most outstanding Anglican New Testament scholars. These originally came out month by month in *Worship* magazine where a second series by the same author is now appearing.

Proclamation: Aids for Interpreting the Lessons of the Church Year. Philadelphia: Fortress Press, 1973ff. A series of twenty-four books (eight each for the three cycles of the new Lutheran lectionary— also similar to the Episcopal) that gives about one printed page of exegesis and another of homiletical suggestions for each reading. The biblical scholars and preachers who contributed to these volumes are among the most distinguished in the country. A second series of twenty-four volumes is now in preparation.

Proclamation Commentaries. Philadelphia: Fortress Press, 1975ff. Commentaries of around 100 pp. on books of the Old and New Testament that give preachers information on the background, structure, and message of the books so that when one book appears in the lectionary for a period the preacher can ascertain how the passage for a particular day fits into the thought of the entire book.

Christian Education and the Bible

At former times this would have been an easy matter to deal with because established church school curricula would have been available to which one could refer, and nothing else would have been necessary. Now, however, there is a great dispute about what Christian Education is, and there is even less agreement about how it should be carried on. It would be impossible in this short space to arbitrate among the various options. One point of view will be set forth in a concise way. Readers who have commitments to other points of view will undoubtedly know where to look for guidance on how to use the Bible in Christian Education programs undertaken with their presuppositions.

The writers assume that it is not enough for students in our church schools—or, more properly, younger members of our congregations—to learn *about* our religion. The crucial thing is for them to acquire Christian faith. It has been pointed out by John Westerhoff (from whose book, *Will Our Children Have Faith?*, most of these ideas are taken) that there are four stages in the development of faith. A child in the preschool and early school years acquires *experienced* faith through the experiences of being a member of a Christian family and belonging to the church. During late childhood and early adolescence *affiliative* faith is acquired in the process of identifying oneself with the institution of the church by learning its lore and being accepted into it. During late adolescence faith often becomes *searching;* it is tested intellectually so that its adequacy may be discovered. If those tests are negotiated successfully, young adults are ready to move into *owned* faith in which they accept the church's faith for themselves and begin to develop styles of life that are consistent with their Christian profession.

A strategy for Christian education based on an intention to facilitate successful movement through these four stages of faith would, on the one hand, provide for understanding of the church's ongoing life day in and day out and would, on the other hand, make special provision for those members of the congregation who are ready to move from one stage of faith to the next. For the ongoing program Westerhoff suggests using the hour before the Sunday liturgy:

> What if a congregation, all ages together, gathered before the morning liturgy? At this time they could welcome new persons, share fellowship together, learn about and minister to each other's needs—all of which are ways of enhancing community life. Second, the people could prepare for the morning ritual by learning hymns, responses, and other aspects of the liturgy, thereby making participation meaningful. Third, the liturgy

could be enhanced if the lectionary (lessons from the Scriptures to be read and preached) was used to provide content for a series of diverse intergenerational educational experiences and discussions among all the worshippers—children, youth, and adults. (*Will Our Children Have Faith?*, pp. 57–58)

Special courses of study would be arranged for those ready to make the transition to a new stage of faith. For adult Christian education Westerhoff recommends, in addition to the intergenerational experiences mentioned above, that short courses should be taken by homogeneous groups to deal with questions they raise; such courses should result in a program of action.

In her book, *Exploring the Bible with Children* a system has been devised by Dorothy Jean Furnish for which the sort of intergenerational concept advocated by Westerhoff is one of the recommended teaching methods. Indeed, her thoughts about what such explorations should accomplish are very compatible with Westerhoff's goal of enabling our children to have faith. Pointing to the inadequacy of such motives as the feeling that children "ought" to study the Bible, the theory that Bible study builds character, the belief that Bible data stored in childhood will be available for later use, or the assumption that the "message" of the Bible can be taught to children, Furnish goes on to say:

We want for our children what we want for ourselves. We want children to begin to develop a sense of being special persons who own a special tradition. We want them to begin to find heroes and heroines in the Judeo-Christian tradition as well as in secular history. We want to open the Bible to them so that God can use it to bring meaning to their lives, at whatever level and in whatever ways this is possible. We want children to know the Bible so that they can be confronted by it. We want the Bible to be an important part of the child's "now" world. And we want all of this to happen in their present, not in their future. (p. 96)

In contrast to contemporary theorists, who contend that children are not ready for religious thinking, and therefore not ready for the Bible, until the late elementary grades, Furnish points out that not all that should be learned about our religion is thinking or concepts. Much of the biblical content is stories. These can be taught to and eagerly learned by relatively young children if appropriate methods are used. Such methods would include first-rate storytelling, art work in relation to the stories, songs about the stories, acting the stories out. The content should not be tested by asking for a playback of the facts, though, nor should the teacher tack on a moral (often very unconvincing) as the meaning of the story.

Children are also able to deal with the meaning of stories on their own level. The teacher can begin by asking what the story means to them, recognizing that there can be no wrong answer to that question. The teacher should also be willing to say what the story means to him or her. When this idea of the plurality of meanings has been established, the teacher can ask, "What do you think the story meant to the first people who ever heard it?" After these questions have been explored, the children are then capable of considering what the story should mean to the church today, at least within their own frame of reference.

Children are also capable of absorbing a lot of biblical background unconsciously if it is put to them in the right way. Many such details can be woven into the telling of a story. Information about the land of the Bible, the customs of biblical times, some of the literary forms of the Bible, and even how the Bible was made can be picked up in this way. During their elementary years children can also begin to acquire some biblical skills such as learning where to find passages in the Bible or how to use a simple concordance or Bible dictionary. Such experiences in studying the Bible will not only result in children knowing about the sacred writings of their religion but will give them a sense of being a part of the community of faith that has its early history recorded in the Bible but which continues to exist today in their own church.

FOR FURTHER READING:

Bennett, Robert A. *God's Work of Liberation: A Journey Through the Old Testament with the Liberation Heroes of Israel.* Wilton, Conn.:

Morehouse-Barlow, 1976. A survey of the content and background of the Old Testament from a liberation perspective, intended for use in secondary schools. A teacher's manual is attached.

Doss, Helen. *Young Readers Book of Bible Stories.* Nashville: Abingdon, 1967. A Bible story book which introduces a great deal of background information inconspicuously into the narration.

Furnish, Dorothy Jean. *Exploring the Bible with Children.* Nashville: Abingdon, 1975. Discussed above.

Miller, Donald E.; Snyder, Graydon F.; and Neff, Robert W. *Using Biblical Simulations.* 2 vols. Valley Forge: Judson Press, 1973–75. A theoretical and practical guide to acting out biblical stories, with background data for each episode and directions for leader and participants.

Walton, Robert C., ed. *A Source Book of the Bible for Teachers.* London: SCM Press, 1970.

Warshaw, Thayer S.; Miller, Betty Lou; Ackerman, James S.; eds. *Bible-Related Curriculum Materials: A Bibliography.* Nashville: Abingdon, 1976. An indispensable list of literary texts related to the books of the Bible to be used by both teachers and students. Compiled for use in courses on the Bible as literature, it lists literary and audiovisual materials that are related to the Bible.

Westerhoff, John, III. *Will Our Children Have Faith?* New York: Seabury Press, 1976. Discussed above.

Personal Study of the Bible

ACQUIRING THE TOOLS

There are many reasons why a Christian might want to study the Bible: one could study in order to teach others, or the study might be a personal discipline undertaken for a particular season in the church year such as Advent or Lent, or it could be an ongoing effort to make oneself better informed as a Christian, or any of a number of other excellent reasons. The aim of Bible study is to hear more clearly what God revealed to the sacred writers and what he reveals through their words to us. To understand what the biblical authors wanted their original audiences to hear we focus on the biblical word within its historical and cultural context. Personal study strives to elucidate the historical or literal meaning of the words, passages, and stories of the Bible.

Only after we have learned what the words meant within their original context can we begin to examine what they might mean to us here and now.

Three major tools are necessary for success in this task: (a) the Bible itself, in at least two or three translations; (b) supporting secondary literature such as Bible dictionaries, commentaries, and other books on historical background and theological interpretation; and (c) one's own native intelligence and unaffected common sense which will put the right questions to the biblical text and trust the answers received to be the plain meaning of the text.

Selection between the many translations available today may be facilitated by reference to the discussion of them in chapter 1. Especially helpful are those editions that have explanatory articles and footnotes, such as the Oxford Annotated Bible (RSV), the Jerusalem Bible, the Annotated New English Bible, and the New American Bible. These different translations are needed by anyone not familiar with the Bible's original languages because no one translation can ever capture all of the nuances of the original. Having the same sentence phrased several different ways insures that we get the real point rather than something suggested by an accident of English phrasing.

The secondary literature is just that: secondary to the primary text which is the Bible itself. A good dictionary of the Bible is invaluable for identifying persons, places, objects, and concepts. Two publishers have issued good one-volume dictionaries, calling them, logically enough, *Harper's Bible Dictionary* and the *Westminster Dictionary of the Bible*. A singular accomplishment for one man is the *Dictionary of the Bible* written exclusively by John L. McKenzie. The standard multi-volume dictionary is *The Interpreter's Dictionary of the Bible* which began as four volumes and now has a supplementary volume to bring it up to date.

Commentaries give verse-by-verse interpretations of biblical books. There are two excellent single-volume commentaries on the entire Bible, *The Interpreter's One-Volume Commentary on the Bible* and *The Jerome Biblical Commentary*. In addition to the verse-by-verse analysis, both of these have valuable introductory essays on each biblical book as well as articles on biblical archaeology, geography, history, law, and so forth. The introductory essay should be read before one ever begins to study a biblical book in order to acquire an outline and overview of the book, as well as to learn its historical and theological background. The commentaries also include bibliographies that guide the reader to further and more detailed reading on the topics under consideration.

The most important tool after the text of Scripture itself is our own intelligence and common sense. That means that we approach the text with an open—but not an empty—mind. We let the plain meaning of the text come forth instead of imposing on the text what we think it ought to mean. This is to say that we must put aside our preconceptions in order to hear what the biblical writer is trying to say. This does not mean that we should approach the Bible without faith, but it does mean that we should approach it with a mind that is open to what is actually being said instead of with an expectation that it will confirm our opinions.

CONVERSATIONS WITH THE BIBLE

The best way of studying the Bible is to do so as though you are carrying on a dialogue with it. Better still, you should imagine youself as conducting an interview. You are holding a conversation with the text, putting questions to it and listening to its answers. The mystery of Bible study is that when we engage in it we enter into a dialogue not only with the words of the text but also with the divine-human encounter to which the words bear witness. Although we begin as the questioner, we soon find that we ourselves are called into question. Often our presuppositions are challenged. Rather than being frightened by this, we should accept it as a sign that we have begun to touch and to be touched by the divine Word.

Interviewing reporters proverbially ask five questions: who, what, when, where, and why. The Bible student must also ask five basic questions. The first is: What are the actual words of the passage? This is to ask whether we have the original text, what the author actually wrote. Finding this out is a highly technical process known as textual criticism (see above pp. 62–65). The amateur student of the Bible can make some decisions by seeing what variant readings are mentioned in the footnotes of the various translations and in the commentaries.

The second question to be put to the text is: What are the literary boundaries that make this passage a distinct unit, or *pericope,* to use the technical term? In other words, how does this passage fit into the outline of the book? Just as a bone can only be understood as part of a skeleton, so a passage must be seen as part of the argument of the whole book. To outline the book we note the chief characters and the progress of the action. Then we see where our bit fits in. If the passage is not narrative but, for instance, a collection of laws or proverbs, we ask what they have in common with one another, what holds them together as a unit.

Our third question concerns the identity of the speaker and the audience. Who is speaking here, to whom does he speak and for what purpose? It is important to find out not only the author's name, but where he comes from and what tradition or point of view he represents. Priests, prophets, kings, sages, and poets all speak different languages and use the literary devices that are common to their "trade." Their audience can also differ. The way a priest addresses the worshipers in the Temple is not the way a prophet speaks to a crowd, a king addresses his subjects, or a teacher talks to pupils. The help this identification of the speaker gives in understanding the passage is like the help we get from knowing whether a scene we see on television is from a newscast, a situation comedy, a dramatic story, or a commercial. The sense we make of it will depend on the purpose for which we think it is being used.

The fourth question is: What did the words of the text mean in their original historical and cultural context? Here the questioner is asking what the words or unit meant in the plain language of the time. The focus is on the literal meaning of the words, phrases, and concepts of the passage at the time it was written.

Finally, our dialogue with the text asks the last question: How was the original plain meaning of the text used later on within the Bible itself and within the Judeo-Christian tradition in the years since? In this way we can come to ask what the text means today. The Bible, as God's living word, means more than its original, historical meaning. This is shown by the retelling of patriarchal stories, the reuse prophets made of older prophecies, and the New Testament recycling of the Hebrew Bible. Each generation hears God's word anew for its own time and circumstances. For contemporary Christians who are products of the historical consciousness of today, the more-than-literal meaning of the Bible can only be sought after one is thoroughly familiar with the plain historical meaning. We cannot step out of our time and place and resort to a timeless sphere where truths are eternal and unconditioned by historical concreteness.

The personal study of the Bible through this question and answer exercise seeks to open our hearts to the inner power and dynamic of the written Word of God. These steps take us from the original meaning to the present meaning of the text. Because God continually reveals his will to his people, we cannot be satisfied with what we assume the Bible is saying to us today. We must seek to test and enrich the word today with what it meant when it was first uttered and when used through the generations.

FOR FURTHER READING:

Aldrich, Ella V., and Camp, Thomas E. *Using Theological Books and Libraries.* Englewood Cliffs, N.J.: Prentice-Hall, Inc., 1963. A valuable guide on how to use a theological library, with comment on the different types and particular titles of books related to Bible study.

Brown, Robert McAfee. *The Bible Speaks to You.* Philadelphia: Westminster Press, 1955. An excellent effort to draw on historical criticism as a way of showing how the theological and moral themes of the Bible speak to young people—and adults—today.

Brueggemann, W. *The Bible Makes Sense.* Atlanta: John Knox Press, 1977. A particularly useful way of getting into the theological thought world of the Bible. It is a "how to" book dealing with the major biblical themes.

Griffin, William Augustus. *Who Do Men Say That I Am?*, Atlanta: Episcopal Radio-TV Foundation, 1972. Two cassettes with a study guide on understanding Jesus in the light of the Old Testament.

Interpretation (A Journal of Bible and Theology), vol. 32 no. 2 (April, 1978). Richmond: Union Theological Seminary in Virginia. This issue of *Interpretation* has several helpful articles on recent Bible translations, useful in comparing the different translations one might use in studying the Bible.

Kaiser, Otto and Kümmel, Werner. *Exegetical Method: A Student's Handbook.* New York: Seabury Press, 1963. A quite practical guide to the method and resources used in studying the Bible. It presupposes that one intends to be a "serious" student of the Bible.

Richardson, Alan, ed. *A Theological Word Book of the Bible.* New York: Macmillan Co., 1950. A useful dictionary-like guide to the theological meaning of terms and concepts.

Verna Dozier is also involved in publishing a cassette presentation on group Bible study for the Episcopal Radio-TV Foundation. It will include a concise summary of the story of the Bible.

The entire King James translation of the Bible has been recorded by Alexander Scourby in sixty-four cassettes for the Episcopal Radio-TV Foundation. The cassettes may be ordered individually, in volumes, or by the entire set.

The Use of the Bible in Private Devotion

The Bible has been at the heart of personal spirituality for many centuries. A number of the psalms, for instance, were written to express the joy of meditating on the Torah day and night. The beginnings of the Christian monastic movement in the Egyptian desert centered around hermits who memorized all of the psalms and filled their days by reciting them. Translations of the Bible into the languages of the people at the time of the Reformation began a strong tradition of lay spirituality that focused on daily Bible reading.

At the same time it must be said that many Christians who have wanted to grow closer to God have set out earnestly on an effort to read the Bible only to become bogged down and discouraged, feeling that they were somehow left outside of an experience that must be reserved for the privileged few.

Sometimes they began with an intention of reading the Bible straight through, "from cover to cover," as the expression goes. This effort may not have lasted past the fifth chapter of Genesis, which is filled with sentences like: "And Mahalaleel lived sixty and five years and begat Jared: and Mahalaleel lived after he begat Jared eight hundred and thirty years, and begat sons and daughters: and all of the days of Mahalaleel were eight hundred ninety and five years: and he died" (Gen. 5:15–17). Whether this or something else happened, they decided that the Bible would have to remain a closed book to them.

Most people would be well advised to get into devotional reading of the Bible on a more modest scale at the beginning than setting out to read all of it straight through. The use of a daily devotional guide that has a Scripture reading of a few verses for each day is a good way to get one's feet wet. *Forward Day by Day*, which is available on the tract racks of most parish churches, is a very good example of this sort of thing. One of its strongest advocates was Duke Ellington:

> Ever since I saw the first copy, this little book has been my daily reading. It is clear, easy to understand, written in the language of the ordinary man, and always says things I want to know.
> (*Music Is My Mistress*, p. 282)

The British-based Bible Reading Fellowship, with American headquarters at Post Office Box M, Winter Park, Florida 32789, publishes daily Bible study guides (Series A Notes) and a daily inspirational booklet called *Salt*. At the time of this writing, both of these plus three books of Christian interest and a newsletter can be ordered from the address above for six dollars per year. This combination is referred to as the "Compass" program.

When one feels ready to try reading the Bible book by book, there are better sequences in which to read than straight through from beginning to end. Since Christians understand the Old Testament through the New, the best place to begin is with the life of Jesus in the Gospel according to Mark. After that it is good to look at the history of the early church in Acts. A few letters of St. Paul may be read after that. One may then turn to Exodus in the Old Testament, Joshua, Judges, 1 and 2 Samuel, and 1 and 2 Kings. After that possibly Amos, Hosea, and Isaiah or Jeremiah. One's own interest will probably be a safe guide after that.

The distinction between Bible study and devotional reading must be remembered. The intention is not so much historical understanding as it is to apply the Bible to one's own life, to engage one's feelings in response to God's Word and his mighty acts. A suggestion that was made by Bishop John Coburn in relation to the prayers of the Bible can be transferred to all devotional reading of the Scriptures: make the readings your own by reading them slowly as if they were addressed to you. This can be done in the Psalms, for instance, by emphasizing all of the pronouns in the first person, as in Psalm 23 in the new Prayer Book:

The Lord is *my* shepherd;
  I shall not be in want.
He makes *me* lie down in green pastures
  and leads *me* beside still waters.
He revives *my* soul
  and guides *me* along right pathways for his Name's sake.

The letters of Paul can be read as though you were a member of the congregation to whom they were written. Sometimes scholars use two Latin terms to refer to two senses of Scripture. They speak of the meaning *extra nos,* "outside of us," which is the objective and historical meaning. They also speak of the meaning *pro nobis,* "for us," which is the subjective and devotional meaning. The two do not always have to be closely related. One does not really have to be convinced that Jesus calmed a storm at sea in order to believe that he can bring peace to our tempestuous lives.

From this effort to make the readings our own to what is technically described as meditation is but a short step. Meditation is an exercise of spiritual response to a passage from the Bible, especially a story from the life of Jesus. The exercise has three steps which have been variously designated by different writers. Bishop Coburn lists the steps this way:

1. To *picture* a Biblical scene,
2. To *ponder* its meaning,
3. To *promise* God something as a result.

The Presiding Bishop, on the other hand, has spoken of these three steps as God in my head, God in my heart, and God in my hands. The first step is to recreate the scene imaginatively. One technique is to imagine that you were one of the characters in the story and think how you would tell what happened to someone else. The next step is to ask what the story means, what God was trying to do, what he is saying to you through the story. Finally, you commit yourself to a concrete action, no matter how small, to implement what you have gained from the meditation.

Sometimes meditation can be done in a group. One particular method has been recommended by Walter Wink. He suggests that members of the group do homework on the historical criticism of the passage and begin their session by discussing the passage exegetically. After that the members of the group try to picture the scene. The next step, which is very effective, draws on a technique used by psychoanalysts trained in the methods of Carl Jung. In the Jungian treatment of dreams the dreamer is not identified exclusively with the self in the dream; each character of the dream is thought to represent one dynamic of the subject's personality. Transferred to group meditation on the Bible, the technique enables members of a group reflecting, for example, on the parable of the Healing of the Paralytic to see that parts of themselves have been healed by Christ as the paralytic was, while other parts of themselves are more like the scribe who objects that the healing was performed on the Sabbath.

In devotional use of the Bible Christians can hear God speaking to them through his Word more directly than almost any other way.

FOR FURTHER READING:

Coburn, John B. *Prayer and Personal Religion.* Layman's Theological Library. Philadelphia: The Westminster Press, 1957. A good simple introduction to the various forms of prayer.

de Dietrich, Suzanne. *Discovering the Bible*. Nashville: Source Publishers, 1953. Both a theoretical and a practical guide for meditation upon Scripture.
––––––. *God's Unfolding Purpose: A Guide to the Study of the Bible*.
Philadelphia: The Westminster Press, 1960. Provides an overall
sweep of the biblical drama together with a section-by-section
guide to the study of and meditation upon the Bible.
Robertson, E. H. *"Take and Read": A Guide to Group Bible Study*.
London: SCM Press, 1961. Examines different types of group Bible
study and suggests which are most appropriate for particular
kinds of groups. Included is a chapter on how to choose a biblical
book for study.
Wink, Walter. *The Bible in Human Transformation: Toward a New
Paradigm for Biblical Study*. Philadelphia: Fortress Press, 1973. This
book not only sets forth the method of group meditation described above but also gives a trenchant analysis of how biblical
study has been subverted from a means of religious growth into
an academic discipline with no personal implications.

The Use of the Bible in Evangelism

At least four kinds of activity are involved in evangelism:
persuading non-Christians to become Christians, recruiting
inactive or unfulfilled members of other Christian bodies for
one's own, assisting late adolescent and young adult members of one's own church to move from testing to owned
faith, and helping adult members of one's own church to
become renewed in their faith. Different uses of the Bible are
appropriate for each of these. Renewal movements are too
numerous to be discussed adequately here. Helping young
people to move from testing to owned faith is discussed in
our treatment of Christian Education. At this point, therefore, the discussion will be limited to helping non-Christians
to become Christians and non-Episcopalians to become
Episcopalians.

For those who do not accept the Christian faith the need is
to show that human life as they have experienced it is described more adequately in the Bible than anywhere else. The
usual way of presenting this is to start with the non-
Christian's sense of alienation—from others, from the uni-

verse, from his or her true self, from God. This may be experienced by that person either in a sense of guilt or in a sense of a lack of meaning to life. In either case the biblical understanding of what it means to be human is often greeted by those who learn it for the first time with a shock of recognition. Such a person can be offered the hope of reconciliation, of alienation overcome, that the New Testament holds out through Jesus Christ. The lay person who attempts to share faith in this way can acquire facility in the biblical message by mastering the chapters in this book on biblical theology or can try to arrange for the non-Christian in question to get in touch with someone who has had more extensive training in the study of the Bible.

Often non-Christians will have to overcome acquired prejudice against the Bible that is the result of inappropriate presentations which they have encountered previously. Then, too, many non-Episcopalians will be dissatisfied with their former church precisely because they cannot accept its literalistic approach to the Bible. The discovery that the Episcopal Church takes the Bible seriously without taking it literally may be the best news they have ever heard. For a long time they may have wanted to be wholehearted Christians and have felt many pangs of guilt because their minds simply were unable to accept the presentation of the Scriptures made by their denomination. To learn that one can be Christian and at the same time have intellectual integrity as a citizen of the twentieth century can be an experience of great relief and release for such persons.

As important as the Bible is to any program of evangelism, it is necessary to remember that more is involved. For Episcopalians evangelism will usually focus on inviting prospective converts to church so that the liturgy can make its impact on them. Those who feel the power of God through the worship of the Book of Common Prayer (including its liturgical use of the Bible) will be drawn to return. When attendance has become a habit for them, they can be invited to receive instruction for membership. After they have been initiated into the church they should be integrated into the life of the congregation by being put to work. After that they should be encouraged to discover other people like themselves who need to hear the Christian Gospel as this church has received it. Conversion is not just a private transaction between an individual and God; it is incorporation into that community of God's people which has its beginning recorded in the Old Testament and its reconstitution as the Christian church recorded in the New and which has its life today in the parishes where Christians gather to worship.

FOR FURTHER READING:

Edwards, O. C., Jr. "An Overview of Evangelism in the Church: New Testament Times to the Present." *Anglican Theological Review*, Supplementary Series, No. 6 (June 1976), pp. 151–69. Also published in *Realities and Visions: The Church's Mission Today*, edited by Furman C. Stough and Urban T. Holmes, III, New York: Seabury Press, 1976, and as a cassette from Episcopal Radio-TV Foundation. An analysis of evangelism and a thesis about methods that are appropriate for the Episcopal Church.

————. *What Is Evangelism?* Atlanta: Episcopal Radio-TV Foundation, 1977. A study course consisting of three cassettes and a study guide for the purpose of analyzing what evangelism is, deciding what are appropriate methods for Episcopalians, and planning a parish program according to principles discussed above.

————. "Evangelism." *Saint Luke's Journal of Theology* 21 (1978): 165–80. An analysis of conversion as one event that has intellectual, moral, psychological, sociological, and metaphysical dimensions. The recognition of this truth is essential to any sound program for evangelism.

The Authority of the Bible for Theology

A naïve view of the relation of the Bible to theology would be that theology consists of setting out in a systematic way all that the Bible has to say on the various topics of Christian belief such as God, Christ, the Holy Spirit, the church, and so forth. Anglicanism has always recognized, however, that three factors are involved in theology: the Bible, Christian tradition, and reason.

The necessity for this fuller view of what constitutes theology can be illustrated by the account in Chapter 4 of the different ways in which the story of Isaac and Esau was understood at different periods in the early history of Israel. The view of reality that a society has is not the same from one period to the next, even though the basic commitments of that society remain the same. As the sociologists of knowledge say, a given culture "constructs reality" differently at different times. The enduring faith, therefore, has to be restated in terms of the presuppositions that are made in each generation.

To say that the *Bible* is authoritative for Christian belief is to say that the church today is in continuity with Israel and the early church, and that it is in essence the same community at a later period in its history. This community's classic and normative experience of Jesus and God in the history of Israel still gives our faith its basic shape today.

Tradition is, among other things, the record of the church's efforts to express the faith of the Bible in terms of the view of reality current in every period of its history. Obviously some of those efforts were more successful than others. The least successful ones were discarded by the church as heresy. The more successful remain authoritative for us today as examples of the way the biblical faith can be rephrased in the thought forms of a later age and also can be extended to comprehend situations and knowledge that had not been envisioned by the biblical writers.

To say that we employ *reason* in theology is not to affirm that we have access to some timeless logic. It is rather to say that we have to state our Christian belief in terms of the understanding of reality that is taken for granted in our own times. Sometimes it also means using the thought forms of our own times to demonstrate the inadequacy of contemporary presuppositions that are inconsistent with full Christian faith.

Psychologists who specialize in the way people learn have shown that every impression our senses receive is sorted by the mind according to whether it is consistent or inconsistent with the understanding of the universe that the mind has already formed. Sensations that are consistent with that picture are assimilated to it. If inconsistent sensations are persistent enough, the picture must be revised to accommodate the new data.

Societies go through much the same process as individuals. The majority of people in a society share a basic idea of the nature of reality. This view is shared so deeply that the average person never thinks of it as a view; the view is assumed to be a direct perception of reality. New information is acquired, however, that not only reminds everyone that the view is only a view and not reality itself; it also shows that the view was an inadequate one. A construction of reality, then, stands in constant need of either legitimation or revision.

Christians make up a subculture within a majority culture. The task of theology is mediating between the historic faith of the church and our society's constantly revised construction of reality. As already noted (p. 73), one of the qualities of a good law is its capacity to be extended to new situations for which it was never intended originally. This same kind of extension of principles of Christian belief growing out of the Bible is called for in a society that assumes that the earth revolves around a sun that is 93,000,000 miles away, that our solar system is part of a minor galaxy within almost an infinity of galaxies, that the universe is billions rather than thousands of years old, that human life evolved from lower life and ultimately from inorganic matter, and so forth and so on.

Theology consists of the construction of such extensions. Needless to say, a good bit of trial and error is involved; some extensions are more adequate or apt than others. Often it is not immediately apparent which are which. Sometimes it takes the church a generation or so to come to a consensus about which proposed extensions were apt and which were blind alleys.

The test of the adequacy of any proposal, however, is the consistency of the extension with what it extends. Is the faith of the Bible still being affirmed in new situations or has "the baby been thrown out with the bath water" somewhere along the line? The Bible, which is the church's adequate account of Jesus and of Israel's experience of God, furnishes the principles that are to be extended to fit new situations. It also serves as the standard against which those extensions have to be tested. Tradition is the history of the apt extensions that have been made through the centuries and thus also furnishes models for making apt extensions. Reason is our society's construction of reality to which the biblical faith must be extended. It takes all three—Bible, tradition, and reason—to have a theology that is adequate according to Anglican standards.

FOR FURTHER READING:

Barr, James. *The Bible in the Modern World.* New York and Evanston: Harper & Row, 1973. An examination of the key concepts in the understanding of biblical authority, a survey of current ways of thinking about that authority, and the constructive proposal of a way to think about it.

Berger, Peter L. *The Sacred Canopy: Elements of a Sociological Theory of Religion.* Garden City, N.Y.: Anchor Books, 1969. An application of the sociology of knowledge to religion. Such an understanding underlies the explanation given above for the constant necessity of theological revision.

Kelsey, David H. *The Uses of Scripture in Recent Theology.* Philadelphia: Fortress Press, 1975. For those with the background to understand it, this is a model of lucid reasoning about how the Bible has been used by theologians in the past and what is involved in treating the Bible as authoritative.

Bringing the Bible to Bear on Moral Decisions

One way of drawing on the Bible for guidance in the moral decisions that we all must make in our daily living would be to comb through it and excerpt all of the statements that recommend one course of action and condemn another—its "thou shalts" and "thou shalt nots"—so that when a situation occurred all we would need to do would be to discover the appropriate regulation. The trouble with doing that is that the outlook of the people who wrote the Bible was not only pretechnological but even prescientific. They came largely from oriental and agrarian cultures. We, on the other hand, have a point of view that is twentieth-century, Western, technological, and urban. The Bible, therefore, not only gives a permanently valid account of divine-human encounters, but also at the same time reflects a culturally conditioned point of view that we no longer share.

The biblical writers, for instance, accept without question a number of institutions and attitudes that are offensive to contemporary moral sensitivities. Slavery and the inferiority of women are no longer accepted. At the same time, contemporary life involves complex judgments that the sacred writers never imagined, such as our ability to disrupt our environment, produce test-tube babies, prolong life, or destroy the universe. We can see some carryover: the demand of prophets like Amos for social justice or the attitude toward God and neighbor in the Ten Commandments still have an obvious relevance. Yet other sections of the Bible—such as, for instance, the bizarre imagery of Daniel—seem to offer little moral guidance to contemporary Christians. Nor does the dietary and cultic legislation of Leviticus (although it is still important for orthodox Jewish practice).

The changing moral demands of new generations, however, should come as no surprise to anyone really familiar with the Bible. Jesus, for instance, preached exclusively to his own people, and he himself observed the Torah. After his resurrection, however, Gentiles as well as Jews were called into the saving fellowship of his church and Jewish customs receded into the background. Acts and the letters of Paul testify to new attitudes and new actions that emerged within the church, not in reaction against the old Israel but in response to the continuing presence of God in the church. Taking this lead from the biblical record itself, the Christian community always looks to God as a present and future reality rather than as one locked into the past. The identity of a Christian today, therefore, is shaped not just by the Bible but also by the church as it tries to live out its vocation in the world of today. The Bible records the encounters of God with the community of his people in their past history. The church today is the latest generation of that community and it is still encountering this same God in the events of current history. Precisely because God is still calling his people onward, we can expect expanding awareness of what is good and what he expects of us. Thus the fact that biblical situations no longer exist and that situations unknown to the biblical world do exist need not paralyze us when we try as Christians to make uniquely modern choices.

The applicability of biblical attitudes to contemporary moral decisions becomes more obvious when we remember that Jesus' standards are not to be thought of as laws that must be obeyed, but as an invitation to experience what life can be like when it is lived in the kingdom (see p. 222). Further, the basic thesis of this book—that the Bible teaches more through stories that have a variety of applications to new situations than through an explicit statement of hard and fast principles—also leads one to expect that biblical moral teaching will appear more in perspectives than in laws. From being immersed in the stories and in Jesus' teaching about the kingdom, the Christian acquires a number of postures toward life, a number of attitudes or perspectives that furnish the context in which any moral decision is made. It is the totality of these perspectives that makes up Christian character. Christian virtues result from the effort to apply these perspectives to particular moral decisions.

At this point a parenthetical remark of great importance needs to be made: The individual Christian is not left completely on his or her own to make decisions. One way of describing the church is to say that it is the community that has biblical perspectives on moral situations and that it is constantly engaged in assessing the ways in which they are applied to contemporary life. All Christian moral choice, then, is made within the Body of Christ and is informed by the Body.

The insights expressed in the last few paragraphs have been stated abstractly and need to be illustrated. Two examples can show how these principles work: technology and revolution. The moral problems of technology have come into existence only within the last century, when technology itself has come into being. One area of moral problems that it poses, that of ecology, has been recognized by the general public for only a decade or so. Yet biblical perspectives can furnish us with the means to make moral decisions even in this brand new field. Here, as elsewhere, all of these perspectives are not neatly consistent with one another but instead balance each other: the Jesus who told us to turn the other cheek is the one who plaited a whip and drove the money changers out of the Temple. The various perspectives can be compared to the laser beams used in holographic photography to create an image that is three-dimensional.

Thus we bring to the issue of technology our perspective on creation. We recognize that the Bible sees creation not just as something that happened in the past, but as an ongoing process in which new realities continually emerge, such as the creation of the people of God and provision for redemption in Christ. More, we see that our expectation of the second coming of Christ orients us toward the future and leads us to believe that the meaning of history will emerge into full clarity only at its end. This means that we can see new technology as part of the ongoing work of creation and rejoice in it. That hope, however, must be tempered by our recognition of the sacredness of creation, by the knowledge that "the earth is the Lord's." It is therefore to be cared for and to be loved. Technology then must be used for the sake of man and of God's creation and can never be treated as an end in itself. Like the Sabbath, it was made for man and not man for it.

By the same token, liberation is a powerful biblical image and the release of the Hebrew people from slavery in Egypt has furnished a biblical grounding for all revolutionary efforts to throw off the bonds of oppression. The biblical demand for justice and the understanding of redemption are also perspectives that influenced a German pastor and theologian, Dietrich Bonhoeffer, to participate in a plot to assassinate Adolf Hitler. For similar reasons the World Council of Churches gave its support a generation later to the efforts of guerrillas of the Third World to overthrow oppressive regimes. At the same time, another perspective of the Bible is that all human life is sacred. Balancing these perspectives against one another is always a difficult task. Yet Christian moral decisions are made by an effort to keep all such perspectives in a proper tension with one another.

FOR FURTHER READING:

Birch, Bruce C., and Rasmussen, Larry D. *Bible and Ethics in the Christian Life*. Minneapolis: Augsburg Publishing House, 1976. This book deals both with the theoretical and practical relationship between the disciplines of ethics and Bible study. Some suggestions are given for using the Bible in helping one make important decisions.

Everding, H. Edward, Jr., and Wilbanks, Dana W. *Decision Making and the Bible*. Valley Forge: Judson Press, 1975. Attempts to provide a practical guide for biblical considerations in making moral decisions. Though meant for average parishioners, it seems more useful as a leaders's guide.

Knox, John. *The Ethic of Jesus in the Teaching of the Church: Its Authority and Its Relevance*. Nashville: Abingdon Press, 1961. A classic essay on taking seriously the ethic of Jesus without being legalistic and moralistic, and on relating the law with the love of God.

Notes

CHAPTER 2

1. *Biblia* can have its origin traced back even further to Byblos, the name of a town on the Palestinian coast from which writing material made from the pulp of the papyrus plant was distributed throughout the ancient Mediterranean world.

CHAPTER 3

1. Since the word *virgin* occurs only in the Greek translation of Isaiah and not in the Hebrew original, Matthew must have used the Greek. The corresponding Hebrew word means "young woman."

2. This plan of God revealed in the Old Testament is what St. Paul means by "mystery," as in Rom. 16:25, 26.

CHAPTER 4

1. This chapter draws heavily on the following works: Hans Frei, *The Eclipse of Biblical Narrative* (New Haven: Yale University Press, 1974), and *The Identity of Jesus Christ* (Philadelphia: Fortress Press, 1975); David Kelsey, *The Uses of the Bible in Recent Theology* (Philadelphia: Fortress Press, 1975); Norman Perrin, *The New Testament: An Introduction* (New York: Harcourt Brace Jovanovich, 1974), pp. 26–34; Paul Ricoeur, *The Symbolism of Evil* (Boston: Beacon Press, 1967).

CHAPTER 5

1. From Elie Wiesel, *The Gates of the Forest* (New York: Holt, Rinehardt & Winston, 1966).

2. Scholars believe that this song, one of the oldest literary fragments in the Old Testament, dates back to the time of the crossing of the Red Sea.

CHAPTER 8

1. For the basic structure of the Fourth Gospel and for its main divergences from the Synoptics, see pp. 31–32.

2. The fictional apocryphal gospels tell many stories of Jesus' childhood, but they are motivated by pious curiosity or theological purposes and are not very edifying.

3. This story has troubled the consciences of many generations of Christians. It is best understood not as a historical reminiscence of Jesus but as an early Christian way of justifying their sharing their Jewish Savior with non-Jews.

4. In his efforts to show that Paul was innocent, Luke went too far in minimizing the differences between the belief of the Pharisees in life after death and Christian belief in the resurrection of Jesus as the basis of their own hope.

5. Suetonius, *The Twelve Caesars,* trans. Robert Graves (Baltimore: Penguin, 1957), Claudius 25.

CHAPTER 9

1. This chapter and the next owe much to Gerhard von Rad, *Old Testament Theology,* 2 vols. (New York: Harper and Row, 1962–65).

2. *The Infancy Story of Thomas,* trans. A. J. B. Higgins, in Edgar Hennecke, *New Testament Apocrypha,* ed. W. Schneemelcher, trans. ed. R. McL. Wilson (Philadelphia: Westminster Press, 1963), I, 394.

CHAPTER 10

1. This recognition, that references to speaking in tongues is a narrative technique used by Luke to indicate the spread of the Spirit-filled community, could be understood by some as questioning the biblical basis for the contemporary charismatic movement. It would be more correct to say that the New Testament warranty for an evaluation of the phenomenon is the fourteenth chapter of 1

Corinthians. There St. Paul discusses ecstatic phenomena at some length. He claims to have experienced them to an extraordinary degree himself and considers them to be good, but he is far more concerned with the welfare of the church than he is with impressive behavior. In Galatians 5:22 he lists the fruit of the Spirit as "love, joy, peace, patience, kindness, goodness, faithfulness, gentleness, self-control." He undoubtedly would consider the presence of these to be far more certain evidence of the activity of the Holy Spirit in the life of a Christian than any ecstatic phenomena or religious experience, although he was grateful for what he had received in that way too.

2. Willi Marxsen, *Introduction to the New Testament* (Philadelphia: Fortress Press, 1968), p. 275.

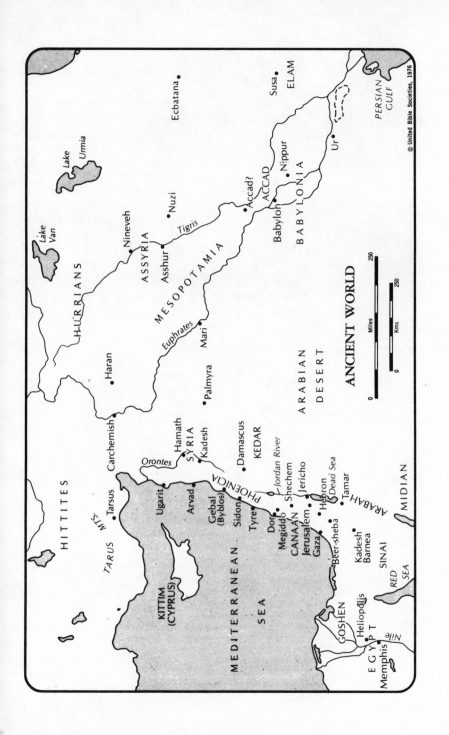

ANCIENT WORLD

Kadesh

Gebal

SIDONIANS
MT. LEBANON
BETHREHOB

SYRIA

Sidon
•Damascus

MT. HERMON

Tyre
Abel •Dan
Hazor MAACAH
Bashan
Cabul GESHUR •Ashtaroth
MT. CARMEL
Dor Megiddo Edrei
Jezreel
Taanach •Romoth
MT. GILBOA Jabesh
Jordan Zarethan
Shechem Jabbok
Gathrimmon Jazer
Joppa Beth •Rabbah
Gezer Horon Bethel AMMONITES
Ashdod Ekron Jericho
Ashkelon Jerusalem •Heshbon
Gath? •Mediba
Gaza Debir Hebron Dibon
Gerar Ziklag? Dead •Aroer
Beersheba Sea
MOABITES
Tamar •Kir Hers

AMALEKITES
•Bozrah
•Kadesh-Barnea

EDOMITES
Sela

The

Negev

The Desert

UNITED ISRAELITE
KINGDOM

0   Miles   60

0   Kms   60

© United Bible Societies, 1976

Eziongeber
GULF OF
AQABA

MEDITERRANEAN SEA

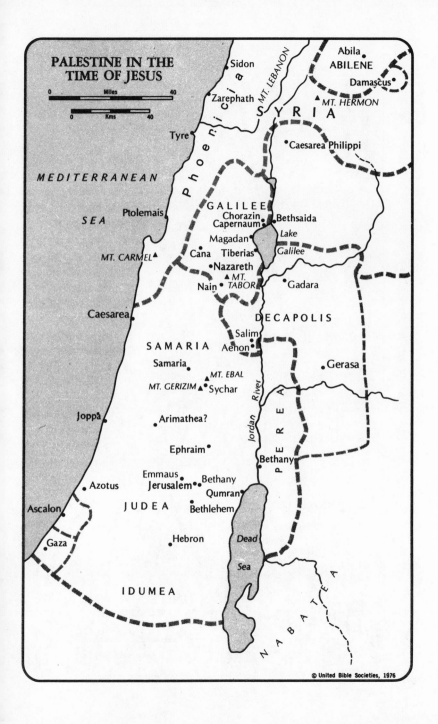

PALESTINE IN THE TIME OF JESUS

Sidon
Zarephath
Tyre
Ptolemais
Chorazin
Capernaum
Bethsaida
Magadan
Cana Tiberias
Nazareth
Nain
Caesarea
Salim
Aenon
Samaria
Sychar
Arimathea?
Ephraim
Emmaus
Jerusalem
Bethany
Qumran
Bethlehem
Azotus
Ascalon
Gaza
Hebron

Abila
ABILENE
Damascus
MT. HERMON
Caesarea Philippi

GALILEE
Lake
Galilee
Gadara

MT. TABOR

DECAPOLIS

Gerasa

MT. EBAL
MT. GERIZIM

SAMARIA

JUDEA

IDUMEA

MEDITERRANEAN

SEA

MT. CARMEL

Joppa

Phoenicia

MT. LEBANON

SYRIA

Jordan River

PEREA

Dead
Sea

NABATEA

Miles
0   40

Kms
0   40

© United Bible Societies, 1976

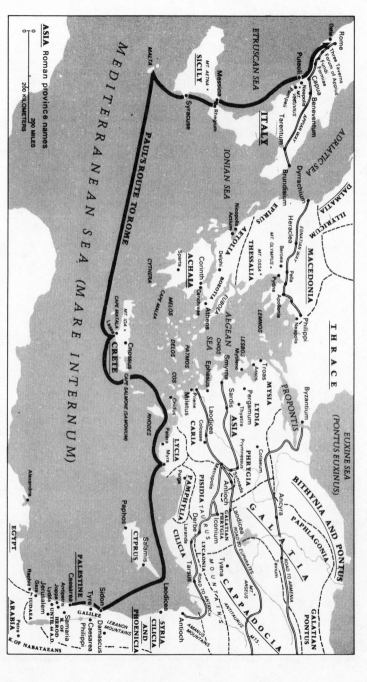

The World of the Apostle Paul

Index of
Biblical References

297

Index

WORK AS ART

WORK AS ART

··········

Idaho Logging as an Aesthetic Moment

Charlene James-Duguid

A Publication in Northwest Folklife,
Louie W. Attebery, General Editor

University of Idaho Press/Moscow, Idaho
1996

Copyright © 1996 University of Idaho Press
Published by the University of Idaho Press
Moscow, Idaho 83844-1107
Printed in the United States of America
All rights reserved

00 99 98 98 96 5 4 3 2 1

Cover photos, left to right: Ted Leach (courtesy, the author), Jake Altmiller (courtesy, Jeff Tinsley, Office of Printing and Photographic Services, Smithsonian Institution), Sharon Barnett (courtesy, Jeff Tinsley, Office of Printing and Photographic Services, Smithsonian Institution). All other photographs are by the author, except where otherwise noted.

Typography by WolfPack

James-Duguid, Charlene, 1942-
     Work as art : Idaho logging as an aesthetic moment / Charlene James-Duguid.
          p.   cm.   —(A Publication in northwest folklife)
     Includes bibliographical references (p. 133) and index.
     ISBN 0-89301-190-8 (cloth)
     1. Logging—Idaho—Orofino. 2. Loggers—Idaho—Orofino—Biography. 3. Orofino (Idaho)—Biography. 4. Orofino (Idaho)—Social life and customs. I. Title. II. Series: Publication in northwest folklife.
SD538.2.I2J35
979.6'88—dc20   95-48839
                                                                                              CIP

There is a great deal of nonsense written about aesthetic experiences on the assumption of their being not only apart from common experience but phenomena of peculiar and special concern to the artist. They are neither. Every man's entire experience of life is the aesthetic experience of sensual contact; and by the degree of a man's immediate sensitivity to such contact rests his inherent right to be an artist. It is that sensitivity, urged to expression by the creative impulse, of which it is perhaps the parent, which determines the artist, and which remains with him as the only guide and rule of beauty in the work he does. One is an artist not by knowing laws, but by feeling beauty so unerringly that his experience of beauty infinitely transcends the limitations of formulae.

Rockwell Kent, "On Aesthetics"

To the memory of
Dorothy Frances Drezdon James

Contents

••••••••••

ILLUSTRATIONS

....

ACKNOWLEDGMENTS

·········

Many people helped write this book with their love and caring. Before I knew Orofino existed, my grandmother Frances Piontkowski, father Sylvester James, and uncle Frank Malecki taught me the value of work. Myron A. Loewinger first accompanied me to Idaho and Michael Kenny listened for hours as I tried to convince him that description spoke for itself. Never more than a phone call away, my patient mother, Dorothy James, heard about a place she did not know but an attitude she knew so well. And home—home is my husband Jim Duguid, who speaks in actions. He built an atmosphere of perfection with craftsmanship creating the ambience for writing. In our simple life of two people together he listened intently, judging whether the nuances of my poetry were grounded in solid reality. To him, and Andrew and Meg, who love him, I offer this book.

Art historian Charles Millard established a realistic, logging-centered definition of aesthetics by saying, "Don't give it labels; show how these people look at their world." In *The Art Spirit,* American artist Robert Henri said, "Art when really understood is the province of every human being. It is simply a question of doing things, anything well. It is not an outside, extra thing." Rockwell Kent's presence pervades this book, as does the work of the University of Idaho Press staff.

To the people of Orofino, I send my deepest appreciation with more than a dedication: I acknowledge that they, more than I, are the authors of this book. Ingrid Ponozzo, the guiding light of Orofino Celebrations Incorporated and a loving human being, shines through, as do the other elders in logging—Joe Richardson and Louie Porter—along with young loggers like Bill Stephenson, who are no longer with us. Many people appear and are acknowledged by name but others were a constant support during my visits. Though they are unnamed, I send my appreciation to them. And to Jim Cochrane, my thanks for his strong injunction, "Don't write anything boring; it's not true of this town." He was so right, for as I learned from the people of Orofino, theirs is a vibrant story.

INTRODUCTION

·········

The Limner

I am a limner—an itinerant portrait painter in the artistic sense—and a limnar—a person who is on the threshold of understanding in the anthropological sense. I am on the periphery of the lives of loggers, but I am central as the painter of their world. As in the early days of America, like a limner I walked into a community in search of exactly the right subjects for these literary images. As a limnar, I stood at the doorway of Idaho lives, always seeking clues for my canvas—this book. With the help of the community, I've recorded the vision of the logging life they are trying to maintain. I have tried to follow the suggestion of Clifford Geertz (1988:10) "find where to stand in the text that is supposed to be at one and the same time an intimate view and a cool assessment."

Clearwater County has its own individual lifestyle and so logging in other regions, in other historical periods, or as described by other writers may differ from my portraits of these long-time residents of the Idaho panhandle during the 1980s and 1990s. As a limner would, I looked for the prosperous and the noble, the fresh and the innocent to portray. I sought those who epitomized the lifestyle of the independent logging contractor and his family. I chose both men and women, because they play equally significant roles in the logging community—men as they perform their jobs and women as they influence tradition and act as organizing agents for the industry.

As these people spoke to me, we all created this image, we all were the authors of this book. Each person mentioned has reviewed and edited his or her presence in the text, and I hope that in addition to portraying this community, I have contributed to a new literary treatment in anthropology. If it has been successful, the distinctions between these people and myself will become unimportant and the sense of authorship and ownership will bring us together. So far the Idaho authors have commented that I've come close to what they want to say about their lives. But if I have failed to create a total image that we share I can look forward to a real-life social drama in which the Idaho authors who are strong in their opinions and solid in their convictions will contradict my findings.

I know that the people of Orofino will be affected by this book; they hope for an elegance, an idealism in the story of their lives, but they also expect it to be truthful, making no excuses for attitudes that may not be currently popular. I have tried to write an intimate, poetic, engaging book without jeopardizing the reality of this way of life. Proposing that we were authors of this work together is a dangerous suggestion since I have included my impressions of events. I hope that my coauthors will take no offense to my liberty with these inclusions.

Anthropological thinking today suggests that more than one voice can be heard (Marcus and Fischer 1986). But there are concerns about how identities are negotiated and documented in the story. According to Marcus (1989), the most venturesome works in the trend of ethnography are concerned with the shaping and transformation of identities of both subjects and ethnographer. These works are causing anthropology to question the way it works.

In an ethnography, reality is altered by the writer's presence. Without knowledge of my position, perception of this book about the loggers and their point of view would be skewed; therefore it is necessary for me to state that I have tried to create a realistic ethnography, but have not concentrated on pan-national values, the international logging economy, or the interplay between loggers and those with political or ecological concerns who contest their way of life.

Originally, I chose Orofino for its festival, Clearwater County Fair and Lumberjack Days. From my first contact with it over fifteen years ago, I believed that it could be an ideal event to paint. My preoccupation at that time was to describe the festival as a way to retain the sense of community while negotiating the dilemmas of diverse lifestyles in a changing world. I saw in those who befriended me—both well-established independent loggers who were members of Orofino Celebrations Incorporated (OCI) and members of the business community—a sense of mission to preserve and live a small community life in contemporary America.

During my early visits, I saw this feeling of community embodied in the annual festival which I believed to be symbolic of their life. But when members of the community saw my intentions, they welcomed me and invited me to learn about the lives they lead day in and day out and I discovered that it was in work, not through play, that the central values of the community emerged. And so, instead of painting a people at play, in celebration, I am now a limner who realizes that meaning in the world of Clearwater County is in real actions and work. The festival is the performance of certain themes, but everyday life holds a meaning that far surpasses festive behavior.

While my position and perspective affect this portrait, I have tried to give full voice to the people of Clearwater County. I've tried to place the loggers' role in a larger artistic context, being sensitive to the shared memories and historical consciousness of loggers. To the community of loggers, history is embodied in the presence of the old-timers. Their memories shape contemporary social and occupational values because though no longer working in the woods, they still play a central role in the aesthetics of logging.

With their straightforward ways, the loggers and the people of Orofino made this portrait possible. They have a sincere desire to inform the world of their beliefs, of the nobility of their occupation, the intensity of their volunteer life, and the richness of their existence. They and I share a belief in negotiating the future in a changing world. I do not thrive in conflict situations; these people ameliorate all conflicts through negotiation as soon as they arise.

The picture of these men and women may seem all too perfect at times. I admit that this community understands stagecraft, perpetually acting out social roles in ways that place a high value on balance. They see themselves as mature, conservative adults of comfortable means but they would not classify themselves as an elite group. That designation is not used in Orofino. Those people portrayed represent the hopes of the community, if not always the reality of its way of life. However, a problem arises in portraying work as art. There are a multitude of jobs in logging that I have not described. The images of the many competent workers in the woods and mills may seem shadowy, for other than the best among them, they were not highlighted on this canvas. As a limner in the artistic sense, I am a portraitist of those who use themselves and their symbols to make a statement about a way of life. But I have also put myself into the picture, for I have stimulated motion, conversation, and thought in the society. At the same time, as a follower of Victor Turner, I know I am a limnar—I am truly on the threshold, a temporary. At this doorway, I felt myself to be outside categories—not male, not female, not young, not old. I never felt that my personal characteristics ever influenced our coauthorship.

I was able to write as an artist poetically and with feelings, not merely mine but often theirs, while as an anthropologist, I tried to capture the meanings they apply to their lives. These people do not speak in categories of politics, economics, language, domestic life, religion, and so forth, and neither does this book. Instead it focuses on individuals who occupy roles in different areas of society. For example, the three County Commissioners typify the workings of county politics; Father Michael Spegele represents an opinion on religion; and Norman and Sharon Baugh describe the way successful marriages are organized. They are all representatives of the community who speak with conviction about specific elements of their life. However, I have not ventured past their descriptions to apply the classical anthropological categories to their world. My goal is to concentrate on descriptions that the community members might have written about themselves. If anything, I hope that the work is seen as a coming together of an anthropologist with a community, and will thereby be considered a contribution to the discipline.

In a literary sense, the portraits contained herein serve as "slices of life." They really happened. Those people reported as saying and doing certain things actually said and did them. My reflections flow in and out of the text without breaks in the action: I have tried to choose each word and phrase precisely, to make real the specific occurrences that took place. I participated in Orofino's life. I spoke the same language, shared the same national economy, and was a part of the same citizenry in a contemporary world. But even though we shared a common culture, I found that a small town milieu and loggers' mentality were far different from the patterns lived in

Washington, D.C., my hometown. The significance of topography in the community's perception of the environment; the stories of logging by the old-timers who are at the heart of the community; the loggers' opinions of work and art; and the special role of women in enhancing the quality of life are important to understand. These demonstrate the nature and satisfaction of work, its aesthetic quality, and the way that work, art, and life meld together. The portraits provide a vehicle for discussing work as art and capture loggers using words like "artist," "emotional," and "perfect." Logging is an art that is created, appreciated, and perpetuated in a natural setting. It is an art of doing and experiencing, always directed toward perfection as suggested by visionary artists like Robert Henri (1984) and Rockwell Kent (1933) and philosophers like Robert Plant Armstrong (1975) and John Dewey (1934).

During my visits to Clearwater County I developed techniques that made my work easier. The townspeople became accustomed to my ever-present notebook and often joked about it. I knew that the telephone was useless and only by getting out and about would I learn what was going on. So I went everywhere—church, shopping, meetings, dinners, schools, cultural organizations, restaurants, and even bars. I'd drop in sometimes with no questions but always kept an option for another visit open. I remembered birthdays with small cakes and sent letters to the editor of the weekly newspaper. I carried a camera and took photos, distributing copies on subsequent visits. And I religiously watched videotapes of logging operations, community plays, high school concerts, and classic logging films like *Charlie the Lonesome Cougar* and *Come and Get It*. Often these became the jumping-off point for a conversation that eventually resulted in a portrait.

I would have failed as a limner if I had produced a lifeless rendition of the times I had spent talking with people, visiting their logging jobs, homes, and families. Orofinoans, those who lived the story while I wrote it, would find it dry and boring. They know that the reality of ordinary life might seem mundane, but they and I hoped that when painted this community and its members would rise above the commonplace.

These portraits are not anonymous or nameless. The people of Orofino like seeing their words in print and their opinions on parade. They like to think of themselves as storytellers, not of tall tales from unknown origins but of episodes from their lives and the lives of those around them. Rarely did they stop at mere description, for they are thoughtful about their existence and often became their own analysts. Their colorful words bring life to this book. Logging, generally seen only as a product-oriented occupation in a physically demanding environment, emerges as having its own social and artistic standards. The timber that is produced, the resulting visual impact on the natural setting, and the manner in which the task is performed all figure significantly into the end result.

The aesthetic, which is a particular brand of the appropriate, fits into the rest of the loggers' existence because work is not segmented out—it is an inseparable part of a balanced life. Work becomes a social outlet and an artistic pursuit when it captures the subtle moments in the lives of these loggers, the intricacies of a logging job, and the beauty of a well-cut stand of trees. This art is ephemeral, never manageable enough for a museum setting, never individual enough for an art historian's critique. It lives in the memories of old-timers and the everyday visions of contemporary loggers. It exists in loggers' conversations about the artistic elements of their work and is strongest when loggers talk about the real artists in the woods, the emotions connected with the passage of time, and the regeneration of their environment. It is a constant struggle for perfection that is understood best by those who live it every day.

And so this book brings together two threads rarely interwoven, the work of logging and the ideal of leading a balanced life. It suggests that work well-done and life well-managed can be defined as art.

I begin this painting with a tribute to Ingrid Ponozzo, a woman who captures the essence of a life in logging. This is a portrait of a proud woman and beautiful woman, always classically dressed, even when conforming to the Lumberjack Days red-and-white color code. She was very well loved.

Near death the last time I saw her, Ingrid demonstrated a quality many Orofino women possess. Beautiful yet frail, still smoking even though she was dying of cancer, and slow about mouthing her answers, she still had a quick wit and was well able to get her point across. Even when it was difficult for her to breathe, she lay there newly manicured, concerned about her appearance while uttering incongruously, "I'm tough." Many Orofino women exhibit this contrast: an important face they show to the world, while underneath they can work with the best of the men. They can take the hardships and are proud of it.

When I last visited Ingrid, her body was barely able to move. My feelings did not allow me to ask relevant questions, so instead I decided to create a story about logging. We pretended to get into a logging truck and she went gladly as she might have with her husband so many years ago. We must find a crew. She winces at some of my suggestions, perhaps remembering long-held rivalries. "No, no," she says, "not on my job." To others she'd say, "Sure, he's okay, I remember him." This woman whom I had admired for so long was at a critical point in her existence and all I could do was invent a deathbed survey of reputation and work habits. Though not intended, it had happened when I had wanted only to bring her some joy, some remembrance.

By the time we got to the imaginary job site with our truck and our crew, she was delighting in the thought of people who had been a part of her world, who had helped her when she was the manager of Lumberjack Days. That time had been filled with work and excitement. She had taken care of the annual festival for over twenty years, diplomatic when the occasion called for it and tyrannical when there was no other way. She was the foundation for the performance of the logging lifestyle and the glue that kept OCI together.

Ingrid Ponozzo, manager of the Orofino Celebrations Incorporated Logging Show, pictured here in 1976, epitomized the significant role of women in the logging industry. She was the driving force of OCI until her death in 1990.

Empty—the sense of loss coming with death—was how Don Ponozzo felt at Ingrid's passing. Until her illness in June, 1990, they had been inseparable. Her feet had hit the floor before his every morning. At 4:00 A.M., she was immaculately dressed, her hair and makeup done to perfection, and she had breakfast ready for him.

Her obituary recited specifics—family survivors, civic positions, Swedish heritage—but could not tell the story of this woman. Ingrid had a sense of elegance needed for so harsh a life and so fledgling an organization as OCI. Her focus was the logging show—she was its center. She set a standard for herself and for women in the logging community—one of style and femininity appropriate to this world.

In the final moments we shared, I tried to bring her joy. She, in turn, gave me information, and much more—a sense of the totality of her own life in Orofino, her life with its people. When she died I wanted to cry but couldn't, because people there don't cry. They told me that, and they told me why: when life is done, it's over. That's the end. You may have personal convictions about an afterlife but in the here and now you must get on with it and return to life. Sometimes life seems barren, but you always remember it regenerates—like the forests that grow, show the beauty of their maturity, and then are gone. There is no reason to ponder the meanings of things; humans can only do their best to deal with them. Ingrid left this world, but she gave me a memory of the fineness of her particular existence.

THE LOGGER'S WORLD

· · · · · · · · ·

Life on an Incline

The Clearwater River Valley is beautiful. It meets the needs of your senses. In the rainy season, your eyes are riveted to its richness and the freshness of the trees. Sharp blue or moody grey, the sky is all sky, without telltale signs of human manufacture. In early morning a mist settles in and you live with green and grey-white surrounding you. It's quiet, the quiet of true quiet. It is what a logger sees and feels, as Tim Barnett would tell you. "To those of us who rise at 4:30 A.M. six days a week and go out to meet the day in its infancy there are no words to adequately describe the feeling and the beauty. This is what keeps us going year after year until we die. You can retire a logger and he will still go back to the woods until he is too old to get there. You show me a logger who doesn't think it's the most beautiful place on earth and I'll show you a man who is not a logger. Try to imagine the sun coming up out of the Rockies over a small lake or stream with elk or deer in the background, birds singing, and life in action all around you, and you will see what we see every day of our lives."

At the Clearwater's shoreline the water sounds like crystal. As you drive on U.S. Highway 12, the road obeys the contour of the river. You feel it with every turn of the wheel. In this place, humans are subjected to nature's design. Going from the valley up to the timberline, you can smell fresh-cut pine, cedar, fir, and other species that thrive here. You see it in growth and scattered in hulks of fallen trees. You see the earth gashed by the unnaturally-colored machinery that has brought these trees down. Traveling up the grade, the uninitiated will fear the heights and the weights that surround them.

Topography is supreme throughout the entire region; it dominates your thoughts. Glaciation during the Pleistocene Epoch created this world and its life, now called the Northern Rocky Mountain Province. The landscape is filled with subtleties that only those who work in the woods understand. Southern and northern exposures cause different rates of timber growth, a feature best known to loggers. The mountains run helter skelter, never in a line. There are no dominant peaks, no trends, no consistency. A myriad of minor crests run in all directions. In all this ambivalence, a sudden ridge or peak towering over its neighbors, the result of faulting or unequal erosion, can surprise you. But the uniformity in heights is much more striking than these solitary anomalies and the only way to know the terrain is to walk, or work, or settle in it, as loggers do.

Bordering the mountains of the western and southern edges of this land are the lava plains of the Columbia and Snake rivers. At the northern limit is Clark's Fork of the Yellowstone River. The area hosts the eastern foothills of the Continental Divide and the Bitterroot Mountains, formed by a fault that is quite out of character with the Northern Rockies (Fenneman, 1931).

Human history has made its mark on the topography of this great mountainous area through place names, which were sometimes poetic and even occasionally scatological, such as Weitas, a derivation of "Wet Ass." Plainly, more whimsy than logic went into these designations; humans often modified the names of earth features in relation to their locales. For example, the Salmon River Mountains are south of the Salmon River, even though that river does not drain that range. The Clearwater Mountains lie between the Salmon River and the North Fork of the Clearwater, and the Coeur d'Alene River is actually the district north of the Clearwater River. To add to the confusion, the entire area is referred to as the Bitterroot, which mountains, in fact, lie to the east and extend from Nez Perce Pass on the south to Lolo Pass on the north.

Native Americans were familiar with the area's enigmatic face. They lived with it, explored it, used it, and made their peace in managing it. Bands of Nez Perce lived in permanent villages along the Clearwater River and it was from there that East Coast nationals Lewis and Clark began adventuring into the region in 1805. They traveled along the Nez Perce and Lolo Indian trails that provided passage through the Bitterroot Range and led westward along the ridges. Only by taking advantage of the ridges' height could these Jeffersonian explorers avoid the forbidding gorges. Their trek down through the Salmon River Valley failed because, like so many of the river valleys, it was too narrow and rugged to follow. Steep grades, impossible to cross, have been a protection for the land. Her impassability prevailed.

Today the only indicators of the Corps of Discovery's presence are highway signs marking the events and hardships Lewis and Clark encountered. Near Orofino the Expedition built five canoes to go by water to the Pacific. The historical importance of their trek is permanently fixed in the minds of its devotees: even though there are no artifacts, they come to see the historical markers and experience the landscape, imagining how it might have been for the early explorers.

After Lewis and Clark, few others ventured into the territory until the 1850s when gold was discovered by Captain Elias D. Pierce along the Clearwater River. Mining was prohibited then because it was in Indian territory, but Pierce returned in 1860 when a treaty allowed miners access. About forty miles from the present town of Orofino, miners made their first significant discovery. Two towns were quickly established, Pierce City and the original Oro Fino City; the latter, located directly on top of deposits of placer ore, was doomed from the beginning. Miners, mostly experienced prospectors from California, continued to move into the region, and the original town of Pierce City existed until 1867. In its heyday the mining region was inhabited by about 15,000 people. It is believed that at least $17 million worth of gold was mined in Idaho during a short period in the early years. The Chinese came to work the areas abandoned by miners and at one time over four hundred Chinese lived in the region (Spencer, 1982).

With the movement of the nation's population westward, conflicts between white settlers and Native Americans occurred. A major confrontation in this region, the Nez Perce War, took place in 1877 when, in a still much-debated battle, General Howard caused the retreat of Chief Joseph. The lands became open to the possibility of townships. In 1895, Nez Perce reservation land that had not previously been allocated for Indian use was officially turned over for settlement, and migrants came to plant crops and establish communities.

Today, the Indian population of Clearwater County remains stable, but few live in the community of Orofino. Most are settled in Kamiah and Lapwai, and a small Indian population lives in Ahsahka, a town adjacent to Orofino that was once an Indian fishing village. The Indian church and cemetery remain, but the Dworshak National Fish Hatchery and a second hatchery built by the U.S. Army Corps of Engineers dominate this section of the river. Farther upriver, near Lewiston, there is a concentrated population of Nez Perce living at Spalding.

The central area of the Bitterroot Mountain Province concerns us most, for here, in the valley of the Clearwater Mountains, is the logging community that I will portray. In 1898, the area was subdivided for homesteads by C. C. Fuller of the Clearwater Improvement Company and with the advent of the *Orofino Courier* in 1899 and a railroad line, Orofino became a true Western town. Timber interests were of little consequence then, for settlers were staking timber claims merely to clear the land for agriculture. But in the early 1900s, companies from the East and Midwest began to look to the West for timber after forested areas in easterly parts of the country were depleted. Prior to the turn of the century, there were practically no laws concerning the forest or its use.

Many settlers situated themselves on terraces, known locally as benches. These are like shelves cut in rock or formed from sediments deposited in narrow, discontinuous bands along the hillsides. These latter exist due to Columbia Plateau lava flows that dammed river valleys and created temporary lakes which deposited sediment at different levels. These temporary lakes also caused streams to cut more laterally across hillsides. Even today, while riding through the area, these benches strike you as a perfect place—a fine landing—to set up housekeeping. Since benches occur on different, discontinuous levels, they provide settlement areas that are private yet neighborly. Many are named for farming, logging, or ranching families who originally settled in the area, such as Carr Bench and Bobbitt Bench.

In such names, topographic features, ideal conditions for settlement, chronology, and social history come together. The terrain forms an earthen kinship chart with settlers who took refuge on the land and gave their names back to it. Miners may have come and gone; towns boomed and busted, but the prosperous lifestyles of farmers remained dominant until the 1920s. Since then, the Clearwater National Forest has become an important feature in the economy. It is ministered over by hundreds of federal stewards who now live in this region.

The community of Orofino, with a current population of approximately four thousand people, was incorporated in 1905, when the population was two hundred and seven. Its early buildings included the Orofino Trading Company and the State Hospital. A school was built in 1910. Originally Orofino served as a supply center for the largely agricultural community. When the first advertised timber sale occurred in 1914 no bids were received, but by 1924 the logging industry had grown and fourteen mills were operating in the region, producing approximately twenty-eight million board feet of lumber that year.

At first, logging families produced lumber for building supplies. They set up small, mobile mills and hauled lumber by wagon. When the supply was depleted, they'd move to another area where other settlers were building communities. Lawrence Olson was one of these men. He and his family operated "O" Mill for several decades and, along with the other pioneers listed in the logging chronology in Appendix B, helped establish the logging industry.

At the same time that individuals were establishing logging operations and mills, Eastern corporations were seeing the potential of Idaho forests. According to Bob Allen, director of the J. Howard Bradbury Logging Museum in Pierce, Idaho, Clearwater County actually developed as a major logging area when Potlatch, a logging company, offered homesteads in this region to encourage the migration of entire families. Some migrants both established homesteads and took up employment with the corporation. Headquarters, Idaho, a company logging town that was established in 1926, provided accommodations for about four hundred bachelor loggers and approximately one hundred and four homes for families. Two trends were occurring simultaneously—the establishment of family-owned businesses and the establishment of company towns.

Many of the independent operations were threatened during the Depression. From 1930 to 1939, much forest land passed from individual owners to the county government in payment of taxes. These were then ceded to the National Forest. In spite of this economic downturn, more people came into the region. When the government instituted work and training programs for young men, many came to the area and learned forest management and logging in the Civilian Conservation Corps (CCC) camps. Local loggers trained these young men and guided them in their understanding of the natural resources of the region.

Even though these early loggers took resources from the forests, they cherished the trees and established a strong fire protection association. The historical writing about the region concentrates on fighting forest fires more than on any other human achievements. There was no forest management plan because cutting was low: there was an embarrassing wealth of timber until 1942, when there was enough logging to warrant government planning.

Technological change has made its mark on the region. With the coming of gas powered saws in the 1940s, logging began to thrive and the "gyppo" system—the operation of small, independent logging contractors and mills—was in full force. About fifty operations were in business, including Johnson at Grangemont, Cardiff at Pierce, Ahsahka Mill at Ahsahka, the Schmidt Brothers at Weippe, and Richardson at Orofino. Of all the mills running at that time, Konkol Mill at Konkolville is the only one still in operation.

Of all the historical events that occurred, the damming of the North Fork of the Clearwater River seems to evoke the most memories. When the Army Corps of Engineers built the Dworshak Dam, many of the homesteads at Bruce's Eddy were flooded out. Even today while boating on the reservoir loggers will point out their old homesteads, now deep under water.

The settlement of this region has been highly homogeneous both occupationally and ethnically. Farmers, ranchers, loggers, and merchants from the Midwest, mostly Michigan and Wisconsin, and the Southeast, specifically West Virginia, settled here. Most current residents trace their heritage not to European ancestors but to states of origin. Ethnically, the town and the county are almost exclusively Euro-American except for the Native American population. Few African Americans or Asian Americans live here as permanent residents. Occasionally, Hispanic migrant workers employed by the major corporations come to the area to plant seedlings in reforestation programs, but they are temporary laborers and do not reside in the town, staying instead at campsites in the federal forest.

A special edition of the local newspaper in 1990, the state's centennial year, recounted the history of the town and the region with historic photos from the early part of this century, providing a vivid picture of past settlers and entrepreneurs. But the appearance of local people has not changed: contemporary newspaper photos depict backhoe operators, fence company employees, grocery store staffs, and purveyors of auto parts sharing the same physical characteristics and stance of early residents.

The popularity of this community, "the best little town by a dam site," is not new. In 1909, a promotional brochure advertised it as potentially one of the most prosperous cities in the region. Today town boosters point to its moderate climate and "banana belt" temperatures as well as its economic opportunities. Commerce has grown and the Orofino business community takes pride in its full range of services and merchandising: two banks, several clothing stores, automobile dealers, motels and trailer camps, cable television service, real estate agents, and building supply firms.

Much of the history of this county is painted on the landscape, in locations named for those who settled here. Some is engraved in the photographs in the small historical society, newspaper

Jake Altmiller boating on Dworshak Reservoir in 1990. Often while out on the reservoir, loggers tell stories of life at the North Fork, a logging community that was submerged when the dam was built. (Courtesy, Jeff Tinsley, Smithsonian Institution.)

files and those kept by the elders of the community. Historical facts and images hold promise for the epic story of the community, but at the moment, there is no comprehensive record of the generations. There are few books about the region and all in all, the story of the social life of Clearwater County has gone untold. Who did what and when often seems to be ephemeral. How it was done, however, is the key. History here is in action, technology, and development, in the changes that have occurred on the landscape.

Human intervention in this region is not without controversy. Those who live here believe that through their intimacy with the Clearwater Forest they have learned to treat it with proper and practical respect. Meanwhile, national environmental groups cry out that familiarity has bred abuse and that only the conservation movement's global understanding will preserve this region and Mother Earth. But in the loggers' view, the land—traversed, intruded upon, and cut down—has been forgiving. It regenerates, remaining elegant and displaying its enduring survival power in new stands of trees with their own special kind of beauty.

This is where the story begins, with the people who live and have lived in the Clearwater Valley. They are a people who believe they understand the proper place of humans in their environment. But I can't tell the story of this region and its people without telling the story of the land, its unique organization, and the way in which humans have adapted to it. From the difficulties that Lewis and Clark experienced to the careful maneuvering required by logging trucks, the land has human transportation and communication are at its mercy.

This community's activities and its social life revolve around nature. It's a place where people comment on the smell of the rain and talking about the weather is not idle conversation. Rain and snow, heat and drought affect their livelihood. A sensible logger who respects the land and who follows environmental regulations can't get a logging truck to and from a job in the mud. Hot weather brings the possibility of forest fires, both destructive to the timber and time-consuming to fight. This community understands the mercurial elements of nature and the difficulties of living in a unique geographical setting. Fear-inspiring gorges add both challenges and breathtaking moments to life. Inclines that are treacherous under a light dusting of snow are all in a day's work.

As it bears up under hazards, the community also relishes the benefits of living and working out-of-doors. The people of Clearwater County never hesitate to point out the incomparable sunsets and sunrises which break over vistas punctuated by solitary peaks. To live here in Clearwater County is to acknowledge nature's supremacy, to draw inspiration from the spirit of the place, and to respect nature's paramount trick, the incline.

It is the incline that is central to life in Orofino, life in logging, and this book. This community respects inclines. Being an Idaho logger means spending most of your life traveling either up or down mountainsides. It means negotiating grades from fifteen to forty-five degrees, and handling enormous weights on foot or in vehicles. You must carry, drag, haul, hoist, and lift, and you must do it throughout your life. You rarely look straight ahead, rarely see great expanses of open land. Instead, you look down into a canyon, or up onto a ridge. You calculate how to build a road that follows the contours of a mountainside so that the incline can be conquered.

But the incline is more than a physical state of potential off-balance. It has permutations. Your entire life conforms to the incline's whims. Time, daily and seasonal, brings you closer to the sun and the sky than it does most men and women. You rise earlier and work longer, out of step with a standard nine to five routine. Your year is not divided into the four seasons of spring, summer, autumn, and winter with a two-week vacation somewhere therein. Instead, your high and low seasons depend on the weather.

In a crew, if you are a sawyer you must look up into a tree to assess the job and evaluate the danger. If setting chokers—the cables chained around logs that are used for hauling—your gaze is directed downward to the ground. After bending and cabling you watch the log being lifted up the hill by the hoister on the landing. If you are a loader operator, positioning the logs on the truck, your view is down at the vehicle, then farther down the mountain where the driver negotiates hairpin curves toward the valley and the mill.

If you work in a sawmill, you watch the log lifting and dropping up and down throughout the process of unloading, removing the bark, and milling it into lumber. The mill's efficiency depends on the levels engineered into it so that the logs have the least horizontal distance to travel on their way into timber products. The longer the distance, the greater the time spent in transport: each foot requires more equipment to carry the heavy loads.

The incline principle translates into everyday life, for some inclines are social. Stories describe the lives of old-time lumberjacks—the bachelor immigrants—in highs and lows. They worked and played equally hard. When in the woods, they were at the height of their craft. While in town, out of their element, they were outsiders drinking, carrying on, and spending money, sometimes plummeting down the economic ladder.

The gyppo logger, working with friends or family members, taking work by the piece instead of the hour, understands the incline and the best places to make money. According to Walter McCulloch (1977:76), a gyppo could outwork and out-earn hourly workers by working at his own pace as long as his energy held out. He banked on his productivity, normally working as long and as hard as he could to conquer the weather and the terrain. He used his wits to bring prosperity to his operation and to his family.

The work habits of the logger influenced by the incline ran counter to the ideas of hourly wages and unionization. His way of meeting the exigencies of economic inclines was to work long and hard, not to join with others in standardizing labor practices. He felt that no outside organizer could understand the ups and downs of weather and terrain and no union could meet the challenges of the incline or set the incline horizontal. Only the logger could negotiate its ups and downs and guarantee his own survival and financial stability for his family. By remaining independent, the logger may appear to be out of balance with the rest of America's working class who don't exist on an incline, but he meets this condition in his own way.

Nowadays you don't hear "riches to rags" stories of men losing their month's pay on a night in town. The lone lumberjack has disappeared. Family men have replaced him in the woods. And gyppos may call one another such, but most prefer to be known to those outside the woods as independent logging contractors or by their occupations—sawyer, loader, or logging truck driver. But the incline principle still applies. Life is still lived at an angle, with social and economic times having their highs and lows. One day work goes well, and you are

A piece of heavy equipment is used to skid logs on a job. This incline is typical of the conditions in which logging jobs take place. (Courtesy, Jeff Tinsley, Smithsonian Institution.)

paid handsomely; another the conditions aren't quite right, and money and satisfaction are scarce.

You are always in jeopardy on the incline. It is synonymous with danger. It is one thing to be sure-footed on level ground and another to be nimble on uneven terrain. Driving a tractor in a field is a far cry from operating a Caterpillar on a hillside, even with the safety of a roll cage. It's easy to be dragged down by others on both a physical and a social incline, and the tumble is quick. Only those who know every inch of the path, those who you know are good in the woods or who have good reputations in the community, will help you on the hillside or the social ladder. No outsider can do that for you.

Accidents on the incline are unpredictable even among the most skilled loggers, and rescue on a slope is ever so much more difficult. When it fails, your passing will be marked for a moment; then everyone will return to the woods and another day on the incline.

Because of the incline principle, loggers and townspeople who share this environment see the world differently. Their terrain—physical, economic, and temporal—necessitates careful navigation. Often social relationships are used to bring balance to an unbalanced world. At work and in recreation the community avoids permanent hierarchies; instead, authority rotates among equals. In crews, with spouses, and in organizations, those most adept on a specific incline at a particular moment, are the people who create the balance.

The incline allows for little leisure. There is no time to relax in either work or social activity. Bodies and minds are always at the ready, concentrating on the next step, anticipating the next move, but never tense—tension can throw you off balance. Day in and day out, in work and in life, you watch your footing. Success occurs when the incline, which will not change, is negotiated. It works when daily social life is negotiated into perfect order, balanced with the lives of others in your community.

The first time you hop into a car and go up the grade of Grangemont Road you know that the twenty-five-mile-an-hour sign means just that. Farther up where the loggers are at their work, you will brave the incline with all its hardships and its challenges. If you watch and listen carefully to the loggers you will learn how it can inspire, for life in the woods transforms work into an art form and logging into an aesthetic moment.

"Good Company" is the social rule in Orofino, which has a reputation as the best little town in the area. It almost seems as if it has a patron protector, a silent guardian maintaining it as the perfect hometown, upholding the needs and values of the community. Such a guardian could be imagined standing on the bridge over the Clearwater River, in a white shirt with a red decal: "Hometown Proud." He breathes every breath for his hometown, standing stubbornly against the onslaught of change. He is fierce, holding a shotgun, and untiring, constantly keeping in his mind the image of his ideal Orofino, a town of great charm yet cosmopolitan amenities.

Paul Pippenger is that guardian. A man of strong convictions, Paul believes his hometown is the best investment he can make. Remembering the promise he made to his father, he has the best intentions, and will do whatever is necessary to guarantee the well-being of his birthplace.

For many men in this region, the father has had a compelling influence on life. Wayne Pippenger, Paul's father, and Louie Porter, Paul's uncle, had been in the logging business together, but the day came when they realized that the mill could not support them both. So, as was decided by the flip of a coin, Louie bought Wayne's interest in the mill.

But Wayne's sense of being a part of the logging community didn't end when he left the woods to become a merchant. Wayne opened a grocery store for profit, but also for service. In a community with severe economic fluctuations, credit was not a luxury but a necessity. For a logger to feed his family in times of unemployment, he needed a sympathetic merchant who understood the work cycle. Wayne was that man. Trusting in the integrity of the loggers, he extended credit, offered services, and began a tradition of concern for the community.

Paul, his son, inherited his commitment to the community and operates his grocery, the Glenwood IGA, as his father would. In Wayne's day, approximately seventy percent of the community were loggers; now the percentage has dropped to about thirty-five percent. There is less fluctuation in the overall economy and in associated buying patterns. But Paul still believes in services like UPS, faxing, film developing, check cashing, moving and storage boxes, lottery tickets, USPO boxes, senior citizen discounts, child-sized shopping carts, recycling bins, coupon exchange boxes, a community meeting room, and a town bulletin board. If a new service is needed, Paul will incorporate it. Every employee wears a shirt reading "Hometown Proud," and Paul sees to it that pride is reflected in service.

Glenwood IGA is open twenty-four hours a day so that loggers are supplied with tobacco, caps, gloves, or even motor oil. That had been Wayne's philosophy: to be there with what they need, when they need it. This attitude made Wayne Pippenger a town father, a man who wanted growth and helped in any way he could. He didn't talk much about his beneficence, but from 1945 to 1975, he was active in everything. Wayne and the other early boosters managed their town without elaborate regulations or discussions. A man's word was his seal not only in a personal business deal but also in the course that the town might take in zoning, utilities, or development.

Paul remembers his dad's traits, sees him as a hero, and acts as his dad would have acted. He sees the need for diversification. Be it a prison, Forest Service facility, or retirement home, Paul is behind anything that makes Orofino a better place. If buildings downtown are dilapidated, he'll buy them, fix them, and rent them to keep the main street alive. He purchases property wisely, but sometimes stretches himself to make sure that a piece of real estate is renovated to add to the appearance of the town. He is realistic, but sometimes opinionated in his support of certain projects and at times this makes him a controversial figure.

Paul joins all the civic organizations and attends all the meetings but says very little and is nearly invisible when it comes to politics. He understands local values and knows that power, or the perception of power, can thwart a project that may be good for the town. You don't demand, insist, or throw your weight around.

Orofino has its social and political intrigues and not everyone in town agrees with Paul's tactics. Not everyone remembers Wayne Pippenger or sees in Paul's actions the qualities of a selfless community supporter. But there is no question that he believes he is following the directives, to the last detail, of his deceased father. As a good son, he always buys a pig and a steer at the county fair and provides a scholarship annually to the high school. If you ask Paul he can easily and automatically state his dream for the future: "A proud community, one for everyone, with people behind all the projects that will make it great. There must be diversity but there is no reason for disharmony. When attacked by the outside world, community support should be strong." Paul will fight for Orofino's well-being, to keep it healthy, strong, and growing. He does not hold public office. He leaves that to others like Roy Clay, restaurateur and mayor of Orofino several times over.

You don't have to go far to see the social life of Orofino. Merely walk out of the Helgeson Suites Hotel and at almost any time of year, in any weather, you are in the center of Orofino's social life by crossing the street to Roy Clay's Ponderosa Restaurant. A great deal of business takes place here and although Roy may not seem like a bona fide city planner, his intuition helped him know what the town needed as a gathering place. Roy's establishment serves as the seat of community activity from informal, early morning coffee discussions to important civic gatherings.

Roy tells his life story in rapid, telegraphic succession. As a young boy he went with his dad into the woods and to work at the "O" Mill camp of Lawrence Olson. He knows logging from those days and his years loading logging trucks. After his experience in logging, he came home to help his uncle run the flight service at the local airport. He broke his foot. He moved to Lewiston. He met and married Rose Lenz. He worked as a carpenter, in dry cleaning, and for Potlatch Forest Industries. He ran the creamery in Orofino. Those jobs held no appeal but when the lunchroom on Michigan Avenue came up for sale, Roy hired two cooks and eagerly began a restaurant.

Roy and Rose thought about a name for the place; "Henry's," Roy's given name, or "Rosie's"? They just weren't right. Then one day when Roy and Rose were riding through the countryside they looked up and saw the surrounding pines in all their glory. Because of the dominance of the Ponderosa pine and its significance in the landscape the name "Ponderosa" was perfect.

For nearly forty years Roy Clay has been changing the eating habits of Orofino by introducing new dishes. Roy also faced changing food consumption habits. Loggers and their families were accustomed to volume—good, hearty, substantial portions—but Roy recognized the need to be health conscious. Today, he serves a goodly-sized, though not embarrassingly large, portion, especially for breakfast—the most active part of the day and best time to see the community in action.

After loggers drop by at about 5:30 A.M. for coffee, contractors and woodsbosses arrive to check out the daily news from the forest. After an hour, they're off to work and their booths, already warmed for the morning, are taken over by the old-timers, retired loggers who can't stay in bed. They drop in to share a cup of coffee and a tale with their buddies. Then they are supplanted by members of the business community—insurance men, bankers, lawyers, and accountants who arrive before going to their offices for a day of paperwork. During each transition, friendly greetings take place and, if necessary, business is transacted.

Do people in this community have massive morning appetites? Not really, few people actually eat breakfast. But they all drink coffee. Roy estimates that each consumer drinks an average of three cups per visit and that the Ponderosa has about 10,000 visits by coffee drinkers in a month.

Later and throughout the morning a steady stream of farmers, in town on business, comes into the coffee shop. But it isn't until noon that the Ponderosa again becomes the community's central gathering place. Orofino closes down between noon and one. Everyone knows that the professional community is at lunch, and if it is urgent to find a local lawyer or realtor, all you do is check the eating establishments.

Throughout the week, the Rotary, Chamber of Commerce, Kiwanis, and other civic and professional organizations hold luncheons in the banquet room. Women's professional groups meet for breakfast, and sororities meet for dinner in the Garden Room. Weekends and evenings are less busy. The Ponderosa is quiet and other watering holes such as the Oasis, Jet Club, and Homestead, which provide music, drinks, and a more lively atmosphere, take over.

Roy observes the territorial patterns of the community by way of the places they choose to sit. Most people who frequent the Ponderosa sit in exactly the same booth or on the same stool at a given time of day. "You can almost set your watch by them," Roy says. "Sometimes an elderly couple from the farming community will stand waiting for their booth even though many others are empty."

Several years ago, Roy bought the adjoining buildings and created a spatial universe that set the social character of the community with different sections of the restaurant consciously defining different social worlds. The coffee shop retains its homey quality, while the Garden Room, plant-drenched and dimly lit, is perfect for women's luncheons and family social occasions. The banquet room comes equipped with an American flag, movie screen, and storage area for club paraphernalia. The Brass Rail is fashioned after a Spokane cocktail lounge, a sophisticated version of the traditional saloon, appropriate for women but comfortable enough for young men from road crews who come in to play a game or two of pool. "But it isn't a beer joint," Roy makes clear.

The back area of the coffee shop, between the booths and the banquet room, has no name or specific decor, but the tables are set up to accommodate the rotating population in the morning. It provides the setting for loggers, town merchants, and politicians to meet.

According to Roy, "People sort themselves out." They understand the atmosphere of each room and choose the appropriate place for the occasion. Because there are no price differences throughout the Ponderosa universe, none of the three areas caters to a specific economic level, but diners dress and act differently as they eat and drink in each sphere. Business is transacted in every room, often by the same people. For example, a local lawyer may visit with her colleagues in the back room of the restaurant, have a casual drink with her clients in the Brass Rail, but take a deposition in the quiet relaxation of the Garden Room.

Roy's tenure as mayor shows the intermingling of personal, social, political, and economic activities, the web so typical of life in Orofino. Roy followed Mayor Albert "Bert" Curtis when he became ill. Bert was no easy act to follow: in over thirty years as mayor, his many accomplishments included bringing considerable economic growth to Orofino with the building of the Dworshak Dam. When Roy took over, his roles as restaurateur and public official complemented each other. As both an entrepreneur and mayor, Roy saw a need to create a downtown that would encourage people to come into Orofino as well as strengthen the bond between the business, logging, and agricultural communities. Roy could not divorce his lives as mayor and restaurateur for neither position had office hours; both were twenty-four-hour-a-day activities. As mayor, he was available whenever his constituents came into the Ponderosa. He used his business skills to manage a city budget of over three million dollars.

To be a leader in Orofino is to listen. Leaders may have to make decisions, but they hope that before their arbitration comes into play everyone will work out the problem on their own. If necessary, they will suggest why the parties should agree to the matter in a certain way. Orofinoans take care of conflicts on a friendly basis. This doesn't mean there are no hard feelings. Some disputed situations have caused grudges between individuals for decades. "People in the community may be 'touchy' when they are personally threatened. But, all in all, they will not buck the system on major issues," at least according to Roy.

Roy Clay, with logging only a shadow in his past, jumped at the opportunity to tell me about Timber Crisis Day—the ultimate demonstration of people committed to the stability of their way of life. Roy proudly offered the Ponderosa as the nerve center for this monumental solidarity rally. Though low-key in most of his comments, Roy became excited when he spoke of that day and described the "scary" atmosphere of a town closed down without logging. That day, the part of Roy that would always be in logging came out.

Roy had seen changes in the logging industry especially with the disappearance of the area's family-operated sawmills. They couldn't stay in business because of high operating costs, smaller timber supply, and the strength of Potlatch Forest Industries. I often heard people describe Potlatch as "the company they loved to hate," but they knew it was irreplaceable in the economy.

By the 1990s Potlatch had improved its image both nationally and in small logging communities by demonstrating a sensitive concern for both the preservation of natural resources and the logging way of life. But on August 7, 1985, Potlatch hadn't yet demonstrated these concerns. Instead, it decided to eliminate its operations in Idaho to make the company more profitable, moving toward closure rapidly. The logging community's only recourse was to take symbolic action. In a quiet, dignified manner, Orofino became a ghost town. No banks, stores, or services operated. Signs read, "Closed to support our logging community." All the churches and civic organizations were involved and differences were set aside. The town was tied up with a yellow ribbon, bright bows symbolizing their unity on every post and tree. A line of trucks eight miles long sat motionless along the major roadway. The local and national media covered the rally, and the evening ceremony held despite heavy rain would be remembered for a long time.

For, what is rain to men who work in worse conditions for over half of the logging season? Even Senator Steve Syms joined them, saying, "If you can stand out here, so can I." As Roy remembered, "It did your heart good, because sometimes loggers think that the retail community doesn't care. The loggers needed this 100 percent participation; without it they couldn't declare war on the mill's closing." The entire community had come together to support its loggers and show that Orofino would no longer exist without them—it would lose an important part of the economy, but also its symbolic identity and its edge over other communities. In Roy's words, "It was a milestone for Orofino." Potlatch reconsidered its decision and the mills did not close.

For the past forty years, Roy has watched the community. For one thing, the population size never seems to change. Aside from periodic fluctuations when construction workers come to the area, it never really grows or decreases. Some segments move away and others arrive, but in Roy's memory, there has been constancy in numbers. Government-related jobs at the dam, hatchery, and prison have helped the economy, but these don't cause it to grow, either. Small industries would be welcomed in Orofino but haven't settled here. The town does attract retirees, though. Roy has seen many former residents returning after having lived elsewhere. "These people will have steady incomes that will contribute to the economy," says Roy, "but because of their age, they may see limited value in contributing to the educational system and community needs related to the young." Only time can tell.

According to Roy, Orofino has yet to come to terms with issues like child care that have traditionally been handled within the home. Families were so close that there was rarely a need for social services; even today women have "grandmommy day," when they take over the care of their children's children. Roy is nostalgic for those days and the closeness of relationships, but he knows that economic pressures and evolving lifestyles will change his town.

Roy is a real town booster. For years he has been a supporter of OCI Lumberjack Days and the Clearwater County Fair. He admits that it is good for his business, but he's always supportive because the Fair is an excellent example of the friendliness and unique quality of Orofino. He says, "It's something special; it shows our logging tradition and the families that support it."

Cindy, Roy's daughter, married into a logging family and as the wife of Fenton Freeman, a Jaype plywood mill supervisor, she is a link between the logging and entrepreneurial communities. Today, many loggers' wives work in town, keeping an eye on business activities while their husbands are in the woods.

The Ponderosa's multiple functions show how this community uses one means to accomplish several goals. There is an economy to the way in which Orofino, a small community with limited resources, operates. Through the ingenuity of its residents it handles many social needs simultaneously in a given situation. The process of overlapping helps Orofino operate smoothly, keeping the community working as a cohesive unit, and handling all eventualities easily with limited personnel and resources. For many Orofinoans, the day begins and ends at the Ponderosa, the hub of communications.

Information is freely given and gladly received there. In conversations during early morning coffee sessions, loggers brief one other on the progress of their jobs, giving details of each step of the logging operation. They negotiate the free loan of privately-owned equipment that is scattered throughout the area, knowing that the favor will be returned later, a reciprocity necessitated by the conditions under which loggers work. Equipment is expensive, and it is difficult for anyone other than a large corporation to have a full complement of machinery. Where ownership is impossible, borrowing and lending are practical alternatives. It all works out in the end.

Loggers who deal with the uncertainties of climatic conditions and changing Forest Service operations depend on up-to-date information, spread through free conversation. They understand that thoughtful planning necessitates daily intelligence and wouldn't miss a morning's informal coffee at the Ponderosa. But the web of information gathering benefits everyone, and so knowledge is not for sale. It depends on who has seen the conditions most recently or has knowledge of the site, or experience with the equipment for the particular job. With that know-how you are designated the expert of the day.

But in a broader sense, loggers think past today's job and take a long-range view of keeping the hillsides bountiful for the future. That's where coffee with the old-timers comes in handy. They talk about their experiences with successful logging operations that spanned long periods of time—not five or ten year increments, but the time necessary for a stand of trees to regenerate. Forty or fifty years is a likely measure of history for a logger. Often an old logger's breakfast conversation revolves around timber stands he knew as a boy, information he conveys to younger men who can use it in the future.

This desire to share information is mandatory, not only because of the length of growing time, but also because of land tenure patterns. Independent contract loggers seldom own the land they work. They pay stumpage, that is, the money agreed upon to cut a specific area in a given period of time. Lands and their yield are actually owned by other individuals, the National Forest Service, or major lumber corporations. It is imperative to know current policies, saleable lots, and, in order to win a job, the bid requirements. All this information is discussed informally over coffee.

Tim Barnett and Ted Leach filled me in over coffee on the principles of having, holding, sharing, and using information and equipment. Both men have been logging contractors and are college-educated in engineering and forestry. Tim and Ted are practical men, but they can become philosophical about time, history, and their part in the stewardship of nature. Tim and Ted, or any number of other local logging contractors, could explain how the area was harvested—when, with what type of equipment, and probably by whom. To them, the quality of the current stand reflects what has been done in years past. Connoisseurship is not a word commonly used in Orofino, but its definition as a "discerning eye" is exactly what these loggers have when they evaluate timber or the results of a logging job.

Orofino uses modern communication devices: telephones, CBs, newspapers, radios, and televisions, but when it comes to essential information, it is transferred personally and face-to-face. Talk is rarely chatter; it is normally focused on daily necessities. Tales are real stories about jobs performed and history written on the landscape. Knowledge is derived from experience and conveyed directly. Ask a question about logging, either current or past, and loggers will answer in great detail, covering all the technology, topography, and environmental concerns. But in addition to talking about logging, conversation is constant, interaction is perpetual, and no one is excluded from the discussion. Information is spread instantaneously without the need for telephones, in part because of the constant interchange that happens in town, on the street, and at the Ponderosa.

The situation is somewhat different for the farming community that lives in this region. In order to find out the differences I spoke to Norman Fitzsimmons, a former county extension agent who is known for having the best understanding of farming in Clearwater County. According to Norman, pioneers using horses in pre-mechanized times changed the face of the land and the economy of the county. They had the same stamina, resilience, and perseverance as the loggers. Even so, a saying goes, "If your money doesn't smell like sawdust, your money is not welcome in Orofino," and so farmers went to Grangeville, Nez Perce, and Lewiston to buy farm equipment and feed.

Today only a small portion of the county's acreage is devoted exclusively to farming, but the amount of land in farming is misleading when determining the number of people who actually farm. Most of the people in the area are part-time farmers with their major means of subsistence in logging, construction, or jobs in town. For many it is good recreation, or, as Norman says, "When they hung up their boots, it was a good way to put food on the table."

Farms generally operated by families are clustered on the highlands above Orofino in Cavendish, Fraser, and Gilbert. Cash crops include barley, green peas, rape, canola, and lentils. Norman claims that even though the soil is not exceptional, the average yield is not far behind the richer counties in the state, a tribute to the skill and care practiced by these Clearwater County farmers. Full-time farmers have been eclipsed by the mystique of the mighty woodsman, but they are also in the shadow of those who harvest the nearby romantic and spectacular Palouse.

Interaction between loggers and farmers is rare because their cyclical and daily schedules don't mesh. The logger's season is best when the ground is hard, either in the dry season or when frozen; the farmer uses wintertime to work in his shop, upgrade and care for his equipment. When the logger must leave the woods because of spring rains and summer fire danger, the farmer is seeding and fertilizing. It's only during fair time that the lives of the logger and the farmer coincide. For farmers it is a chance to show their stuff. "It's a time when neighbors get together to demonstrate community spirit regardless of their occupation. They get together to appreciate one another," says Norman, "and prices for prize livestock at Fair time are higher than in any other community." Norman feels that this, in itself, is a show of support for agriculture in a community that has historically focused on logging.

During their off season, loggers can gather to share information at the Ponderosa and the other restaurants in town, but not so the farmers. They may share information when called upon, "but rarely do they go out of their way to join in a gathering of talkers," says Norman. In the past, agricultural business was transacted at Grange meetings, along with socials and card parties, but about ten years ago these organizations lost their hold on members; today farmers only meet on rare occasions.

According to Norman, farmers also differ from loggers in their spending and saving patterns. They can meet their basic subsistence needs from the land with less expensive, longer-lasting equipment. "But farmers are also very conservative, they don't spend money when the only way to survive is not to spend money," says Norman. "Often their money is tied up in assets, not cash, and so they can't spend it. They are less likely to buy snowmobiles and fancy rigs so often found in the yards of logging families."

One similarity farmers and loggers do share is that women form one half of the production team. Even though there is "women's work," women receive respect. According to Norman, "Spouse abuse does not occur, divorce rates are low, and children are considered important members of the unit. Farmers pride themselves on having stronger family ties than any other occupational group in the area."

Farmers are also more conservative regarding changes in technology. A logger will search out new mechanical innovations while farmers, especially old-timers, are reluctant to accept any type of change. For example there was slow acceptance of chemical farming when it was introduced in the 1960s. Farmers felt that these additives would burn the crops. Norman proved that there was value in the new technique only through extensive demonstration. And often, even though the new way proved successful, Norman was confronted with other skeptics when new pests arrived and the farmers' beliefs were vindicated. Norman quotes them as saying, "We didn't have these problems until you, an old weed-fighting fool, came." Norman's good-natured reaction to criticism was, "Well, these farmers may not be progressive, but they sure are persistent."

Newcomers who were non-farmers trying their hand at agriculture began arriving in the 1970s. "They didn't know that you need a bunch of money to make agriculture break even in this region. Many lost their land or handed it over to absentee owners and farmed it as tenants." In 1983 the depression hit and with no support from a stable, financial unit, the newcomers all but disappeared.

The current, second wave of agricultural immigrants—sophisticated, urban newcomers generally looking for a second source of income—tried cultivating grapes. But Norman says, "they have two strikes against them." First, the region is known to have a climate that promotes many fungus-caused diseases that can attack grapes. Second, farmers in the surrounding areas rich in wheat fields, though not heavy users of aircraft spraying, use 24D, a basic weed control chemical that can devastate grapes if it drifts with the wind. Questions arise as to the rights of the long-time agriculturalists who exist by farming and those of newcomers who do not gain their subsistence from the soil but wish only to supplement their incomes. The problem is thorny and has yet to be resolved. Farmers are sharing the difficulties of loggers when confronted with a diversifying economy and environmental issues.

Norman responded immediately to my questions about the aesthetics of farming. "It may be a science, but it is so very much an art. There is a green thumb. Looking at a field, knowing when and how it was worked is like playing a piano, like being a Liberace." And how could he recognize these artists? "By looking at the front gate; that gate will tell you how the fields look. They predict straight or crooked rows and skips, the little things that count in good farming."

Norman's last comment put me back in touch with life on an incline. "This community levels everyone; there are no stars. Loggers enjoy the limelight but it was against the rules, against the nature of the community, to say that they are the sole population and the important one, everyone in this community is important."

The community teaches these values to their young at home but also through the schools. I visited the high school to see how this transmission takes place. Skip Wilson, the dedicated principal of Orofino High School, is responsible for preparing Orofino's youth for life. His are the choices to be made for them and the community; a mighty job for a man who has never left Orofino. He was born and raised in this area, went to school at OHS, saw his father work in the timber industry, coached here, and took office about fifteen years ago. He's seen the children of farmers, loggers, and government employees grow up. He has experience in farming and driving a truck. He has had experience in the woods, even if it is limited. Skip knows of the dangers and the deaths in logging and feels concern for the young men who choose it as a profession. Nowadays, the young people, strong and able for work in logging, leave for greener pastures, and Skip felt that perhaps through education logging may return as a major industry. The glories of the 1950s and the virgin timber may be gone, but because of reforestation, government employment in timber, and new techniques to produce sustained yield, the forest will provide a decent living for some young people willing to work.

The situation is better with more safety consciousness and fewer accidents, but improvement is still necessary, and so Skip and members of the logging community devised a course in woods knowledge and forest management. This course would have looked at biology and ecology but would also have taught actual work in the woods. The course was planned to be coeducational and would have begun with no preconceived notions about the environment. It would have been action-oriented, with experience with cables and chokers, but would also have emphasized ethics and safety. Even Potlatch Forest Industries wanted to become a partner, by offering grants for teacher training. However, as with many of the best plans, the course in woods knowledge, although brilliant and appropriate in concept, was never offered.

The student body of Orofino High School is no different from that of any other school, according to Skip, but approximately thirty percent come from families that are involved in logging. Sons follow their fathers into the woods and are able to get jobs at an early age. Approximately forty percent of all the students are bound for additional education and, of that number, twenty percent will finish college, but the rest will go into the labor market immediately after graduation. A few will remain in Orofino, but often graduates leave for non-skilled jobs in larger cities in the Pacific Northwest. Orofino High School meets state requirements, but it must also meet the needs of the majority—students not bound for college. Since the faculty is small, it cannot provide all the vocational and academic needs as well as special education and individual programs.

Skip's one wish is to motivate the students, but other things seem more important to them. A new rig can intrude on good grades or a college education: students may go into debt just to buy a 4x4 or a customized truck. Skip is sincere about his concerns and honest about his evaluation of the problems of Orofino, many of which may be widespread nationally. As he sees it, students are losing their self-worth and good feelings about themselves. Skip believes that drug and alcohol abuses are tied less to occupation than to social and recreational issues. He acknowledges the hard-working, hard-drinking, hard-playing stereotype so often attached to loggers, but he doesn't believe that it is a factor in current abuses.

And what about the future of the graduates of Orofino High School? Although the area is product-oriented with logging, farming, and merchandizing, small industry has never been a part of the landscape. Government employment may be a possibility for some students, but the job market is small and often draws from outside the area. Where once production from natural resources was the economic base, in the future, service industries may predominate. Are the school and student body prepared? According to Skip, that's hard to say. But then why does Skip have hopes for this region, why does he stay in Orofino? "It's a great place to raise your kids; secure, with no robberies or rapes. You can leave your door open while you're on vacation. You know your kids are associating with people just like you. Someone will help you in need. There is a good moral basis in the community. Parents are concerned about their children and are supportive of school policies and discipline. The bottom line is that all of us—the school, the parents, and the community—are working to grow better citizens."

Orofino High School is proud of its successes, as evidenced by the students who go off to the United States military academies—West Point, Annapolis, and Colorado Springs. Scholarships to these are the epitome of success in Orofino. But the general education for most students appears to concentrate on physical development and vocational training, preparing them for life as it is lived here in Orofino. This means the educational choices are complementary to the region, but perhaps not to the rest of the country.

Often a dedicated teacher will set the direction for student choices. For example, several years ago the music teacher, Darold Kludt, was able to coalesce the teenage musicians into a jazz band that gained recognition in the Northwest. Generally, though, the high school must address a more basic issue: the problem of preparing the students with the rudiments for success in a working-class world.

Several weeks after my conversation with Skip Wilson, I attended the Orofino High School graduation where Governor Cecil Andrus, considered a native son, gave the commencement address. Many people think of him not as the governor but as a young millworker or the past president of OCI who had the courage to paint the flagpole for Lumberjack Days after it had already been erected. He used the occasion to designate Orofino a "Gem Community." "Cece," as he is known locally, doesn't doubt his support in this clearly Democratic region. In 1990, during his fourth run for re-election, he garnered seventy-three percent of the votes in Clearwater County.

The graduation was a fine occasion. Almost everyone in the community was there since in one way or another they knew or were related to a graduate. There were smiling faces, and for good reason: not only were they graduating, but they were being honored by the presence of the governor. The stage setting seemed to speak of the community: instead of bouquets of flowers, it was dotted with pine trees of various species. And just as the decor was unique, the event took on a quality indigenous to the people. For one, it started on time, to the moment. Some of the parents may not have been seated and the formally-clad ushers had not finished their jobs, but the occasion began on time, as do all events in Orofino.

Throughout the ceremony, speech after speech followed the same theme, that of looking back on young lives. There was a degree of nostalgia you might not expect from high school students who were so young. It was topped off by a slide presentation in which each student's graduation photo was preceded by his or her baby picture. It was like the parlor game, "Where are they now?" There were howls, laughs, and sighs as the current appearance of the person was flashed on the screen. For many of these students, this would be their first and last graduation, their only appearance in cap and gown, and they, their families, and the community were proud of their high school accomplishments.

Scholarships and awards given by service organizations were many and varied; some went for academic achievement, but often grants were given for advanced vocational training. The highlight of the evening was the awarding of a full scholarship to the United States Naval Academy to Kenny Weller Jr., the son of a local logging contractor.

Again and again there were words from the elders praising these young people for past achievements but also stressing their role in a changing world. They were encouraged "to make this world a better place through the smallest actions and the biggest dreams." But perhaps the best of all the night's quotable quotes was the governor's. It captured the challenge and quandary of these particular graduates. He said, "As you leave here, you will be entering a world in which you don't know everyone you meet in a day." This statement had profound implications for the young in a community that thrives on the intensity of interaction. Anonymity is an accepted fact in urban society, but not in Orofino.

The evening ended without much ado, not even a recessional. It was over, so why continue the ceremony, why remove the graduates from their families with a pompous closing. Instead, graduates bounded off the stage as families flocked to it. It was over. Many would leave Orofino and have to find their own way, but those young people who stayed in Orofino could rest securely in the fact that their elders were in charge of all the spheres of their community.

For example, Father Mike Spegele was in charge when I went to visit him to find out something about the religious convictions of the town. Instead of a description of religiosity I found out far more about Father Mike, a missionary of the Order of the Precious Blood. Perhaps he's stuck in the sixties—that would be just fine with him. It was a good era, one of fire, fervor, and activism, of doing God's work for civil rights down in the trenches. But for the past twelve years, Father Mike has been in Orofino ministering to the two hundred families who attend St. Theresa's Roman Catholic Church. At seventy-five, nothing is new to him; he's marched for civil rights in the Midwest, fought to keep a linden tree, and been denounced for being too ecumenical. Yet, so far, the people here have accepted him and congregate to his ministry. By his own admission, he says, "I'm not afraid of the devil himself."

His Sunday is more active than that of many people who are nowhere near his age. It begins at the first Mass followed by a parish coffee hour; it continues through to confessions and Mass at the prison, and finishes up with visits to those who are sick and unable to leave their homes. Every one of his sermons is a tour de force. They are never drawn from the crib sheets prepared by the diocese. He never has them, as he says, "in a can"—each is spontaneous. Father Mike never knows what he'll say until he gets to the pulpit. On this particular Sunday he spoke about civil rights and his participation in demonstrations for black equality. In a community without an African American presence, it was doubtful that the congregation had much awareness of the times he spoke about. Nonetheless, he spoke with a passion and enthusiasm nurtured by a captive audience.

Father Mike's concerns for the community are wide-ranging. For one, there seems to be no way to gather the ministers together. For another, there are a large number of fundamentalist persuasions of which he admits, "Of course, they know the Bible and we don't." Other sources had told me that many of these ministers were loggers who were equipped to help woodsworkers cope with the daily problems of unemployment and alcoholism as well as devotion to God.

Father Mike's church was moved to a new building five years ago. Because of the help of a prominent parishioner, a mill owner, it has a fresh touch of modernity and beautiful woodwork about it. But the execution has the Father Spegele mark all over it. When Father Mike came to Orofino, the church was nearly inert, so he fired the Church Board, disbanded the Building Committee, and placed all power in a newly-constituted, vital, and active Parish Council that he picked personally. Most of the administrative work done for the church is done through voluntary committees, and the good father has a "loaves and fishes" ability with finances. Economic setbacks don't seem to affect the church, and the debt on the new building is paid. Approximately twenty logging families belong to the parish. Father Mike feels that they work hard, have good, strong families, and are extremely generous to the church. All in all, they are "outspoken with a rough exterior but they are good-hearted."

For his next challenge, and there must always be a challenge for Father Mike, he wants to create an awareness of internationalism and combat the local conservatism. To do this, the church has begun Oktoberfest celebrations reminiscent of the festivals of Father Mike's birthplace and during the Fair he has introduced the community, which doesn't have much ethnic orientation, to ethnic foods. With a booth that offers unlikely cuisine to a typical Idaho palate, the church tries to spread the word that there are other places and other nations outside Clearwater County.

Father Mike shows no timidity in his opinions. He sees an issue and speaks up. As a "man of God," he demonstrates his beliefs unswervingly. For example, during a session of the Idaho legislature there was debate over abortion rights. Father Mike entreated his parishioners to work toward passage of a flawless pro-life bill. To bring home the severity of the issue, he asked every Catholic to abstain from one meal every Wednesday and to spend ten minutes each day in concentrated prayer. For a man who must have his contract renewed every year in order to stay in this diocesan role, Father Mike is surprisingly opinionated. He would never change his views even though they would put his position in jeopardy. And retirement? That's a thing of tomorrow. For now Father Mike has his heart set on a retreat, with a stirring Catholic preacher coming from afar to "charge up" his parishioners. The question is, who could top Father Mike's ability at oration? His is a God-given talent for exhortation.

Father Mike's role as a religious leader and Catholicism's spiritual, practical, and social nature in this community may be only one facet of its religious life. Loggers, a realistic group of people, don't seem to hold to a strong tie with religion or the ways it seems to lessen the hardships of daily travails. They do everything in their power to control their own fate. They are self-reliant. But Father Mike, another strong, rugged individualist, seems perfectly suited for work in St. Theresa's Roman Catholic Church with those who appreciate his religious guidance.

The Clearwater County Commissioners of 1990. The board room is decorated with murals illustrating the logging images of the county. From left to right: X. E. "Bus" Durant, Jim Wilson, and Don Ponozzo.

So many people seemed suited for their positions, as if they had been put on a long time ago and were like well-worn shoes. The Clearwater County Commissioners of the early 1990s, X. E. "Bus" Durant, Don Ponozzo, and Jim Wilson, fit that description. They meet every Monday morning and continue into the afternoon if any petitioners show up. With Alice Hardy, the county welfare officer and secretary of the commissioners, fielding phone calls, pouring coffee, and clarifying legal points, they carry on business and seal the fate of the territory. None of the three members stands out, nor would they try to. They follow the guidelines of county government. (Mika, Duncombe, Holden, and Poinelli: 1987) There is no dissent even though they might not agree on a particular matter. They've been elected again and again, and see no reason to lock horns. Two Democrats and an improbable Republican, three honorable men with only one goal: the good of the county, the peace of the place.

The meeting proceeds simply. A citizen comes in to be heard and if it is an issue concerning members of the county staff, they are called from their offices to come and clarify a matter. The commissioners act as interpreters of the regulations of the outside world to these petitioners.

They have the ultimate authority and power to levy taxes over approximately 10,000 inhabitants in a 2,236 square mile region of Idaho and have proven their competence in the political arena. They and their predecessors must have made the right decisions, because Clearwater County is still intact; its highways are good, waterways clean, and school district graduating fine young people. There is always the possibility of conflict but chances are that most of the issues are immediate, personal, and handled without the need for future debate. Committee reports are never requested.

On this particular day, June 4, 1990, five people appeared before the committee, each with a different problem but all focused on the same goal, advisement from these men. Why should a young man, representing his fifteen friends, challenge the council with a lawsuit on assessments that they thought were excessive? He knows that it is an empty threat and that the honorable men will be sage enough to set him straight in a kindly elders' fashion. In this friendly atmosphere the commissioners could tell a petitioner he would have to sell his soul and they would be acknowledged authorities on the matter. Without malice they explain, it's just something you have to do, you must pay the assessment. Their advisory is gentle but unequivocal: be a good citizen, conform. It's not great news, but all in all, the petitioner didn't waste much time; he was first in line; he could come in his work clothes, and he parked his rig right outside without paying as much as a nickel—there are no parking meters. In less than an hour, he could be back on the job, and in the course of the afternoon, earn enough to pay the added assessment.

The issues never seem too troublesome for the commissioners, and it's even a delight to sit on the board. Should the commission give Bob Burnham and the "No-Name Fishing Club" an endorsement? Is it just another group looking for county money? Well, not quite. The anglers have already received $4,000 from the Fish and Game Department. With it they will improve Campbell's Pond by putting in new picnic tables making it an even more popular place for families to fish. Bob merely wants the right to tell the newspaper that he has appeared before them and they think it is a good idea. With that in his pocket, Burnham is sure that volunteers will come to help with the job. Volunteers do this as they do so many other projects: cleaning the city and the highway, repairing scenic areas, and being all-around good neighbors.

Next the sheriff comes in and assures the commissioners that an accurate tabulation of compensatory time is being kept. Then, George Summers, supervisor of the county highway commission, presents his request for a Radio Shack computer. It's denied. Fine, he'll be retiring in April, he says, and someone younger can computerize the inventory. He'll spend the remainder of his time on the job finding an efficient way to keep the hillside at Bobbitt Bench from sliding off. His on-the-job know-how provides techniques to fix problems, keeps the entire county highway system in good order, saving money by not contracting it out. George talks about his staff; putting the best operator on the new John Deere gets a lot more work done.

Orofino · 35

Despite all his loyalty and community spirit, George lets the commission know again that in April, when he turns sixty-two, he's "history," gone, retired. Of course the commissioners respond that it will be impossible to do without him. The discussion closes; everyone will just wait and see. A man's decision is his own, and there's no changing it once it's made. How will they replace him? What does it take to be the supervisor of highways in Clearwater County? According to George, "just a man with a lot of experience, even if he's a guy's [guy who's] got a forgettable [forgetful] mind."

Finally, Bill Snook, the town gadfly, comes in with an apology for misinterpreting a recent local issue to the newspaper. The commissioners know that this won't be the last time, Bill will find another issue and he knows that the town of Orofino will expect it of him.

All these matters are dispensed with deliberately, but without extended discussion. Simultaneously, the commissioners have taken care of mail that has accumulated since last week, giving it to Alice for disposition. During the session, I began to wonder, what is behind it all? How are they dealing with the governance of the county? When asked, they responded that first and foremost they are concerned with the proper use of county monies. Second, they feel that they must symbolize the county's image both with their sound judgment as well as with their own good conduct. Each has an impeccable reputation in the community. But let no one misunderstand, they are not pushovers—they are a decision-making board and the budgetary officers for the county, accountable to the state.

There are some difficult issues that they know will become more trying in the future. For example, an area of growing concern is the indigence law. Any person can appeal to the district court to be declared indigent, thus relieving him or her of debt. A woman living here to be near her husband while he is in the state prison may have an accident or financial difficulties and be declared indigent. Then the county is expected to pay her bills. Initially, the coming of the prison meant more jobs and a potential boost to the economy; this was an unforeseen problem. Now the commissioners must deal with the social aftermath of the new facility.

But their financial concerns don't stop at the personal problems of any one resident. They are charged with managing the three-million-dollar annual budget of the county. Sales and liquor taxes bring in revenue, but so does money coming from the timber industry. Currently, the federal government owns over seventy percent of the land in the county and receives a payment when timber is cut from the area. So the commissioners, two of whom have been loggers, must also concern themselves with the economic fate of logging.

It is good sense and the ability to handle the most delicate situations without official action that makes the commission work. Once elected, commissioners are generally re-elected again and again until they decide to retire. Creating an atmosphere of responsiveness, a casual informality that breaks down barriers between the powerful and those that must petition power, these men carry on a congenial county government. But how do they negotiate grievances? They listen to all the individuals involved and based on the facts they uncover, they come up with a decision. It is a highly personalized process, but most importantly, everyone is treated equally.

The commissioners talked about road and bridge maintenance, zoning, unforeseen emergencies, and solid waste disposal, but social problems never came up. Yet everyone knows that periodically the police will find a marijuana patch someplace in the outback, and that there is alcoholism and family abuse. The commissioners don't deal with city issues, either. The city, an incorporated entity, has its own mayor and municipal government. And besides, the commissioners are busy with the committee meeting of a five-county cooperative for central Idaho, which also gives good service to the residents of their county.

When asked what makes a good commissioner, they jokingly highlight the characteristics they themselves have: they are U.S. citizens, they are good listeners, they are highly intelligent—said with knee-slapping joviality—and they accept the role of decision-makers. Judging from my observation of their meeting, a commissioner must also have a heightened sense of diplomacy, or in their words, "Have the ability to tell someone to go to hell and make them look forward to it."

These men, all of whom hold or have held important roles in the business community, are not complacent. They know that the future means change and that it is going to require a good dose of common sense. They acknowledge that every day, those in authority must learn that the rules and the laws are changing. The society of yesterday, the halcyon days when small-town America could remove itself from the travails of urban society, are gone.

Each commissioner has his own view of his honorable position. For example, "Bus," the token Republican, the only elected Republican in Clearwater County, banks on his common sense to help him make a proper decision. He tries to be non-partisan, "mostly friendly," hold no negative feelings, and in both intent and appearance, shows no favoritism. At the same time he realizes, "you can't satisfy everyone," especially when you realize that "everyone is related to everyone else and everyone is involved in absolutely everything."

Jim Wilson is active in the Clearwater County Resource Coalition and an avid supporter of the role, rights, and sensitivities of loggers. He feels that "loggers are environmentalists," that from long years of experience they have a grasp of natural resources that no amount of armchair study or laboratory work can provide. But somewhere down the line there must be a settlement of forest issues. He feels that management of lands is an important issue and that the people of Clearwater County, "rugged individualists" living in a locale of natural beauty and resources, are the best stewards of the land.

He, "Bus," and Don all know that they need a diversification of industry to supplement the logging industry. But they all agree that there's no place they'd rather live. "It's the best kept secret in the West; all we need is a little better economy," says Don. Comparing the county and state to the world outside the Clearwater River Basin, the general feeling of the commissioners is that Idaho is well-protected from the problems of other states. They are as well-informed as need be and they don't need any more regulations. The commissioners' wholehearted boosterism is common in Orofino and Clearwater County. They and Alice qualify as quotable supporters of Clearwater County, "We live in Paradise. We're not ignorant, not rural rubes. We wouldn't trade this country for anything."

After the meeting, I ran into Don Ponozzo at the Ponderosa. No sooner had I sat down than Don was off, booth-hopping to talk to Joe McCarthy, one of the real pioneers in the region. Don's conversation was short, but when he returned to our booth he was glowing from his encounter.

He began to talk about the history of the area and the pride that people have in their elderly, early founders. Don knew about the historical comings and goings of the region in both logging and political happenings. "It was an interesting place and fascinating time, those early days when most of the business and decision-making was a function of personality," said Don. "If people didn't like you, you'd better move on," he said.

Don arrived in Orofino in 1948 from Michigan with other Michiganders. Two years prior, in 1946, Andy Konkol, "the Pollock" from Wisconsin, had settled here. Even though Andy's Polish ancestry was mentioned, generally European ethnic backgrounds didn't matter much. Most people were known by the state from which they came. West Virginians settled here, as did Mississippians, but their origins, other than previous state affiliations, were unknown.

Most of these early independent loggers contractors had been married before their move to Idaho. Since that migration, there have been many instances of members of logging families marrying within their occupational group. Often the sister of a contractor will marry the owner of a logging truck company, or the daughter of a sawyer will marry a man who works in a sawmill.

Don's description of the changes in the community focused on both the topography and the personal interests of the early town fathers. "Before the road through the section called Hollywood had been paved, it was difficult, a real job to come down into the valley." The paving of Grangemont Road in 1970 made all the difference in the ability of more people to get to town. Issues such as access to town and an area's official designation as city or county have always been important. Often it was the men in the logging profession, those who owned and operated the sawmills and their adjacent properties, that haggled over the decisions on land use and annexation of a section of Orofino.

If an area is designated as part of the city, the residents must pay city taxes and are entitled to city services. If not so designated, the residents do not pay taxes but still have access to certain services and benefits of the town by mere fact of proximity. On several occasions this has been the source of controversy in the city council. For example, the area called Riverside, on the south side of the river, was suggested for annexation several years ago. There was a bitter debate. I asked if perhaps it was a section in which just one segment of the society lived. "No," Don said, "It was mixed: loggers, merchants, lots of Potlatch folks, and government workers." Don, by his own admission "a broken down gyppo," was in the thick of these discussions as a member of the city council. He successfully combined professions in logging and politics as a bridge between the town, its governance, and the independent logging contractors. As such he demonstrates another important feature of this life. A logger is not absolved from being a citizen of the town. He cannot live totally in the woods. He must take an interest and have input into the local decision-making process; otherwise loggers would have no say in the operation of their home community. A life in logging is one in nature, but it is also one in which the town is an important reference point for the logger.

I mentioned to Don that the governor of Idaho would be in town soon. The governor may be "Cece" to the people of Orofino, but to me he was the former Secretary of the Interior. Don, his long-time friend, assured me that he would be happy to fill me in on his experiences as a logger.

There was no question that when Governor Cecil Andrus entered the city council chambers he combined the right proportion of gubernatorial *savoir faire* and down-home warmth. It was natural, the way he shook hands and greeted his constituents joking about "we old-timers." Cecil Andrus had lived in Orofino twenty-five years before, when it was known as an important logging town with independent contract outfits and privately owned sawmills in full operation. He could speak fondly of his years here, but today the future was on his mind with a ceremony to designate Orofino a "Gem Community," to give it seed money and then potentially $300,000 in commercial grants. It was Orofino's opportunity to work with the state on economic development, and the governor was sure he could count on his friends to lead the way.

He used political rhetoric, but knowing the town, he could personalize it. He could assign phrases like "Can-Do Attitude," "sell-quality of the community," "taking the dips out of the economy," "put your money where your mouth is," and "the economy is the best ever," each to a specific member of the audience. The governor was optimistic because of the financial infusion provided by leading citizens and the forward-looking attitude of the mayor, Paul Decelle. But the underpinnings of Orofino's tomorrows rest in the hands and, more aptly put, in the hearts, of two women; one senior in her knowledge of the town and its need, and one young, effervescent, and exuberant about Orofino's future.

Harriet Reece is grey-haired and bespeckled now, but once she was a young girl who was the first Clearwater County Lumberjack Days royalty. She is no longer the editor of the *Clearwater Tribune,* but has every intention of staying right in the center of community affairs. She has the data from which the future will be planned. She was on the development committee of the community and the Board of Directors of the planning committee for the new retirement home. At every turn, Harriet could pull out the materials I needed to make sense of population trends that had affected Orofino. She knows the history; with the newspaper her livelihood for many years, she is a living scrapbook of community events and personalities. She understood the segments of the community that have demonstrated political activism, those that have influenced state politics, and those that have put forth effort to help the town compete and win many state facilities. She was going to do her best to assist in any way possible to make a near-perfect place just a little bit better.

Her counterpart, Janet Kayler, was pert, energetic, and ready to put Orofino on the map. She was ready to "Big Mac it"—that is, find a fast food franchise to set up here that might bring tourists and settlers to Orofino. Janet would have tried anything. In the early 1990s, she worked for the Chamber of Commerce and "Orofino Unlimited," but she was also committed to the community. Her involvement with timber was much more manicured than most. At that time, she and her husband Jeff operated a hand-raised Christmas tree farm. Seemingly ironic in this land of naturally growing pines, Fantasy Farm sits on Highway 12—it and she seem midway along in the transition between logging and a new diversified economy. Still tied to the land and the best resources that the area has to offer, her enterprise both in the office and at the farm demonstrates what she hopes Orofino is doing—transforming itself from a place of the rough and tough, mechanically-oriented sites of massive growth to operations of a more delicate, "cultured" occupation.

Janet believed negotiating lifestyles will be the only way to ameliorate the tensions that might occur when economic change takes place. The undercurrents of diversification may be difficult and shocking to some, especially to those who see this area relying exclusively on timber. She and many others felt that it will be necessary for the town to turn to other means of survival; tourism, government facilities, retirement services, and anything other than "dirty" industries are options. But beneath all the choices are the decisions that must be made concerning the use of the land. Timber concerns change the landscape that the tourist industry wants to keep pristine. Government agencies bring a bureaucratic mentality that may not be compatible with this region of practical people who learn by doing. Retirees may help stabilize the economy, but what will their ultimate support for education and youth services be?

Each year, the Chamber of Commerce brings potential investors from the state to northern Idaho in hopes that they will settle here but so far, the area has attracted mostly individuals, professionals, especially Californians who are escaping their frenetic way of life. But they rarely become involved and often when they do, their suggestions are contradictory to an understanding of the environment, existing production, and commonly held local values.

Nevertheless, Janet sees signs that there may be positive growth. Each day a few more people call for visitor information. And the proliferation of festivals and celebrations like

"Mid-Summer Cruz," capitalizing on the passion for 1950s vintage automobiles, and "Old Fashioned Sunday," highlighting artisans making cottage industry crafts, have been successful. The change in Orofino is striking in the videotape entitled *Celebrate Orofino* that emphasizes tourism with a vengeance: the golf course, steel-head fishing, hunting, and the festivals. The visitors interviewed state that "It was one of the friendliest places they had ever visited," "It was beautiful," and "It had a lot of advantages." But these emphases were totally different from the interests of the logging community that seem to typify Orofino. Why were there two images of Orofino? Where were they coming from? Or was this new image a creation that was a hoped-for evolution?

The dilemma of identity is ever-present in Orofino today. In reality, only a portion of the community worked in logging throughout its history, but the community hung its communal *persona* on logging. It provided the imagery, excellent logos, heroes, and contests that no other community in the area could claim. But should Orofino relinquish this image in favor of diversity? Would diversity provide a new image over time, or would Orofino become just another small town in the West? Janet couldn't spend all her time pondering questions that will only have answers in the next century, but she was concerned. She was looking for answers that would make the community thrive. She saw the value in the old image, but as a part of the younger generation continued to seek ways to make the community grow quickly. Should they open the doors to immigration? She, the city council, and the merchants understand the problems of unrestricted welcomes. The newcomers, so far, had been accommodated. The new professional class had been accepted into the community and into its organizations. But it is impossible to say whether tensions could arise in the future.

Orofino may no longer be one town, but several; no longer a place holding onto one set of occupational values. It may be difficult to find a consensus on where to go next. Throughout Western history, communities the size of Orofino have become ghost towns when their industrial base experienced hard times. Janet, Harriet, and many other boosters won't let that happen to Orofino.

In finding the best solution perhaps the town should remain the way Lydia Dennis, a newcomer to Orofino, describes it. A retiree from Maine and active in community development throughout her life, she said: "I love it here in Orofino. It's like living in the 1950s and thank God, it's off the beaten path. Regardless of where you try to retire in the East, you're trapped in a town that's a bedroom community for some large metropolis. And it's safe. People drop in; kids on their way home from school bring their projects to show you. There are groups to join and groups to start." Her apt analysis of Orofino could be correct. It may be a town captured as much by time and as it is by place.

THE ELDERS

The Past Revered

When visitors come to Orofino, they will without exception be introduced to one of the elders, the old-timers. Social history here is measured in decades, not in centuries. But among the elders it is often difficult to sense history as being time past because these individuals give the impression that time has stood still. Technology may have changed, but to them it is as if all of time is collapsed into the present and logging standards have remained the same. Older people are revered as an important feature of community life.

The elderly men and women exemplify the roles and talents that were necessary in the profession. They are the sages for the aesthetics of the industry, from whom contemporary loggers learn their craft and feelings about logging. They pass on a tradition, not only in stories but also in the standards for work and life that they expect from all woodsworkers. Speaking with them is frequently less like going back in time than living fully in the actions that make a logger successful in the woods regardless of time period.

I began my visits with Joy Boles. She reveled in remembering Headquarters. Today, Headquarters, the Potlatch Forest Industries base camp for logging operations, is all but abandoned. But thirty years ago, it was a thriving community, a company town with homes for over eighty-five families and nearly four hundred single loggers. In its heyday, it had a variety store, school, restaurant, grocery, church, and community hall.

Joy Boles, over seventy years old when we spoke, remembered those buildings, but her eyes really lit up when she remembered "the way of life at the end of the road." Joy's husband, Wallace, was the logging superintendent and *ex officio* mayor, making sure that the community ran smoothly and that the loggers' home life added to their productivity.

Potlatch maintained other company towns, one of which is described by Keith Peterson (1987), but they were generally attached to the sawmills. Headquarters was a logging town without a mill that provided the necessities for community life prompted by the changes in woodswork during the decades from 1940 to 1960. The horse loggers had disappeared with the coming of logging trucks, and so had the river pigs—loggers skilled at handling logs carried down the river to the mills before truck logging.

Joy remembered the single men who lived among the families in the camp. "They were so respectful, those unattached lumberjacks. Often, they were European-born, generally known only as The Finns. They may have had harsh nicknames like *Broomface,* but they always lowered their eyes when a woman walked past. Granted, after a Saturday night in town they might spend a day drying out, but they were gentlemen to the end."

Following World War II many of the loggers were family men often educated in engineering or forestry. They didn't want to take up the ways attributed to the old stereotype of immigrants who had nowhere to call home and no one to call family. Joy's memories of Headquarters were of a near-perfect existence where ladies played bridge and she read her *New Yorker* every week for the twenty years that they had lived there. There was fresh milk from their own dairy and a school for the children. Judy Kilmer, Joy's daughter and executive secretary for Potlatch, remembers her childhood at Headquarters fondly. "All the kids loved Headquarters; we had everything we needed and friends that couldn't be beat. It was a sad day if your friend's dad left Potlatch employment and they had to move away. It was the ideal childhood. We didn't even want to go away on vacation."

The lives of the superintendent and his wife were filled with responsibilities. While Wallace had to make decisions on community allocations, Joy, the school teacher, went about creating a social atmosphere in the camp that was cultured even in this rugged environment. Christmas programs, community dances, card parties, and hospitality calls on new families were all a part of life, fostered through the efforts of the women. "Everybody was your friend, if you liked them or not, because in an isolated community, surrounded by a dangerous environment, teamwork was critical in both work and social life. The work was hard and danger was always present, but the women made sure that there was time for refinement." They were proud of the way they managed to uphold culture in the wild, but equally proud of the logging standards that their husbands maintained. Loggers took their occupational tradition seriously, and becoming skilled was a personal commitment. Men who were good at their jobs were revered, while the women were not only expected to meet the requirements of a wife, but expected themselves to be the instruments of social life, civilizing the camps.

If you compare the photographs of the early bachelor camps to the camps in which women had an influence, you can see the difference. Earlier camps were sturdy and liveable, but obviously for temporary habitation. In family camps where women's hands were at work, flowers abounded in gardens, kitchens were utilitarian but delightfully chintz, and sofas and chairs were covered with doilies. This female touch altered the camp so that the distinction between workplaces and living places was hazy. A loaded logging truck might be parked next to a patch of pansies or a man might collect firewood for his hearth during lunchtime on a logging job.

There was no separation between living and logging. A man could watch a sawyer and know his level of skill, but so could his wife. From long years of exposure, she could see how he determined the balance points and how straight and true his cut might be. She could judge logging skills as ably as her husband. Joy Boles said that winter provided the real test of skill and artistry. Conditions required the very best sawyer with excellent coordination and a kinesthetic sense, described locally as knowing where to be when. She'd learned her husband's criterion for being good at logging—"You only get a rating of *good* if you grow old doing it."

Logging was Headquarters and Headquarters was home. Joy, like the other women in the community, formed not only a family but a corporate unit with their husbands. Faye Porter, another revered woman in the community, shared many of Joy's feelings about pride in home and logging.

The Porters' story began when Louie Porter needed boots and asked his employer for part of his wages. The employer gave Louie "half of everything that he owned, which was pocket change, and one half of his business." From that inauspicious beginning, Louie built a business and eventually processed some of the best white pine in the region.

Louie met Faye walking down the road to visit her grandmother. Theirs was an instant attraction. They wanted to get married immediately but had to wait three years until they had enough money to get a license. They had been together for nearly sixty years when he died in 1991.

"It was tough going in those days," said Louie when I interviewed the Porters. "You made one dollar for cutting and splitting a cord of wood." But throughout our three-way conversation I had a feeling that they wouldn't have traded their life for any other. This was especially true when they spoke of the time they ran their logging operation at Poor Man Creek. Old photographs show a kitchen ready for feeding fifteen to twenty lumberjacks a day and capture Faye's perpetual preoccupation with flowers and her unquenchable need to have a garden.

The standard day began at 4:00 A.M. when Louie would get up and look over the job. By six he would have a plan for the day, and then it was time to go to the cookhouse for breakfast; by seven Louie and his crew were hard at work. Faye did the washing for the camp, shopped for groceries and machine parts in Orofino, tended her garden, and took lunch out to him on the job. At 4:00 P.M., the work day ended. In the evenings the crew sat around and "told lies, played poker, and smoked." Faye says, "We truly did think a lot of our men and always enjoyed them; some of them still come to see me, even today, all these years later."

The Porters were prosperous. They had seven camps and were for some years one of the largest independent operations in the area. Louie who had one of the finest reputations in the region as a logger, employer, and individual, said that when he was sixteen he decided "this is what I'm going to do," and he never changed his mind. "You get tired but not of logging; it gets into your blood and you don't want to do anything else." He treated his men fairly, but everyone on the crew had to produce. "To be good you had to be ambitious, have know-how, and a clean cut appearance. You didn't need much muscle but you needed a lot of brains," said Louie.

Faye was the flunkie—the person who does everything. Without her, the creature comforts would have gone untended. She was the mainstay of the entire operation and ran it with both the gentle hand of a mother and the determination of a general. As was true then, and is today, it took a man and woman working together to make a logging business succeed.

Louie and Faye enjoyed talking about the past and the exploits of their youth. Once, Louie challenged a man with a power saw. He had confidence in himself but also in the widely-known fact that the early saws were unreliable. The time for the contest came and the power saw wouldn't start. Louie's opponent had to wait for parts and by the time they came, Louie and his old, manual cross-cut saw had processed 18,000 feet of timber.

Louie had a wealth of information and opinions about the old days. For one, he felt that the sons of logging families were always better workers because the craft was passed down from generation to generation. When asked about the one overriding feature of success in logging Louie didn't hesitate, he said, "It's the roads. You must keep them well-tended. At night you water them to keep the dust down. Any job is only as good as your road." For Louie, "There is no way to learn logging out of a book; you must grow up in the brush and learn it by experience. Education is good for business but it doesn't make a logger out of you; having a degree is as good as having rocks in the head. Logging takes experience and hard work, and the best school is doing it."

I asked Louie who were some of the finest loggers he'd known. "Well, there was Abner Cowger; he was strong, had know-how and wasn't afraid of any work. He handled big timbers like toothpicks. Tim Barnett's mother was another, one of the best that there was. Women can be, you know. They aren't quite strong enough to do sustained work like a logger can, but some are really good with machinery and in the woods."

The Porters also succeeded with their showloads for the Fair, winning first prize with a load of Ponderosa pine. Louie thought it was by far the prettiest timber. And his criteria for beauty? "Its bark is smooth; it's a yellow-gold color, and in the forest it stands out and glistens," he said. Louie and his crew worked for a month to pick out the finest trees. They found seven or eight with no defects, big, round, and straight with limbs only at the top. They felled the trees one at a time and positioned the truck as near as possible so the bark would not be damaged. It was a real honor to be on the showload crew. It called for special, caring men.

When I asked Louie and other loggers what they thought was their most memorable experience in the woods, I was surprised at their answers. Often they did not recall a triumph, but instead would relate the time that someone was killed. Louie told me about Lesco Reece, who had been killed when a dead tree fell over. For Louie this was an exceptional tragedy, for he liked all his men and did everything he could for them—they had always been like family to Louie and Faye.

A load of logs decorated for the Clearwater County Fair and Logging Show parade. Because of their size, only three logs could be loaded safely and according to road regulations. (Courtesy, Jeff Tinsley, Smithsonian Institution.)

The Porters retired and lived a comfortable existence until Louie died. Their home near a creek had the natural elements so much a part of the region, but in their backyard, Faye's garden sang with flowers and herbs in designs that recalled a British country garden. The Porters had lived in untamed conditions, and yet they had always had that sense of flair, that sense of good taste that is so often ignored in describing a life in logging.

Just as Faye tended their garden religiously, Louie maintained equally precise standards for work in the woods. "You don't cut it all down and don't let the big corporations brainwash younger people to think that there's a reason to clearcut—cut down entire areas completely.

When you do a job you leave the small trees and you clean up the remains. A good job should look like a park when you're done. Looking like a park, that's the answer."

Before his death, Louie spent one afternoon a week with the "Luncheon Group." Every Wednesday around noon at the Konkolville Restaurant, an amazing exchange took place. Sometimes several hundred years of logging history were represented when the old-timers got together to talk and "tell lies." On one particular day, November 20, 1990, Mel Snook, logging contractor, Mel McClain, scaler, and Joe Richardson, former mill owner, all in their eighties, were examining a piece of Brazilwood with serpentine edges. They had seen a lot of timber species, but this one was different. The sliver of wood had been a joke—Joe's bit of humor to see if Mel McClain had any idea of how you would scale or estimate the yield of a piece that did not have a regular, circular perimeter. It opened a conversation on the roles of these three men in early logging.

In many respects, the timber industry is one of estimates. You cannot follow a specific piece of timber through the entire process, so there must be some way to account for payment at various stages of work. Scaling is based on the need for someone to verify the piecework quantities. It is a mathematical and technical skill in an industry of indefinite measures. The scaler converts irregular cylinders—logs—into the number of board feet that can be produced from them. But, as Mel McClain said, "These skills are not enough, you have to grow up knowing how to do it. You can be a school dropout but gain a reputation as an educated guesser, because it's experience that educates." Joe said, "It's a business that is chuck full of educated guessers."

Scalers work in several locations—in the woods and at the landings to verify the output of sawyers and in the mills to determine the potential of each log for lumber. It's not an easy task, because the sawyer and the contractor want the highest possible estimates while mill owner wants the lowest possible number since this will mean greater profit for him if the lumber produces more than the minimum that has been scaled. All in all, each party wants fairness in the scaling process.

Accuracy is not someplace in between the desires of the men at the beginning and those at the end of the process. Instead, it depends largely on getting the best scaler with the finest reputation for fairness and knowledge of the potential of each piece of timber. It sounds easy—measure the circumference and the length, and apply a formula that tells you how many board feet of what lengths are possible. Not so, for just as Joe's piece of Brazilwood demonstrated an unusual case of extreme outer irregularities, every tree that is cut must be examined for its unique features that would make it difficult to mill into lumber. Is there disease that must be cut out? Are there outer flaws that must be removed in the sawmill? Are the dimensions compatible with current marketable goods? Is the scaler scaling up or down to a fraction of an inch in each log's potential?

The scaler had been, and still is, the man in the middle. And during this Wednesday luncheon, Mel McClain, even though retired, was still taking the ribbing handed out to those in his profession. The men with the "long thumbs" as they were often called, make mistakes. These errors could cost as much as $30,000 for a job. This would be an impossible margin for a mill owner to absorb. But generally scalers—the decision-makers on quantity—were fair. They learned early in their careers to be impartial, even though they are in the employ of one side or the other. It is on the basis of being fair that they gain their reputations, but even so, the scaler will have certain tendencies in the way he does his job. If you are contracting a scaler you know that you can get someone who scales in a certain way. There is a limited range of arbitrariness in his decisions, but you can still find a slight margin if you find the right scaler.

As these three men discussed the intricacies of scaling, I realized that logging, because of its built-in inaccuracies, was an occupation that prized and rewarded men with good reputations. These men go back a long time and have had their differences of opinion, yet they still joke and jab at one another. They are always supportive and don't hesitate to praise one another's reputations. Says Mel Snook of Joe, "He had the best reputation for treating people right." Says Joe Richardson of Mel, "Oh, well, he was always a politician," and both of them say of Mel McClain, "For a scaler, he's a pretty straight guy."

Sometimes they just mention a name and start to laugh, remembering the colorful characters of the past. There was Tom King, who rarely wore shoes in town. He was fearless and he would do anything for a thrill, but he was also known for his safety record. He would go into an uncharted area and inspect the brush for danger before a crew arrived at work.

They remember "Butterfly Pete," who rolled the log in *Charlie the Lonesome Cougar*. Often when they mention others, like "Cream Puff Dave," "Dirty Shirt Smith," "Hambone Smith," and "Broomface," they know the stories so well that just the name conjures up a volume of memories. These three men, pillars of the industry, with their in-depth knowledge of the values that were at the heart of the logging industry, passed down the colorful monikers and tales of these men of folkloric interest from the past.

Loggers in whatever category—sawyer, loader, mill operator, or logging truck driver—must trust that people will deal honestly with the imprecision of the industry. They must have knowledge and experience to make the proper judgments and to develop a profitable business relationship. If there is a dispute, the parties have to be able to discuss it and make alterations that satisfy the standards of both fairness and of good working relationships. Not only did individuals have a certain reputation in the community, but their relationships had a soundness that was long-standing. Logging is a profession of continuous communication and interaction over decades, not just years.

Conversations with old-timers show that the stereotype of the "hard-working, hard-playing, and hard-drinking logger" is only one side of logging. The men of the logging community of Clearwater County have a thick and luxuriant veneer of sophistication about them. The complex interweaving of these men and their values is not the product of a lone lumberjack. "Yes, we worked all the time because we didn't know anything else," said Joe. "We worked because we were doing it for ourselves." But the lives of early loggers in Clearwater County point not only to individuals working for personal gain but also to relationships. The story of Idaho logging is incomplete if it is peopled only with romantic characters. The real men are less colorful than those of Bunyanesque myth, but they are far more notable. As men at the foundation of the industry, their contribution is not for colorful imagery but in the philosophy and the values they set for logging.

But that's not to say they don't like to talk about the colorful characters. Mel Snook is especially adept at storytelling and keeping records of the past. Mel still works on his ranch in the mornings and, like others his age, settles in to work on his memoirs in the afternoon. His home is filled with family portraits, plants, and piles of logging photos. Agnes, his wife of over sixty years, was recently deceased, but she had built a lifestyle of taste and style as had so many other women in the spouse-owned and operated logging camps of the 1940s and 1950s.

OCI Lumberjack Days program photos show Mel acting as the judge for the contests, newspaper articles say he was the man who single-handedly kept the show going after the fairgrounds had flooded in 1948. He proposed the auction of prize winning logs and, along with Potlatch Forests and Joe Richardson, was a major donor. "It was a show for us, not for the tourists, and we had to make a go of it," said Mel.

Mel hadn't changed much in size or weight from those early photographs. He was still straight and in control, more so than many of the old-timers who are bent, with limbs twisted from overuse. Mel had started in the woods with his father; he was cutting cordwood in his early teens. By the time he had finished the eighth grade he was working a ten-hour day at fourteen cents an hour for the Panhandle Lumber Company. When Mel turned eighteen, his dad and a friend bought a truck and a team of horses and began gyppoing. His brother came into the business with them and by 1922, it was a stable concern and they began to employ more men. Because the company needed a business manager, Mel attended Northwestern Business College. The company prospered, and Mel eventually took over as one of the major logging contractors in the area. From time to time he probably employed every logger in the Orofino region.

Mel was successful, but as was true throughout the lives of many loggers, there were economic ups and downs. He remembers a time when his dad lost the logging sleigh and horses. They were so poor that they went to a family that had cows and asked for a pail of milk for the baby, but that was the only charity they would accept. Even though the church had offered money, the Snook family was going to make it on their own. "Doing for yourself" and "preparedness" seem to be the themes running throughout Mel's conversation. "If you can handle yourself, you don't have trouble. You want to learn everything you can and do all you can."

Mel spoke briefly about union organizers who showed up in this region. He remembers their recommended scheme for labor: Do what your job describes, do it for a designated time, and do it on a standard that is set by the union that has the interests of all workers at heart. The plan didn't fit this industry, where a logger can do everything. He can cross over to just about any job. The union also suggested that there was a division between the employer and the employee, one that loggers who worked side by side with their bosses did not see. "When the union guy came around and told you to slow up, you began to question the union's motives," said Mel.

Mel remembers the technological changes in the industry. In about 1944, manual sawing was replaced by power saws. It was quite a revolution. The old sawyers claimed that they could out saw the new equipment. Even though they could not physically saw faster, the amount of maintenance required by the power saw often set its production back and meant that manual sawyers were, in fact, more efficient. Albert Altmiller, a woodsworker and sawyer, became the mechanical genius of the region. He was inventive with the big and cumbersome early McCullough chainsaws that often needed two men to operate them. They had handles on both sides. In front of a salesman, Albert said, "I know a way to fix it." He cut the end off of one side of the saw so that the handle could be eliminated.

Mel remembered thinking from the very beginning that the power saw wouldn't be success-ful until the man who operated it owned it. That man and not an absentee owner would do the thinking, and changing, and making it better. He would make it his own both by possessing it and by understanding it. Eventually that happened, and it changed the course of the history of the power saws.

Not only does Mel get credit for having one of the best memories of the technological changes, he was also the first person who used the word "artist" to describe the woodsworkers to me. He began by telling me of the categories of jobs in the woods. When he began talking about the early top loaders—the best men at loading logs on a truck—he said, "Now that Canada Joe, he was a real artist." Mel couldn't find the words to be eloquent enough about this man and loading crews in general. It called for skill and balance to keep those unmanageable logs moving onto the top of the hauling truck. It was hard enough to begin with, but logging in the winter, that was the real test of a man. Mel said, "And the blacksmiths, they were real artists in days before acetylene welding. The work was very heavy, but they could get it perfect. Well, talk about artistry, most of the people in the early days of logging could do everything, and they could do it right."

To be an artist in logging was a physical feat, but it was also a mental skill. The actions took strength to perform, but in order to get the operation done you had to have logic and under-standing of physics. "Being strong doesn't help if you can't figure out where and how to get a load balanced. The whole operation both in the old days and today is a team thing," said Mel.

Prior to the development of trucks constructed specifically for logging, standard vehicles like this Dodge were used for hauling. Because conventional trucks had shorter beds, logs were cut to smaller lengths. This load was entered into the parade by White Pine Lumber. (Courtesy, the estate of Carroll Brock.)

"Every man knows his job. They look out for each other—a very special kind of friendship develops on those crews, one based on the balance of life and death."

Mel captured the essence of creativity in the industry. He introduced the idea "that operations in the woods were the best research lab, and gyppo loggers were the best research department that any merchandiser could have." He remembers the hard tires on trucks in the 1920s and the way in which loggers kept adapting their trucks. "They'd use junk and sometimes invent parts to replace those that broke," he says. Loggers kept on learning about machinery, and by the 1930s many were not only woodsworkers but also qualified as excellent mechanics. Finally, manufacturers took their ideas and produced trucks designed specifically for logging. The first bona fide logging trucks had no cabs or lights and were used only on short hauls.

Mel also taught me the origin of the logger's rendition of the word "haywire." In the early days when machinery broke down, loggers would fix it with baling wire, practical only for short-term use. The loggers who then failed to finish the repair properly were not considered very good and were called "haywire outfits."

Looking back on the early days of logging, Mel believes that people were different then. "They were taught to work and they worked. Men and women weren't looking for easy things. Adversity makes you strong, and everyone can remember the tough days." Mel always keeps his word and feels that the old values are the best values. There are things in modern society that he can't condone and will be outspoken about. "Today people want the easy way out and aren't willing to take the consequences of their actions," he contends, and he feels that people must return to valuing life, family, and other human beings.

Mel still owns over five hundred acres of land and logs it as he has for forty-five years. He is selective so that the secondary growth looks like a real forest. He's proud of the care, the artistry with which he has harvested his land. "If you're careful about the diameter of tree that you cut, you can have a nice little forest in forty or fifty years." Knowing him, Mel "Boss" Snook will be there, at one hundred and thirty-eight years of age, felling his trees and skidding them down for loading. His work will be a joy to him and will bring pleasure to those able to see the art in his work.

Joe Richardson had every right to be there too, in the woods until he was a hundred, but reality doesn't always follow the path of a good story. Joe died in 1993. Joe Richardson thought I was truly stupid. How can anyone from Wisconsin not know why an eagle is the symbol of the J. I. Case steam engine company? Of course my stupidity about the iconography of machinery was not my only shortcoming. I didn't know the heiress of the Case corporation, and she lives in Washington, D.C., where I now make my home. And I couldn't get logging terminology correct nor date certain logging practices accurately.

Yet, Joe took time with me and tried again and again to explain what was really important in logging. For Joe, there was little reason to talk about vague feelings or outlandish hyperbole when you could be talking about real machines and productive activities. His knowledge spanned sixty years and touched the full range of occupational and community roles. He was there and knew why certain events happened. He was there and didn't hesitate to refute the "histories" of other writers. He was there and didn't need to pretend, nor did he let others get away with it.

Often, Jim Cochrane would accompany me on my visits to Joe; I think that somehow he would be my go-between. The two, though years apart in age, had much the same outlook. They were able to speak the same language, one that depended on the concrete elements of the workings of the world around them. I kept trying to look underneath their comments for a different level than the realism of these down-to-earth men. My approach probably exasperated them, but they tolerated it anyway.

Joe's background was in sawmilling, but he also had technological curiosity. His dad had logged with steam, and he could remember the 1876 Corliss steam engine, a technological breakthrough. Its valve system was shown at the World's Fair in the same year Edison invented the light bulb, when General Grant was president. Information comes from Joe in a soft voice, with little emphasis on any one topic but always with a steady stream of history. But when he speaks of J. I. Case steam engines, there is something added in his tone. Why has he been collecting them for so long? The answer is simple, of course—"Because they are the best-looking."

I said to Joe, "The governor is in town." He replies, "So. He used to work for me before this political thing. He ran the green chain that carried green lumber up to be cut at Riverside Lumber. He was a pretty good mechanic in those days." Joe measures a man for what he can do, not for what position he has attained.

After I had earned the right, by paying attention to his history, Joe ended the mystery about why J. I. Case adopted the eagle. During the Civil War the regiment from Wisconsin used an eagle on their regimental flag. It was drawn from an actual eagle that had been given to the regiment by a Native American. The eagle survived the war and was brought back to Madison to live in the State House. It was asphyxiated during a fire there, but its remains were taken to a taxidermist, stuffed, and kept in memory of the Wisconsin regiment.

In logging, Joe was a man who dispelled the myth of the lumberjack. He was a fine businessman and he ran his mill with honesty, integrity, and good business acumen. His reputation was in management, not the type that is taught in a graduate department of business but rather in knowing how to handle his men and the resources at his disposal. Joe was a mill owner, so his professional life was somewhat removed from work in the woods. But he remembered with great relish the early years he spent in the forest protection service when he was responsible for building lookout towers—not an easy task in an era without roads to the sites.

Joe looked back on his life in forest industry mostly from the vantage point of technology and the developments in machinery that occurred. His unparalleled collection of J. I. Case steam machinery demonstrated that he was a connoisseur of mechanical beauty. He took these treasures to steam engine exhibitions throughout the country and was known for the care with which his restorations were done. Joe also had a real love for wood. Each room in his home was paneled with exceptional examples of native timber cut in his mill. It was his way of living with the fruits of his profession.

Joe exemplified a life in logging that understands all the technicalities of the industry. It was a life based on good order and precision, one that had an appreciation for the finer things of life and the finest products of the forest industry. He was a perfectionist in everything he did and yet claimed that his life had been based on "doing what we had to do."

He found an incomparable degree of satisfaction in the fact that you could harvest the trees you planted yourself and then take that wood and turn it into a beautiful object. Perhaps it was a spinning wheel for a niece or a picture frame for a photo of his J. I. Case steam engine. His wood-working was ingenious. His shop was filled with unique tools and devices for doing impossible tasks in wood, and regardless of the product, his creations were as perfect as Joe could make them.

But even before Mel Snook could cut, Mel McClain could scale, and Joe could mill, another logging professional would be in the woods. Cruisers like Frank Randol would be the first to have completed their jobs. Many said that Frank Randol was the best cruiser that the county had ever had, but when we spoke, he began by telling me I should have met George Harlan who "was the best cruiser that the county had ever had." After evidencing the appropriate degree of humility, he laid out his claim to his excellent reputation. "Forty-eight years of tramping for Potlatch. I've seen every-thing from white pine logging with horses to helicopter operations. And you'd think that I could retire; no, I'm still doing two hundred and fifty sections a year for these real estate people. Whenever someone wants to sell land they call me to estimate the timber on that lot. A lot people think its a cinch, but finding the corners—the boundary markers of the section—that isn't always easy."

Cruisers and the process of cruising are indispensable to corporations, independent log-gers, and land owners alike. They are estimators *extraordinaire.* The cruiser's role is to estimate the number of board feet that can be logged in a given stand of timber before it is cut. Cruisers like Frank Randol, who at seventy-five looks fifty, are always out in the woods. According to him, he never gets sick because "I wear wool clothes and eat onions." He likes the out-of-doors and finds it a healthy place to be: "In this country it's too cold for germs anyway," he says. But he believes that going from the age of physical labor to the machine age has affected people's health by making them sedentary and sickly.

Frank has seen billions of feet of timber in his time. Cruisers look at everything in the woods; it is their determination as to the yield of an area by species and quantity that will set the price, settle an estate, or fix the bid for the timber. Much of the territory in this region is surveyed by mapping techniques that have varied from time to time. The maps of yesteryear were not nearly as accurate as they are today. This means that land disputes over the actual boundaries are common. Often Frank cannot depend on records, even official ones, to be accurate. He has to go out on the land and find the original markers at the perimeters. But regardless of the technical advances, the equipment, and the maps, the job is only as good as the cruiser.

As a cruiser, you must train your eye. You are looking at many factors all at the same time—species, width, height, and condition of the potential timber. While cruising, you also get a sense of the difficulties that the logging crew will encounter in harvesting a specific stand. Frank will tell you that a good cruiser has the right perspective on the stand and that "I size up the timber even before I get to it." There are certain technical procedures that you follow in this job. When you cruise you go in a straight line, looking on either side of that line for the marketable species. You can cruise and estimate anywhere between 20 and 100 percent of the stand depending on the specifications of the owner. Normally you cover forty acres as the best estimable percentage of a six-hundred-and-forty-acre section. From your observation you draw a map and then put together a chart that shows what's on the land. The chart is like a grid that itemizes the number of species and specific trees in each square. The percentage of territory covered and the amount of marketable timber the cruiser says is on that portion is used to estimate the yield of the entire area.

The cruiser has a truly discriminating eye and he knows dimension and species at a glance. Everyone works at the skill, but according to Frank, "You have to have a natural inclination toward it. There's an art to it all." Cruisers enjoy the challenge of seeing how accurate their estimates are, and want to perfect themselves. They will check how close they came to the actual production of the stand when it is measured in the mill. Frank is often right on target.

Today, aerial cruising enhanced by computers is possible. It is a technique suggested by government agencies. But for Frank the only way to really get an accurate estimate is to be in direct contact with the trees. Anyone can identify the species and the quantities from above, but no one can tell conditions of a stand unless you are close to it and look at the terrain to determine the amount of time necessary to harvest it. There are only three cruisers left in the area, and cruising is becoming a lost art. Other than cruising with an old-timer, there is no way to learn the craft. If the new technology replaces traditional cruising, a great skill and an outstanding practice of woodsmanship will be gone.

How did Frank Randol become a good cruiser? Why did Potlatch keep him on the job for forty-eight years? Throughout our conversation the critical elements of his job emerged. He knew the importance of concentration and observation. Not only could he look, he could *see,* which was more a matter of insight than eyesight. His perception of space, distance, and density are excellent. Frank's talent and the talent of many woodsworkers depends on "being there." They have been on site for long periods of time and the forest is familiar to them. Finally, Frank keeps moving. Cruising is done at a swift pace and not a matter of a leisurely saunter through the forest. "What good is a cruiser if you're paying him by the hour and it takes him longer to estimate than it would to have someone come out and just saw?" says Frank.

The work of the cruiser is typical of other roles in a life in logging. It involves constantly trying to make sure that approximations are as accurate as possible. It is the measure of exactness, not the margin of error, that everyone in the woods works on. The cruiser is an estimator, the scaler is an estimator, the independent logging contractor must have a good sense of estimating, for it is on this basis that he will place a bid for a job. Any errors along the line by someone not well trained in his craft can set the entire process off kilter. On the other hand, when all of the estimators are on target there is both financial certitude and a pride that lets each man know he is right. Being accurate is an important measure of a man in the logging industry.

A conversation with Frank Randol is not an easy encounter. For example, he asked me, "If you have never been in a place, how would you know if you were lost?" I realized that with no point of reference I would be disoriented and could not trust my perception of direction. But for Frank, who cruised in unknown territory often, it means something very different. Not knowing your exact location does not mean you are lost. It means that you are at a place that may be unrecognizable but no different from any other place. You have the confidence that here or anywhere, you can manage, you can cope. You are in a place and if you don't have to be somewhere else by a certain time you'll be there in that place, until you get to somewhere else. This idea seems to bring together the sense of place and time that typified this occupation and region. You can take all the time you want in a place, you are in command of it, you are not lost, you are just taking longer to get back to where you came from.

Frank's idea tossed me upside down; I was truly a limnar on the threshold of this world that doesn't allow for being lost. And if our conversations were cryptic, my encounters with Uncle Boyd were labyrinthian.

Talking to old-timers, men now in their seventies and eighties, offers a set of unusual challenges. They have time on their hands and are retired, and unhurried about their ways. Conversations must be carried on with patience and the sense that they will go their own direction.

Logging may have been their occupation but these senior men have preoccupations that can range from collecting antique cars and steam engines to gold mining. Often they have rivalries, making the interviewer step gingerly and use information received from one carefully with another. You've met many of these men: Joe Richardson, the kind-hearted curmudgeon; Frank Randol, the philosophical cruiser; Louie Porter, who believed that logging was a family endeavor; and Mel Snook, the diplomat *par excellence;* all important parts of the development of the logging industry.

But I would like to introduce an elder who is a story unto himself—Uncle Boyd Olson, a farmer, logger, and closet gold miner. He is certain that some day he will find the Lost Dutchman Mine. His thoughts come out in spurts and you have to write them down on separate sheets of paper to organize them. He talks about horse logging, early flumes (troughs used to bring logs down the mountain), family history, settlements, his travels, his future, and his current problems. His staccato delivery makes it nearly impossible to follow all the threads. He has written pamphlets on horse logging and holds onto a stand of trees that's just perfect for showing the old mastery of this technique. A few years back, his dream was to document this art form. He wanted to find a professional cameraman and recreate the entire process down to the type of trees that were harvested and the type of horses that were used. The bridles and tools must come out of a museum to make it authentic. He'd construct a gin pole—a tall tree used as a fulcrum to lift the logs onto the sled. His teamster would be an old guy, someone who knew exactly how to handle horses in the woods. "They're still around, you know," says Uncle Boyd. Often when he retells his dream, I wonder what might actually happen if Uncle Boyd and all the old-timers were brought together, whether they could ever agree on how the job should be done.

Uncle Boyd's stories are free-form, with no rhyme or reason. Finding a script, a coherent discourse in his words was difficult. He'd start a story by saying, "Butterfly Pete was a great man on river drives in the early thirties. He never fell off a log." And that was it, all there was to that story. He provided a challenge to me and introduced the questions of what interviews are actually all about.

To give an example of Uncle Boyd's conversation: In the space of a few minutes he told a story about cables, horse logging, and moving small mills. Then he referred to old-timers like Leonard Cardiff, the famous lumberman. He used quotes like, "Better move fast or you'll get killed." He talked about the ten-day men who were just that—wanderers who stayed for ten days on any job and then went off to greener pastures. He maintained that "Michigan Bill could do anything." Finally he asserted that "swear words make writing robust."

Uncle Boyd gladly speaks to visitors who want to know about the old days. In my role of limner, his was the most difficult portrait to paint, each sitting full of fits and starts. The fragmentation of his stories added to their charm, but I am at a loss as to how to document his conversations. I have yet to put Uncle Boyd's comments into perspective. Perhaps both his choice of episodes and method of presentation suggest the need to look carefully at the role of an Uncle Boyd in the story of logging. Nonetheless, a conversation with Uncle Boyd was always an occasion, as was a visit with Bill Cummings.

Bill Cummings has done it all. His construction company would tackle any project—roads, septic tanks, or moving houses. He's done more hauling than he wants to remember. His lowboys—nine-axle trailers—could be seen throughout the region running all over the place.

Though he was raised in Orofino, on Canada Hill to be exact, he has been as much a man of the world as you will find in this community. He was in the service during World War II and has a wealth of experience from his time away. But today at over seventy, Bill is content to relax on his property, to survey the land, and make sure that it is tended in the way a natural environment must be. Along with his home and equipment buildings, Bill has a shed that contains bits and pieces of the lives of six different families. His is an informal repository for things that are too precious to throw away and yet too distant from necessity to keep up close. His own treasures include a 1930 Caterpillar, a 1923 Mack truck, and an antique automobile.

Bill's philosophy is based on the life he has led. He feels, "Anyone can learn anything. You have to have some ability, but what you really need is determination and desire. When I was growing up, everybody was poor so we had to start working and trying to outdo everyone else. Here stands ten men, nine fall down and one walks on." Bill has run a lot of crews, and those men who were good showed determination. Another of Bill's work-related axioms is "Even though you want to get a job done, never get in too big a hurry; if you do, you'll never get there." Bill believes that a good man has to have the right attitude. Discipline is paramount; you have to be clean and have a haircut.

Some things about modern life don't thrill Bill. For example, once on a job, his Caterpillar was wrecked and fell into a waterway. Bill knew it would take one hour to get the wrecked machine out, but a week to get the permission from the highway department to do it, so he just got on with the job. In a sense Bill Cummings has spent a life alongside of logging. He has sometimes worked in it, but always has known that the services of someone good in construction and engineering were invaluable to the logger. Loggers didn't want to handle these jobs, but Bill could, and he was always there when needed.

According to Bill, a good boss is always a good listener and teacher, and one of the best had been Frank Fromelt, who came up often in conversation with loggers. He was honest and hard-working and went out of his way to give jobs to people who needed them. He would have gone to the brink of bankruptcy before letting any of his employees down.

Frank liked driving new cars. On one occasion he went to Lewiston for a new car wearing logging clothes. To him, going to Lewiston was no reason to change his clothes. When he arrived at the dealership, the salesmen ignored him—just walked past him as if he didn't exist. Finally, a receptionist came from the office and asked if she could be of help. Frank asked for the owner, who recognized Frank immediately. Frank took cash from his pocket and said, "I want a Chrysler Imperial Le Baron, and I want this young woman to have credit for the sale." The owner told Frank she couldn't get commissions as a receptionist. Frank said, "No commission for her, no car for me." Of course the owner changed his mind and the young woman received a bonus. There are several variations on this story, which is told to pay tribute to Frank as well as to give a pointed example of an important attitude. It's not what you look like that counts, it's what you've done. And you always reward those who do the job regardless of what their positions are said to be officially.

Again, as so often during this field experience, what the people of Orofino look upon as everyday fare struck terror in my heart. Bill decided to take me up the incline to show me Orofino from the top of the ridge. There were several ways to go, the safest of which would be to walk. Even though the terrain was steep, a slow walk up the hill would have been enjoyable. Instead, he put me on the back of a four-wheel, all-terrain vehicle. With every foot we climbed, I felt as if we would go tumbling down the hill with the vehicle plummeting after us. I held on. We got to the top, I took three photos, and we began to descend. Finally, we were down, and it was time to ride through town in his restored Model A Ford—almost as if I were being rewarded. We got in and putted through Orofino, waving to every passerby.

Clearwater County has recently become aware of the fascination outsiders have for logging and residents have begun to tell their story to visitors. Bob Allen, a retired Potlatch woodsworker, is one of those who has taken on the task. For many years Bert Curtis's cabin stood at Headquarters abandoned, used principally to store old records and logging paraphernalia. No one thought a logging museum was a priority except Bob Allen. When I first met Bob, we had a conversation in an empty lot on Main Street in Pierce, Idaho. Curtis's cabin was still at Headquarters. Bob had no money, but he was convinced that the area needed a logging museum. Somehow he'd get the cabin moved and get his version of the logging story installed. Six months later it had been done. A foundation had been laid, the cabin was moved, and a storage building was in place. As an added attraction, a sawfiling shack, a former Potlatch building used to sharpen crosscut saws, was donated by logging contractor Ron Beck and was moved to the site. If ever the logging "can-do" mentality was in evidence, Bob's six-month odyssey from Headquarters to Pierce, from shambles to order, and from logger to museum director, was it. He received some services and a financial donation from Potlatch. His friends, mostly logging contractors in Pierce, had equipment and men sent to help move the building. Volunteers often appeared out of the blue. On a Sunday afternoon ten or so loggers would show up just to help out, never with a schedule and never with sign-in sheets; they'd all just dig in. Now Pierce has a logging museum. Bob isn't concerned about staff, because as is true of so many other projects in Clearwater County, there will be plenty of volunteers to come in to help. "It's something they like to do when they feel a part of the operation," says Bob.

How did Bob get involved in this massive undertaking? Bob says he always liked history, but his wife says it was inevitable. "He was forever coming home with junk, with stuff. I'd walk into my living room and find an old switchboard sitting there. Every day it was something else. Now, luckily, I have my house back and all those things are down at the museum. But sooner or later, he'll run out of space and they'll be cropping up again." But artifacts are only one part of the museum. With his background and that of the loggers who drop in, a visit to the museum is like stepping into living history. There are facts and stories swirling around the room, information that rarely appears in publications because it is too common and matter of fact, so seemingly inconsequential.

Bob has identified some of the sacred icons of the logging life, such as flumes, long wooden channels built on stilts as the pathways for logs downhill to the waterways. Finding the remains of one over a stream as you drive down the highway is reason to pause, look, and marvel at an entire era that is gone. Bob has the early notes from the Beaver Creek flume and as a self-educated engineer he intends to build it. Bob will tell the story of the excitement and splendor of log drives. You waited all year for a drive to happen and you had only one chance to do the job right. You had your best men there and it was high drama, a performance of the art of logging in its finest form.

Bob will also uphold the memories of fine Potlatch supervisors. The museum is named for the first, J. Howard Bradbury, a man who always appreciated the worker. Bob will have information about Wallace Boles when he was at Headquarters. "He was one of the finest men around. He paid you for every hour you worked during a time when workers often felt cheated by their employers." Bob is untrained in the workings of museums, but since he has often learned by doing, he feels that becoming a museum director will be an automatic process. And the desire is there. He's always been able to put his wishes into reality. "When you want to do it so badly, it's play and not work. As you're doing it you have in your imagination the finished product and what it will be like. You may operate by the seat of your pants, but the vision is always there, and it happens," he says.

Bob, like many others, mentioned the Hutchins brothers and their mill at Weippe. "They made it work because it's all theirs; their money and their computer. The programming was done by a high school dropout, and it works; it works better than the one in the corporate mill." According to Bob, "A degree doesn't say you can do something, it only says you can go to school."

Bob loved every minute in woods, but it wasn't the cutting down of trees that fascinated him. Bob was always concerned with the state of nature. He would put a kink in a road just to save a special stand of quaking aspens. He'd construct ditches to ensure water quality and would seed skidding roads to finish off a job even if it wasn't required. He wanted the environment to be attractive, and it was part of his job not only to use its resources but to keep it beautiful.

Bob and his wife claimed that they never argued. His work was important to him, and she believed in him, so she believed in it as well. He was a good provider, and judging from the appearance of their spread, he handled his personal life in the same manner that he did his work in the woods—every feature was perfect. And in true logger fashion, he gives Jeanette credit for the beauty of their home—the gardens and the country-club clipped grass, the freshly painted house and outbuildings, and the vehicles parked in even rows. Bob was concerned with visual appearances. He would obviously apply this same discriminating eye to the development of the museum.

Bob started me thinking about several important issues, for example: What if environmentalists left the logging industry alone, removed themselves from the issues? Would loggers come in and cut down all the trees? Would they take shortcuts to boost their individual earnings, or would that be against the philosophy and the aesthetics of those who take pride in logging? And exactly how does Potlatch, the major logging corporation, fit into the picture given to me by the independent logging contractors?

And why was I surprised when Bob spoke of imagination and intuition? Weren't all loggers like the lumberjacks of the past—hard-drinking and insensitive? How could this be? Bob was a man in the logging industry talking to me as would someone in the arts—about creativity. Bob and the other respected elders are a force in this community, living examples that life and art and work in logging are bound inextricably, and that the hopes for the future may, in fact, be embodied in the past.

LOGGERS TODAY

The Tradition Continues

Working, and doing it right, was a repeated theme in my conversations with today's loggers. They never flinch at how hard a job might be or how long it might take. It was the outcome, always the outcome, that propelled them through difficult and often uncertain conditions. Challenges were welcomed, changes from routine, but then again there is so little routine in their lives. It was as if every day was an occasion for the loggers to build stories, just as the elders had, of their occupational exploits.

It is inevitable that Norman and Sharon Baugh appear together in the book, for they are inseparable. At dinner in the Garden Room of the Ponderosa, the Baughs arrived looking less like loggers and more like Sun Valley skiers going out for a night on the town—casual chic with not a crease, not a wrinkle. They cut a fine figure and they knew it. They were ready for this interview. They wanted to be heard because they knew they were one of the prominent families in the area, supportive of the logging tradition. Even so, they would never have boasted of it to me or anyone in the community.

"Everybody works," was the theme in their household. Everyone is continually moving, not putting in hours, but accomplishing tasks. Thinking of working from 8:00 A.M. to 5:00 P.M. doesn't make any sense to the Baughs; work must be done when the conditions call for it, so you clean when something is dirty and drive a truck when the conditions are right. To spend your life in an office shuffling paper is just not work since words on paper have little to do with reality. And paperwork produces only a report, a memo, or a book, good to be read, but rarely acted upon. Or, if acted upon, they are modified drastically, because reality and words on paper are miles apart.

There is a division of labor in their family. Norman runs the truck. Sharon makes sure they have allocated their finances in the proper way. Norman tells a story about going out with his grandsons that demonstrates this division. It was a moderately muddy day and one of his grandsons wanted Norman to put on the chains. The conditions didn't warrant it, so Norman said no. The grandson thought a moment and said, "You're right, Papa-grams. They cost a lot of money and Grandma doesn't want us to wear them out." Sharon responded, "Sure, everyone knows that Grandma is tight." In practice this may not be true, for everyone tells Sharon what they want, and she finds a way to satisfy all of their needs while making ends meet. As Norman says, "It's my job to make the money and hers to see if it is enough."

Sharon feels that she shares her role with many logging wives. A husband and wife are a team; there is a camaraderie. They are usually together, or if they can't be, they know exactly where to find the other, in case an emergency arises. They don't complain, and they don't argue.

How do they handle situations in which there are several possible answers, for example, when it comes time to choose a new logging truck? Both Sharon and Norman go shopping. Norman has his favorite brand but could be convinced to try another. Sharon feels that if he is happy with one brand he should stick with it. Norman is undecided. Sharon states her opinion and adds, "If you get a different brand and you're not happy, don't complain. I won't say I told you so, and you won't complain." That's the end of it; Sharon states her position, Norman makes the decision, and from that point on he lives with the choice. There is no argument over the decision-making process, nor would there be any argument in the future, because they would both live up to their word. It's a simple process, says Sharon, "If you agree beforehand not to argue about it, you won't argue."

Shopping for machine parts is a critical task for logging wives. The process is not easy since the rigs are complex and have specific parts needs. At one time there were more local parts stores, but their numbers have dwindled and wives find it necessary to make longer trips to get a correct part. Sometimes they must drive as far as Spokane, four hours away, but it is their job as part of the team. When the husband needs a part he will tell his wife as specifically as possible, using both the part name and describing the technicalities associated with the problem. Normally parts shop owners know the drivers and their rigs and how they operate. The salesman and wife will discuss what's needed and determine how to solve the problem.

Driving a logging truck is Norman's livelihood, but it is also central to his total existence. He does it right, he does it to perfection, and he feels good about it and about himself. "It's not only a job; it is doing your job with a little bit of extra skill. It's picking up the residue on a log landing so that when you leave, it looks well-maintained. It's not only the work you do, but it's the world you live in. You do things as best as you can and then one day, you die," says Norman.

Of all the challenges Norman has had in his career the one he is proudest of meeting was moving the Peck Bridge. Originally this bridge had been located at the town of Myrtle, but due to the ingenuity of Bud Deyo's crew and Norman's driving skill, this massive, seemingly immovable structure, which could carry the heavy weight of huge logging trucks, was picked up and repositioned at another site on the Clearwater River. Norman has the photographs to prove he had done it.

Bud, who felt it wasn't all that big or all that heavy, approached Norman, who said "Sure we will move it." Bud and Norman decided to weld one end onto the truck bunk and place the other end on the tilt deck trailer so they could carry all one hundred and ten feet of it down the highway to its new location. Sharon rode in another rig with "Wide Load" signs. The bridge was relatively well-balanced—in fact, it was easier than hauling logs which are often top heavy. It was a job that had to be done, and they did it.

Norman is proud about moving the bridge for two reasons: first, because the community wanted it moved and he could oblige; second, because so many people said it couldn't be done. One company thought it might be done, but it would cost $20,000. Instead, according to Norman, "a bunch of dumb gyppos" accomplished this engineering feat. To add to the accomplishment, as Norman said with pride, "We only had to back the truck up once to position it."

Many of the people in the logging community, men like Norman, distrust theoreticians. Norman has a brilliance in execution that doesn't come from formulae or from mechanical sketches, and he doesn't trust people who spend most of their time with abstract information on paper or computers, data that they cannot see or feel. There is a significant difference between being on-site, experiencing every sensation of the job, and being in an office. At a desk you assume that conditions are as they are reported on paper and that a particular technique will work. This assumption may not be correct.

This often applies to road building. It's one thing to plan a road because you see what the contours are and what must be done. It's quite another to see it only in a written description. Often road planners don't fully know the conditions, or if they do, they don't get out every day to see how the road is holding up. The logging truck drivers do. They don't need a written report on the roads. They feel them. They experience the wear that the roads are subjected to when they take load after load from the job to the mill. Many logging truck drivers can give a full report on the conditions and status of all the roads in the county at any given time.

Norman prizes his independence. Owning his own truck is being his own boss. Sure, he is responsible to the contractor and the mill owner for whom he is driving, but they know his talents, and he's appreciated. Retirement is not an option for Norman. He can't imagine what it would be like. "Many drivers are still good, still in their prime, even though they are in their seventies. So why would I even think of quitting?"

Other drivers who have gained notice in the area, like the Greene family and Dwayne Opdahl, to name a few, don't want to "get out of the saddle." These men don't want to retire. Their skills may lessen slightly with age, but for driving logging trucks the skills they really need—perception of weight and knowledge of truck performance on different terrain—will be with them to their graves.

Over and over again Norman repeated that many men have the mistaken idea that if you are a long-haul driver you can naturally drive a logging truck. It's dangerous to believe this. The principles are totally different and often it is one of these drivers who will come down a grade too fast and flip a load of logs. When that happens the truck is wrecked by the weight of the logs and the roadway is a mess.

Family life for a driver is not easy. When their daughters were growing up, Norman often couldn't attend school programs or other family events. But neither the Baughs nor their daughters feel that they were cheated of their family life. In fact, Tammy, their youngest daughter, resided with them while she finished college, and Brenda and her family live down the road in Julietta. The Baughs enjoy their life. When they married, they were both young and intended even then to grow old together. They can talk to one another about anything, from the technicalities of a job and the repairs necessary to the wonders of an antique toy truck they might have seen. As we finished our conversation, Sharon saw that I was still perplexed at how their marriage worked. As we left the restaurant and Sharon and Norman went off to their truck, she called out to me. "Oh, Charlene, if we ever have a fight, I'll call you and tell you what it was about." That was four years ago and the call has never come.

Sharon and Norman Baugh are not the only examples of a negotiated marriage, a choice well made and carried through life. Sharon Barnett has been married to Tim Barnett for over thirty years and was a co-owner in their logging business. For over ten years she has been the manager of Orofino Celebrations Incorporated. Through the years that I've know her, Sharon has shown herself in many moods: frivolous, grouchy, efficient, and lighthearted. She strikes a pose when confronted with a question that she doesn't want to answer and has a "no-nonsense" way about her. Her tee shirt that states, "I'm Sharon Barnett, Don't Mess With Me," is right on the mark.

Sharon can talk about logging and the tribulations of running the office of a logging company, but she can also bubble with excitement when talking about her role as a woman supporting the logging industry. I asked, "What is it like to be the wife of a logger?" "It means washing diapers on a washboard in the creek and shooting bears when you have to," she said in a deep-throated laugh, referring to her early years at Big Island. But then with more distance and resolve, she said, "You just live with him."

She remembered flagging machinery and carrying the oversized-vehicle signs ahead of a truck with two children in diapers in 104 degree heat. She remembered running two emergency radios for twenty-four hours a day. She did what had to be done, and since she was cheap to hire—working for nothing—she was always the designated flunkie, the all-around provider of services. "Everything was good on the North Fork," she said. Sharon and Tim lived across from the Altmillers on Elk Creek. She didn't want to move to town even though she had no telephone, washing machine, or grocery store nearby. They lived in a trailer house, and Sharon loved it, especially the freedom of an environment in which a herd of deer played in her back yard. But, because Sharon is as determined as she is, there were times she had to take matters into her own

Sharon Barnett, who with her husband is an independent logging contractor, makes a statement about herself on her OCI shirt. It reads, "I'm Sharon Barnett, Don't Mess With Me!" As the manager of the Logging Show for over 10 years, Sharon organized the team of volunteers, both men and women, who sponsored it. The show has been held every September since the 1940s. (Courtesy: Jeff Tinsley, Smithsonian Institution.)

hands. When the logging trucks speeding by caused her newly cleaned house to be covered with dust, Sharon took a broom and hit the trucks. Drivers quickly realized that slowing down was in their best interest.

Early in their marriage, Sharon, a city girl, went with Tim to the woods. He didn't let her sit on the sidelines; instead he expected her to skid logs—a job that calls for dragging them along the ground to where they are to be loaded. She ended up on a Caterpillar on a steep grade screaming at the top of her lungs but skidding those logs as best she could.

Sharon never knew where she was in the woods and Tim's directions were typical of those for someone at home in the pines—"Turn right at the stump, then turn at the tree with the red mark." That was the extent of Tim's instructions; he never told her precisely where she was or where she was going. She recalls once wandering for hours when taking a picnic lunch to Tim and a crew in a meadow. Driving a white Chevy pickup truck she would stop, look around, and then circle the meadow again and again. After the third rotation, one of the crew came out of a stand of trees. He had seen her going through her cycle but she hadn't been able to spy him. For that particular crew, she was a city girl evermore.

Most pronounced in our interview was Sharon's reaction to my question about "things feminine." Her eyebrows wrinkled and she registered a look of total disbelief, as if masculinity and femininity were measures of no consequence. She responded that she loved fashion and clothes and that she was a fine seamstress. But this answer was a token response to a question that had no place in her life.

Co-ownership of the business means exactly that. When Sharon and Tim married they began to operate the logging company together. He handled the work in the woods, while Sharon was responsible for everything else. She kept the books and did all the accounting. She was the nerve center, always near the radio in case supplies were needed or a disaster occurred. Women are in charge of crisis management. A report of a lost hunter, child, or horse, the need for the volunteer fire department or an emergency medical unit, could come in and reciprocity in the logging community comes into full play. Nothing is too valuable to share if someone is in need of help. In a disaster, everyone—friends and rivals alike—bands together, offering the necessary equipment and services to set things right again. Even Potlatch will send out a helicopter, free of charge, to help an independent logger in trouble. For people who always live with danger, there is little time to ask questions or count chits. "You don't stop to think if you should or you shouldn't," says Sharon. For loggers, every problem is a life or death situation and there are no manuals for saving a man with a broken back who is pinned under a piece of heavy equipment. "You just do everything you can, be as creative as you need to be to save a life," she said. When a disaster is declared the radio quiets—it is off limits to anyone other than those solving the problem.

Sharon portrays herself as a woman in charge of her destiny and her world. She has no need to be liberated, for she has never been dependent. She has no need to pursue a career, for she has always had one. She has no need to prove herself, for she is who she is and will never change.

Women are in the forefront of supporting their husbands and their industry through Federated Women in Timber (FWIT), a political and educational force throughout the Northwest. They lobby for the greater use of paper products and create teaching kits for forest management. Many women feel that they transcend their domestic roles through this organization. These women, not their husbands, meet with congressional leaders to foster support for the timber industry. They mount letter writing campaigns, analyze legislation, participate in forest planning meetings, stage local protests, and offer scholarships for forestry students. They are untiring in their efforts to teach the positive benefits of logging and combat the attitude that loggers are detrimental to the environment. The state organizations in Alaska, California, Idaho, Montana, Oregon, Washington, and Wyoming believe in the power of the grassroots approach. Congressional figures who are eager to discuss issues with Federated Women in Timber have said that theirs may be the most effective home-grown organization in the country. The members weave together their strong commitment to their families, communities, and the logging industry.

Sharon is proud of Tim, everything about him. "But don't tell him I said so," she says, as if this admission might put her at a disadvantage. "He's very intelligent and can do anything. He concentrates on it—that makes it possible. He's always sacrificing for someone else, and in the woods you can't beat him. He understands the woods." But perhaps Sharon's own feelings are the most telling. I asked, "What's it like, Sharon, what's it really like?" She replied, "Life is good with a logger. Every day is different."

Tim began logging under the tutelage of his father and his mother. As Louie Porter said, "She was one of the best loggers around." She would drive the skidder and as a young boy Tim would be there to help. He gained a sense of this place from early on, and now, he says, "You have to live here to understand it." Contemporary loggers like Tim have a strong desire to maintain the standards of the past. He feels that unfortunately many of the people who migrate to the area do not understand it. Those who come in government service, even though they have experience with the environment, don't seem to understand that much of what happens today in Clearwater County occurs because it harks back to history through ties with its old-timers.

For most of his life Tim was a woodsboss—the supervisor of a crew—with daily contact with the men who are employed by Kenny Weller. He saw their performance and progress in the woods and also knew when their personal lives were in difficulty. Many of the people in this book seem to lead trouble-free existences. They are well-established revered elders or the masters of important skills. But a large majority of loggers have problems, often financial, because the working season is restricted to nine months. If a woodsworker has not prepared for the three-month layoff, he and his family could have economic difficulties. Tim feels this period of unemployment leads to alcohol abuse and family disputes. He recalls that when Potlatch shut down for six months there was a rash of domestic violence. In contrast to what seem to be the ideal marriages reported so far, Tim said few people in this region marry only once, but according to Tim "The ones who stick to their spouses are much better off."

Tim also feels that in addition to the threat of unemployment, the dangerous nature of the occupation creates social problems. "Some women can't handle being married to a logger. For twelve, fourteen, eighteen, or twenty hours of the day their husbands are in the woods. The radios help some, but there is a lot of anxiety for a woman. Those who don't understand logging or want no part of the out-of-doors, can't sustain this type of married life," he said. On the other hand, women like his mother and Sharon work alongside their husbands as a form of self-preservation.

Tim is honest about the lives of loggers and their tribulations, but he also knows and has seen their sensitive side. "Some of them might be rough and rowdy, fight like the devil on Saturday night, and still move a bird's nest or take a squirrel off a job so it won't be harmed. They may go out to shoot game and yet pick up a baby elk and keep it safe. They're rough in nature, but they've got gentle in them."

Tim was there when Johnny Altmiller was killed. Johnny was married to Tim's sister, who was about to have a baby. He and a friend had been fishing on the North Fork and were missing. The search was done at a feverish pitch and with a concentration charged with emotional energy. Tim remembers the feeling of it, the perseverance, the desperation of men trying to find their friends.

Finally the bodies were found. Both men had drowned. They were laid on the ground and the coroner was called while the search party stood around. Tim couldn't believe what he saw and heard. The searchers were talking casually about hunting and fishing and swapping information about the woods. They were acting as if nothing had happened, as if no tragedy had occurred. Tim was young and had never experienced a death in the woods before. He thought this situation was an insult to his brother-in-law, and he got angry.

One of the elderly men took Tim aside and put him in touch with the reality of the situation. "But it's over; he's dead," said the old-timer. That was the fact. The search had been frantic because that is what loggers do: they hope against hope that they can allay disaster, but when it's over, when death comes, they accept it and go on with life. Loggers go back into the woods and back to their jobs, since nothing can be done about death except let it rest.

Tim's picture of logging is an honest view of the men he has known and the problems they have had. He sees no reason why they should be different from who they are. He also realizes "They live here because they don't fit the pattern—they'd die in the city." He and the younger loggers like Mick McLaughlin have no allusions about their lives.

Mick McLaughlin had taken me down to the Poe Ranch in Peck. The incline was so steep it seemed as if you could fall out of the truck. A hard hat, thermos, and flashlight clattered around in the cab as we descended the treacherous pitted road. We went over gravel, through stream beds, and into an actual logging area. He spoke to me about the crew and the ages of the men who worked for him. Several were in their sixties and no one was under thirty-five. The criterion for choosing a good worker according to Mick is, "If he's middle-aged and not banged up he must be a good worker."

Mick explained that each job has a signature. It can be read, and it tells a story. Loggers know this story and tell it in terms of good work habits and the resulting visual and environmental effects. The job site makes a statement about the understanding that the independent logging contractor has about the land and the quality of work he expects from his crew. On this site, Mick will leave a certain percentage of good trees, thinning out the bad ones and taking them to the mill. But the net result is that in thirty years this hillside will be healthier than it is now.

As we rode through the site I saw letters painted on the ends of the logs, the initials of the last names of the crew members—the sawyer, skidder, and bucker (the man who cuts the felled logs into standard lengths). The crew would be paid by the amount of timber they had cut and these marks would verify their output. Like so many other practices in logging, everything is worked out in a very simple system. People don't walk around with pencils and paper, yet they have accurate records of business dealings.

Mick could also tell exactly what his crew had done throughout the day with one fast pass through the job. He knew that at the end of the day they had been playing around because the equipment was parked so close together that it looked as if a tracked cat and a skidder were copulating. Mick follows one cardinal rule: "Never lose touch with your loggers. Never let them think or feel that you don't care or that you are in a different world while they are on the job. Never remove yourself from the guts of your profession, working in the woods."

As part of his contract with Poe, the land owner, Mick's company sells the timber to a mill. This is where experience and a long history of living in the community comes in handy. Mick knows how to deal with the mill operators. He knows what kind of job each mill does, its requirements for cutting, and its ability for getting the most lumber out of the timber. He knows whether a bit more money will compensate for a milling situation that is not ideal. In other words, Mick knows the web of skills and relationships and how to operate within this net.

In the 1950s Mick's parents, Bruce and Marguerite, came to Orofino from Michigan where Mick's grandfather had been in logging. Even as a young boy Mick would get up before sunrise to go with his dad to the woods. He says jokingly that he believes this was to keep him out of his mother's hair. Regardless of the reason, their days together created a close bond between father and son. Mick grew up in Orofino and went to Boise State University, where he was a football star and studied to become a teacher. Instead, family ties brought him home. He missed his father and wanted to reestablish the close contact they had in his younger years.

Bruce McLaughlin Sr. admits that he was afraid to fell his first tree when he came from Michigan because the Idaho trees were so much bigger than the ones in the Midwest. Until Bruce was sixty, he never had a mishap in the woods, but then he fell off a skidder and hurt his back. Today he limps slightly from a car accident, but continues to work.

Bruce entrusts management of the business to his son and daughter-in-law. At great cost Mick bought a sophisticated new delimber which cuts down trees and removes tree limbs in one operation, to help the business grow and to keep up with changes in the industry. Mick knows that logging today takes not only the traditional skills of the woodsworker but also a good knowledge of business. The fourth generation of McLaughlins in logging, Bruce III, now in his teens, thinks he wants to be out in the woods instead of in school and may have already caught logging fever.

Mick and his wife Mary Ann are concerned about building support for the logging industry. In addition to operating McLaughlin Logging, they are at the heart of OCI. Mick often acts as a spokesperson for the industry and has been quoted on his view of logging. "Loggers have changed from the old ways of thinking that there was no end of forests and lands to the modern realization that we must protect our way of life. We'd better plan for productive forests tomorrow. Working and living in the woods makes us aware of the need for some pristine areas. We realize that there are some areas where logging and habitat cannot co-exist and all machines should stay out. Our knowledge comes from experience and should be part of the deliberation processes when the forest environment is considered. We loggers have a real stake in the future of the industry, we also appreciate outdoor recreation, wildlife, and the beauties of nature. We want it to be there for our kids, too."

There is a sense of light-hearted ebullience about Mick. Everyone enjoys his company. But there is also a seriousness underlying this demeanor. He and Mary Ann demonstrate an integrity of spirit in both their professional and family lives. They continue to try to do the right thing for the profession, for their community, and for their family. They introduce innovations into the company whenever possible, they watch the quality of their jobs, they care for their crews, and they try to guarantee a good life in a well-maintained natural setting.

Seeing Mick with his son, a red-headed, Norman Rockwellian lad, is like hearing an echo of the relationship he must have had with his own dad. In a matter-of-fact way, the eldest McLaughlin says he wants to die in the woods; he doesn't want to die of cancer or something else. In the woods is the best way to go, and he'll be out there for the rest of his life. The senior Bruce entrusts the running of the business to his son because he knows that Mick will do the right thing. Mick wants the business to grow. He knows that logging today takes not only the skills of the woodsworker but also the knowledge of a businessman. The family tradition continues.

Judging from Bruce III's tie to his dad and his passion for the woods, he has already caught the fever of a life in logging. So the line of McLaughlins will continue in the Clearwater County timber industry.

After the work in the woods by independent logging contractors like the McLaughlin family, timber goes to sawmills. They efficiently take trees from raw to smooth, from unmanageable to manageable, transforming an irregular natural cylindrical object into a uniform piece of lumber through technical knowledge and skill. Each tree is different in weight, length, and imperfection. Proper tools, saws, gloves and other equipment are required to do the best job.

Going to Triplett's Mill is like traveling back through time. Down a lane, past a house painted the yellowest yellow, you find the sawmill surrounded by logging trucks. Triplett's Mill occupies a specialized niche. When the large corporate mills became more concerned with output, their equipment became less able to take logs of various sizes. The major producers had to contract with smaller, more specialized mills to get this timber cut.

Triplett's handles large-size cedar and uses equipment and techniques that appear, to the uninitiated, to be closer to old-fashioned, manual operations than to automated technology. The carriage for the saw blade runs automatically, but the mill sawyer—the man who controls the cuts—must eyeball the positioning for the cut. Two men at the end of the line lift the sawed boards off the track and place them on a pile. The operation is simple, working without the computers, lasers, or chain conveyers typical in other mills in the region.

If you don't understand mill construction, Triplett's appears to be little more than a shed with a few exterior walls. The light level is intense in critical areas where cutting takes place, but non-existent in other parts of the operation. Speed, safety, and efficiency are necessities in the operation but because of the varied dimensions of the logs and the specialized attention necessary in cutting, there isn't a production-line mentality. The millworkers dress in warm jackets and wear gloves, earplugs, and hats. There is no pretense about appearance. They dress to meet the elements, because even under the cover of a roof, the mill offers little shelter, and the noise level is intense. Lifting, carrying, bending, and hauling are the only way to get the work done. Other than the saw carriage and the conveyor chains, there are no mechanical devices in the mill to get the job done.

Triplett's Mill is a great deal more modern than early sawmills which were built on eight-foot high timbers that allowed all the debris to fall underneath. Fire was a hazard since debarkers and chippers—the equipment used to remove bark, clean the logs, and cut residue into small shavings—had not been invented. None of the remnants of the lumber were saved for reuse as chips, sawdust and hog fuel. Often the accumulation of debris led to nighttime fires when a stray spark ignited the rubbish. Tripplett's is constructed on cement with a clean-out chain underneath the saw that carries away the debris. Nothing is wasted. Timber as long as twenty-six feet comes in at one end and goes out as lumber on the other. Meanwhile all the byproducts of milling are collected for other uses. There is a pattern and consistency of sound and motion in the mill operation regardless of time period or level of technology. The trucks bring in the logs, the loader feeds them onto the intake chain in a continuous motion, the sawyer moves the saw in constant successions, and the men remove the boards at a regular pace. Other men stack the lumber so that it doesn't back up at the saw and then another convoy of trucks takes the lumber away from the mill. The day has a pattern to it that cannot and does not vary. The conditions become a part of the life of the mill workers. Physical exertion, weather, and consistency in the process surround the mill workers.

The Konkolville Lumber Company, one of the longest continuously-run operations in Clearwater County, owns not only a mill but an entire town. Even though the mill, restaurant, cocktail lounge, motel, and family homestead are not within Orofino city limits they occupy a unique place in the geography and politics of Orofino. The family has been active in the Republican party and are strong supporters of the Catholic church. Andrew Konkol, the patriarch of the family, arrived from Wisconsin in 1946 and began a small sawmill at Cow Creek. He moved to Orofino Creek and established Konkolville and built housing for his employees; and today even though it is not a company town, many of the employees have worked with Konkol for years and feel an affinity and a loyalty for the Konkols.

After Andrew died, his family continued the business, and now his son Don is president and manager of the corporation. It is the only local mill that takes the timber through the entire process including kiln drying and planing the lumber. Not only do the Konkols operate the mill, but they also own and selectively harvest timber lands in the region. Their goal is to put their acreage into an intensive forest management scheme that is both practical and profitable.

In the 1950s there were twenty-three mills in the county, but now, Konkol is one of a handful of remaining independent operations. Konkol's mill uses techniques that were in operation since the 1950s but has also added new technology throughout the years. Currently it is run by electric motors, but prior to the 1950s it, like most of the mills, operated on steam. Konkol's is not the most specialized nor is it the most automated mill in the region; instead it retains both manual and automated operations and depends on the physical talents and skills of its work force.

Konkol's mill is managed by Dale Richardson, son of Joe Richardson, the owner of Riverside Lumber Company, which closed several decades ago. Since most of the men and women employed at Konkol's are young and unskilled, Dale Richardson uses both his milling expertise and his good-natured approach to people in running the operation. Long years of experience have taught him the trade of milling and how to manage people. In fact, many say that when Dale went from running a lifter to running the plant, he single-handedly turned the mill's production around and increased output by thirty-five percent without new equipment and without firing anyone.

He worked on building morale by eliminating all the desk-bound jobs and having management get out into the mill and take part in the physical work. Dale says, "As we see it, pushing paper around and consulting isn't a job; here you don't tell someone how to do something unless you can actually do it yourself." Dale understands the business practices as well as the physical production of lumber and how to manage the capital at hand. He changed the operation so that even without the sophisticated computerization used at the Potlatch mill in Lewiston, Konkol's remains a viable business enterprise.

"Every sawmill is different—it depends on who built it," says Dale. It may be a combination that uses band saw, circular saw, trim saw operators, filers and boiler engineers, but success depends on a team working in unison in the same place at the same time doing individualized jobs to produce a product. The team element of the mill is obvious; even though each of the isolated functions stands out as a highly-specialized skill, the production of lumber is more than the ability to set up a pattern of cutting. Running a sawmill may be a matter of dollars and cents—timber coming in and lumber going out—but it is also a business based on a complex web of social relationships and values which influence the sawmill as well as all the operations that are a part of the logging industry.

For example, the head saw sharpener occupies a position of great importance, because the condition of the saw is critical. The blade must be sharp but it must also have the proper tension to keep it on the wheel. Every three days the master sharpener works on the blade for approximately four hours. This is a job that must be accomplished but it is also considered a part of the art form of the taking care of the saw blade. If the filer doesn't do the job correctly, it affects the work of the sawyer and all the other workers down the line. Although there are filer's manuals, each filer does the job differently, with personal flair. Many have learned from other filers, "Some guy who found a better way to do it by using some angle that works best," says Dale. A filer's success never comes overnight; it takes years to become a real master. But when success comes, it is measured in whether the sharper's saws cut just a bit faster and more accurately than another's saw. There is no question about skill; it can be measured quantitatively.

Lumber graders also occupy a specialized role in the mill. According to Dale, "They learn by doing. They learn with every piece of wood that they touch." In grading, as in everything else in logging, accuracy is the key. There can be little tolerance for deviation in this industry of educated estimators.

Of all the jobs in the mill, the millwright plays the key role in the operation. He is essentially a mechanic but he takes care of everything. A good one needs a special kind of knack and Dale has seen "good and bad mechanics covering the entire spectrum of intelligence." Again and again I heard loggers in a variety of positions comment that it is not how intelligent you are but how well you do your job that counts. The combination of a second sense and how you hone that skill at a particular endeavor adds up to your ability and becomes the basis for your reputation.

Dale, like others who train and supervise people, is good at his job because he himself can do everything—from operating all the equipment to fixing it and even performing the manual labor needed to make the mill operate. He may not be as good at a specific task as someone who specializes in it, but he is competent all around and knows why jobs are done in a certain way. The combination of these traits allows him to innovate in the operation when the need arises. Dale knows and has seen the levels of competence of timber workers. He believes that he can tell the caliber of a worker at a glance, a skill he learned from the old-timers. Dale commented, "Now you ask the 'old man' [Joe Richardson]. He could tell you all about a man before he got out of his truck. He'd just get a feeling about someone by noticing the way they handled themselves. It was that first impression that they gave. If they were watching everything, he knew that they'd be good on the job."

Life in logging is based on intense observation and knowing exactly what is going on around you. This talent is critical in an industry with so many possible dangers. Being observant is the way to stay alive. "This fact is better motivation than any OSHA standard," says Dale. "For example, guards—the railings that keep people out of the path of equipment—don't protect a man if he is careless. On the other hand, some people can work without guards and never be harmed. The men who are the best workers think a lot more and are just plain safer."

Dale trains and manages fifty-eight people. And so I asked him, "What is your technique?" He said, "I chew them out when they do something wrong." He says it's the best way there is. Dale's been "piling boards" for forty years but knows that if he retired and just sat around watching television he'd die in six months. His passion for logging is more muted than those who could not give up going into the woods, but he does convey the necessity of perpetual motion and the sense of keeping busy that characterizes the town and the logging community.

Dale, like his father Joe, is very self-possessed. He answers questions directly and honestly and doesn't pull any punches. This is how sawmills operated; there is no need to be overly technical, overly cerebral, or try to impress the listener with the mill's productivity or his own skills. Every once in a while he gives a funny grin and throws in an off-hand comment that shows the wry wit about him. This too, is a part of life in logging.

Hutchins Timberline Lumber is another family-owned and operated mill. It was established by two brothers, Leslie and Lawrence Hutchins, and now Leslie's sons, Elwin and Emerald, manage the operation. There are three mills; each has its own claim to fame. The most unique one is actually in the building that houses the machinery that was used to build the other two mills. It is a miniature model of a traditional operation that is manned by a six-inch-tall sawyer

Members of the Hutchins family pose outside of their mill, Timberline Lumber Inc., in Weippe, Idaho. This family-owned and -operated sawmill is often used as an example of the finest blend of modern technology and traditional logging values. (Courtesy, Jeff Tinsley, Smithsonian Institution.)

and produces tongue-depressor-sized timber. It carries on all the operations of an old-time mill of the 1950s to the delight of the brothers and their guests. And there are always guests because Hutchins mill has an open door, and the brothers have a friendly handshake for anyone passing through Weippe, Idaho.

Their first mill, built in 1947, was a circle sawmill like their model. Originally it had a log slip or pathway from the mill pond to the log deck. The pond man would put a cable chocker—the metal chains used for hauling—around three or four logs, then go up to the deck and pull them up by a cable winch. He would roll the logs down the log deck and then go back down to the pond for another drag of logs. After a few years the log slip was replaced by a log conveyor, called a bull chain, with a cradle that carried the logs one at a time up into the mill, where air-activated kickers—mechanical jaws—pushed the log out of the conveyor onto the log deck. Then the conveyor would start again and bring up another log just like the model mill.

The first mill or "old mill" ran by a diesel engine and lots of man-power. The turndown man who rolled the log onto the carriage and then turned the log over after the sawyer had cut off one side of the log was on the log deck. The setter—the man who positioned the log—rode the carriage. He would operate the dogs, the metal grips that held the log on the carriage and set the size for the board to be cut. After the log was fastened on the carriage, the sawyer would signal the size he intended to cut to the setter. The setter had to know the cant sizes—the angles of the cut and lumber run sizes—dimensions for all thicknesses of the lumber so that the cut would be correct.

Vast improvements have been made in the second, rebuilt mill. The sawyer has control of the log with a push of a lever. He loads a log onto the carriage, rolls it around until he finds the desired position, and pushes a button to dog or hold the log firm. He pushes another button to move the log ahead on the carriage until the log is hit by a red laser line that shows the placement of the saw line. The mill sawyer hits the compute button for the computer to figure out the best cant and size boards for the size lumber to be cut. This set works within 0.002 of an inch in accuracy. All this work is done from an enclosed, climate-controlled cab. There are television monitors mounted where the sawyer can observe and control the flow of lumber through the mill. The mastery of the Hutchins operation was proven when they built the equipment for the mill on site in the mill's shop without outside engineers. The care with which it was done is obvious when you walk the catwalks and look at the structure. There is no waste, no sign of imperfect workmanship. The welding is functional. The plywood is plumb. The utilitarian sparseness does what it should do—cut logs efficiently with a minimum of waste and a maximum of safety.

Just as the miniature mill delights visitors with its diminutive perfection, so too the Hutchins' human-sized operation also delights. When you walk past the equipment and the operators you get a feeling of properness. When you look closely, you see workmen dressed with a sense of style, with pride in the logging trade. Shirts are pressed; not a button is missing or a tail hanging. These men stand and walk differently from the men in other mills.

The crew at Hutchins knows that any time a visitor learns of the new techniques of milling in the region, they will hear of Hutchins Timberline Lumber. It is not the technology created by a large corporation and exported to a smaller mill that is a history-making phenomenon. Instead, it is the machinery and procedures built by these men themselves to improve a small family-operated mill that has gained a regional reputation.

Throughout its construction, the mill never closed. With careful planning based on practical knowledge, the brothers transferred parts of their crew to the construction of the new mill while other members of the crew manned the old equipment. Having many talents and knowing about a lot of things has always been a part of the loggers' tradition in the woods, and you can see it vividly in the Hutchins mill. They built it, they work it, they clean it, and all three operations are done to perfection. The value of this personal investment shines in a comparison of Hutchins with the large corporate mill in both general appearance and hard-core statistics.

At the end of each ten-hour shift the ten crewmen gather around a small personal computer terminal and punch up their output without asking the aid of a computer specialist or business manager. They gather there before going home for this one bit of quantitative information. They worked a good day, they did the job right, and now they merely verify their productivity. The screen reads 197,000 board feet for a ten-man crew. In comparison, the output of a major computerized mill with a greater economic base and an elaborately outfitted operation is 267,000 board feet, produced by sixty-five men in a ten-hour shift. If this is a typical day, it means that it takes more than six times as many men to produce less than twice as much lumber in the corporate mill. The major milling operation may be bigger, look more efficient, and have heavy-duty computers and massive loaders, but the Hutchins family proves that it is the men and not the machines that count.

In the corporate mill, men are often dressed in shabby undershirts and listen to taped music. They push buttons almost as if their job was a token move to keep the unions satisfied that automation had not totally replaced the workers. These men show little interest in the timber or the job and are passing time until work is done. Throughout the day if their equipment fails, they call a specialist to repair it. Before going home they don't gather to see output, because electronic messages flash continuously on a board that keeps workers updated with instantaneous records for every board as it is cut.

The Hutchins don't think much about being in the age of automation. They believe in doing a good job with the tools and talents at their disposal. Who was the decision-maker? Who took the chance? Did they discuss the landmark change with their employees? How long have their employees been with them? You could ask these questions to discover the process, but the results are obvious. The Hutchins and their millworkers have pride in their work, both as individuals and as a team, and surpass the production of the larger mill. They, like others in the logging industry in this region of Clearwater County, hold onto an attitude of pride and independence.

There are pleasures in logging, the Hutchins mill being one and the gracefulness of a stand of beautifully cut trees another. But the difficulties of life are constant, and reminders of how they can affect individuals are ever-present. Chet Donley, by his own admission, hasn't had an easy life. There are times he isn't very proud of, but now those are over. He is a woods supervisor for Potlatch Forest Industries as well as the pastor of his own church and a singer in the service of God. With his wife, Jeanne, he has traveled through the area with his tapes and microphone, praising the Lord in song. He is born again, on the right track, and staying there. For the time being, he'll work in the woods, but eventually perhaps he and Jeanne will get into their motor home and travel the country with his religious message.

During our day-long ride past logging jobs, Chet filled me in on the economic situation of the logging industry and its problems. We discussed the turnarounds of recent years and the attempts by the forest and paper products industry to stay in the market in the face of the ever-growing use of plastics. A switch to plastic shopping bags may be of little consequence to an urbanite but to a logger this can mean disaster. Throughout the day Chet was careful to be sure that I understood, from Potlatch's point of view, the specific practices that were taking place.

Logging was the topic, but our conversation really revolved around Chet's commitment to a new life of spirituality. Chet was a product of a logging life, hard work and long hours. Years ago, without drawing attention to his problem and while still doing a good job, he began to drink and spend his evenings at the Brass Rail. During the fall of 1984, he had thrown his life away, and he knew it. Talking about it many years later, he still registers disbelief that he could have let something like that happen. The remorse is there, but more importantly, so is the optimism. He's grateful that he asked for help, went to the rehabilitation center, and returned with new dedication to his job, his family, and his religious beliefs.

Chet feels that working conditions are such that many men get little sleep and spend much of their time in rigs or in the woods alone. They know the stories of the immigrant-bachelor loggers from Scandinavian countries, the hard-drinking Finns and Swedes. But they also know that this is no excuse to over-indulge in alcohol. Now life is different, they are family men with responsibilities and, better yet, with the possibilities of a good life. And yet drinking problems do happen to some of them. For Chet, religion was a solution.

Other loggers are also committed to religion. Phil Bonner, known as a good sawyer, is also a minister in a neighboring community. He followed the path of his father Emmett, who had worked for the Porters and then founded a church. Phil and his wife Jan are trying to revitalize family life in the area; their young people's group activities are well-known. With musical programs and social opportunities they've begun to draw teenagers and their families together.

Although many of the hardships of the past are over, logging is still a difficult life; it means commuting, leaving one's family, and living on that economic incline. Alternatives for making the life easier are few, but religion and personal commitment to God are one. Chet, Jeanne, Phil, Jan, and others who have involved themselves in religion have found an answer that seems to carry them through the long rides and economic uncertainties of living in a logging community. Religion sustains them in their work.

They, like many others, are concerned that the depression of the 1980s took many good woodsworkers, young men who had learned their craft from seasoned loggers, away from the area. If a new crop of woodsworkers are to develop, it will have to result from a combination of on-the-job training and school courses developed by loggers. These loggers know the problems and the hard work needed to sustain a life in logging. Living with the history of the occupation is the one most compelling way of committing to this life: the respect that is paid to elders in the profession, its history and sense of pride, and its creativity in the technological innovation of their coworkers carry the loggers a long way. Sometimes the pride in tradition, less than a century old, is embodied in the old-timers, those who were learning and inventing as they were doing. Sometimes it is a more elusive feature, an attitude that makes these Northwest loggers grow taller when they say that they are woodsworkers.

The importance of this pride was reinforced to me by outsiders Tony and Marie Shank, of Marion, South Carolina. The Shanks own a timber dealership firm called "Swampfox Logging." In the South, the system of logging is different from the West. The mills don't buy all the land and the newer mills don't have a land base, so dealerships help to furnish the timber. Different dealers supply mills with wood at different times and work as middlemen to negotiate the work arrangements.

While I was visiting Marion, Tony registered concern for the timber practices that occur in the South and the need to change the current logging and environmental situation. I began to talk about the loggers of Clearwater County. Tony's immediate response concerned their nobility, the fact that theirs was logging at its best. He didn't know their specific practices, but with their mythic reputation they impressed him as heroes in the industry. To find out why he thought their tradition was rich, I asked Tony what made a hero and if he had any heroes in logging. At first he was at a loss but later, as if he had been thinking hard about the question, he said, "You asked me about heroes; yes, there was one, old Roy. He taught me everything that I know." As we spoke, Tony went on to tell of this early logger's part in the Southern tradition of logging before power. He had a respect for timber as well as a respect for work. His jobs were done right, and he was always on schedule, well-equipped, and responsible in performing an operation. To good loggers, their work is done in one way, with care for nature, reputation, and open communication between all the parties involved. Regardless of whether it is Roy in South Carolina or Tim, Mick, Ted, Kingsley, and the rest of their coworkers in Idaho, logging is more than merely cutting down trees, it is a profession with a strong tradition and standards for occupational excellence.

BEYOND WORK

Performances in a Logging Community

You might think that after the work day is done, the people of Clearwater County would want to relax. Instead they extend work into leisure time by building on an extensive system of community group action. Often it is the women who spearhead these after-hour volunteer work activities. Women figure prominently when leisure time contributes to the well-being of the community.

I went to the women to find out how they lived. From conversations with the respected elderly women I knew that their role was to be the backbone of the community and to introduce the necessary embellishments to life. As Joy and Faye had added zest to early logging enterprises, to daily life and in the celebrations that they managed, so contemporary women play the same role.

These women come from a different orientation, one that I don't share. Some are pioneers but have no ethnic memory, while I am the product of a long Polish tradition. Others are wives, mothers, and homemakers, roles I've never experienced fully. Some belong to women's organizations which I have never joined because of an erratic work and travel schedule. Others are co-owners with their husbands in logging operations; I've never owned a business. Still others are teenage girls vying for a place among the Fair and Lumberjack Days royalty. I have never been a teenage queen. I could not depend on a natural affinity with Orofino women based on similar life experiences, but I tried to be sensitive to what they said about the degree of commitment, the problems of isolation, and their view of the roles that they are expected to occupy. I appreciate the self-reliance they convey, their concern for the pressures of their husbands' jobs, and the need to be central to the family unit while being self-determined individuals.

These women, both those in logging and those in town activities, have their own sense of artistry in their lives. Women in logging often emphasize work and its rewards, while those who are oriented to the town spend a great deal of energy on creating a "cultured" way of life in Orofino, with such examples as a community theater, chorus, and other cultural organizations. Like most of the social action in town, these are run by voluntary, non-profit groups using local talent and resources. No one social group dominates; instead, individuals participate as the occasion arises. The women who manage these endeavors and are untiring in their volunteer efforts. They work beyond work.

On the main street of town, FISH Inc., an arm of the Christian Church, runs a thrift shop. The indomitable Laura Holzhey was there whenever it was open until she moved to Spokane in 1994. She believed in the world-wide movement to help others and thought first of helping those near at hand with the donations of merchandise that come from the community.

Self-reliance seems to be Laura's *modus operandi*. It is her answer to life's travails, both for herself and for those she helps. Emergencies occur, and when this happens she feels people need the aid of friends. But once the problem is over and you are back on your feet, you repay the help with your first few checks. Laura is no stranger to the difficulties of living in this region. She and her husband Charlie, to whom she was married more than fifty years, combined family, cowboying, and logging from 1947 to 1957.

She grew up in Washington's west coast timber area and knows that you are never far from the words of the woods. "Even for a sophisticated woman, they get into your language and they become a part of you—you and your husband," says Laura. "You're never far from his work either; you know about the new inventions created in the woods because he tells you about his buddy who had a bright idea that day. And you see his technique, his ability to fell a tree, to place it just right, because there in your own backyard is the winter's fuel supply."

Laura remembers being responsible for the family's economic well-being. Financial planning is nearly impossible, but "to eat like bears" when the money is there and starve the rest of the year is no answer. Laura learned the truth about the financial uncertainties of logging quickly, and so she taught school part of the time while Charlie also ran a farm.

Laura never worried about what kind of job she had, what type of work she was expected to do. "You don't define what it is, what you do, if it's productive. You don't even worry if you like it or not. You do it because that is what life has store for you."

The lives of women have changed since Laura lived a somewhat solitary life. Today women have more opportunities to gather together, but theirs is not a world of talking about the woods. Their meetings are a more intimate time, a time of companionship in the difficult world of logging, a time of supporting and displaying the work of logging to others.

After getting their husbands off to work, their children ready for school, and their own lives in order, a group of women who work in town businesses head for The Bakery, where they chat over coffee. It's their time. It's not gossip, since they never impugn the character of others or talk behind their palms about what they've heard through the grapevine. Instead they enjoy being with one another. Often they describe changes that are going on in their personal lives: a daughter who is getting married, a son who will graduate, a parent coming to visit for the holidays, or a festival that must be planned. It's satisfying, it meets their needs before they go off to work. They wouldn't miss a morning at The Bakery. If someone does, her companions are immediately concerned about her.

The morning coffee gathering, from left to right: Mary Wagner, Jane Greene, Janet Burnham, Shanna Roedy, Dita Happ, and Melissa Stewart. (Courtesy, Fran Ciarlo.)

The group is informal with no dues, no officers, no regulations. Its membership evolves as women leave town for other jobs and others arrive. Everyone is welcome—that is, if you are a woman and show up at The Bakery between 7:30 A.M. and 8:15 A.M. The group has no agenda, no political aspirations, and does not seek recognition, but its members make things happen for their families, for logging, and for the town. These women are first and foremost a part of their family group. They are working women out of necessity, not because their job is considered a career. Conversation revolves around hearth and home, not Orofino's business.

Support group? This term is foreign to them, for they derive support and satisfaction in their lives from their families, not from this group. If the group never met again, their primary focus, their families, would not change. But since they do get together, why not make the most of it. They are not tied by kinship, but they extend invitations to one another for family celebrations, showers, birthday parties, and weddings. They also share personal effects. Dresses, jewelry, and books change hands as if these women were going into a sister's room and borrowing something for the day. Theirs is not as visible a reciprocity, or on as grand a scale as their husbands', but in many ways it is similar. No object is too precious to reserve for yourself alone, and there is no urgency about its return. In this group they are perhaps not as close as a family, but each member is definitely dear to the others in her own way.

When someone leaves there is a wholehearted farewell with a cake and gifts to send that woman on her way. There is always the hope that someday she will return and take up membership as if she hadn't left. The group extends this feeling to women like myself who come for only a short time. Without knowing exactly why, when I return to Orofino, I am automatically a part of the women's group. I don't pay any dues other than buying coffee for the group when the spirit moves me. Jane, Janet, Mary, and the other women who gather are constantly busy with volunteer activities, and in the morning when they meet and bring me into their circle they always have something to share.

Other groups of women, more formal in their organization, gather in the evenings at precisely orchestrated dinner parties in the Garden Room. They exude an aura of femininity. It is a sophisticated world filled with flowers, gifts, and polite conversation. The evening I attended was a special night for the monthly dinner for the Beta Sigma Phi sorority. The "secret sisters," who had been surprising each other with bibelots at the dinners throughout the year, would be revealed. Of course, recipients suspected who their sisters were from the taste in gifts, but there was always the excitement of knowing whether you had been correct all along. Gift giving is often labeled conspicuous in a consumptive society, but in this group giving gifts transcends the mere display of monetary wealth. The women are truly concerned about reflecting their own personalities and the personality of the recipient through the gift. Often the presents are handmade, showing the skills of the giver, and always the gift is well-tuned to the temperament of the recipient.

Beta Sigma Phi is a national sorority with membership chapters and sub-chapters based on the length of involvement a woman has had with the organization. The individual groups perform social services throughout the year, sponsoring young women for scholarships and community recognition and raising money for worthwhile causes. But in addition to making contributions to the community, they value the friendships developed through the sorority. These are professional women who dress and look the part. Theirs is a world of offices, schools, libraries, and flower shops. They are known for their skill in cartography, ability to teach homemaking, and talent in raising princesses for the annual celebration. They can sing, dance, and act. They sponsor a concert series and a city beautification project; they continue the job of women who lived in the early logging camps who took it upon themselves to civilize the wilds.

Doreen and Peggy, members of Beta Sigma Phi, shared their feelings about the town and life with me. They understand the needs of the community, and help the culturing process by reading national magazines, hosting foreign exchange students, and thinking of themselves as unofficial ambassadors of the region to the outside world. They know the stereotype of a man's world that had been associated with the area, and in their own fashion they try to preserve a sense of social propriety. If there is a wedding, all the members of the sorority are invited. They are friends who would share the joy of the occasion, but they also know how to follow the rules of Emily Post.

Their husbands love them for being women: feminine, dressed, and bejewelled. They are raising their children to fit into a society outside of Orofino, especially if the children are daughters. The men can handle sons, but daughters must be cultivated. This sense of the finer things in life has influenced Orofino's economic growth. Over the past ten years the number of shops in Orofino oriented toward gift giving and being fashionable has grown significantly. The main street has changed from the avenue where most of the merchandizing was related to necessities in to a place to buy luxuries. Before, a few craft objects had been sold in the variety store. Now, the influence of women who look outside of the community for style has begun to spread and gift shops dot each block.

Diversification of the town economy occurs in part because women have entered into their own version of cottage industries and are beginning to fill the town with objects that are more decorative and less utilitarian. These women are having an influence in fashion and home decor and are setting new standards by creating a demand for objects of art that have little relationship to the logging world; flowers instead of pines and porcelain figurines instead of carved animals are becoming vogue. Their husbands' professions support these secondary decorative industries. The women of Beta Sigma Phi see themselves going about their daily tasks and seeking the company of other women for occasions of celebration, but their desire for sophistication in Orofino is becoming a part of the town's economic diversification.

Women make it in Orofino; they are successful. They start businesses, run organizations, and hold prominent positions inside and outside the community. They are not afraid to be different, to try the unusual. Susan Petree, owner of Empire Realty Services, is one of these women. Susie dresses tastefully but is not preoccupied with fashion. She enjoys good food and entertainment but can be happy in a tent with a can of beans cooked over an open fire.

Susie is part of the community and yet an outsider. She was born and raised in Seattle. She is feminine, but can drive an off-road vehicle with the best of the men. She is a member of the Orofino Civic Theatre and often directs its plays. In "Witness for the Prosecution" she played Carter, the male curmudgeon and assistant to the defense attorney. She opened the show wearing a three-piece suit, men's oxford shoes, and a bow tie, and played her part to perfection.

Everyone knows that it is Susan, and they admire her spunk for playing a male character while others in the play are typecast—the detective character is a sheriff's deputy, the forensic specialist character is the local pharmacist, and the bailiff character is a former official at the state prison. But Susie is trying something totally different, playing a man. The play is a success with enthusiastic audiences, but that is always the case. It is as if the theatre group is proof that the town qualifies as a full-fledged modern community. It is as good as Lewiston, as good as Spokane or Seattle, different only because it is smaller. And what is the basis for artistic success? Just as in other areas of life and work, it is based on doing the best that you can, working hard, and meeting your own standards for perfection. You don't compare your production to Broadway. You do as well as you can and you strive for perfection in your own sphere. Neither the town of Orofino nor the logging community that exists here bases its outlook on comparisons. Doing according to your ability is the real yardstick and on that basis the theatre productions are as good as you can see anywhere.

Orofino also counts on females to be symbols of the community to the outside world as queen and princesses of Lumberjack Days. These women are singled out to represent the best of womanhood in the community and are expected to perform for all members of their gender group. Three young women are off on their first adventure to Kendrick, a town of four hundred and eighty people forty miles from Orofino, to ride in the Locust Blossom parade and celebration. What was paramount in their minds on this first outing? Actually, little more than to learn how to wave. The formula was elbow, elbow, wrist, wrist, with just the proper figure-eight flow. Add to that "smile all the time," "stomach in and chest out," "don't be stuck up," and "be on time," and the girls have all the rules of the royalty game. The crowd would be responsive, and other girls, especially the younger ones, would idolize them.

It was too early in the season for Orofino to have its royalty float, so they would ride atop the same white Ford truck that had brought them to Kendrick. All were dressed in red shirts and white cotton slacks; there was little to mark the queen as distinct from the princesses except for a tiny heart in her crown and the fact that unconsciously the two lesser royalty always flanked the queen. Later in the season they would all wear the same formal dresses from the J. C. Penney's overstock outlet in Lewiston. But today and for the remainder of the summer festivals they would wear sports attire donated by Orofino merchants.

Tammy Baugh, chaperon and the young president of OCI, knows the obligations and intricacies of royalty. She doesn't hesitate to remind them that last year's girls were stars, nor does she hesitate to give examples of less than regal trios and her frustration over difficult past royalty. She is a veteran of OCI, having joined her first committee eight years ago and risen through the ranks. Tammy had invented a tradition of stopping at the Kendrick Cafe for donuts on the way to the first parade. The girls go into the restroom one by one to put on their crowns, but when they come back out the customers are indifferent—no one makes much of these three girls dressed exactly alike, wearing crowns. But Tammy watches for their ability to carry it off.

A second tradition was created two years before when the former president, Mick McLaughlin, began calling the royalty "My Girls." As a remembrance they had given him a framed picture. Last year's royalty gave then-president Fenton Freeman a video tape of "His Girls." Tammy

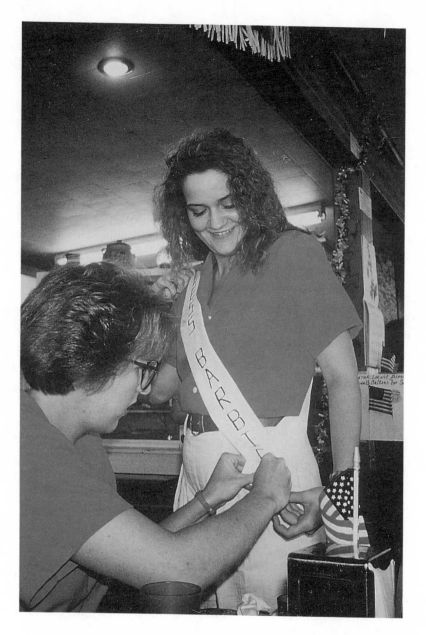

Tammy Baugh-Gilmer, long-time member and past president of OCI, adjusts the sash of Barbie Butler, OCI royalty, during their stop for morning coffee.

Baugh let it be known at this first outing that this had become an accepted practice, something to begin thinking about, a tradition that should not be broken. Tammy has a dream for another tradition which she wants to become a reality: she hopes to draw together all of the royalty alumnae for a gala presentation in five years when OCI celebrates its 50th anniversary.

What distinguishes these girls and their predecessors from other young women in Orofino? Aside from living in a logging community, the Orofino royalty need not be a part of the logging industry; however, they are expected to demonstrate talent, charm, and answer a question on current events. It is difficult to say what sets these girls apart. They are normal teenagers, perhaps a bit prettier, a trifle smarter, and a smidgen more socially connected than other teenagers, but criteria for queenship are hard to define.

In 1989, Tracy Johnson, Amy Reed, and Mary Jo Hall, the stellar court, were always together. They had been long-time friends and reigning throughout the year intensified their friendship. For Tracy it was a dream come true. Since she was six years old she had imagined becoming royalty for Lumberjack Days. She loved the reality of it but also learned early on that it entailed a great deal of work. Mary Jo stated that if she were giving advice to a new member of royalty it would be to not get "uppity." When you are representing the town you have to be someone else, maybe someone a little bit more than just yourself: "You are Clearwater County." They all agreed that "to be queen it is not necessary to be beautiful but to be inherently nice." "Once you are royalty people are always watching you, especially the younger children. The twirlers and the little girls in the parade want to be just like you. You are something special; your gown shows it, your manners show it," said the queen.

While the queen reigns she is someone special, someone painted with the romance of a bygone time and an imaginary place. She knows that she has responsibilities and must work at them. Making the posters and selling the tickets, helping with the registration and the record keeping are part of your job. It doesn't absolve the queen from being either a good daughter or a brilliant student, since it is only a temporary state of being more than you are—but not better, or above the rest. That's what Orofino expects of its royalty.

And just to be sure the temporary nature of the role is fully understood by the rest of the community, the queen and princesses undergo a transformation back to normal status. In a final act at the logging show celebration, the royalty can expect to be thrown into the birling pond, the place used for log-rolling contests. You can struggle and feign not wanting the dunk, but it must happen. After donuts in Kendrick, Tracy, Amy, and Mary Jo go into the cafe restroom and emerge as new royalty. At the end of the logging show and a cleansing in the birling pond, they reemerge as Tracy, Amy, and Mary Jo, normal young women in the community. They will keep their crowns and gowns, but the royal ride is over, and they are back to reality, back to equal status among the other young people of Orofino.

Just as these young girls experience "a time out of time"—the festival period defined by anthropologists as a suspension of reality, the ideal time, the perfect time—so too the town shines as a picture-perfect logging community during OCI Lumberjack Days. The spectacle of competitive logging may draw the crowds, but it is the intensity of the behind-the-scenes activities that are the mark of the Clearwater County Fair and Lumberjack Days. It is an occasion for the town to exhibit its ideals of cooperation, reciprocity, a concern for logging, and the triumph of perfection in work. Bureaucracy be damned in Orofino. No one here needs to be reminded of their job; no one keeps elaborate schedules of what has to be done—especially if you are a member of OCI and you are planning for the Clearwater County Fair and Lumberjack Days. Work proceeds smoothly because everyone knows their role, speaks little about it, and merely does their job. This is the key to all work and volunteer activities, and it allows organizations to operate smoothly and without controversy.

Without a bureaucratic overlay, the job gets done. Discussions are kept to a minimum, and there is an ever-present underlying trust that one's compatriots have the talent to do the job and will keep their word by doing it. Teamwork is key to incorporating inexperienced members into the group. With more encouragement than direction, these young people learn by doing and quickly take over control of major offices. The individual tasks can be arduous and taxing, but the organization never feels this stress since it has total confidence that the members will perform. Orofino Celebrations Incorporated has successfully sponsored the community logging show for nearly fifty years and many of its members appear in this book as central figures in the world of logging, but others are insurance agents, bankers, and real estate agents—part of the business community. All have a common desire to maintain the logging component of the festival and the lifestyle of Orofino.

To see the success of this approach one need only attend an OCI meeting. Members gather in the White Pine Building to plan the September program; throughout the evening, loggers still in work clothes arrive from the woods. They are greeted by the group as they go to the refrigerator for a can of beer and then to settle down to business. The committee reports begin. The treasurer says they are solvent and that there is enough money to produce the September show. Each committee chairperson makes a comment and is subjected to good-natured kidding, but there is an obvious sameness in their reports. Even though the show is rapidly approaching , the comments are all the same: "No problem," "We're ready," "A piece of cake." Without detailed discussion, the members automatically assume that the tasks associated with the committees are going smoothly. No one brings up problems, though they might exist in the background. No chairperson admits that he or she is having difficulties getting materials or organizing their part of the operation. Somehow, in some way, the volunteers will commandeer the necessary resources either on their own, from their businesses, or from major corporations

OROFINO LUMBERJACK DAYS

AND CLEARWATER COUNTY FAIR

September 16, 17, 18, 19

1982

At Orofino, Idaho

Free Admission
To Fair Exhibits
Logging Shows
Auctions

1982 Theme: "Tomorrow And Forever"

1982 Royalty
Queen Leann Harrell
Center

Princess Caren Cantrell
Left

Princess Theresa Brown
Right

★ 2 Dances - Friday And Saturday

★ Old Timers Social

★ Lumberjack Breakfast

★ Lumberjack Run For Fun

★ Fair Exhibits

★ Carnival

★ Two Big Logging Shows

★ Horse Pulling Truck &
Skidder Driving

★ Two Big Parades

★ Friday Lumberjack
Luncheon IOOF Hall

★ Two Auctions

The "Super Logger" Legend Lives "Tomorrow & Forever" At Orofino

Each year, posters and flyers similar to this one blanket Clearwater County. A theme such as "Tomorrow and Forever" is the focus of the floats in the parade. A variety of events take place during the festival, as is evident from the poster.

in the area. OCI and Lumberjack Days are never refused, regardless of the magnitude of the request.

In Orofino, volunteerism means giving what you have in material or services regardless of who you are or what is requested. If the Rotary needs help at the hot dog stand, you are there regardless of your position in the business community. If a community function needs a cherry-picker—a crane with a bucket to lift a man up—Washington Water Power will have it there free of charge and on schedule. If the logs for the show have to be peeled, the Potlatch mill at Jaype will take care of it. Requests are made person-to-person because paperwork is generally associated with a waste of time and is seen as a source of aggravation.

Since you don't attain status through wealth or by birth in Orofino but through volunteerism, newcomers want to be part of the system. No one receives a phone call or a visit soliciting help; instead volunteer opportunities are listed in the *Clearwater Tribune*. Whether it is picking up highway litter on Cleanup Day or helping a local church run a bake sale, it is a part of community action and it is how one becomes an integral part of the community. Newcomers quickly see that Orofinoans are always busy and are rarely at home. Instead they are out in service to their community.

This high degree of community action is contrary to the notion that rural residents lead dull and uneventful lives by urban standards; however, it also has its drawbacks. Organizations are always finding new reasons to use volunteer help, and everyone takes a turn in political, social, and cultural arenas to benefit the town. Working on a plethora of volunteer activities can lead to burnout: workers must take a break and may find it necessary to drop out for a time. Everyone understands that a temporary rest is needed and that after a respite they will be right back in the thick of things again, for Orofino is built on volunteerism.

Making the Clearwater County Fair and Lumberjack Days happen is a jewel in the crown of civic activities. The festival offers a good performance, even if it is a fictionalized version of work, for it embraces the logging traditions as they have been handed down and will be passed on to future generations. During the years I attended, I looked upon the event as a wonderful "time out of time," a celebration of a tradition. I wanted to believe Grimes when he said that it was "good fiction—a celebration of social and metaphysical fiction in which questions about reality were irrelevant." I wanted it "to be a mode of embracing the past that draws the future and past to itself" (Roland Grimes, 1982:150).

Initially I viewed Lumberjack Days as a major representative feature of logging culture. I believed that it spoke symbolically for all of life in the community until I realized it was work, not play, that counted in Orofino. The performers, most of whom are from outside the area, are not real artists but are only shells compared to authentic loggers. They put on performances in town after town in hopes of winning prize money and then move on to the next to repeat their show.

Jake Altmiller performing during the preliminaries of the 1990 logging show. Jake is observed by a professional logging show contest judge, who travels the circuit throughout the Northwest. Even at his age, Jake is considered one of the finest loggers in this region.

Woodsworkers rarely enter the competitions, even though they feel they might be able to beat the performers. Many sawyers, for example, feel that it just takes too long to sharpen the chain or practice for a brief competition that isn't based on actual work in the woods. Instead they continue to express themselves through accomplishing their daily tasks well, and they gain personal gratification from a job well done instead of from the applause of the crowd. Authentic art takes place in the landscape among the loggers who do their jobs and in the community interactions among the residents who organize the Fair.

I realized the festival was a metaphor for the community's belief in work when I began talking to residents, visiting logging jobs, and riding on logging trucks. It was the behind-the-scenes authentic loggers and community members who used the event to reinforce their beliefs in the profession and in community values. The true festival is the camaraderie of the loggers and townspeople working together on the event and producing it with skill. The crafts of correctly erecting the climbing pole, getting things done efficiently, or cleaning up after the events are actually what logging and art are all about. The Clearwater County Fair and Lumberjack Days is a reaffirmation of their lives, a once-a-year intensified statement about work as an artistic form and as part of a worldview of community.

The festival performance did not tell the story of logging or demonstrate the skills and talents of loggers as I had learned them. It was an unrealistic portrayal of a way of life based on stereotypes instead of actualities. It was not a performance done by symbolically acting out an entire lifeway in a weekend, but instead one in which occupational skills were subjected to the demands of audience expectations and an external performance style, a style that was far more spectacle than real. Artistry was occurring, but it was behind the scenes, that of volunteers preparing for the events.

Work, not spectacle, becomes an artistic form in the woods or at the festival as a part of the intellectual framework and worldview of the community. The loggers and logging contractors live with this aesthetic in the woods and apply it to the behind-the-scenes operation of the festival. Sawyers, log truck drivers, loader operators, and woodsbosses can all point to characteristics of quality work in much the same way as an art historian can point to the exceptional qualities of a classical painting or a fine sculpture. The festival merely provides another opportunity to demonstrate this artistry. When loggers put experience into action with spontaneity and innovation, it is not the object that speaks of art, but the artistic processes that operate in their lives.

I saw this process vividly during a logging show that was being held in Lewiston. Tim Barnett couldn't help it. He had to take over as he had so often in the past. In his quiet way he just takes charge. He and Ted Leach have been working on the arena for the Timber Show for days, and it is obvious that the birling pond will fall in if they don't do something about it. Although the Potlatch Corporation papermakers' union had the best of intentions, they don't understand the physics of building a birling pond, making it stand, and most importantly, holding water for the contests.

Neither Tim nor Ted have built a pond nor prepared an entire arena before, but that doesn't stop them. They have worked in the woods with machinery and materials for a cumulative total of seventy years, and if something has to be done, they can do it. They know their materials and the capability of their equipment. Engineering means merely making materials do what you want them to do, creating something that works.

Both Tim and Ted have owned logging companies at one time or another in their careers. Now in their fifties, they still work in the woods, but as supervisors for other logging contractors. Their workload probably hasn't lessened any in the years since they gave up ownership. Their concern for their crews, their involvement in proper timber management, and their decision-making roles in cost and production persist even though they are no longer independent logging contractors. These attitudes don't leave you; they are ingrained after the long years becoming an expert logger.

Both men have taken their knocks. They have worked hard and sometimes have not realized all the benefits of their labors. But through it all, their pride in their profession has translated not only into a job well done but also into actions that show others what a job well done should be. Either might have been a miner or farmer. They would have thrown themselves just as readily into those jobs. But they are loggers, up and out early in the morning, checking equipment, making sure that their men are safe and working.

Here in the arena, Tim spends the week figuring out what to do. He and Ted translate what they know about logging, logging shows, and the manipulation of men and machines into building a birling pond. They study the space, pace it off, look at the overhead lines, figure out where the underground dangers might be, and evaluate the tactics to use. Should they weld the stanchions or bury them more deeply? Should they use another layer of plastic sheeting in the pond or would one suffice? How would they raise the two eighty-foot climbing poles? Without plans or blueprints, they set about their work. Driving machinery, even pieces that they have never worked before, Tim and Ted make the arena ready for the show. The facility for operating machines is almost a gift; some men have it and some don't. The gifted don't need training or a break-in period, they just get on and get at it.

During the process I observe Tim and Ted pacing, looking, and saying little, seemingly having the knowledge of earth, water, and air, not from books but from years of seeing them react as they work. Years of knowledge are being applied to preparing the show arena. Contending with conditions and handling equipment in the tradition of men who can build sawmills out of their heads, Ted and Tim know that success will be measured in the human reaction to their work. Just as in the woods where they must negotiate the demands of their employees, their employers, the Forest Service, state safety supervisors, and local communities that see their logging jobs every day, Tim and Ted factor the audience and contestants into their equation for a good show arena.

Time management, team meetings, and flow charts are terms and practices unnecessary to Tim, Ted, and their cohorts during the festival performances and on the job in the woods. The point is to do the job right with as little fuss as possible. Their objective is timeless, not trendy; it is product-oriented, not process-preoccupied. Operating manuals are unnecessary; plans—typed, labeled, and diagrammed—are a waste of time when you know what works and what doesn't.

After pacing, there is only one solution when the job isn't going quite right. You pick up a shovel and begin to do it single-handedly. You don't issue orders for others to do it. And as you accomplish this goal, you do it with artistry as well as with sweat. To be an accomplished artist one must have expertise in many areas.

Sharon Barnett is the fan most loyal to Tim and most enthusiastic about his artistry. When the climbing poles are raised, Tim does it with one try, using big equipment to get a delicate job done. For Sharon, it's like painting the Sistine Chapel; the whole town should be there to see her husband's competence and his manipulation of machinery.

After a week of work and several alterations to the original plan, the arena is ready. Tim has lost fifteen pounds in the process, Ted a comparable amount, and the entire crew has lost several nights' sleep, but the task is accomplished and the audience will see that the loggers of Orofino know how to stage an event to perfection.

One of the most important symbols of logging that goes on display during the festival, the ultimate masterpiece of this logging community, is the showload. I had heard about the characteristics of a prize-winning load of logs, but I never realized the time, money, and effort it took. Sharon Baugh introduced me to the beauty and the emotional importance of the showload in 1980. Sharon had passed the trucks being prepared for the logging parade. She stopped. She had to see the logs that were even, proportioned, and perfectly loaded. Each vehicle showed the best of a particular species—white pine, yellow pine, or cedar. And the group of men looking on knew it, too. She paused in her story, not knowing whether it would be embarrassing to continue. A nostalgic look captured her. As if experiencing a thing of beauty, Sharon was transported from the living room in which we sat to visualizing loads in parades of the past. "It's awfully hard to find good logs these days; the Forest Service helps for the parade, but good trees are getting harder and harder to find. Sure the youngsters can see the ordinary loads coming through town. There's a talent to loading them too, but most of that work is done for production, and you can't take the time to produce real beauty. But my grandsons, I want them to see what these forests can produce and how much we appreciate it. Those loads brought tears to my eyes."

Naively and perhaps with less delicacy than the situation demanded I said, "But Sharon, you can't push back time; if you keep cutting trees, you lose the good stands." Firmly, Sharon replied, "You'd better join Women in Timber; they'll teach you something about forest management—the facts—the facts that Washington doesn't understand." With that, our conversation was over, but I knew that the next day Sharon would take her grandchildren to the staging area, to see those loads of logs before the parade. She'd point out each and every detail of their natural grandeur and the artistry with which the loggers of Orofino had put them on display.

It was several years before I realized that what Sharon was talking about was a work of art. Other people helped me understand the technical dimensions necessary in the showload. These included rating elements and points based on safety, appearance, and quality. In each category specific practices were given points; for example, for safety the main characteristics were secure binders—thick fabric straps and stakes—metal retainers holding a compact well-balanced load. For appearance the logs were to have uniform size and length and be cut straight and be free of bark scuffs or loading marks. The logs themselves were to be of high quality, free of defects, and in conformity to standard mill lengths for the type of load it was.

Of the one hundred points, the trees themselves rated forty points, but the way in which they had been handled, the way in which the load was created and conformed to all of the safety standards added up the majority of the judging criteria—sixty points. Even though the truck itself was not rated, Norman Baugh, Sharon's husband, let me know that it was the pride of the driver to make their trucks sparkle. It was the driver's part in this creation; his are the finishing touches. He will be driving the load, and for him, even though it is not in the official judging rules, the appearance of the truck makes an impression on the crowd. I had heard often about the characteristics of the prize-winning load of logs for the Lumberjack Parade but did not have an opportunity to truly understand this artistry until ten years later.

On September 14, 1990, Chet Donley of Potlatch Forest Industries took me to watch a showload being prepared. Only then did I see that for a few minutes of inspection in the parade, days of toil went into their preparation. Chet warned me that the current timber harvest didn't allow for the true perfection of log loads of the past, but I was still excited about seeing the perfect load.

The intensity of this expectation had developed in me over the years. At first, all log loads looked the same to me, some perhaps a bit more evenly matched than others, but essentially all falling into the same general category. I had developed a certain sense of the aesthetics in architecture, furniture, and visual arts, but I had never applied this to a load of logs, and I was totally unaware of the process. How was a load of logs created? Was there a genius underlying the work? Was the thought process a part of any timber code, or did the loggers do what was expedient to put together the load?

Chet and I traveled up Grangemont Road, passed places that were familiar to me—the school, the homes of loggers and log truck drivers. We drove off the pavement, onto gravel, and finally onto the logging road. The area had been "clear-cut," a term and practice that linguistically and aesthetically cries out as if to say that the land has been raped. The slopes are barren and all signs of silviculture gone. Chet has prepared me for this and has taken the precaution of explaining the various opinions on this practice.

Throughout this drive and on my many trips to Idaho, I have been exposed to the controversies that rage over forest management. My Eastern, academic opinions and the Western pragmatic opinions were at odds. But for now, in looking at the preparation of the show load, let me say only that I have experienced concern from many quarters of the logging community about clear-cutting. Independent logging contractors and corporate CEOs alike are sensitive to finding rational, judicious uses of timber resources. The clear-cut from which the prize logs were taken may not have been pleasing to the eye, but it had been done with the intent of replanting in the current tradition of good forest management. What we were seeing was a temporary situation that would be remedied once the land was prepared and saplings were seeded.

Nine yellow pines had already been cut and skidded, brought to the landing with a Caterpillar. The process had begun the day before when the sawyers and skidder operator, working throughout the day, had brought the trees down. Some might say that there is nothing as beautiful as a growing stand of trees, but the task of these hardworking men was to turn the raw, natural materials into something equally beautiful, into a work of art—an image of perfection, the showload.

Potlatch provided the timber and crew. Its very best men were here. Two sawyers, a loader operator, and a woodsboss all knew their jobs, both the mundane, daily acts of logging, and this specialized occasion of preparing a showload. This finished job would come under scrutiny by the entire community. The truck used to carry the load and its driver, Dwayne Opdahl, one of the very best in the region, were also a part of this attempt at perfection. Before the parade the truck would be cleaned and polished and become a part of the image. Pride in their vehicle was ever-present for log truck drivers.

Art and science, beauty and practicality, finesse and precision blended that afternoon. Nine trees had been cut in the hopes that nine sections from those trees, each thirty-five feet long, could be found to put on the load. There was little room for experimentation. They were dealing with massive weights. Every move meant more time spent on the process as well as the possibility of a mishap. They had only one afternoon to prepare the load. Each loaded log weighed approximately 9,000 pounds, but added together the load could not exceed the legal road limit of 80,000 pounds. Thus, eight logs might seem to be too meager a load, whereas nine could be too great for road safety.

Aesthetically the load must be beautiful; legally it must be within the limit to travel on the highway; practically it must be cut to dimensions that a potential buyer at the auction could process in his mill. Its aesthetic beauty had to match its practical usefulness because, even now, the showload crew knew that the best potential buyer would be a veneer company that had exact specifications for the logs they mill. Dave Kludt, in charge of logging safety for the Associated Logging Contractors, was there. His job was to see that the highest safety standards were being met.

The necessities of the current situation as well as years of experience came into play when the men calculated how to cut the logs. As a team, the sawyers spoke to the loader, a man with years of experience in placing logs on trucks. In his everyday role this man was responsible for speed and proper balance of logs on trucks trying to make as many trips to and from the mill as possible. Today he was calculating how to load not only for efficiency, but also for beauty. He wanted to be sure not to scar the logs, yet have them balanced. Even before the loading, a discussion was held on the seemingly minor matter of whether the retaining posts on the truck that was coming to carry the load were curved or straight. This would make a difference in the appearance but also in the dimensions of the logs that were cut.

The Potlatch crew preparing the show load in 1990: Bill Stephenson with saw; George Payne, crew chief, watching; and Kingsley Steinbruecker, on the ground. Stephenson was killed shortly afterward in a logging accident.

The loader operator also wanted to hide the bad spots, not because they were unmarketable but because they seemed less sightly than other parts of the bark of the logs that would be on parade. As a loader operator, he had to make important decisions. For the sake of balance and image, should he try to reposition the logs, chancing that the bark would be damaged, or was the lesser of two evils that of having an imperfect surface visible?

Throughout the afternoon a transformation took place. Logs, laying helter-skelter on the ground amidst underbrush and gravel, were being turned into pristine cylinders, transforming a natural object into art. For loggers, the progress of their work was an aesthetic moment. The sawyers, Kingsley Steinbruecker and Bill Stephenson, concern themselves daily with safety, efficiency, and accuracy, for off-sized logs cannot go through the mills easily. This principal was applied to the showload, but with added diligence. All the logs were to be the same length on the load. That meant that whenever the truck moved from place to place picking up the logs, one of those already positioned would move. It was necessary for the sawyers to hop on top of the load and cut them to even out the ends. Sawing too much would mean that the logs would be off-size for the mill; sawing too little might mean that they would not appear even. An added problem was that since the saw bar was only thirty-eight inches long, it was nearly impossible to cut the bottom logs a second time.

Positioning the logs on the truck was a technical nightmare, but the sawyers and loader operator seemed to have the instinct to make any error correctable. They would use imprecision as an interim step toward this perfect showload. In the end the logs would be thirty-five feet long, and "they won't be off an inch," said Chet. Once the job began, there may have been several opinions, but few discussions, and no controversies. The woodsboss worked with the rest of the men, jumping atop the load when it was necessary, watching from a distance when only the person performing the work could control the product.

When loggers speak of the prize-winning load of logs or the performances at the logging show, when they recall the log drives or grandeur of a beautifully harvested stand, these loggers are sensing not only the object but the process that made it possible. That process, like the recollections of early logging with horses or the log drives that still have a romantic ring for the loggers, is as much a part of the art of logging as the product itself. Transitory and ephemeral though they may be, the loggers hold on to these thoughts. When they put their experience into action, it is not only the object but the artistic process that lives.

It is at the auction of both the showload and other useful items after the parade that the power of the logs comes into play again. As the prized possession of the community the showload will be the greatest draw for bids. The year 1990 hadn't been a very good one for logging in Clearwater County. Even though it had been difficult, that didn't mean that the Lumberjack Days would suffer. Everyone gave it their all, as usual.

This day of Lumberjack Days, Tim Barnett was a judge and Sharon was the manager of the show. Tim went to the preliminaries early, then caught a cup of coffee and a donut at the Ponderosa. Sharon picked up Bobbi Samuels and together they began to set up for the activities. By midday, Tim and Sharon had passed each other on the grounds several times, but both were too busy to talk. When the showloads and the floats carrying the other auction goods to the arena arrived, Sharon took her place in the announcer's booth and Tim took his with his buddies in the stands. The refreshment trailer was open, and those who knew about it took advantage of the libations intended to loosen up even the tightest bidder.

Tim and Sharon had discussed their plans for bidding late the night before. Both agreed that perhaps this year, like many other loggers, they'd lay off a bit, and let some of the others in the community pick up the goods. Bidding on the lesser items—sandwiches or flowers—would be just right as a gesture of community support. Their strategy was set. No unnecessary purchases. Tim, sitting with the guys, joined in their joking and kept his own counsel about his bidding. Some of the other loggers were in the same financial boat, and everyone was being cautious, or so they thought. It had been a bad year all around.

The bidding began with few surprises; useful objects went for double their market value. The auctioneer, Bill Crutcher, one-time county commissioner, had fun with the crowd, bringing up community leaders and asking for personal items to be auctioned. Don Ponozzo's socks brought a few dollars. To the auctioneer and to Don, it was worth the laugh.

But then, the legendary Barnett-Finke bidding war began. Les Schwab had donated a set of truck tires that both men wanted. Even though they could have purchased the same tires the next day, they both wanted them then and there. It got to the point that it didn't matter how much the tires cost, the war was on. Not to be outdone, Sharon decided she wanted a mailbox. She wouldn't let it go regardless of the unlimited resources of the other bidder. Sharon knew that if it aggravates you to spend, you don't belong here, especially since the proceeds went to next year's show.

At the auction, some people bid only on practical things that they could use, perhaps paying a bit more but knowing that the extra dollars will go to next year's logging show. Others bid on firewood or objects to contribute to charity. Others concentrated on the special loads of logs, and still others didn't bid at all. But throughout the afternoon, bidding or not, the members of the community are on display for the rest of the town.

As auctioneer, Bill Crutcher squeezed the last dollar from reluctant townsfolk. Sometimes the action was brisk, generally caused by a bidding war, often between two women who wanted a specialty item like a hand-painted mailbox or hand-carved bowl. At times it was slow, but everything was sold and often for three or four times its worth. It's not uncommon for a high bidder, or even just someone caught just sticking up their hand, to get a rousing round of applause.

Ted Leach, independent logging contractor, acts as the auctioneer for the OCI timber sale in 1990. He often performs with the theatre group and sings at celebrations. He wears the official Orofino Lumberjack Days tee-shirt.

Crutcher is an expert performer, knowing exactly when to lighten up the crowd, engendering in them a pride of community by saying, "Oh, our guests this weekend come worldwide; we even have people from Walla Walla, that sure is the end of the world." He causes purchases by taking bids when none were offered, knowing that the non-bidding individual will purchase the object regardless. He knows the way to prompt someone to shake their head, or point their finger which in his mind, but not in theirs, is a legitimate bid. Bill is especially hard on politicians, commenting on their bald pates and making them go higher just for the honor of standing up and being recognized as a candidate for office. "Just rub that bald head of yours and see what happens," is a frequent comment of Crutcher's. He allows access to the microphone only if he can fine the user a hundred dollars if he mentions his campaign. Governor Cecil Andrus, a past resident of Orofino, attended the festivities and was often in evidence during the weekend. At the auction he barely escaped making a contribution. Bill stretches the limits of social decorum, but never too far.

It is apparent that the largest donations come from selling the showloads that have been in the parade. Through the years it has been the timber mills that have bid, and made the contributions that have allowed the weekend to flourish. When more mills were in operation, the number of showloads and ferocity of bidding was greater. Now, with only three operating mills in the county, much of the responsibility falls to Potlatch, the major timber corporation in the region, to use its wealth to support the weekend. In 1990, Potlatch and its employees played a crucial part in the festival. Potlatch donated a load of logs, bought it back at the market rate, and then donated it back to be sold again. Thus their total contribution of log donation, bid, and re-donation figured to thousands of dollars. Currently, no other mill in the region can afford this type of beneficence.

The auction is a good way to recognize those people and organizations which are prominent in this logging community. Along with the livestock auction of the Clearwater County Fair, it provides an opportunity for members of the community to gain recognition if they wish, but this is not the sole reason for purchases. Instead, members of the community feel an obligation to redistribute the community wealth.

The auction is a performance that the community puts on each year, a performance of the reality of the community's economics, but always in the spirit of friendship. The community becomes a cast of characters expecting a level of performance and communication. The play that results is a theater piece of the community. The beauty of the showload, the excitement of the bidding, and the work of the volunteers who put the logging community on display to the world, speak loudly of the pride in perfection felt in Clearwater County.

WORK AS ART

Lessons on a Ridge

To unravel the two threads of art and work in the loggers' world requires establishing a definition of art—no easy task since definitions abound. On the other hand, work for a logger represents not only actual physical activity, but also a certain pride in the industry that surpasses mere manual labor.

Loggers themselves use the term art for their work, even though traditional art objects, such as a painting in a museum or a play on Broadway, are not produced. Art appears on logging trucks, in the woods, in the subtle work motions of each logger and in the patterned perfection of everyday life. Only individuals who understand and react emotionally to the visual significance of logging images can truly appreciate these aspects of work as art. If you have the eye, however, they can be perceived in daily occurrences and can be seen in the processes by which certain effects are created and achieved.

John Dewey (1934) suggested that art is not an object but an experience—one with its own feelings and way of thinking. If he is correct then the loggers, men who are continuously examining their inner experiences with nature, are true artists. For the logger it is the experience and not merely the product that is the aesthetic moment. Logging constitutes an art form under this definition. Aspects of aesthetics can be applied to situations in logging that have not traditionally been considered part of the artistic sphere because, to the loggers, these experiences demonstrate a striving for perfection and prompt emotional responses.

In the following conversations, logging is described by old-timers and contemporary loggers in Clearwater County as being beyond physical labor and is seen as a ground for aesthetic experience. To avoid predisposing the individuals I talked with to the idea that their work was art, I did not use the terms art or artists in our conversations. However, many loggers volunteered the term themselves when talking about a particularly skilled logger or a logging operation.

My first experience of the depth of feeling loggers demonstrate for their work and their need for perfection to sustain the beauty of the logging lifeway came in a lesson from Tim Barnett and Ted Leach on a ridge. It was a May day when we stepped out of Ted's pickup and looked across a canyon. The day had started when Tim and Ted met me at 6 A.M. at the Ponderosa Restaurant to give me a lesson in history and art. I imagined they would hark back to the pioneers and old-timers or significant historical events. Instead they chose to instruct me in the right place—in the woods—with practical and specific information.

To Tim and Ted, history and place are inseparable. History is place. History is logging and regrowth. History is recognizing that what you see today is temporary and only a small part of the cycle of life. It is seeing the stages through which each timbered area has gone. That is history.

Art to Tim and Ted is a stand of handsome trees and their proper care. They made sure that I could recognize the "thrifty" trees, ones that were both healthy and using the resources. We stopped at stands to look at species density, crown development, limb balance, and general composition. Discussing the relative ages of the trees led Tim to think about one of his logging heroes, Ray Saylor. Years ago, Ray and Tim had been sitting in silence on a landing, next to a road Ray had swamped—cut through the forest—forty years before. Ray was silent, even more so than usual for a man of few words. Tim remembered the silence. Tim asked the older logger why he didn't have anything to say. Ray replied that fifty years ago he had logged the area across the canyon and now it was ready to be cut again. For him, it signaled the passage of time, his aging. The next day Saylor retired from logging. He had gone full circle. He had measured his personal aging and phases of life through the timber stands and not with birthdays.

That day we rode through time, and through an emotional process that only those who have worked in the woods and have seen the forest regeneration can truly understand. Often government service workers and Forest Service personnel don't stay in the region for the thirty-five years it takes to see the complete process, but Tim and Ted had and they were aware of what time could do to the region. Knowing that when they died, there would be no recognition for their work—no highway signs, no parks or roads named after them—these two men still revelled in the part they had played in stewardship of the land. "Everything you've done in thirty-five years of work goes with you," said Tim. "But maybe other good loggers coming after you, will look at a stand of trees, remember that you had done the job, and see in its regrowth how well you had done it. You live only in their memories, at least that is your hope. History is mine now but when I go it is theirs." It is as if they were both adding, "That's my gift to history and art. I logged it and I'm proud. I don't need a record of my jobs; I can take a pickup and drive there, I can see my own history."

To be good at making a living a logger must know which trees to cut and which to leave standing. A successful logger must have the experience to know that if a tree is growing well, it should be left for future harvest to produce a better, more valuable yield. He must know by looks: know by the bark and the crown, by its shape and its density. There is a complexity and specificity in the aesthetics of the logger's eye. We were looking at trees that were harvestable, but we were also seeing them as objects that had a sense of beauty about them. In fact, Ted said that to him "thrifty" meant in essence "pretty." So, you save a "pretty" tree.

This ordinary morning had become a profound one for me. We were not looking at timber, we were looking at aesthetics in the way loggers recreate a natural environment. The woods-bosses know how to look at these trees; so do the artistic sawyers. The boss gives a general picture to the sawyer indicating the way in which the job should be done, but he doesn't mark the trees. It is the sawyer who makes the decisions.

Ted Leach's legacy to logging is his concern and the courses he teaches for the young sawyers coming into the profession. "It's an attitude," says Ted. "For three days I don't let them touch a saw. I teach them how to walk around and size up a tree, its lean and limb structure. I show them how to analyze imperfections. I help them see what effect it will have when it falls. I try to build confidence in them and a sense that work and living are one. Habits cross over, and if you are a good worker you have a good life." He teaches that woodsworking should be combined with the aesthetic in a complete life. "If you have no pride in yourself, you have no pride in your work. It all boils down to pride. You don't tear up the woods; you play a part in preparing it for its reproduction." Ted says "Work and life values equate. I can show you this. The way a logger works is the same way he treats his wife and kids." When he tests young loggers in class, he judges the look, the aesthetics of their work as well as their production.

Tim Barnett confirmed my belief that work, to the loggers of Clearwater County, is an art form. Privately, his feeling is that if left to do a job the way they believe is proper, the loggers would do it right for both the industry and nature. In public presentations he is well-spoken, firm, dedicated, and politically articulate concerning timber interests and environmental sensibilities. Seeing only this side of Tim, one might think his advocacy sprang primarily from economic motivation, but that is not the case. He is walking in the footsteps of the elders and carrying out not only the mission of economic viability for himself and those in his profession, but also an aesthetic that has been transmitted to him throughout his youth.

Driving through the logging areas, walking around a job and remembering back to days in the 1970s—not so long ago by logging standards—Tim was less political and more artistic in his descriptions. His words were chosen with precision and flowed directly from what he saw. As he looked across the canyon, a stand of trees echoed back the story of the past to him through their beauty. In a natural setting as magnificent as Idaho, this is not surprising, but Tim's interpretation of beauty had an added dimension because of the potential for natural beauty to be altered by the loggers. Historically loggers have approached logging with respect and reverence, harvesting trees for human survival. But there was also the potential for new beauty in the future.

Landscape painters give us the impression that it is the untouched, virgin wilderness that resonates with near-godly perfection. Tim taught me that the hand of man, when applied properly to nature, can create a setting with its own special kind of beauty. If ill-applied it speaks of greed, but when seen as an artistic creation of conscientious loggers who care about its perpetuation, the natural surroundings can demonstrate the artistry of human intervention. Tim knows this, and feels it. He practices it every day and showed me on that ridge that day. History and artistry reside together. Logging is an aesthetic moment, both as it appears on the landscape in the skills of its artisans and as a historical statement about beauty in nature.

Sometimes loggers speak in terms of the art of their occupation. They focus on the inventiveness and creativity in the many operations necessary to perform a job, from sharpening a saw chain to producing a balanced load of logs. The product surpasses the mere accomplishment of the job, and the best loggers receive among themselves recognition akin to that of an artist. Loggers have used a common experience to develop a sense of quality that is above and beyond the mundane. Whether it is in a natural or technological object, or in an experience derived from the setting, or in the performance of physical labor, the source of quality is the result of striving for perfection. The standards that have been applied to an object or experience set it apart from other objects and experiences. Emotions or emotional quality—the ability to move the viewer—are associated with the object or experience, and there is close adherence to the standards, if not the technology, of the past.

Loggers identify masters such as Jake Altmiller and Kingsley Steinbruecker, objects of art such as the showload, exemplary technique, and the application of creativity and invention. To hear a logger say, "It's my world: I built this road, I cut that stand of trees, I can't leave it," sums up the tie between man and his environment, his need to tend it carefully, and his sense of the artistry in doing it. And as is so often case, loggers look to the elders as the true artists.

As the logging hero of Clearwater County, Jake Altmiller has answered hundreds of questions from people ranging from school children doing a *Foxfire*-type book to the public relations director of the Idaho Centennial Logging Show. In his responses Jake will not tell his age, adding to a mystique that has become more important to others than to him. Jake Altmiller is slight, stooped, and looks nothing like the current Bull of the Woods, Mel Lentz, the national logging champion. They are separated by a half century in clothing, speech, and style, but both have an unparalleled talent to cut through logs with blinding speed. Jake is certain that Clearwater County has the best sawyers in the nation. "We have good sawyers here; they sharpen their chains right" is Jake's standard answer to what makes a good sawyer. It is the chain, always the chain, done to perfection.

Jake takes his role as a famous sawyer seriously. He always appears in the same green coat and hat, always in black logger pants with red suspenders and a plaid shirt. There is nothing contrived about this outfit, it's just the practical way any good lumberjack would dress. It has an air of dignity about it, like the cream of today's crop of woodsmen. Their clothing may be old, their collars frayed, but it is always clean, practical, and well-fitting. At the national finals in Lewiston, Jake participated in an exhibition. He sawed through one log with the skill and ease the audience is accustomed to seeing. It was a straight, clean, artful cut. In contrast, some younger competitors are beginning to "dude up." One wore neon chartreuse, skintight running leotards for the choker setting contest and looked more like a modern-day Olympiad than a lumberjack when he struggled with the metal chain binders.

Jake, originally born a farmer, learned his skill in the woods first with a cross-cut saw and then with a power saw. He also participated in professional logging contests and made his way into final after final, often winning first prize. Unlike other competitors, he didn't climb, chop, or throw an axe; he just cut through a log and the crowd loved it. After a performance he returned home and went back to the woods on logging jobs.

Jake remembers he was in the Navy in Algeria when power saws first came into use. He couldn't imagine what they would be like. He had heard that Joe Cox had observed a beetle girdling a tree and had developed a device called an Oregon chain based on the same principle. Jake couldn't fathom it. Sure it had to have a motor, but how else was it constructed? Did the blade

Jake Altmiller performing with a crosscut saw in an OCI Logging Show in the 1940s. (Courtesy, the estate of Carroll Brock.)

travel back and forth? He never thought that it would be a chain around a bar and that the teeth of the chain were be akin to those of the beetle chewing through the bark. When he returned from the service, Jake gravitated to the invention.

Jake recalled his first eighty-five pound power saw. It didn't have a filter and the carburetor would plug up; the sparkplug would get magnetized and cause trouble. Every night the dirt had to be blown out and the saw cleaned. "Some people didn't think these new-fangled saws were worth it," said Jake. Often the time saved using the power saw was taken up with mechanical repairs. In his logging camp days, in the evenings Jake honed his chain and prepared several others for the next day. "It takes a lot of time to put a chain into good condition, take off a lot of it so there is less resistance, so it can carry more sawdust, so it can go faster."

In the woods Jake and other sawyers practiced the art of felling trees at the proper angle to the skidder. To make any money you had to be efficient, and Jake was capable of felling for two Caterpillar tractors at the same time. He was paid by the board foot and knew his paycheck would reflect the care he took in his work and the extra chain he had as a replacement for use in the afternoons.

Jake is the epitome of "lumberjack pride"—a phrase used often by Mick McLaughlin. Jake and his wife Barbara live in a modest home on one of the benches. Their home is not stylish or urban chic, but everything is in good order. Their garden is exceptional, and their meals, as Barbara says, "come from the land." Beets in vinegar, corn, potatoes, apple tarts, and even the venison had not too long ago been a part of the Idaho environment.

Barbara is proud of her garden, and rightly so. She had a scrapbook of photographs of the produce and the ribbons she had won. A pumpkin, 220 pounds in weight, and apples from seeds of trees from the Wolf River in Wisconsin made her "prideful." In her quiet way, Mrs. Altmiller had never quite become accustomed to being the wife of a local legend. She was simple and subdued. She didn't know quite what to make of it when she and Jake were chosen as the Grand Marshalls of the 1990 Logging Show, yet she so enjoys talking about Jake's movie career. For a town as obscure as Orofino, there has been considerable public notice of it, especially in the movies. Although kept anonymous, it has been featured in the film *The Big Sky,* in which Jake played a French riverman. To this day he and Barbara remember it as quite an experience.

Jake recalls the changes he has seen but also the stories of those who retained the old ways. For example, Jake's brother-in-law Clarence Roby stayed with the crosscut saw a little longer than most. But when he switched, this expert with a crosscut turned out to be an excellent power sawyer as well. Often, in early competition in the everyday work in the woods between power and manual sawyers, the old style won because of maintenance difficulties with the early power saws.

Changes in clothing and equipment had taken place in the past fifty years, but for Jake, though he would never go back to a manual saw, lifestyle has not. Jake and Barbara worked hard, they raised their children, attended family reunions, planted their garden, and did a little hunting. The question is, what qualified him for the role of a local symbol of the sawyer's profession? Trends come and go, but Jake remains Jake. Looking back at photographs taken in the 50s, 60s, 70s, and today shows that he has never tried to follow any fashion in style or attitude. Solid, never varying in his opinion that the chain is all, Jake was and is for the community their symbol of the logger.

Del Roby, photographed in the 1940s. A logger from a well-known family of woodsmen and competitors, Roby wields an early chain saw, significantly heavier and larger than those used today. Although they were more efficient than manual tools, when power saws were introduced over five decades ago they were large and cumbersome. (Courtesy, the estate of Carroll Brock.)

His awards did not make him special. Others may be younger, faster, or stronger sawyers, so why Jake? Why did everyone suggest that he was the man who epitomized logging? Jake stuck to one thing, being a fine sawyer. He believed in the technology of a fine chain and had been consistent in his competition in the logging shows. He has missed only one since the inception of the logging show in 1946 because of an automobile accident. Jake did what he did well, and everyone appreciated that trait. He had also consented to being the consummate performer, appearing in every show, and quietly plying his skill.

He and Barbara were typical of other loggers in this region, less aware of their European antecedents than their American ancestors. They spoke of 1950 and their early married years together in a one-room cabin. They worked hard. Their life was the same as everyone else's. They were not special; they were on the same plane with everyone else, not winners or losers, merely players in the community.

They, as others in their age group, had gone through the Depression, surviving by depending on their garden. Jake had worked in the woods in the 1930s and remembered the "foreigners" who didn't have people here. They were the Swedes and Finns who, according to Jake, eventually died out. In his memory it was as if an entire generation of unmarried lumberjacks disappeared and a new breed of family men took their places.

He had worked for Ray Coon for twenty years and even though for three years he worked as a sawboss, he always kept his saw with him to trim limbs, knots, and broken log ends on log decks and landings. He thought of himself in the same category as Paul Leeper, the great skidder operator: "He never seemed fast but never got hung up, he never broke up a tree, and always seemed to do his job with a minimum of movement."

Jake also proclaimed the beauties of the top-loader's art, as had other veteran loggers. The top-loader's skill is most apparent when you look at the log loads. Not only can an expert loader handle more in one day than any other man, his loads look good—they are built up square, the ends are even and balanced and the face log fits in the notch so that the entire load can be transported easily.

Praise for others permeates Jake's comments. Others always seemed to be doing a great job. Human skills at manipulating logs were perfected with new inventions, like the skidding carriage. And why? Because if you needed a better or safer way of doing something, "you invented it yourself," said Jake. "A real artist was Don Christenson," says Jake. "I never saw a man handle a piece of equipment as easily as Don could. He could cross cut, load, and line skid, truck drive and Cat skid. And he was an expert mechanic too. He was from the old school. He learned mainly from experience. He invented a skidding carriage that is now sold internationally."

Jake talked about technique in logging show competition. "You have to be careful if you are the first on a log. Check the saw, put your hand on the cylinder to make sure it's hot, and get your feet planted so you don't have to move." In the woods you have to use good judgment and make sure your path is clear. But over and over again, Jake and others emphasized the differences between performance and speed in a controlled setting versus work in the woods, where skill is characterized by good judgment. Performance is meant to please crowds, not get a job done, and the cuts are little more than spectacular moments that have very little to do with work in the woods. Many contestants do not work in the woods; they are a part of the entertainment, not a part of the craft.

And what about the education of a sawyer? Jake would happily teach a young man all he knew—"be careful and alert." He would willingly let a young man follow him around in the woods and learn from observing. Would the youngster make a good sawyer? That would be difficult to know until you got him into the woods and watched to see whether the lifestyle grew on him. Says Jake, "Some seemed hopeless, were awful slow to start, but after two or three years they got the swing of it. You have to be a sticker to be a logger. Today there are schools, but if it doesn't appeal to you, you won't want to do it and will never do it right." Time and perseverance—in the woods and in performance, but also in those silent times when you do nothing more interesting than sharpen your chain—that's what makes a good sawyer.

"And family ties help," says Jake. He had seven brothers, and they were all woodsworkers. The Altmillers married the Robys and the Barnetts and the Burches, all of whom are known to be important members of the logging network. Today they are still logging families and interconnect with one another, a functional dynasty of timber arts.

Jake is used as a symbol of the sawyer's art in the local newspapers and in promotional pamphlets. He is a classical version of the lumberjack, but there are no fool-hardy adventure stories in Jake's life. The big theme of his life is not going on heroic quests; it is working hard, day in and day out, and having a sense of honesty and integrity, earning a reputation as a human being as well as a master sawyer. As others have said, he is not only a good logger, Jake is also a good man. In his life, no one keeps score except Jake. He has an eye for filing and sharpening chains. He has learned all the angles and can make it cut fast and not bind. That is a very specific talent. But Jake's life in logging is seen as more than just filing skills. Jake knows what to do in the woods. He has taught others and has been a subtle inspiration to generations of young sawyers in Clearwater County.

Kingsley Steinbruecker bases his life on learning from Jake and believing in similar values. Active in the Clearwater Resource Coalition and an outspoken advocate for the logging way of life, he's also well-liked, a humorous guy, full of pranks, who can turn a time-consuming, difficult job into a jovial outing. That is, until it comes time to actually do the sawing.

Kingsley is the complete sawyer, proud of his work and demanding of himself and those who work with him. Everyone knows that with Kingsley on the crew, things will be done correctly. He is careful and concerned about the appearance of the job and exacting about the technique applied to each operation. Kingsley is the first in his family to choose logging as a profession, but as a young boy logging was always an influence in his life. He was in constant contact with the Altmiller brothers. Kings' dad went hunting with them frequently and the young boy would tag along. When it was time to build a fire, he would watch the Altmillers prepare the wood. They were always generous with their knowledge, letting him ask questions, but more importantly, allowing him to watch how they plied their craft. He remembers it so well, admitting that he learned more by listening while sitting around the camp fire than talking. He was like "a mouse in the corner." So, too, he remembers and is proud of the fact that they used to call him "The Kingfisher."

He had done well in high school, and though it surprised his family, instead of continuing on to college he got a job in the woods. He stayed with it and learned to do well in difficult situations. Every time he was unsure of himself he would ask himself, "How would Jake do it?" He'd think about it and decide, "Jake would do it this way."

Good sawyers rarely divulge how to sharpen a chain. While Kings was learning he remembered that the Altmillers would say, "that the main thing is to get it sharp." But in order to do this he would sharpen and sharpen. He would change techniques and finally, by trial and error and perhaps sneaking a look at an expert's chains, he learned.

Kings said that after about seven or eight years on the job he began to feel comfortable and gain competence. He still learns something new every day since his is an evolving art that demands that the artist be open to new challenges, always finding ways to invent techniques that will produce a better performance and a better product. Three cardinal rules that Kings holds are: "Never use anyone else's tools; be sure that yours are running right; and always, even on the most rugged of jobs, give it a delicate, soft touch."

Pam, Kingsley's wife, who is the niece of logger Don Ponozzo, tells the story of Kingsley's expertise. She appreciates the artistry that he, someone from a non-logging family, has developed. As the story goes, friends of theirs had a home in a meadow with a large propane tank near it. They asked Kings to fell a tree that was situated between the two. The tree was in a position that put the house or tank in jeopardy if it fell the wrong way. Kingsley evaluated the situation and felt that he could bring down the tree without harming either. He prepared his cut and readied two men to pull on a rope attached to the tree when he called out that they should do so. In the performance Kings added a bit of intrigue—just enough so that the owner of the property would feel "rattled" and Kings could make a good story when the feat had been accomplished. The owner wanted to be "too technical." Kings felt he would go wrong if technique overshadowed his intuition of how to do the job.

For the first half hour Kingsley made a "big game" out of the occasion. He even made the owner, who was afraid of heights, climb up the tree and tie a guide rope around it. All the while

Kingsley was concentrating on the stump which he knew would tell him how to make the cut. To add to the excitement, he asked the owner to stand exactly where the tree would hit. He made his cut and yelled for the owner to move. They pulled the rope and the tree fell, the tips of its branches gently kissing the edge of the tank as it hit the ground, in exactly the spot the owner had moved from moments earlier.

Throughout the process, there had been no talk of insurance or liability. It had been a "gentlemen's agreement," with no written contract or request for payment. For Kingsley, it was a challenge, but he also acknowledged that if he had any doubt about his ability to succeed, he wouldn't have attempted it. The property owner, in turn, trusted that he knew his capabilities. Both sides knew that there was no way to put a monetary value on this type of specialized operation, or at least, in this country and between these parties, there were no prices set.

Instead, they all knew that it had created a bond. Kingsley would never ask for a return on the job but knew that if the occasion arose, reciprocity would occur. And it did. Pam and their daughter were riding at Red River some months later and one of their horses threw a shoe. They asked for help from the property owner and were given the owner's best horse to ride back. It was a return in kind and in quality for the day of the "big game."

Words come easy to Kingsley; he uses them wisely and has been called upon often to represent the logging industry. His statements are sincere and possess clarity when he is speaking of the political issues attendant with logging as well as when he speaks of it as an art. For Kingsley, to be a good sawyer means to have a neat, nice fluid motion. Everything about the action should look easy. In fact, he claims that before he became a sawyer, when all his knowledge was gained from watching the Altmillers, he had no idea that logging was hard work.

In life as in work, the Steinbrueckers seek and attain a quality of life that begins with creating an environment in the natural setting that pleases the eye. Because logging is a seasonal occupation, they bought a rundown homestead and began ranching. The cattle are gone now, but the homestead might easily appear in a copy of *Architectural Digest*. When you drive up High Valley Road, not knowing exactly which spread to stop at, all you have to ask yourself is what would the home of a sawyer committed to artistry look like? The answer comes easily. Without the need for an address painted on a mailbox, you would know that a family concerned with visual impact must live on this particular spread. The house, even though it is under renovation, is orderly. Construction materials are neatly organized, tarpaulins are secured, and equipment is out of the weather. As you look out the large windows across the finely-cut meadow toward the out-buildings, you can see that there has been care given to every visual element. The barn and sheds are roofed, repaired, and painted, as if maintenance is perpetual. A pride in their homestead is exemplified in the way it is kept up. In both their living and their work, fine woods' artists seek perfection.

Kingsley begins his day at 4:30 A.M. when he leaves for coffee at the Ponderosa. There, with other loggers, he finds out what is happening—where current jobs are being done, how many logs are being processed, and what new ideas are coming out. Then he goes to his job as a sawyer. In an area as large as forty square miles, he can find the job with the vaguest directions. Once there, he selectively logs out the right timber to get the best production out of the stand now, while maintaining its appearance and potential yield for the future.

Kingsley feels that there is no substitute for experience. Logging couldn't be done better with computers or formulas. In fact, he claims that occasionally men committed to a textbook approach will come back to him and admit that "the book just doesn't work." He believes in the need for a "methodical manner," one in which there is no room for mistakes but one learned through experience, not in a classroom. So many areas are so rugged that a sawyer needs forethought. Kingsley says, "You can't have a guy who does a big mess. You pace it off, you walk it, before you form your idea." And if you're really good, the supervisor comes to you, as he does to Kingsley, to ask for a plan to log a region.

In Kingsley's own words, he's like a modern day John Henry competing against modern technology. There are regions where advanced machinery can't operate, and he must go in and do the job. But like the fate of other independent, self-motivated men of legend and real life, Kingsley sees the current problems. He worries that his profession is becoming a lost art, that loggers are turning to other things and that mothers don't want their sons in the woods. The physical risks that woodsworkers have to take were in the past financially worth it, but are no longer, and in the past ten years, the pay for a good sawyer has not increased in proportion to the cost of living.

Kingsley commented on the teamwork necessary for specialized tasks, like preparing the showload. The job is orchestrated but no one gives orders because everyone knows what everyone else is thinking and knows that they are thinking ahead. Because of their long years of experience, they will come up with the same conclusions on how to accomplish the job. The team works at the level of psychic unity.

To Kingsley, the best crew he has ever been on was one with Bill Stephenson, John Curtis, and Paul Cleveland. It was smooth and they knew in one day that everything was right, that regardless of the strip to be cut they would come together in a good, hard-working relationship. They would go the extra mile to help one another and have a good time in the process. "You have to have a good time because the job is hard and you don't want to make it any harder by not getting along," he says.

Returning to the question of how a sawyer can survive, Kings enumerated his tenets: "Show pride in your work. Build a good reputation, it is your way of life. Don't worry about your physical size or muscular attributes, but stay in good shape. Don't be afraid of hard work. Take advantage of education but count on experience, 'being there,' to get the job done. Keep a sharp, clear mind."

Finally, he said, "Learn from the old-timers. They became experts by doing, and the best bet for a young logger is to work with someone who knows the country. The Altmillers took time with me when I was a youngster. They never lost their temper or made a young fellow afraid to ask questions. And the biggest secret to success is to have a good teacher." Kingsley Steinbruecker seeks perfection. He is meticulous with his tools and his clothing. Says Kingsley the artist, "Everything has to feel right and be right—in a heartbeat."

Kingsley's feelings are not unique among the younger men who work in the woods. Others in different specialties feel the same about their way of life. For example, Mike and Darlene Lee lead a simple life, in a modest, rented home in Orofino. When you enter from a cold and rainy night you appreciate that it is warm and toasty. Like many other houses in the region, the Lee home is heated with a wood-burning stove always kept supplied by Mike's enterprise. He and woodsworkers cut, split, and supply their stoves for the cold. The Lee home seems like a communication nerve center. There are two CB radios, an ambulance scanner, and a hand-held radio for constant communication with Orofino's volunteer Fire Department.

Mike Lee, always ready for fire emergencies, looks tired. He went on a 2:00 A.M. call the night before and he expects to be called out again. The department is small—only twenty-eight men—but it prides itself on being one of the best. These men know the local terrain and many of them are loggers. Their greatest value rests in their ability to get to an emergency without elaborate directions in any location, regardless of how remote. Once there, they can examine the situation and can devise a system for taking care of any emergency, any accident, any fire.

Darlene is the tiniest "drink of water" you can imagine, perhaps five feet tall, slight, freckled, with a halo of pale carrot-red hair. When not cooking at The Bakery, she's working for OCI or at grandmothering for her daughter. To my surprise, Darlene mentioned that she had grown up among nine other families in the logging camp of Frank Fromelt. Frank, to many in this area, is a hero. In his quiet way he made sure that the town of Pierce, and especially its children, were protected and loved. According to Darlene, she "needed a little spoiled," and it was Frank that did the spoiling. Grandpa Frank was 150 percent behind the kids and, as a tribute, Pierce High School dedicated their yearbook to him. Darlene brought it out with pride to show me a picture of this old-time logging hero. From him she learned that even if you start poor, you work at being nothing but the best. Darlene feels that Frank became prominent because he was dedicated and worked day and night. "There was no better human being."

Here, in the Lee living room, the influence of Frank Fromelt and other early independent logging contractors shines. Mike and Darlene perpetuate the practices and attitudes they found in men like Frank Fromelt. As they both agree, "It's a hard life, but a good life even though life for a logger has changed and today it takes two to make a living."

Darlene and Mike both rise at about 1 A.M.; she is always up to prepare breakfast and see Mike off. As a loader operator, he is on the job for about twelve hours and is the first to arrive and the last to leave. If you add to that one hour of travel time each way, sometimes more in the winter, you have a fourteen-hour or more day, and there is always the possibility of a night emergency call which leaves Mike little time to sleep.

The annual cycle, as well as the daily one, follows the whims of the weather. Loggers work from May through October, but not much during November before the freeze. When December comes and the ground is hard again they will work until approximately Valentine's Day. Then they have layoff time, and they allow themselves the luxury of rest, or they do a little mechanical work in the company shop. The daily schedule also operates without reference to calendar or clock with times based on daybreak and nightfall.

For Mike, working the loader is the epitome of high status in the woods. Felling trees may be most dangerous, a logger might lose one or two sawyer friends each year to accidents in the woods, but it is the loader operator who can make or break a job. He plays the role of the daily go-between for the men and the boss. "Every day is different in the woods, different for the logger," says Mike. He is proud of that fact, because associated with it is the understanding that he, as a logger, must meet new challenges each day. Concentration is the key to much of what has made Mike a success. He has been working in the woods for thirteen years. In that time he has learned to be fast and efficient at his job, but most importantly, he has learned always to be cautious. He knows exactly where every crew member is at all times during the logging operation. "Your equipment is expensive and that is a consideration, but the lives around you are irreplaceable. As a loader you are hoisting approximately 15,000 pounds with each swing of the crane's arm. One false move can damage a truck or kill a man." Mike has never lost a man.

Knowledge of species, size, and length also play an important part in any loader's talent. Eyeballing a lift of timber, the loader is responsible for making sure that it balances properly on the truck. This must be done instantaneously without the aid of charts or blueprints. The only flow charts are in the loader's head, imprinted there through years of practice. "You can't learn how out of a book," says Mike. "There is an art to all of it, and part of that art is based on routine, speed, efficiency, and knowing the woods. And one of the best of them all is Jake Altmiller."

I was surprised that Mike, who is so much younger, would bring up Jake. "Jake is amazing. He never has a wasted movement. He never gets excited and yet he can outsaw anyone." Mike continued, "Felling timber is definitely an art. You have to know where the log is going to fall. You want it as near to the skid trail as possible. To do that you have to know how to make different cuts and where to put your wedges." But according to Mike, you can't believe everything you hear about talent—"There is more timber skidded in the restaurants in town over coffee than in the woods," he said.

Mike was thoughtful and paused often during our conversation as if weighing his words. He believes in what he and his fellow loggers are doing, in the fact that they are applying decades of knowledge and using well-honed skills in their profession. He is a part of a team, not only on a logging crew but in the total scheme of the logging tradition. One of his most memorable experiences occurred when he became a part of the logging truck convoy to Darby, Montana. As supporters of the timber industry, he and hundreds of loggers throughout the region took loads to a mill that was about to close. It, and the town, were in dire straits for if the mill closed, the town was doomed. Mike and others carried logs to Montana to keep the mill open. To see fifteen miles of logging trucks traveling on the highway and into the mill's yard was truly a sight to behold. Teamwork pays off, in the woods and in major crises as well. If the future means more demonstrations, Mike Lee will be right in the middle of them with his compatriots.

But success can't happen if loggers' intentions are sporadic or if their lives are disorganized. Life must be lived dependably day by day. Routine is essential. There is a proper mix of men doing their specific tasks to the best of their ability, and a system that supports their striving for excellence. According to Mike, "you have to care about your job, have pride in it, and that means doing it better all the time. You rarely criticize others because everyone knows what's expected." Everyone knows the expectations and the procedures that are to be followed to achieve a goal.

You might think that with the little time they have at their disposal, the Lees would turn down other volunteer opportunities. Not so: they also devote time to the OCI Logging Show, in the thick of the planning and as valued members of the Board.

"What is beautiful?" I asked Mike. Without hesitation he replied, "If you do a good job, that's beautiful. You should take a look at the job we did at Greer Grade three years ago. It looks really nice. You can't even see where we had to put in roads." He continued, "You should look at logging just like farming, but it takes longer. You make sure that in years to come you can go into that area and enjoy it. There's nothing prettier than walking on a landing you've worked and seeing elk and bear among the newly planted trees."

What about the future for the Lees? As far as Mike is concerned, he will "keep loading logs." He wants a reputation for being the best. Even though he knows that there is less money in his profession than there was in the 1970s, it is something he wants to do. He loves what he is doing, and for him retirement doesn't even figure into his future.

Truck driving is another art, especially when you are hauling 80,000 pounds of unwieldy logs down sharp inclines on dirt roads. Norman Baugh is an artist who takes pride in every aspect of driving his truck, from improving the equipment to concerning himself with road safety. He, like other drivers, can't really say why, but regardless of the hardships, they want to "drive truck." Its aesthetic may be elusive, but to these professionals, its satisfaction is never ending.

Norman consumes Pepsi after Pepsi when driving. His Kenworth truck is named Pepsi and his CB handle is Pepsi. He had his first one of the day at the cafe in Deary one early, cloudy day in May when we went out hauling. The rain had caused work in the woods to slow down since it is nearly impossible to keep equipment functioning in mud. In fact, it would be environmentally irresponsible to rut the terrain during the rainy season. And so for a week the work of sawyers, woodsbosses, loaders, truckers, and mills ground almost to a standstill.

There are many technical elements to truck driving. With the legal weight limit at 80,000 pounds, it is critical that the man loading your rig get as close to that weight as possible without surpassing it. The loader needs an eye and a touch so that the weight is right and the load is balanced in such a way that it is not top-heavy. When the load is positioned properly between the stakes, the truck is easier to handle on the road. Also, a properly loaded truck is economically beneficial to the trucker because hauling payment is determined by weight. If a load exceeds the limit and the truck is stopped at a weighing station, the driver could be fined several hundred dollars for the overage. If the load is unbalanced and difficult to drive, the trip takes longer, making it impossible to haul an additional load that day. The unloading order of trucks to the mill is done in rotation. If you were at the yard at precisely 6 A.M. and dumped the load, reorganized your truck, and got back on the road for another load, you might get an additional trip in that day. This is the ideal, but the driver never knows if chains will have to be put on in mud or other circumstances might occur to slow him down.

The cab of the truck is comfortable, a necessity for anyone who spends up to eighteen hours on the road in a day. It has fifteen gears, a two-speed rear end, and more gauges than I can count. Both seats have sturdy shock absorbers. Eighteen hours a day, for thirty-one years, beginning at age nineteen—that is Norman's history. He has taken a lot of vibration and a lot of knocks. The modern trucks like this Kenworth are a driver's delight, but it takes a good driver and mechanic to understand both how to handle and maintain them. Driver-owners watch the competitions at logging fairs to see how a new model operates; often they will buy a truck with some demonstration miles on it because it has been shaken down and the bugs are worked out of it. Buying new means never buying the untested, and buying second-hand means knowing the driving and maintenance reputation of the previous owner.

Norman stays away from some of the latest technology because it causes nothing but trouble. Trucks designed in factories, without an understanding of the conditions under which they are driven, often just don't work. Norman does most of his own mechanical repairs on this 425-horse-power machine. Often, instead of getting a replacement part even under the guarantee, he will invent a new piece. After all, if the original part broke it must have been incorrectly designed and a second one of the same design will break as well. "If it's not engineered right, you change it and don't wait for a company improvement." And for Norman's taste, "they still don't make a logging truck right for Idaho. The roads are such, the incline such, that you have to steer more than in other regions."

Skill meets economy again in the ability to drive the truck. It is not unusual to use thirty or forty gallons of diesel on a run, and it is the master driver who can cut down consumption by using finely-honed braking and shifting techniques. Our drive that day took us up Swamp Creek, past Bishop Creek and Elk River to the logging site, and down again to Bennett's mill in Princeton, Idaho. At each mile marker, Norman radios his exact location so other truckers in the vicinity will proceed with caution. There are always greetings on the CB, short and personal and humorous, and then, when the drivers are in sight, a wave. These passersby are parts of a complicated economic arrangement. If all drivers work together, they can increase their daily income, but working against each other does little more than foul up the orderly progression of trucks going up to the loader and back down to the mill.

When a truck arrives at the deck for loading, safe drivers like Norman take off their visor caps and put on a hard hat. The loader places the logs on the bed. Norman fills out a small slip of paper, staples it to the face of a log, sprays initials on it, tightens and checks the wrappers—heavy fabric straps that secure the logs in place—and takes off.

If the crew is efficient, it takes less than ten minutes to load these logs. Each member of this crew knows his job: the sawyers who cut down the tree, the hookers who attach it to the line, and loader operator who finally places it on the truck keep moving as truck after truck appears.

At the mill yard, the sensation of the weight of the load is striking as a quaking occurs during the unloading. A machine like a giant claw attacks the logs and pulls them off onto the ground. The entire truck rocks from side to side and the enormity of the weight is a constant reminder that a mishap on the road or in the yard could crush the driver, a dangerous situation that the driver lives with daily.

Norman talks about drivers. "Teaching only goes so far. Some drivers have it and others don't; it's the same way with all equipment operators—skidders, cats, and top loaders. When you see a driver you can tell immediately how skilled he is." Norman learned on the job by riding with another driver for three days. He was hooked, he was a driver. Some might want to put him into a category of, as he says, "dumb trucker"—Norman knows that. But Norman is his own boss and is proud of the job he does.

During the past three decades, Norman and Sharon have operated as a team, often living in a camper near a job site, abandoning their home in Orofino to be together on the road. They have shared the hours and the jolts. Both are outspoken about their love of this way of life and their appreciation of the beauty they see in it. Norman believes there are particular elements that make one man a real artist instead of just another driver or skidder operator or sawyer. For the logging truck driver it includes something as seemingly inconsequential as washing the tires of his truck in a special way. This separates the true perfectionist from the also-rans. Norman is forthright about his skills and his opinions. He prides himself on his driving ability, but is not proud.

Neither is Ted Leach, but he does except respect and a high standard in his relationships with others. Over a drink at the Brass Rail, I was chastised soundly, and rightly so, for transgressing one of the basic tenets of logging life—"Always do what you say." During a previous visit that year, I had told Ted Leach that I would go with him to Cow Creek to see the job that he was proudest of having completed, but I didn't. Because of my having broken this appointment, Ted was now not totally convinced of my commitment, but he was willing to take a chance and talk to me a second time. With my apology and promise to keep my word, we proceeded.

Ted's technical knowledge was impeccable, but he also had an important philosophical orientation to impart. He took logging out of the merely physical realm and placed it into the category of a noble profession. Ted had worked at Cow Creek between 1986 and 1988. It was a highly visible site with a county road running through the middle. Ted held to the goal, central to his work, that it was possible to use logging technology to keep an area pleasing to the eye, environmentally balanced, and still obtain high production. While some tradeoffs were required at various points, he was able to demonstrate that a high degree of output, environmental ethics, and an attractive visual result are not mutually exclusive. Cow Creek was an ideal stand to demonstrate this. It had inherently good production potential and could be used to show proper ecological procedures. For Ted, accomplishing his goal was a political as well as an artistic statement.

Ted is also an analyst of the concept of work as art. Precision and forethought are two of the critical characteristics of a life in logging. Each sawyer has a style that marks his work, and this style is a manifestation of how he uses his time. From the moment his alarm goes off until he goes to bed each night, his artistry is expressed in the precision and forethought he applies throughout the day. How he uses his time, regardless of extenuating circumstances, individually stamps his work to such an extent that Ted stated he could tell who has cut a stand of trees just by looking at the logs on the ground and the remaining stumps.

During the course of our conversation, I asked, "Who is the classiest, the most stylish woodsworker you know?" While Ted was giving concentrated thought to this question, Donna, his wife, chimed in, "You'd have to consider Ted for that honor. He's a professional. He's proud. He leaves a stand looking good. He doesn't destroy young timber. He's an environmentalist." Donna was speaking from wifely pride, but also from first-hand knowledge. Perhaps Ted's background in forestry makes him more sensitive to the requirements of good timber management, but when you hear him talk about his work, it is also obvious that his degree may have been merely a welcomed addition to an already highly-developed sense of appropriateness in the woods. He's a "bug" on soil erosion and doesn't let anything—weather, boss, crew, or equipment failure—stand in his way to avoid it. Donna had been in the woods with Ted frequently when he had been with the Forest Service, and Ted had taught her how to look at logging. She knows of Ted's concerns for this way of life and that he speaks out for a logging way of life. But underneath all the strength of conviction is an untiring commitment to the woods and especially to the young men who enter into the profession.

Ted is a born teacher and scholarly in his approach. From insurance company tables he discovered that sawyers were one of the most accident-prone occupational groups. To increase safety in the woods, he developed a course that teaches the techniques of sawing to young sawyers. At the core of his course is the belief that good sawing technique is only one element of job safety. Workers also have to be good at their lives so Ted prepares them to fashion a lifestyle in addition to honing their manual skills.

The students are taught first to observe, then to prepare an area to avoid dangerous pitfalls. Ted tries to instill in them habits that transcend the job and extend into their everyday lives including getting up on time, getting their equipment ready at home before going to a job, being properly dressed for weather conditions, and having a sense of the appropriate, the proper, in all they do.

In logging there are ways of approaching a job that everyone expects. For example, the bucker is the man on the crew who should have the landing clear and ready to go. The rest of the team counts on that and on the fact that he will set the proper footing for them. On a good team the bucker will do his best to get everything organized, but if the workload is too great, the team members don't just sit in the rig, they will help him out. This spirit becomes a part of the life and the art of the logger.

Accidents can still happen, even after taking proper care and receiving training. For example there can be a dead tree—a snag—in a stand that can fall at the slightest provocation. Snags lose their branches and will make very little sound until they hit the ground. The careful sawyer cuts out the snags before clearing a stand of trees, but the dangers of working in the woods are ever present, and any sawyer could be in the wrong place at the wrong time. A skilled and careful logger may be preoccupied with other work, he may be fixing a saw or preparing for another cut. His earplugs may block out noises and, before he can react, a falling tree may end his life.

What do those who are left behind do? They go on. Friends participate in the religious memorial and then go back to the woods. According to Ted, the widow generally has one of two reactions. Some wives are dedicated and continue on in a logger's world; others want out. They leave the past behind and never return.

It may be an art to learn the necessary skills to allay disaster, but it is also an art to construct your life to live with potential tragedies. This is a part of the world of the logger. Again and again,

I marvelled at the ability of the people in the community to speak gently but dispassionately about death. It lives with them.

Ted is concerned with these tragedies but also feels deeply about the tragedies of history. Chinese Diggings, the ingenious mining techniques used by the Chinese at the abandoned fields in the area, came up in our conversation. The fact that much of it was destroyed, that this unbelievable technological accomplishment was erased by a logging job, was criminal according to Ted. It sticks in his mind, he feels that history was destroyed, a technological tradition lost. The Chinese were in Clearwater County, they showed phenomenal skill and creativity, and they should be included in the panorama of history of northern Idaho.

Several years after our conversation, I sent Ted a copy of my memory of our meeting and draft for his review. He wrote back, "Your interpretation of our talks makes me appear to be a VIP. I have never thought of myself that way but as a cog in the wheel that keeps things going. It's nice to get some recognition for my efforts but to stay focused I need to be in the trenches and get my hands dirty."

This personal philosophy, which seems to be the credo of many loggers working and living in Clearwater County, echoes through the forests. We are not special, we do our job, we do it to the best of our ability. We wouldn't give up our life in logging. It is beautiful, it is precious, a thing beautifully done—truly a work of art.

EPILOGUE

·········

After the Tale Was Told

My job as a limner came to a close in 1991, when I painted the portrait of this community and showed the art of logging through the people's lives. They read eagerly the original version of this work deposited in the Clearwater Memorial Library. People who appeared in the book as personalities called with corrections, generally on technical matters, rarely on the central issue, their work and their lives.

But lives, unlike paintings, change. The loggers' attitude toward their work, which evokes aesthetic experiences, remains embedded in the painting. But the reality of everyday existence is subject to the vagaries of economics, politics, and the very basic health and aging issues to which we are all prey.

Some of the major figures like Joe Richardson have passed away, others like Don Ponozzo have moved south to warmer, retirement communities. Among the younger generation, Ted Leach has continued in logging, helping his son with their operation. He and Donna weathered their son Stanley's near-electrocution while on a job, marvelling at his amazing recovery. But Sharon and Tim Barnett, a die-hard timber couple, sold their home, purchased a recreational vehicle, and have been traveling throughout the country learning about the rest of America. Yet, to them, Orofino still is and will remain their sentimental home base.

Tammy Baugh married Craig Gilmer; they have a lovely infant daughter, and Craig was the president of OCI in 1993. In her holiday letter, Tammy wrote, "Megan has already helped chaperon six parades. She has a little OCI shirt that reads 'Future OCI member.' Everyone thought I should have had future royalty, member, and president printed on it. Between her parents, she has lots of shoes to fill."

The Altmillers are happy and healthy and write, "We are still as busy as ever, keeping our place up. There is always more to do than we can. We don't go far from home. Not much excitement around here. We enjoy our grandchildren a lot. Grandpa sings to them and tells them stories about the old days. Sure would like to travel and see the country and visit far-away relatives and friends, but our garden of orchard, grapes, berries, chickens and lawn keeps us very busy."

The lives of the individuals have changed, but ever so slowly, ever so much in the same direction—births, deaths, gardens, and festivals. Regardless of what has happened economically and politically, for the most part, the loggers of Clearwater County seem to stay on the landscape in a life with the environment. The natural surroundings keep a hold on these people. The artistry that combines history, people, and the woods is still there even though it has been altered. Those outside of the timber industry are attempting to curtail logging, while those inside the industry continue to try to keep it alive.

For the loggers change is often difficult because to them, art and work exist in one sphere in which a normal, everyday life is an aesthetic experience. Work and life are part of the same space with work operating as a frame of mind, not only the movement of bones and muscles in a physical act. The logger's seasoned eye must still be satisfied by the visual impact of the incline, the look of a stand of fine trees, and the qualities demonstrated by a fine sawyer as he fells. And by the sense of "place," the ever-present atmosphere that sinks into the mind, making environment a prominent part of how these people see that their existence doesn't change.

Camaraderie, the belief in the traditions of the elders, and the necessity for fairness in an industry where exactitude is prized but difficult to attain, continue to be the accepted values. And always, the cold, the hard and the factual—there are no false hopes or cloudy visions of what is real. Hypothetical situations are rarely discussed. Every question has a "yes" or a "no" answer. "Maybe" doesn't work here. You can weigh the facts, and there is an excellent chance that you can control your own destiny.

Yet outside forces and the conditions of the logging industry affect every aspect of life, from the purchase of computerized equipment to the installation of parking meters in downtown Orofino. It affects volunteerism and the ability of the community to spend time in non-paid pursuits. The flexibility of logging allows a logger the luxury to work at his own pace when the conditions are right and to work not at all if the conditions are wrong. But with no work at all, he and his family cannot contribute to community organizations.

Today, there is a danger that logging, in a style sensitive to the natural surroundings as practiced by many of the loggers portrayed here, may be in jeopardy. It may become obsolete if the large corporations find that selective logging is not economically viable and that it is necessary to buy land for tree-producing lots similar to those in other parts of the country. Or government policy may preempt the timber industry from obtaining the stumpage necessary to stay alive.

For a short while, harvesting Pacific Yew from which taxol, a potential cure for cancer, was extracted presented a hopeful possibility. But once the natural ingredients are synthesized, it won't take long for the new jobs to disappear. And all the time, the battle over who owns the title "environmentalist" rages. Is it the preservationist, committed to saving every green stem on the landscape, or the logger, believing that his knowledge of when and what to cut is the answer to healthy timberlands and the high sustainable yields of the future?

And the women, what will the women do when their husbands' image is altered? What of the independent, self-actuated individuals, proud of their profession, when they are merely unemployed outdoors men? What happens when a family has nothing to offer to their children to keep them in this locale instead of moving to more major Western population centers? Can building a home for your daughter with your own hands and sweat, like the Barnetts did, keep her from leaving the community?

Loggers are reevaluating their occupation. They want to maintain extended families with a stable and settled lifestyle. They want to depend on women for family life, business partnerships, and cultural activities. They want friendships based on necessity and shared attitudes that persist for long periods of time as is evidenced in the enjoyment of the gatherings of elders. Loggers in Clearwater County wonder about the survival of their lifestyle, but they have little doubt that they want to keep it.

Logging is an industry that goes through constant changes—economic, technological, and ideological. It has been bombarded with invectives from environmental groups and in response has developed its own lobbying groups. But these problems plague the industry as a whole and little has been done for the individual logger to help him and his family lead the life they have chosen. These loggers merely continue on, watching the waves of opinion change, getting involved in governmental policy when necessary, and seeing forest supervisor after forest supervisor come and go. They know which politicians will favor their position that proper logging is as important a practice in natural resource management as not logging at all. They know that market forces and the rise and fall of interest rates come into play as lumber shortages and new home construction move their economic fortunes and popularity quotients up and down.

Positive and negative influences come and go. Technology may allow loggers to X-ray trees before cutting. The major corporate mill may or may not close in 1996. And the laws that protect certain animal species, such as the spotted owl, may come under scrutiny to be either renewed or be abolished. Timber sales may increase with certain administrations and decrease under others. But these are problems of the industry as a whole. Little can be said about the individual logger and the way he and his family lead their lives. All I can say is that they seem to be there, in Clearwater County, every time I call.

In recent years, the logging industry has picked up the message of building a public image that is successfully used by the paper products industry's recycling advertisements. It knows that it is necessary to state in clear, direct terms what their industry is all about. It is about homes, and furniture, about the necessities of life produced with natural, biodegradable materials that put the environment at less risk than those made of plastics and synthetics. The Idaho

Forest Industries Association began talking to their critics in 1991, and has recently hired a wildlife biologist to provide advice on ecological issues. It has garnered support by demonstrating its concern. All in all, the total harvest remains constant but it is shifting to private land instead of counting on public timber sales.

These outside influences affect logging's aesthetics, which rest in the fact that there can be no division between life, work, and art. The sense of doing, joy of accomplishment, and predisposition to work results in beauty. In the simplest terms, for the logger, aesthetics is doing your work properly, using your tools to their best advantage, living up to the standards set by earlier generations, and appreciating the natural and social world around you.

The source for this sense of quality is practical. There is an efficiency and understanding of work in an artistic milieu that is not removed from daily life. Standards for excellence can be verbalized. Emotions are associated with the experience of logging. The work of art lives in individualized experience such as loading a logging truck, making a perfect cut, or producing a logging show that meets all the standards of a perfect logging show.

Art is not isolated or removed but is a way of perpetuating continuity with the past and interjecting the quest for flawless workmanship into an entire life. Work is a perpetual state of being busy; things must be done and you continue to do them. Work is less a matter of labor than a matter of meeting commitments. And the Clearwater River Valley is a perfect setting for this type of life. It allows human inhabitants to feel inseparable from nature as if forms and faces become part of the terrain. The human images are never intrusive elements in the environment and every figure blends with everyone else.

Carla Laws, a real estate agent who comes from a logging family, captured life in Clearwater County. She said, "You're not caught in this lifestyle. You aren't stuck here; if you want to leave you can. You are here in this region because you want to be even though there are jobs in other places. You are here because you like it." Carla continued, "In this county, we take care of what is wrong; no government intervention will clear up a problem here, we must do it ourselves. People like living here. And you can't think badly about it. Because if you do, you'll winterkill."

APPENDIX A

• • • • • • • • •

Maps

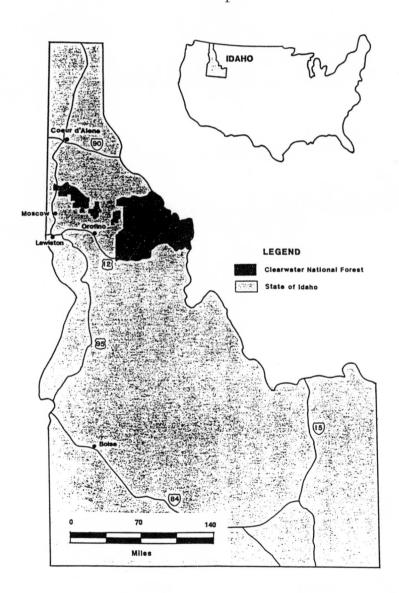

Figure 1. Location map showing the state of Idaho and the Clearwater National Forest.

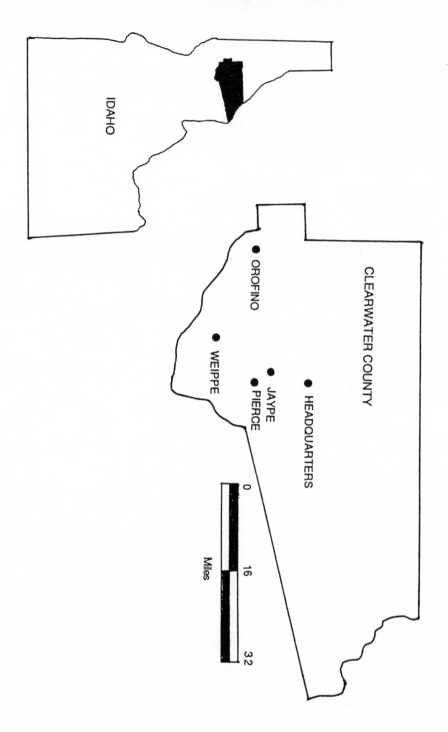

Figure 2. Map of Clearwater County, Idaho, and logging communities

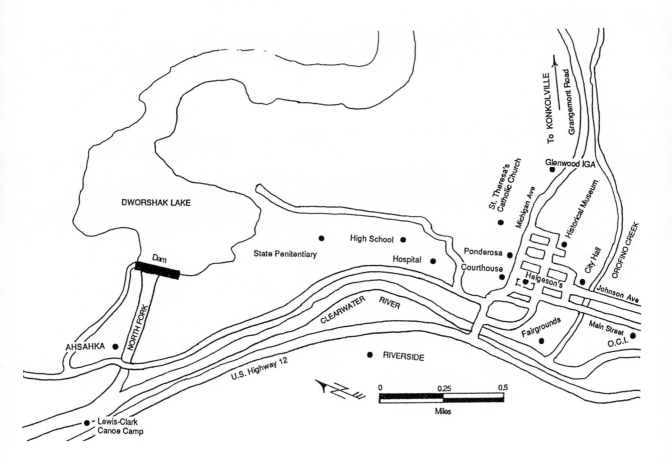

DWORSHAK LAKE

Dam

State Penitentiary

High School

Hospital

AHSAHKA

NORTH FORK

CLEARWATER RIVER

U.S. Highway 12

RIVERSIDE

Lewis-Clark
Canoe Camp

St. Theresa's
Catholic Church

Michigan Ave

Glenwood IGA

Historical Museum

To KONKOLVILLE

Grangemont Road

OROFINO CREEK

Ponderosa

Courthouse

City Hall

Helgeson's

Johnson Ave

Fairgrounds

Main Street

O.C.I.

0   0.25   0.5

Miles

Figure 3. Sketch map of Orofino, Idaho

Chronology of Logging in Clearwater County

Prepared with the assistance of Tim and Sharon Barnett.

FIRST ERA—BEGINNING AND DEVELOPING IN THE 1930S: THE PIONEERS

Leonard Cardiff (deceased)
Owner of Cardiff Lumber Company and Sawmill at Pierce, Idaho, which operated from the 1930s to the 1950s. Established the town of Cardiff.

Lawrence Olson (deceased)
Owner of "O" Mill, which operated in the 1930s and 1940s.

Frank Fromelt (deceased)
Owner of Fromelt Logging Company, which operated from 1935 to 1970.

Joe Mc Carthy (retired)
Owner of White Pine Lumber, which operated in the 1940s and 1950s.

Lewis N. Porter (deceased)
Owner of L. N. Porter Logging, which operated from the 1940s to the 1970s.

Jake Altmiller (retired)
Sawyer for numerous logging companies and finished career with R. F. Coon Logging. Sawed from the 1940s through the 1970s.

Joe Richardson (deceased)
Owner of Riverside Lumber, which operated from the 1940s to the early 1980s.

Andrew "Andy" Konkol (deceased)
Owner of Konkolville Lumber, which operated from the 1930s through the 1970s. Son continues sawmill operation.

Albert "Bert" Curtis (deceased)
Superintendent of Clearwater Potlatch Timber Protective Association (CPTPA). Mayor of Orofino. Involved in community politics from the 1940s to the 1960s.

Mel Snook (retired)
Owner of Snook Logging, which operated in the 1940s and 1950s. State legislator.

Ralph Space (deceased)
National Forest Service superintendent.

Bill Cummings (retired)

Cummings Road Construction and Contracting, which operated from the 1950s to the 1970s.

SECOND ERA: THE 1950S

Ray Coon (active)

R. F. Coon Logging, operating from the 1950s to the present.

Carl Finke (deceased)

In 1947, founded Finke Logging, which is currently operated by sons Jim and "Butch."

Don Ponozzo (retired)

Owner of Ponozzo Logging, which operated between 1950s and 1980s. County commissioner.

Bruce McLaughlin, Senior (active)

From the 1950s to the present, operated McLaughlin Logging which is currently run by his son, Mick.

Tim and Sharon Barnett (retired)

Owners of Barnett Logging, which operated from the 1950s to the 1990s.

THIRD ERA: CURRENTLY INVOLVED IN LOGGING

Don Konkol (active)

Owner of Konkolville Lumber, established by father Andy.

Gail Triplett (active)

Owner of Triplett Lumber and Triplett Logging, which operated from the 1950s to the present. Trippco Inc. owned by son, Ross.

Emerald and Elwin Hutchins (active)

Timberline Lumber Company operated from 1960s to present.

Ted Leach (active)

Past owner of Leach Logging, which operated from 1960s to 1980s. Currently woods supervisor. Son Stanley now runs the business.

Ken Weller (active)

Owner of K. J. Weller Logging Inc., which has been operating from the 1960s to the present.

Cliff Kleer (active)

Owner of Kleer Logging Company, which has been operating from the 1970s to the present.

Gary Medley (active)

Owner of Medley Logging, which operated in the 1970s and 1980s. Currently active in land development.

Kenny Coon (active)

Owner of K. M. C. Trucking, which began operation in the 1980s.

"Butch" Finke (active)

Took over Finke Logging Inc. from Carl Finke in the 1970s.

Alex Irby (active)

Woods superintendent for Konkolville Lumber Company since the 1980s. Active in CPTPA for much of his career.

"Mick" McLaughlin (active)

McLaughlin Logging Company with father Bruce, since the 1980s.

Chet and Cindy Barnett (active)

Barnett Logging Company, purchased company from uncle, Tim Barnett, in the 1980s.

Darold Stanton (active)

Owner of Darold Stanton Logging Company, which began operation in the 1980s.

Steve Barham (active)

In partnership with father, Ernie, in business established three years ago.

BIBLIOGRAPHY

·········

Abiodun, Rowland. "The Future of African Art Studies: An African Perspective." In *African Art Studies: The State of the Discipline*. Washington, D.C.: National Museum of African Art, 1990.

Abrahams, Roger. "Toward a Sociological Theory of Folklore: Performing Services." In *Working Americans: Contemporary Approaches to Occupational Folklife*, edited by Robert H. Byington. Los Angeles: California Folklore Society, 1978.

Agar, Michael H. *Independents Declared: The Dilemmas of Independent Trucking*. Washington, D.C.: Smithsonian Institution Press, 1986.

Applebaum, Herbert. *Royal Blue: The Culture of Construction Workers*. New York: Holt, Rinehart, and Winston, 1981.

Armstrong, Robert Plant. *The Affecting Presence: An Essay in Humanistic Anthropology*. Urbana: University of Illinois Press, 1975.

————. *Wellspring: On the Myth and Source of Culture*. Berkeley: University of California Press, 1975.

Bauman, Richard. *Story, Performance, and Event: Contextual Studies of Oral Narrative*. Cambridge: Cambridge University Press, 1986.

Clifford, James. "On Ethnographic Authority." In *The Predicament of Culture: Twentieth-Century Ethnography, Literature, and Art*. Cambridge and London: Harvard University Press, 1988.

Clifford, James and George E. Marcus. *Writing Culture: The Poetics and Politics of Ethnography*. Berkeley: University of California Press, 1986.

Collingwood, R.G. *The Principles of Art*. Oxford: Clarendon Press, 1938.

Curtis, Albert B. *White Pines and Fires: Cooperative Forestry in Idaho*. Moscow: University of Idaho Press, 1983.

Dewey, John. *Art as Experience*. New York: Putnam, 1934.

Falassi, Alessandro. "Festival: Definition and Morphology." In *Time Out of Time: Essays on the Festival*, edited by Alessandro Falassi. Albuquerque: University of New Mexico Press, 1987.

Fenneman, N. M. *Physiography of Western United States*. New York: McGraw-Hill, 1931.

Geertz, Clifford. *Works and Lives: The Anthropologist as Author*. Stanford: Stanford University Press, 1988.

Glassie, Henry. *Passing the Time in Ballymenone: Culture and History of an Ulster Community*. Philadelphia: University of Pennsylvania Press, 1982.

Halberman, Michael. "Nez Perces: With Their Land Went Their Freedom." *Lewiston Tribune* 2 February 1990, page 1.

Hauser, Arnold. *The Sociology of Art*. Chicago and London: University of Chicago Press, 1983.

Henri, Robert. *The Art Spirit*. New York: Icon Editions of Harper & Row, Publishers, Inc., 1984.

James-Duguid, Charlene. "Orofino Lumberjack Days." In *Idaho Folklife: Homesteads to Headstones*, edited by Louie W. Attebery. Salt Lake City: University of Utah Press, 1985.

Kent, Rockwell and Carl Zigrosser. *Rockwellkentiana: Few Words and Many Pictures*. New York: Harcourt, Brace & Company, 1933.

Lindgren, W. *Geological Reconnaissance Across the Bitterroot Range*. Washington, D.C.: U.S. Geological Survey Professional Paper 27, 1904.

Marcus, George and Michael M. J. Fischer. *Anthropology as Cultural Critique: An Experimental Moment in the Human Sciences*. Chicago and London: University of Chicago Press, 1986.

McCarl, Robert S. "A Theoretical Hypothesis." In *Working Americans: Contemporary Approaches to Occupational Folklife,* edited by Robert H. Byington. Los Angeles: California Folklore Society, 1978.

McCulloch, Walter. *Woods Words: A Comprehensive Dictionary of Logging Terms*. Corvallis: The Oregon Historical Society, 1977.

Mika, Cynthia, Sydney Duncombe, Chuck Holden, and Tony Poinelli. *Handbook for County Officials in Idaho: 8th Edition*. Boise: University of Idaho Bureau of Public Affairs Research, 1987.

Olson, Boyd. *Horse Logging on Freeman Creek*. Lewiston: Lewiston Printing, 1985.

Peterson, Keith C. *Company Town: Potlatch, Idaho, and the Potlatch Lumber Company*. Pullman, Washington and Moscow, Idaho: Washington State University Press and Latah County Historical Society Press, 1987.

Plath, David W. *Long Engagements: Maturity in Modern Japan*. Stanford: Stanford University Press, 1980.

Robbins, William G. *Hard Times in Paradise: Coos Bay, Oregon, 1850-1986*. Seattle and London: University of Washington Press, 1988.

Sanjek, Roger. "On Ethnographic Validity." In *Fieldnotes: The Makings of Anthropology*, edited by Roger Sanjek. Ithaca and London: Cornell University Press, 1990.

Spencer, Robert. "History of Orofino" (mimeo), 1982.

Turnbull, Colin. "Liminality: A Synthesis of Subjective and Objective Experiences." In *By Means of Performance: Intercultural Studies of Theatre and Ritual,* edited by Richard Schechner and Willa Apel. New York: Cambridge University Press, 1990.

Turner, Victor W. "The Spirit of Celebration." In *The Celebration of Society: Perspectives on Contemporary Cultural Performance,* edited by Frank E. Manning. Bowling Green, Ohio: Bowling Green University Popular Press, 1983.

——— "Dewey, Dilthey, and Drama: An Essay in the Anthropology of Experience." In *The Anthropology of Experience.* Urbana and Chicago: University of Illinois Press, 1986.

Vlach, John Michael. *Plain Painters: Making Sense of American Folk Art*. Washington D.C. and London: Smithsonian Institution Press, 1988.

Glossary

....

barker. A man or piece of modern equipment that peels bark off of timber.

birl. The sport of rolling logs in water that was at one time an important skill of loggers during the days of the log drives on the rivers.

board foot. Measure for timber and sawlogs. Generally timber is bought and sold in measurements of 1,000 board feet.

bucker. The woodsworker who cuts trees that have been felled into standard-sized lengths that can be transported on logging trucks.

bull cook. The person in the camp who does odd jobs.

Bull of the Woods. The top man in the woods; the champion at a logging competition.

buncher. The man or piece of modern equipment that gathers logs up at a specific place, generally the landing of a logging job, from which they will be loaded onto logging trucks.

calks. The spikes on the bottoms of logging boots that add stable footing on logs. Sometimes these are called "corks."

cant. The way in which a log is turned in order to cut it efficiently in a sawmill.

cat face. A scarred or damaged part of tree where the bark has been peeled off accidentally. Generally does not affect the quality of the lumber but does not give a good appearance to the logs on the truck in logging show competitions.

choker. Metal device that acts as an adjustable clamp on cables so that they can be tied around logs and dragged from place to place.

choker setter. Man who places the cables around felled trees so that they can be dragged or skidded to the location for loading.

clear-cut. An area in which all of the timber has been removed.

clearing. An opening in the forest.

company town. A community in which all land, homes, and services, except the post office, are owned and operated by the company.

contract logging. Small, independently owned and operated logging company that does work for larger corporations.

corner. The basic point in land survey used to determine boundaries of property.

crown. The living branches of a standing tree.

cruise. To do a timber inventory by walking through the area and estimating the quantity of the timber. The person who performs this job is called a cruiser.

DBH. Diameter breast high or approximately four and one-half feet from ground at which trees are measured.

deck. The flat area at which logs are piled ready for transport.

drive. To send logs down river. The last drive in this region occurred in the 1970s.

duff. Natural litter such as moss and needles that lay on top of the ground in the forest.

fell. To cut timber.

faller. Person who cuts timber.

family camp. Logging camp with accommodations for families as well as single men.

felled and bucked. Timber that has been cut down and sawed into standard lengths in the woods and made ready for transport.

filing shack. A special shed that allows a great deal of natural light so that filers of saw blades can file efficiently.

flatlander. Anyone who is from outside of the region and not considered native to the area.

flume. A trough that was filled with water that carried logs down the mountainside.

flunkie. The person in the camp who did menial jobs such as waiting on tables and washing dishes.

government sale. Stumpage that is purchased from federal lands such as U.S. Forest Service or Bureau of Land Management.

grade. An incline. The quality of a log or lumber cut from it.

gypo or gyppo. Small logging contractor. Sometimes used as a derogatory term by outsiders but generally composed of a single family or group of friends working together.

harvesting. Current terminology used for logging.

haywire outfit. An organization which would use lighter gage cable than the job demands, in other words a derogatory term for company that does not do a job properly.

hoot owl. To work a shift that begins as near to daylight as possible. Often applied to times of year when it necessary to work before the heat of the day makes work in the woods dangerous.

I.W.W. International Workers of the World that originated in Chicago in 1905 and attempted to make inroads into logging in the late 1910s. Did not prove popular with loggers and little hear of it since that time.

landing. Flat ground or collecting area for logs prior to being loaded onto logging trucks.

log. A cut section of timber that generally measures 32 feet long.

log grades. The levels of quality applied to logs as it is applied throughout the logging and milling process.

lumberjack. A term applied to loggers generally by those outside of the industry and seen by insiders to be a romanticized or fictionalized term.

mill. A sawmill where cut timber is turned into lumber.

old growth. Virgin timber that presumably has never been cut.

Ponderosa pine. Name generally applied to western yellow pine.

rig. Term applied to a wide variety of tools, machines, or vehicles.

saw bar. The flat steel frame around which the chain on a power saw runs.

scale. To measure the number of board feet in a log. The individual who does this job is called a scaler and it is his figures that determine the prices paid for making logs.

snag. A standing dead tree that is dangerous because it can fall at any time or ignite and cause forest fires. Sometimes called a "widowmaker" because it or branches from it can fall and be a hazard to loggers below.

stumpage. Standing timber or the price paid for timber that will be cut.

top-loader. The person who is in charge of the loading operation on a landing.

wanigan. A raft with a tent on it that accompanied the crews on the log drives down the river.

woodsboss. A superintendent or top man on logging job.

wrapper. A chain, cable or thick fabric strap that is used to tie logs to a truck so that the load can be transported safely.

For a comprehensive listing of terms related to logging see: Walter F. McCulloch, *Woods Words: A Comprehensive Dictionary of Loggers Terms.*

Index

....